MANAGEMENT LAUREATES:
A COLLECTION OF AUTOBIOGRAPHICAL ESSAYS

EDITED BY

ARTHUR G. BEDEIAN

Ourso College of Business Administration,
Louisiana State University, USA

MANAGEMENT LAUREATES

Series Editor: Arthur G. Bedeian

Previous Volumes 1–5: Management Laureates: A collection of autobiographical essays

MANAGEMENT LAUREATES   VOLUME 6

MANAGEMENT LAUREATES:

A Collection of Autobiographical Essays

By

JOHN CHILD	JAMES G. HUNT
GEORGE B. GRAEN	THOMAS A. KOCHAN
DONALD C. HAMBRICK	RICHARD T. MOWDAY
MICHAEL A. HITT	GREG R. OLDHAM

2002

JAI
An Imprint of Elsevier Science

Amsterdam – London – New York – Oxford – Paris – Shannon – Tokyo

ELSEVIER SCIENCE Ltd
The Boulevard, Langford Lane
Kidlington, Oxford OX5 1GB, UK

First edition 2002

Library of Congress Cataloging in Publication Data
A catalog record from the Library of Congress has been applied for.

British Library Cataloguing in Publication Data
A catalogue record from the British Library has been applied for.

ISBN: 0-7623-0487-1

⊗ The paper used in this publication meets the requirements of ANSI/NISO Z39.48-1992 (Permanence of Paper).
Printed in The Netherlands.

CONTENTS

LIST OF CONTRIBUTORS

Arthur G. Bedeian   Department of Management, Louisiana State University, Louisiana, USA

John Child   Birmingham Business School, University of Birmingham, Birmingham, UK

George B. Graen   College of Business Administration, University of Louisiana at Lafayette, USA

Donald C. Hambrick   Graduate School of Business, Columbia University, New York, USA

Michael A. Hitt   College of Business, Arizona State University, Arizona, USA

James G. Hunt   College of Business Administration, Texas Tech University, Texas, USA

Thomas A. Kochan   Sloan School of Management, Massachusetts Institute of Technology, Massachusetts, USA

Greg R. Oldham   Department of Business Administration, University of Illinois, Illinois, USA

Richard T. Mowday   Lundquist College of Business Administration, University of Oregon, Oregon, USA

PREFACE

"Little by little it has become clear to me that every great philosophy has been the confession of its maker, as it were his involuntary and unconscious autobiography."

– Friedrich W. Nietzsche, *Beyond Good and Evil (1886)*

As with its predecessors, the sixth volume of *Management Laureates: A Collection of Autobiographical Essays* continues in the belief that it is difficult to fully understand an individual's work without knowing a great deal about the person behind that work. To this end, the *Management Laureates* series has sought to provide insight into the personal and intellectual lives – the frustrations and triumphs – of the management discipline's leading thinkers. Although I have now worked with over 60 of the highest achievers in the management discipline on their autobiographies, I continue to be intrigued by the various pathways each traveled through life and the many intangibles that brought them to their current condition. When first contemplating the possibility of compiling a series of volumes containing the autobiographies of the management discipline's most distinguished laureates (in about 1989), I had hoped to gain not only behind-the-scenes insights into the discipline's historical development, but also a deeper understanding of what management is and is becoming. In the ensuing years, I have become aware of what others before me have long realized, and I would affirm with Paul Valéry (1939/1958), "There is no theory that is not a fragment, carefully prepared, of some autobiography" (p. 58).

The difficulty and hesitancy of preparing a self-portrait of one's life should not be underestimated. In "Confessions and Autobiography", Stephen Spender (1962) says the challenge faced by autobiographers is that when we consider ourselves as subjects we are confronted not by one life, but by two. The first of these lives is our social or historic self as seen by others and is more or less the sum of our achievements, appearances, and personal relationships. In this public self, we are free to recount our visible actions and explain how we have become the person we are at present and, thus, to reflect the image we would like others to see. In short, the task is to give meaning to our own tale. There is also, however, the privileged self, known only to ourselves as seen from inside our own existence. Here, in the words of Georges Gusdorf (1956/1980), the "artist and model" coincide, as we become the historian of ourselves. In this sense, to be true to ourselves, we must enter an impartial dialogue with our innermost being. In doing so, the difficulty of achieving such a self-communion must be confronted. Indeed, as Gusdorf realized, "the dialogue of a life with itself in search of its own absolute" is much like wrestling with our own shadow, certain only of never completely grasping hold of it (p. 48).

The inherent limitations of autobiographical memories cannot, however, be denied. Directly stated, "life stories are not simple veridical reports about what 'really happened' in a person's life" (McAdams, 1998, p. 1129). Beyond engaging in solitary recall to support a specific self-view, autobiographers may selectively recall particular events or experiences to present a particular self-image or to fulfill identity-related goals. Moreover, memories can be fallible and incomplete, as well as susceptible to a wide range of cognitive and social influences. At the same time, research indicates that memories of personally important episodes from an individual's past, episodes that are enduring aspects of one's self-concept, are more likely to be accurately recalled than more general events (Thorne, 2000).

Perhaps more importantly for our purposes, the perspective of the privileged self noted above enables self-reflexive autobiographic accounts to access inner thoughts that are unobtainable from other sources. By requiring that their authors reconstitute their lives at a distance, so as to achieve an identity across time, autobiographies represent a unique means for conveying self-knowledge as one interprets one's life in its totality. I do not mean to suggest that autobiographers are thus exempt from the failures of memory or motivational pressures to see themselves in the most desirable manner possible. Rather I argue for the need to go beyond such difficulties and realize that the very fallibility or partiality of an autobiographic account is part of its inimitable value, for as Burnett (1982/1984) has observed, "the author has chosen his own ground, patterned his own experiences, and has painted a self-portrait which is more revealing than any photograph" (p. 11).

In an autobiography past events are re-remembered in terms of present events or outcomes. Recollections of the past based on current appraisals have been said to comprise "screen memories" (Freud, 1899/1955). The rendering of such memories underscores three key elements. First, as acknowledged by the contributing laureates, after examining and articulating the contours of their lives, none is the person they were before. Being forced at the moment of composition to look back and correlate their lives and work, each has grown in ways that they could not have previously imagined. Second, as the reader will soon recognize in the unfolding of each of the following narratives, there are inextricable links in the laureates' lives between their present selves, past selves, past events and past circumstances. Third, as the reader will also quickly appreciate, each laureate tells his story from the perspective of his time and distinctive culture and, as is clear, societal change affects people's lives. This is not to say that each narrative does not possess its own distinctive leitmotifs or that their authors were not essential agents in creating their own situations, but rather that, to a certain extent, their lives were each shaped by the terrain where their lives were lived.

In sum, and in relation to the final point above, each of the volumes in the *Management Laureates* series permits readers to examine trans-historic and time-specific social policies, practices, and structures created and experienced by succeeding generations of management scholars. In doing so, they offer to bring to all who read them an increased appreciation, through an understanding of other lives in other times and places, of the evolving nature of the management discipline, as well as of each person's share in the on-going human drama of life. Beyond this, the autobiographies in this and its predecessor volumes are a contribution to the history of management, and in the years to come will not only serve to fulfill the historian's desire to recall the past, but in Gusdorf's (1956/1980) words, satisfy "more or less [the] anguished disquiet of the mind anxious to recover and redeem lost time in fixing it forever" (p. 37).

As in preceding volumes, editorial intervention has been kept at a minimum. Once again, all essays are preceded by a photograph and conclude with a complete bibliography of their author's published works. Laureates remained free to choose their manner of presentation and the aspects of their lives they wished to emphasize.

Special thanks goes to the contributing laureates. I hope that they will find satisfaction in the immortality that their essays provide. All have hereby gained a medium of access that will allow them, decades from now, to speak to those management scholars who will be heirs to their intellectual legacy.

Arthur G. Bedeian
October 2001

REFERENCES

Burnett, J. (1984). Autobiographies as history. In: J. Burnett (Ed.), *Useful toil: Autobiographies of Working People from the 1820s to the 1920s* (pp. 9–19). Harmondsworth, Middlesex, ENG: Penguin. (Original work published 1982)

Freud, S. (1955). Screen memories. (J. Strachey, Trans.). In: J. Strachey (Ed.), *The Standard Edition of the Complete Psychological Works of Sigmund Freud* (Vol. 3, pp. 303–322). London: Hogarth Press. (Original work published 1899)

Gusdorf, G. (1980). Conditions and limits of autobiography (J. Olney, Trans.). In: J. Olney (Ed.), *Autobiography: Essays Theoretical and Critical*. Princeton, NJ: Princeton University Press. (Original work published 1956)

McAdams, D. P. (1998). The role of defense in the life story. *Journal of Personality, 66*, 1125–1146.

Spender, S. (1962). *The making of a poem*. New York: Norton.

Thorne, A. Personal memory telling and personality development. *Personality and Social Psychology Review, 4*, 45–56.

Valéry, P. (1958). *The art of poetry* (S. Folliot, Trans.). New York: Pantheon. (Original work published 1938)

If I have seen farther, it is by
standing on the shoulders of giants.

Sir Issac Newton

John Child

MIX CONTEXT AND CHOICE, AND ADD A LARGE DOSE OF SERENDIPITY

John Child

What we do is conditioned by the context from which we come and in which we live. However, lucky breaks or coincidences come along from time to time, and these offer us an opportunity to make significant choices of our own. As you will see, I have enjoyed more than my fair share of such serendipity.

CHILDHOOD AND YOUTH

I was born in Manchester, England on November 10, 1940 in the middle of an air raid. I can't say that I was conscious of the danger, but who knows what deep effects these events have. My father was British. He was serving in the army at the time, though far more interested in history than fighting. He had previously studied history in Germany where he witnessed the burning of "un-German" books on May 10, 1933. This was the saddest day of his entire life, he later said. With fluency in the language, he was before long seconded to work on a programme of 'black propaganda' aimed at sapping German civilian morale; which was all rather incongruous with the fact that my mother was German. Her parents lived in Berlin throughout the war, and during the whole of that time the only contact she had with them was very occasionally via the Red Cross. As Allied bombing intensified and eventually Berlin was taken by storm, we had no idea whether my grandparents were still alive or not. They survived, and that lucky break led to one of my most vivid early memories, of travelling by train to Berlin at the end of the war with my mother and arriving in a totally devastated cityscape to find grandparents, aunt and their house mercifully all in one piece.

Management Laureates, Volume 6, pages 1–52.
Copyright © 2002 by Elsevier Science Ltd.
All rights of reproduction in any form reserved.
ISBN: 0-7623-0487-1

Two early formative influences that have impacted on my work are history and dual identity. After the war, my father was able to continue his interests in political history, first at the research department of the British Foreign Office and later as official historian to the Cabinet Office. Books on history were part of my environment right through my formative years. Before I could even read, the shapes and colours of historical atlases fascinated me. An early photograph, taken at the age of three, has me sitting with an open atlas. Turning the pages, like the frames of an early movie, presented a picture of continuous flux, of disequilibrium punctuated by the periodic major settlement – Westphalia, Utrecht, the Congress of Vienna, Versailles. Nothing seemed to stabilize for very long. At that time, one consistent factor seemed to be how the red of the British Empire spread remorselessly through the pages, 1776 notwithstanding. Yet, twenty years later it had all but disappeared. Historical atlases are also a constant reminder that any country, however much territory it takes up, is but one of the hundreds of other colours that make up the world. I can remember wondering about those large mysterious spaces like China that seemed to be accorded far fewer pages and detail than their size warranted. Shouldn't we know more about them? Actually the biggest mystery was Greenland; why wasn't that huge space covered with towns? A three-year old does not have any conception of permafrost.

The German side of my identity had to be suppressed during the war. I never acquired the language properly, because it would not have been very wise to have a little boy running around at the time speaking German. Apparently, I had the embarrassing habit of inviting the other occupants of buses and trains to visit our home; just imagine the consequences if I had done this in German in 1943! Nevertheless, a dual cultural identity has always been there and has, I'm sure, led to the dualism and tension in my thinking that others have noted (Loveridge, 1998). The British individualism in me inclines naturally towards choice while the German part inclines more naturally towards order and external determination. A mixed identity has led to a certain emotional detachment from the British environment in which I grew up, but at the same time it stimulated the life-long interest in other cultures that came to have a significant influence on my work. I have always looked to find colleagues and friends around the world as much as in my own country. This is reflected in the many collaborative research relationships I have enjoyed.

In 1945 my parents moved to Streatham, a suburb of London, next door to the district of 'Balham, Gateway to the South' immortalised by Peter Sellars. I started my schooling at Streatham Grammar School. Despite its name, this was actually a boys' private non-boarding preparatory school. It provided a very traditional form of education, emphasizing the virtues of discipline and hard work as the means to achievement. Achievement amounted to a combination of character formation and getting a place in a good high school. Graphologists discern character from one's handwriting, but the school assumed the reverse: that good handwriting conveys good character. So it insisted on its younger pupils spending many hours acquiring copperplate writing by using copybooks. The result was certainly a legible hand, of which I used to be quite proud though it has become a redundant competence in these days of computers. The school's Victorian method of cultivating handwriting reflected the highly standardized educational methods that were still commonly applied at the time. When, however, it came to fostering middle class modes of speech, the teachers' best efforts were frustrated. Try as they did to eradicate their pupils' London cockney accents, they failed to overcome the environment in which the boys lived. Cockney was considered to be a manifestation of working class culture, which did not suit the elitist tone that grammar schools cultivated. Ironically, a cockney accent has today become quite *de rigueur* among young whiz kids in the financial sector, entertainers and sports celebrities; money has brought respectability.

My parents moved to the county of Surrey, just south of London, in 1951. That year, I was admitted to Purley Grammar School having passed the national examinations that at the time determined admittance to different categories of secondary school in England and Wales. Grammar schools combined a high standard of academic work with a wide range of sporting and extra-curricula activities. Teachers worked closely with pupils in running these. 'Form masters' served as personal tutors if boys ran into difficulties. Teachers and pupils came together at the start of each school day for assembly, which comprised hymns, a reading by a senior boy, prayers and announcements from the headmaster. Each lunch table had a teacher presiding. There was a real sense of community.

This closeness between teacher and student was of huge benefit to the boys' academic and personal development, and it also provided rapid feedback to the staff when problems arose. It bridged the authority and status gap that would otherwise have been quite pronounced in an organization of around 800 students and staff. In fact, the sense of community promoted an acceptance of the teachers' role and so lent legitimacy to their authority. Channels were available to surface and mitigate the frustration and stress that school students inevitably experience as part of finding their own equilibrium, especially in an achievement-oriented atmosphere. Later on, at Cambridge University, I studied in a similar system that continues to operate through the 31 colleges. Right from the start at Cambridge, you become a 'member' of a college and are made to feel one. Paradoxically, the traditional status distinctions between the college faculty ('Fellows') and students are continually bridged by social proximity and frequent communication. Fellows and students have rooms next door to one another. They share meals together in the same dining hall. They join in periodic college rituals. This approach combines a collective identity and sense of community, based on British tradition, with an emphasis on all-round achievement. It is meritocracy with a human face, and it can be extremely effective. In recent years, many progressive corporations have been seeking to apply a similar philosophy.

Several friends and I founded a school newspaper, which we titled '*The Novelty*'. I think we felt it was time to say, rather in advance of Monty Python, 'and now for something completely different'. *The Novelty* ran for several years until its title became a complete misnomer and we all got too tied up with studying for the school-leaving exams. Because it numbered a brilliant cover designer and really quite entertaining writers, our group decided that I was better out of harm's way getting new copy rather than writing it, and pulling it together as Editor. Nonetheless, I managed to sneak in my regular editorials, most of which our 'sponsoring' teacher had to persuade me to make it more politically correct, as well as an interminable travelogue drawn from summer holidays taken abroad with my parents. The challenge of editing *The Novelty* was actually very poor preparation for my later role as Editor-in-Chief of *Organization Studies*. With *The Novelty*, I was continually doing the rounds asking for copy, refusing very little, and trying with the utmost persuasion to get it in on time. It's the opposite with a major international journal. Submissions are constantly coming in, the large majority have to be rejected, and the problem of time is one of frustrated authors wondering whether their manuscript will ever appear. Thank goodness, we did not bother with external reviewers for *The Novelty*!

I wanted to combine maths with economics within the portfolio of subjects to be taken as a prelude to university entry, but the former was classified as a science subject and the latter as an arts subject, so their timetabling clashed. Combinations across the so-called 'arts' and 'science' divide were not encouraged. I opted for economics, but without the higher maths that today is so essential to it. This was undoubtedly a factor in my later retreat from the subject. I had actually performed better at maths and the sciences than other subjects and would certainly have become a scientist if the standard of the school's teaching in those subjects had matched that on the arts' side. In keeping with this scientific inclination, my passion in those days was with what could rather grandly be called 'aerodynamics': designing and flying model aircraft. A group of school colleagues 'went flying' most evenings and weekends, when daylight and British weather permitted.

A FIRST TASTE OF THE REAL WORLD (1959)

At the age of 17, I was offered a place at the London School of Economics. I decided to put this on ice for a year and in the meantime to take the entrance examinations for Oxford and Cambridge. My motivation was a mixture of wanting to study at a sufficient distance from home to guarantee some independence and the effect of many years of looking up at the board of honour in the school hall listing graduates who had gone to Oxbridge. The choice between the two universities was purely arbitrary. The Cambridge exams were held in December 1958 and those at Oxford a month later. So, I ended up with Cambridge, due to start there in October 1959.

I had been heavily cocooned from the outside world by the strongly defined school system and ethos through which I had progressed with a high degree of certainty year-by-year. I had worked within the system and it had looked after me. Maybe this was the reason that I did not do anything more adventurous while waiting to go up to Cambridge than take a temporary job working in the British government's Passport Office. Looking back, I certainly regret not having used the time to better advantage, especially through foreign travel. On the other hand, the Passport Office provided me with my first real-life experience of a work organization. It revealed some of the things that go on within the black box that neoclassical economists assume an organization to be, and how these can directly affect economic parameters such as productivity.

I worked for some months in the section that prepared new passports. We received completed application forms that were supposed to have already been checked, though some dubious cases could still get through to us. Our job was to complete the passport by hand, affix the applicant's photograph, record each case and then pass it on for final inspection. We experienced a high degree of independence as a section; in current parlance we possessed the features of an autonomous working group. When I was shown what to do, it was made very clear that I was not expected to complete more than about 100 passports in a seven-hour day. Everyone gave me friendly assurances that I would cope fine – 'just take your time'. It did not take long to discover what was going on; the autonomous working group was controlling its output. It would have been quite easy even for a novice like me to prepare at least 120 new passports each day. There was one man, Martin, who broke ranks and regularly completed 180 passports. He was a conscientious, quiet man, whose life was simply made hell. Nobody chatted with him and no one invited him to join them for lunch in the canteen. Whereas the final checkers would often correct minor errors for us without returning the passport, in Martin's case they literally made a song and dance of the matter, waltzing back to his desk and shaming him in front of everyone else. These collective sanctions were cruel and distasteful, but I have to admit that I never had the courage even to think of breaking ranks and busting the group norm. What the members of the group were doing was completely rational from their standpoint, particularly as there was no danger that their informal practices would threaten their employment. They were quite simply maximizing their cost-benefit equation given the flat rate of payment they were offered. It was fascinating for me to read later on, at university, the graphic accounts of informal work group controls by industrial anthropologists and sociologists such as Orvis Collins and Donald Roy that rang very true to this first impressionable experience.

The only skills I learned in the Passport Office were those of a master forger. The inspectors would often correct errors in our work with the careful use of a sharp razor blade and carefully re-smoothed paper, which of course was of excellent quality as befits a passport issued on behalf of the Queen. We clerks were encouraged to correct our own minor errors through applying the same skills. As they say, anything you learn may come in useful one day!

UNIVERSITY OF CAMBRIDGE (1959–1965)

I had taken the entrance examination for a group of Cambridge colleges that included my first choice, St. John's, in December 1958. My chosen subject was history, but the exam also included a general extended essay and a paper in Latin. I had gladly forgotten my Latin of several years before and did so badly in that part of the exam that I was sure I had flunked. The Latin requirement was abolished a few years later and today there are no entrance exams. Well, they accepted me and I decided to change subjects and study economics. It seemed to offer better career prospects and one could in any case enjoyably study history as a leisure activity (which few would say of economics).

Whether this decision was a mistake I shall never know, but it certainly had considerable consequences for my choice of career. In the Cambridge system, an undergraduate's closest intellectual relations are normally with his or her college supervisor. You attend lectures and classes, but your interaction with experienced and generally great minds takes place in the weekly supervision. There you have to justify the written work you have submitted beforehand and you are encouraged to examine theories, issues and debates critically. In St. John's College, I had two supervisors in economics, Robin Matthews, who later became the Drummond Professor of Economics at Oxford, and Aubrey Silberston, who later became Professor of Economics at Imperial College, London. Matthews was a macro theorist working on the theory of economic growth. Silberston was a micro economist known at the time for his empirical research on patents and the motor industry. Matthews was my supervisor during my first year and Silberston took over subsequently when Matthews went on leave.

The transition in supervisor was critical for me because it reinforced two other factors that came together during my first year. One was that the

Cambridge syllabus assumed no prior knowledge of the subject. I had studied economics for two years at school and, frankly, became bored with going over the same ground. I might have been more tolerant of the heroic and atomistic assumptions about human behaviour contained in economic theory if they had been novel to me. They were not, so they became vulnerable to a critical attitude that was sharpened by the second factor: further exposure to the real world of work. The influence of the Passport Office experience was mightily reinforced when in December 1959 members of the first-year class of 130 or so were asked whether we would be interested in a Christmas vacation 'industrial tour'. This was being organized by Professor E. A. G. (Austin) Robinson at Cambridge with the help of Professor Sargant Florence who was Professor Emeritus of Commerce at the University of Birmingham. Five of us signed up. The tour was an eye-opener. Professor Florence had selected six of the most enlightened employers in the Birmingham area. He came with us and we had access both to top managers and to shopfloor workers. Here were employers, several of them direct descendants of founding Quaker families, who were sincere in wanting to promote both the wellbeing and the voice of their employees. They had employee participation, they recognized trade unions, and they paid reasonably well. Yet, much of the work being done, be it hand-assembling electrical plugs or packing chocolate boxes into cartons, was repetitive and monotonous. People had to get through the day either by chatting with their colleagues or daydreaming. The only way to survive psychologically was to disengage from the repetitive physical movements being performed minute to minute.

The experience of this tour was a challenge to our little group of privileged students coming from Cambridge. It led to us asking ourselves some rather big questions. Was this deadening kind of working life the best that industrial societies could offer the majority of their citizens? What lay behind it? Was it the economic system or something apparently more politically neutral, namely modern technology? If the latter, did Marxism or Capitalism really make enough difference to suffer the Cold War for? Were attempts at encouraging industrial participation, such as we had seen the employers make, futile if all people wanted to do at the end of the day was to get as far away from their work as possible clutching their pay packets? And more immediately for us, why didn't economists have anything to say about the matter? Although at that time the notion of enriching jobs was not yet widely discussed, we concluded it was the work itself that seemed to be the problem, not the fact that people worked for capitalist employers. After all, work at the Passport Office had been pretty monotonous and that was for a government agency. The employees we talked to in Birmingham had generally stayed with their companies for a long time, and thought well of their employers. So the blame did not seem to rest with capitalism.

An opportunity to study questions like these came just at the right time, in a clear example of serendipity. For in 1960, starting with the second year of the economics 'tripos' (i.e. degree programme), new subjects were introduced. These included industrial sociology, political sociology and a 'Paper Three' which aspired to draw upon both disciplines in treating subjects like the modern corporation, labour mobility and consumer behavior. This was a revolution for the Economics Faculty at Cambridge. We were told that it had been put back for several years by an indiscretion on the part of Talcott Parsons. When delivering the annual Alfred Marshall Lectures, he had outraged the economics establishment by claiming that Keynes's general theory and, by implication, economics as a whole, formed just a sub-system within his, Parsons's, more comprehensive model of the social system. As it was, dark rumours filtered down to us undergraduates that a senior professor in the Faculty had sworn that any student daring to take the new papers would be awarded a first class honours degree over her dead body. Such was the unease in the faculty that only a few years later sociology was moved away from economics to a new faculty of Social and Political Sciences.

Given my frame of mind, the advent of sociology was a godsend. I took every paper I could and was eventually awarded a 'double first' despite the veiled threats. My economics supervisor at St. John's College, Aubrey Silberston was sympathetic to the focus on industrial sociology and corporate organization that had now come into my curriculum. His support at this stage was critical. Aubrey's breadth of interest and far-sightedness are reflected in the fact that back in the 1950s he had written one of the first monographs urging the introduction of management studies into British universities. The College appointed David Lockwood as its first supervisor in sociology. His deep appreciation of the subject's founding fathers, especially Max Weber, and the theoretically sensitive scholarship he had demonstrated in his classic study of *The Blackcoated Worker*, made a deep impression during the hour or so I enjoyed with him every week. Those early days of sociology in Cambridge were in the hands of a small but distinguished group of faculty which, as well as Lockwood, included Ed Shils, T. H. Marshall, John Goldthorpe, Philip Abrams and Michael Young. Shils invited Talcott Parsons back for visits, which he was brave enough to accept, and they were a thrill for us.

One day in June 1961, with the year's exams over, my roommate in St. John's College asked me whether I would mind looking after his fiancée's friend, Elizabeth, who wanted to visit Cambridge with her the following Sunday. I accepted, without too much enthusiasm. Sunday arrived, a gloriously sunny day. So after showing Elizabeth around some of the principal college attractions, I decided to risk taking her, in the afternoon, three miles out of Cambridge to the Orchard Teahouse in Grantchester. The risk lay in the fact that our transport was to be a 1939 Morgan three-wheeler auto, which I shared with another student. It regularly broke down and sometimes had to be abandoned if, at a weekend, there were no repair shops open. This happened in London about a year later and when my co-owner returned he found the car had been stripped – RIP. On this Sunday, however, all went well and I could even show off a little as the open-top two-seater cruised down Trumpington Road into the countryside. Taking tea on the Orchard's lawns beside the River Cam began to work its magic. We discovered that we lived close by in Surrey and had a common interest in tennis. More to the point, her house had a tennis court to which I was invited. That was the start of a relationship that is now of 40 years standing as I write, 36 of them in marriage.

You need a lot of patience and tolerance in a long marriage. I had the good fortune to discover that same summer, in a rather unfortunate manner, that Liz had plenty of both. The Morgan, which had previously not been put to anything more strenuous than the flat countryside of Cambridgeshire, became a very different proposition when it came to tackling the hills of Surrey. Several times, I took Liz out to a country pub, a favourite being the General Wolfe in Westerham just over the county boundary in Kent. Getting back meant a climb up onto the North Downs. Each time the single back wheel on the Morgan, which was driven by an enlarged bicycle chain, slipped forward in its sprocket under the strain. I never found a way of tightening it sufficiently. As soon as we got up onto the flat, the chain came off. Liz had to sit there pushing the foot brake pedal down to hold the car steady while I put the chain back on and readjusted the rear wheel. It was dark, the nights were quite cool and when eventually I re-emerged my hands were caked in grease and oil. It was not exactly good preparation for a romantic end to the evening. Why I didn't have the sense to get some plastic gloves, I shall never know. Or better still hire a taxi.

Graduating in 1962, I stayed on at Cambridge to undertake research for a Ph.D. with John Goldthorpe of King's College as supervisor. My topic started out as an investigation of the turmoil in writing on industry and management that had been created by the advent of the contingency perspective. Scholars like Joan Woodward, Tom Burns, Tom Lupton, and subsequently Paul Lawrence and the Aston Group, were coming to the conclusion from their empirical studies that which mode of organization and set of management practices were effective depended on the situation. In other words, that it was seriously misleading to prescribe best practices without regard to the context.

This seemed to pose a revolutionary challenge to the management education of the time which, despite early critiques from people like Herbert Simon, was relying on universalistic principles of organization, human relations, and leadership. I conducted an investigation that focused on 35 of the colleges offering what was then the one nationwide British postgraduate diploma in management studies. I used questionnaires and syllabuses for factual information and personal interviews to solicit opinion on issues such as how to interpret the state of management knowledge and what was best to present to students. The interview programme led to my first meeting with Derek Pugh, David Hickson, Bob Hinings and their colleagues in the Aston Group. It became apparent that management education in Britain was indeed in turmoil. There were huge differences in what students were being offered under the rubric of a supposedly standardized qualification, ranging from the dispensing of simple 'one-best-ways' to sophisticated context-sensitive analysis in places like Aston.

History, however, raised its voice again. John Goldthorpe had studied history and was keenly interested in the way that history and sociology could contribute to each other. I had not shaken off my earlier background in the subject. With his encouragement, my research as a journey of discovery led back into the past. For what was coming under fire was a quite extensive and longstanding body of thinking on management and organization. Its self-assured dogmatic quality at least gave managers something to hold on to. Even a critic like Joan Woodward expressed concern that her work would undermine principles and practices which managers had previously taken for granted. So, at the very least, my thesis had to have an introduction on how this body of management thinking had developed.

What started as a historical introduction to the study began to take over the whole enterprise. I unearthed more and more fascinating material on the historical development of management at the hands of the so-called management movement. These were the business people, managers and academics who from the earliest years of the twentieth century wrote and spoke on behalf of the emerging occupation of management. They were concerned to develop a body of technical knowledge relevant to the emerging occupational group and at the same time to claim legitimacy for its use of business assets without owning them. The notion of managerial professionalism, claiming possession of relevant systematic knowledge and a sense of social responsibility, both superior to that of bad 'old-style' employers, was advanced very early on as a justification for the growth of managerial power in large corporations. These claims coloured views about leadership, organization and the fundamental nature of relationships at work that became incorporated into textbooks and other teaching materials on the subject. It emerged that historically the balance of attention given by the management movement to technical issues rather than those of social responsibility varied according to the social expectations placed on business at the time. Following both world wars, for example, there was acute criticism of business and vocal demands for something better. At those times, the amount of attention to managerial legitimacy, and the sense of urgency accompanying this, rose markedly. The historical part of my doctoral research eventually comprised the larger volume of a two-volume thesis. It was published in 1969 as a book titled *British Management Thought.*

The natural theoretical perspective for the analysis of British management thought was that provided by the sociology of knowledge. Here, Reinhard Bendix's comparative historical study of managerial ideology was extremely helpful in demonstrating how this had legitimated managerial authority. I was interested in how the technical content of management thinking related to its legitimatory function, as well as how the balance between the two might change along with the context. Max Weber's analysis of the interplay of both ideas and material forces in driving social development opened the way to understanding these issues. Material forces leading to the development of the modern corporation created a separate role for management, which had to be serviced by its own relevant body of technical knowledge. At the same time, the newly emergent authority of managers as agents required legitimation, and this continues to be reflected in contemporary concerns about corporate govern-ance. The concept of management's social role therefore developed as a result of the economic and technological forces that gave rise to the modern corporation, but only in part. The other part was the product of ideals themselves, some founded upon religious conviction, as with the Quaker employers who actively promoted a moral approach to management, and some coming from other sources such as the Fabian socialist Sidney Webb, who wished to see the development of a more socially responsible capitalism. Management thought resulted from a dynamic historical process in which sense-makers on behalf of management were interpreting the changing context in which managers worked, often doing so in the light of their own preferred ideals.

This was a very broad framework within which to work, and I found it quite a daunting task to interpret specific shifts in my qualitative material over time. Although today I might have benefited from the statistical packages for content analysis, they could not replace judgement in relating the content of a wide-ranging body of knowledge to changes in a diffuse context. When my anxiety had reached a particularly high pitch, a friend reassuringly pointed out that I enjoyed the luxury of being the only person who had ever accessed the materials on which I was working, or was likely to for the next fifty years. So, he said, stop worrying and enjoy the experience of being a pioneer. Certainly, unwrapping parcels of unbound and long forgotten management journals and speeches, thickly covered with the dust of neglect in the British Museum Reading Room, brought a special excitement, though a vacuum cleaner would have been a useful accessory to the process. I wonder when they will next be unwrapped?

With the benefit of hindsight, I can appreciate the importance of this study because it concerns the fundamental question of what justifies management, its power and privileges. Nowadays, these issues tend to fall between the interstices of business school syllabuses, divided as they usually are into functional and other specialties. Nevertheless, the growing social concern about managerial accountability, and the attention some companies are giving to corporate social responsibility, are signs of how these are becoming dominant questions for the 21st century.

ROLLS-ROYCE (1965–1966)

Nearing the end of writing the Ph.D. thesis, I had to make a big choice. Should I stay in the superb, wonderfully agreeable, yet rarefied world of Cambridge after six years, and indeed remain in the educational system that had borne me along for twenty years? Or was it now time to escape the 'gilded cage' into that 'real world' of business and industry that I had glimpsed with fascination during the 1959 Birmingham tour? In the end, I felt it was now or never for me to break out, so I went to work for Rolls-Royce's Oil Engine Division. As the name suggests, the division's product was diesel engines, together with some contract work for the much larger Aero Engine Division, and it employed about 2,600 people. It was located in Shrewsbury, the county town of Shropshire about forty miles north west of Birmingham. Although the head of systems analysis had recruited me, I was placed under the charge of the personnel department and this turned out to give me considerable scope.

Liz and I had married in July 1965 and our first home was a rented upper floor of a late Victorian house in Kennedy Road, a leafy road in Shrewsbury that winds down to the River Severn. The house had character, but at a cost. It was constructed over a spring, which meant that in the winter our clothes were perpetually damp. They had piped water in British towns by the end of the 19th century, so why on earth build directly over a spring? Anyway, we enjoyed the environment. In everyday terms, getting to the shops or the railway station was an extremely pleasant experience. It was a short walk down to the river, then up the other side through the Quarry Park, past the ancient town walls and into the town. The Park contained a large sunken flower garden called The Dingle. The head gardener at the time was Percy Thrower, who had already achieved media fame, and The Dingle claimed to host the best annual flower show in the U.K. Shrewsbury was a strategic town in the days when the English were colonizing Wales, with a medieval castle and many old black and white buildings. Even the railway station was built to match the castle. But can you imagine that even as late as the 1960s, permission was still being given to pull some of these historic buildings down in order to construct plate-glass fronted shops?

The two years I spent with Rolls-Royce significantly broadened my understanding in four principal ways. First, an extended period of working in the engineering shops instilled a deep respect for the capabilities of the people working there, and particularly a realization of how managers failed either to appreciate or engage these. Second, my subsequent work in the Company took me much further into organizational design. Third, the implementation of this work brought home some basic lessons of carrying through organizational change. Fourth, the process through which management decided on that change provided a direct insight into my later formulation of the strategic choice perspective. I have particularly to thank the Oil Engine Division's Personnel Director, Barney Mathias, to whom I reported, for affording me these experiences. I guess he was not quite sure what to do with me and saw no harm in letting me have my head.

I still vividly recalled the brief shopfloor visits of 1959 industrial tour and wanted to learn more. So before being assigned other duties, I requested an extended period of four months working in the engineering shops, with enough prior training in the apprentice school so that I could at least turn a lathe or operate a grinding machine. Barney agreed. Almost everything that I had read from participant observation studies in America and the U.K. now came to life. In my thesis I had criticized the patronizing assumption of many writers of the time on workplace 'human relations' that much employee behavior was non-rational. As you will read later, that almost cost me my Ph.D. In the Shrewsbury factory, the workers were systematically controlling output for the quite rational purpose of optimising their economic gain. Given the large incentive element in their pay, this behavior ensured a reasonably stable weekly family wage. Also by adhering to the output norms agreed with time study officers, it reduced the risk that tasks would be retimed and pay rates cut.

The biggest eye-opener, however, lay in the failure of management to enlist the contribution of a highly talented workforce. I believe that with some encouragement, the workers would have been willing to make available the tacit knowledge that their skill and experience had built up. Many were extremely responsible people, active in the town as church wardens, scout masters, voluntary workers and, in one case, member of the town council. Managers, however, appeared totally unconcerned to relate to the workers. Virtually the only time managers came through the workshops was when they took visitors around. Because they did not know anyone by name, these occasional events were clearly embarrassing for them and offensive for the employees. Nor did the foremen provide a conduit for vertical communication. They were older men who had been 'made up' from the shop floor with a clear indication that this was their last stage before retirement, not a move into the 'management'. It is not surprising that they kept their peace with the workers and were largely invisible. This was a shop floor neglected by management, without effective communication, or any mechanisms for encouraging workers to contribute to improvement. It did not take an expert to see that the factory was seriously underachieving.

The greater part of my time at Rolls-Royce was spent working on part of a company-wide 'systems survey' that had been initiated in anticipation of major new investment in IBM 360 series mainframe computers. The company wanted to examine in detail how best to use the new IT capabilities to enhance its management and operations. This was, in effect, an exercise in company-wide organizational redesign, looking afresh at tasks, information requirements, file storage needs, communication nets, and so forth. A young engineer called Clive Singleton-Turner and I were given the job of coming up with a full systems design for the Oil Engine Division's direct customer-related activities. The Division had no marketing function. Instead, there were six different departments – sales, contracts, installation engineering, invoice and shipping, despatch, spares and service – all of which could be speaking to the same customer with different voices. With such an organizational mess, it was not difficult for us to see that our main contribution would have to be to sort out the confusion by reorganizing these activities into a unified system. We then had to work on the information and file requirements for this system. The end result would be to design and establish a new marketing function.

This was easier said than done, for two reasons. First, neither Clive nor I had any experience of tackling this kind of project. Second, there were obviously going to be some major sensitivities in bringing together six separate departments that came under the aegis of four different divisional functional directors. At first we fortified ourselves with the heady wine of definitions of marketing as the 'leading edge' of the company and similar stuff put out by the professional institutes and textbooks. That helped to provide some self-belief, but it did not tell us what to do. There was really only one option in this situation: we had to go out and talk to the people in the various departments. That's what we did. Without clear thoughts of our own we sought those of others. So we simply asked, 'What problems do you experience? How would you like things to improve? What do you suggest?'

Clive and I were just one team out of three working on the systems survey in the Oil Engine Division. Another team worked on systems for the engineering function. And there was Nigel whose task was to look into production. This is where the lesson starts. Nigel was brought in from IBM with a strong systems background. He was a professional. But what happened? Nigel didn't bother to talk to anyone. He came up with his textbook solution and said, 'Here we are guys, this is the best solution and this is what we're going to do.' The guys threw it out. Whereas Clive and I, anxious about our ignorance, had gone round talking with almost everyone. So we came up with a proposal that owed a lot to suggestions made by the eventual users, and they felt that they owned it. The reorganization was implemented even though the company's investment in new computers was delayed for financial reasons. This was one of the most important experiential lessons I have ever learned. If you want to bring about change that will work, you have to talk to the people involved. They are valuable sources of tacit knowledge. More than that, they need to have a sense of ownership because they are the people who are going to live with the change and make it work.

The Rolls-Royce systems survey was a big initiative for the company. It aimed to achieve major change on the back of advanced technology, so it was a bit of a leap in the dark. It generated a lot of discussion and debate within management, and we were in a good position to observe the processes that went on. In contrast to what is implied in many textbooks, I came to realize that arriving at agreed solutions is not really a matter of a rational decision reached after weighing up relevant contingencies. The managers in Shrewsbury did not agree on the importance of different contingent requirements and they were not clear about their organizational implications. Just as studies of decision making on open-ended issues generally show, the people involved adopted positions that were motivated largely by concern about who is going to win or lose from potential outcomes. This means what is eventually decided may be a compromise that is less than optimum on purely technical grounds. On the other hand, this downside can be more than balanced by a positive motivational factor if the outcome is one people are prepared to buy into. It may be a solution that is workable rather than a technically better one that nobody will accept. This experience of the political and social processes behind decision making on organization was the direct trigger for my thinking on strategic choice a few years later.

There was a period of inactivity following the completion of the systems survey due largely to the company's delay in making new investment in the light of an economic downturn. I also became increasingly frustrated at the absence of any pay progression because the company, heavily dependent on government aero engine contracts, was rigidly implementing a government initiated national pay freeze. I had originally intended to stay with the company for five years before making up my mind whether to stay in industry or not, because I was still in my mid-20s. The decision to leave was due to another instance of serendipity. For just at the time I was kicking my heels and grumbling about pay, the Aston Group in nearby Birmingham advertised a research fellowship to work on their growing programme of organizational research. I applied and was recruited by Derek Pugh.

There was one further project before leaving. I had nagged Barney Mathias about the plight of the foremen, so he let me spend my last few weeks preparing a report on the subject. I was able to see most of the 101 foremen in the factory and it was a chastening experience. Here were men (I can't recall a single woman) who were sitting on an accumulation of some 3,000 years of experience, yet they had in effect been relegated to fetchers and carriers of parts and messages. Many said to me, 'you're the first person in years who has taken any interest in us and asked what we do'. The same approach as the systems survey led to a report that was full of sensible recommendations largely coming from the foremen themselves. The Personnel Director promised that something would be done. I do not know exactly what follow up there was, but I made sure that every foreman received a copy of my report. Deep impressions last and, together with Bruce Partridge, I later returned to the study of supervisors and first-line managers in British industry in the research we conducted for the book *Lost Managers* (1982). Unfortunately, much of the story repeated itself. We concluded that supervisors were 'lost' both as potential contributors to managements that did not accept them and in the sense of having no clear identity to define their position either at work or in the wider community.

During my first few months at Rolls-Royce, and with Liz's forbearance, I managed to complete the write up of my Ph.D. The examination was far from straightforward. There was nobody else in the Faculty of Economics at Cambridge deemed to have the expertise or standing to serve as internal examiner, so the University appointed Dr. Cyril Sofer, a social psychologist, who was heading the Management Studies Group in the Faculty of Engineering. Professor Tom Lupton was appointed as the external examiner. Sofer asked me to modify my critical analysis of Elton Mayo and the human relations movement that I had made in the light both of industrial field studies and the more balanced treatment of conflict offered by the then almost unknown work of Mary Parker Follett. I declined, whereupon Sofer refused to pass the thesis. Fortunately, Lupton's assessment was favourable, so the work was sent to Professor Tom Burns for a third opinion. I waited for three exceedingly anxious months before Burns gave the OK. Doctoral students often express concern about external examiners on the principle of 'the devil you know'. I tell them how grateful I was to mine.

THE ASTON PROGRAMME (1966–1973)

I had been in real doubt about whether to apply for the research fellowship at Aston and move back so soon into academia. I turned for advice to Don Conlon, senior lecturer in management at the then Wolverhampton College of Technology. I had interviewed Don in the college survey for my Ph.D. and got to know him better when he ran a junior managers course for Rolls-Royce and two other companies. I asked whether I could seek his advice, and he took me through the pros and cons, patiently and thoroughly. By the end of that day, I decided that I would apply for the Aston job. That's how I came to join the Aston Programme – a near thing! It has often proved salutary to remind myself that the huge service Don did for me could be just as important in their turn for the young people who knock on my door or send me an e-mail wanting to discuss a problem, just when I feel I cannot possibly afford the time.

The person appointed to the research fellowship was to conduct a replication of the first Aston study of 46 organizations in the English Midlands, principally to check its conclusions in a nation-wide sample. This later became known as the 'National Study'. Derek Pugh and David Hickson, who then led the Aston Programme, have in their contributions to previous volumes of *Management Laureates* described the philosophy of the Aston Programme and how this was implemented through research protocols of the highest order. I am not sure how Derek and David would classify the organization of the Aston Programme in terms of their own concepts. I think it combined the best of the 'personnel bureaucracy', and the professional team. The members were carefully selected and motivated by a combination of intellectual challenge and a strong team identity. The same room layout was maintained in each of the programme's various locations, designed to promote intensive interaction but also allow for personal concentration or reflection. All the members of the Group worked in the same large room, with a 'quiet room' adjacent in which to reflect or talk with visitors. There was also a secretarial room. Though Group members at this stage in the programme now specialised on three principal projects, and there were several doctoral students, every effort was made to keep communications and the exchange of ideas open. Latitude to develop our projects was combined with the need to justify proposals through presentation and collective discussion, and to work to rigorous research protocols.

Another strength of Aston University in those days lay in its pioneering of inter-disciplinary teaching. It established what I believe was the first behavioural science undergraduate programme in Britain, which was extremely satisfying to teach and also attracted excellent students. As well as lecturing on the history of management thought for this programme, I organized an inter-disciplinary workshop for fourth-year students who returned considerably matured from an internship year. During their internship, they had to undertake a research project that counted for 25% of their final grade. They therefore had plenty of experience and material from which to contribute to the workshop, which turned out to be so stimulating that other members of faculty soon asked if they could attend. Lex Donaldson was a member of this class, and Stewart Clegg would have been had I stayed at Aston for an additional year.

The funding available to conduct the National Study came to just £7,800. Yet we wanted both to include more cases than the first Aston study and extend its scope beyond replication by investigating organizational structuring in relation to performance and managerial behavior. We managed to do this on a financial shoestring through forming academic strategic alliances that traded complementarities. Four faculty members joined the project from two colleges, later to become universities, in Manchester and London. They welcomed the opportunity to receive on-the-project research training and a share in publication. In return, they extended our geographical coverage, North and South. At Derek's insistence, we all went through intense training, which included conducting trial interviews in real firms whose managers had agreed to help. The early interviews in the study were conducted in tandem with a more experienced member of the team. Derek always emphasized the importance of meticulously recording all the information we were given, the value of learning from the unexpected, and the transparency of procedures for the reporting of findings. Hours, indeed many days, were spent discussing the interpretation of results gathered from multiple interviews and documents. Both structured and unstructured data were carefully written up in separate schedules and filed by case and category of variable.

The Aston Group was a tightly knit community able to concentrate single-mindedly on research and generate a hothouse intellectual atmosphere. Its first home was a physical hot house too, at least in summer, being a below pavement basement lit through glass ceiling panels. By the time I joined, the Group had moved to the upper floor of a building that still housed a youth club. I should explain that Aston University was at the time expanding through the redevelopment of a run-down inner city zone of Birmingham. Additional space to house research units was available in buildings awaiting demolition or refurbishment, space that also offered an undisturbed working environment; at least, usually undisturbed. One day, not long after I joined the Group, I was going to have dinner in Birmingham with some friends whom I had met on the Wolverhampton College management course. I thought it might be interesting for them to see where I now worked. I led them up the bare concrete stairs, over a pair of teenagers in deep embrace, and then opened the door of the main workroom. I immediately closed it again with considerable embarrassment, saying something like 'sorry, they're in the middle of a discussion'. For a senior member of the Group was jumping up and down on a table in the middle of the room exclaiming 'I'm never going to do any research ever again!' That was the hot house. Thank goodness he did not mean it.

The intellectual camaraderie of the Aston Group was reinforced by close family friendships, which were spontaneously extended to newcomers such as Liz and me. The highlight of the Group's social year was the annual summer picnic for all the families, which each of us in turn had the responsibility of organizing. When our turn came, we were still living out in Shropshire, though now in a house we had bought in Wellington. Shropshire has a great deal of unspoilt hill country. We were able to scout out a secluded spot beforehand that was only accessible literally via 'crossing a stream by the stepping stones' (this predated Deng Xiao Ping's famous aphorism), then walking up the hill on the other side. I think some of the party were beginning to wonder what kind of traipse we were taking them on. But we soon reached the intended spot, a glade sloping gently down to the stream. Framed by birches, this provided a beautiful picnic area, complete with an impromptu cricket match in a neighbouring grass field. The more adventurous could climb up further to the top of the hill for a great view.

Aston University had made a serious error in prevaricating over a Chair for Derek Pugh. So in September 1968 he moved to the London Business School [LBS] in his 'home town', where he soon occupied the prestigious Chair in Organizational Behavior. I went with him as a Senior Research Officer to continue working on the National Project. As the project proceeded, however, I grew more concerned about its theoretical underpinning. The first generation of Aston researchers had set out to identify and operationalize dimensions of organization, rather than to theorize their possible interconnections and how these might arise. They preferred an inductive approach to theory-building rather than 'a priori postulation'. Nevertheless, the programme was going forward on the basis of an implicit theory, which was basically that there was a link between environment, context (principally ownership, size and technology), organizational structure, group characteristics, and individual behavior, such that each of these factors importantly shaped the next one. It was a variant of contingency theory.

My experience in Rolls-Royce did not sit easily with this elegantly simple but deterministic view. It left out the vital elements of interpretation, a priori preference, debate, and the management of change. There was considerable discussion within the Oil Engine Division about the competitive domain (environment) in which it should place itself. The options were debated and different departments argued for their own preferred options. So the organization's environment was not simply a given objective factor; it was all along being interpreted and even disputed. Nor was there a single evident organizational design solution for the particular context. In the event, the proposals that were put forward were ones deemed to be 'workable', and this to a large extent meant 'acceptable' to the different departmental stakeholders. Also whether a particular organizational solution was acceptable depended partly on how the process leading up to it was handled, in other words on the management of change. Prompted by this unease, I developed the so-called 'strategic choice' perspective, initially as a working paper of 1970 and later published in *Sociology* (1972). The notion of strategic does not deny the force of contingency theory, as some have thought, but rather qualifies its determinism by introducing the process of choice that accords with the realities I had observed at first-hand. Judging by the influence the concept has had, its formulation was not only timely it also provided a more balanced perspective on organization. In my own view, the most important corollary of strategic choice lies in the way it legitimises participation in setting up organizational arrangements, rather then assuming that they are a technical matter best left to the 'experts'.

Ray Loveridge was a lecturer at the LBS and Malcolm Warner later joined the research group that Derek Pugh established there. The three of us convened the Industrial Sociology Section of the British Sociological Association. The meetings thrived and attracted participation well beyond the limits of London. Some of the papers presented to its meetings were published in collected volumes, one of them being *Man and Organization*, which I edited in 1973 (the title would hardly be acceptable today!). When Ray and I both moved away to Aston University in 1973, we handed the convenorship over to our friendly rivals at Imperial College: Celia Davies, Arthur Francis and Sandra Dawson.

Eventually, Aston University did decide to create a Chair of Organizational Behavior in 1972. The leading personae in the Aston Programme had by now moved elsewhere: Derek Pugh to London, David Hickson to the Bradford Management Centre via Alberta, and Bob Hinings also via Alberta (where he later returned) to Birmingham University. So, with Derek's encouragement, I applied. I was on an untenured research contract, with a wife now at home looking after our two year-old son, Martin, soon to be followed by a daughter, Caroline. It seemed responsible to go for the additional pay and security, and the prospect of returning to Aston in a leadership role was intriguing. Aston, however, did not enjoy the prestige or facilities of an LBS or other international school. Its fame in business and management education rested on just one research programme that was now spreading, but also in a sense diluting, around the world. So, as before, I sought further advice, this time from Professor Jim Ball, the Director of LBS. He made two observations that swayed my decision. First, I should not feel that I was in any way letting the LBS down. Yes, he would be sad to see me go, but it was healthy for LBS to take in, develop and then lose good young faculty so long as the cycle was always maintained. This was a way for an academic institution to be re-invigorated by new young blood and for a prestigious school to play its part in developing leaders for the rest of the system. His second point was that it was extremely satisfying, and much less stressful, to help move a business school up the rankings than it was to maintain an exposed position at the top. This encouraged me to go ahead, and on May 1, 1973 I moved back to Aston, where I remained for the next 18 years.

Only Diana Pheysey was left at Aston from the former research team and there were few teaching faculty in the subject area either. Rather than immediately rebuilding a new research group, we decided that the next three years would be best spent enhancing the legacy of the Aston Programme by consolidating existing data and publishing further results. I continued to write up the findings of the National Project and joined with Alfred Keiser, then at the Free University Berlin, in extending its methodology to comparisons between Britain and Germany. We, as one post-Aston branch, did friendly battle with another in the persons of David Hickson and his colleagues over the 'culture-free' thesis of organization. With the help of Pat Clark, who still works at Aston in research administration, I also put together a database of 26 studies around the world that had employed Aston Programme methodology.

The collaboration with Ray Loveridge and Malcolm Warner had already borne fruit in another extension of the Aston Programme, to take in occupational interest associations – labor unions and professional associations. The three of us developed a theoretical analysis of how such associations were organized and the tensions this had to contain, which Malcolm and Lex Donaldson went on to examine empirically. This is a line of enquiry that I think has been insufficiently built upon since. This was the first of a wider range of collaborations that were to mark much of my later work.

The Aston Group came as near to the ideal of a community of professional practice as I have ever experienced in my whole career. Derek and David have had a hugely positive influence on the formation of everyone who has worked with them. They taught us all the highest standards of professional research and instilled in us a deep belief in the sacred mission of universities to create knowledge. Some people may have an impression of the Aston Group as cliquey and self-referential. I think that it is closer to the truth to say that people who worked on the programme or studied under its members have a deep sense of identity that stems from both the professionalism and personal support that was its hallmark.

OB AND WORK ORGANIZATION (1973–1989)

The 1970s were also spent building what was formally called the Organizational Sociology and Psychology Group. Several of the faculty who joined – Peter Clark, Diane Hosking and Hugh Wilmott – later went on to become chaired professors elsewhere. We spent a lot of time in the early days developing the group's culture and identity. Godfrey Williams organized a faculty research discussion group, with great enthusiasm. This met in our homes in the evenings, and it played a significant role in our mutual learning and group culture-building. Godfrey was a dedicated Christian and the epitome of gentle kindness. He died tragically of Hodgkin's Disease at the age of only 31, something we could never really come to terms with. We also made progress with introducing new courses, establishing a doctoral programme and running regular research seminars.

In 1977, at the invitation of Anant Neghandi, I spent six months of leave in the United States, based at Kent State University. The University thought it was a good idea to put Brits together, and I therefore shared a large university apartment with J-C Spender. J-C has an extraordinarily original mind. Reminiscent of Einstein, J-C was forever sketching new ideas on the back of envelopes, or more usually on Burger King napkins (we preferred their relish to that of the competition!). For me, this was liberating stuff. It encouraged me to think on an altogether broader plane than before. J-C is also a perfectionist and was struggling at the time to reduce his mammoth doctoral thesis from the 1,000 pages it then occupied. Later on, this formed the basis for his path-breaking book on *Managerial Recipes* published in 1989.

There is actually a story behind that book which I hope J-C won't mind my telling. J-C received his Ph.D. from the Manchester Business School in the early 1980s, but then delayed and delayed submitting his dissertation for publication because he felt that he had still not got the text quite right. This was despite the constant urging of his friends. When J-C became a candidate for a Chair at Glasgow University, Peter Grinyer (his former head of department) and I both independently wrote in our reference letters that the University should make publication of a book from J-C's thesis a condition of offering him the post, for which he was thoroughly qualified. This did the trick and it was one of the best things I have ever done. Soon after, the book at last saw the light of day. It was a turning point both for J-C and the field of strategic management. Most readers will be aware of the tremendous contribution that J-C has made since through a steady stream of publications.

The stay in the USA was for me very enriching both academically and personally. With plenty of time on our hands, J-C and I toured around in a huge and very aggressive red Chevy gas-guzzler, presenting seminars at many Midwestern, Eastern and Canadian Schools. I also had opportunities to fly to the west coast and parts of the South. It was a privilege to meet people like Paul Lawrence, James March, Ray Miles, Henry Mintzberg, Karlene Roberts, Stan Seashore and William Foote Whyte, whose work had been so inspiring, as well as to renew friendships with Mike Aiken, Martin Evans, Bill Glueck, Jerry Hage, Ed Lawler, Charles Perrow, Jim Price and others who had previously visited Aston or the London Business School. Just as exciting was the opportunity to get to know the upcoming generation of now leading scholars in organizational studies and related fields, such as Howard Aldrich, Jeff Pfeffer and Chuck Snow. Closer to home in Ohio, friendships grew with, among others, Orlando Behling, Janet Fulk, Steve Kerr, Anant Neghandi, Bernie Reimann, and Chet Schriesheim. Towards the end of my stay, the students at Kent State staged a partial occupation of the campus erecting what they called 'Tent City'. They were protesting against what they perceived as the authorities' attempt to eradicate the memory of the May 1970 National Guard killings by erecting a second gymnasium on the same site. It was difficult to see why the university even needed a second gymnasium, because it was already very well provided for. Passions rose and radical leaders like Jerry Rubin returned to the scene with an impressive quality of oratory.

One of the more important lessons I learned from participation in the American system concerned the professional way in which doctoral pro-grammes were organized. The candidates benefited from features that were unknown in Britain at the time, such as preparatory courses, the supervisory support of several committee members, and the requirement that students demonstrate their readiness to undertake a research investigation through the presentation of a detailed research proposal. We began to introduce some of these features in the OB Group at Aston, and also sought to develop a community of doctoral scholars through attracting those with shared interests, encouraging them to relate their work to that of ongoing projects. The inclusion of doctoral students in research groups had proved its worth in the latter days of the Aston Programme. Towards the end of the 1970s, we brought together a group of doctoral students specializing on the organization of the professions. With the assistance and encouragement of Janet Fulk (now at the University of Southern California) who was visiting us, this focus gave rise to a particularly exciting set of seminars, courses and publications.

My wife, Liz, also decided to register as a part-time Ph.D. student at Aston. Her subject was development among pre-school children, and she built upon the research she had done into maternal deprivation at Cambridge while I was taking my Ph.D., although her subjects there had been Rhesus monkeys. We like to think that the lively presence of our own two young children was also an inspiration for Liz's study, though they certainly competed for her time and energy! Anyway, the outcome was highly successful with the external examiner from Cambridge stating that it was the best Ph.D. thesis he had ever read.

By the mid-1970s, I felt I had to resolve the dissonance in my work between the contributions I had made within a contingency framework and the pull towards power and process contained in my essay on strategic choice. Without wishing to deny the relevance of contingency theory, I perceived it as opening only one window onto a complex world. In particular, it overlooked the dynamics that give rise to organizational design outcomes. There was also a tussle underway between the narrow managerial orientation implicit in the work I had done on organizational design and the broader sociological appreciation I had inherited from my Ph.D. and strengthened by my Roll-Royce experience. I achieved some resolution of the problem through moving closer again to the study of specific work situations while at the same time broadening my frame to take account of the sociological context, in particular social class and national setting. This shift was accomplished through several new streams of work.

I began to move to the dynamics of how organizations develop over time in an essay written in 1975 with Alfred Kieser and eventually published in the long-delayed *Handbook of Organizational Design* (1981) edited by Nystrom and Starbuck. Soon after, I started to work with a more specific focus on changes in the organizational position of two occupational categories – professionals and first-line managers – and how this was affecting their relation to management. Both these categories accounted for significant numbers of organizational members, yet organizational scholars had not given them much attention. The work on professionals followed on from the study of occupational associations and was conducted in collaboration with Janet Fulk.

It also linked in with the research underway by the group of doctoral students at Aston. We analysed the changing bases of professional control in a joint article appearing in *Work and Occupations* (May 1982). I also reviewed the evidence on the extent to which professionals working in business corporations were likely to experience conflict with management over the organization of work, their priorities and career advancement in an article appearing in the *International Yearbook of Organization Studies* (1982).

Towards the end of the 1970s, Bruce Partridge and I undertook the research into industrial supervisors that I mentioned earlier. As with professionals, we wanted to give closer attention to specific work situations with a view to understanding the role of action within them in relation to the formal structuring captured by the Aston Group's methodology. We considered that informal action by people in workplaces, even that running counter to managerial rules, can be regarded as part of the structuring process and, indeed, essential to the continued maintenance of working relationships. The research on industrial supervisors explored these themes, together with the social identity, class position and unionisation of people occupying a significant internal organizational boundary. In the plants investigated, we found that, although they were designated first-line managers, most supervisors were marginalized, unhappy and unable to realize their potential contribution (*Lost Managers*, 1982).

Working with Alfred Kieser provided a big incentive to bring the international dimension into my work. Other members of the former Aston Group were doing this, David Hickson in particular, and there was always the dual identity factor somewhere in the deeper recesses of my mind. I embarked on two studies comparing organization and management in British and West German companies in order to examine the respective relevance of contingency and socio-cultural factors within two capitalist economies that were then comparable in size, stage of industrial development and dependence on foreign trade. Their consistent disparity in industrial performance was naturally also of interest. The results of the work with Kieser challenged the 'culture-free' hypothesis that David Hickson and his colleagues had advanced on the basis of pure contingency analysis. Writing in a chapter for *Organizations: Like and Unlike* (1979) and in an article for *Organization Studies* (1982), we concluded that while there were contingency effects, an adequate explanation required attention to other factors of an institutional and cultural nature. Such factors demonstrated the significance of history and social embeddedness. With Mike Fores, Ian Glover and Peter Lawrence, I also explored the historical origins of differences in British and German work organization, and how it related partly to the Anglo-Saxon concept of professional specialization, in an article that appeared in *Sociology* (1983). My paper in *Research in Organizational Behavior* (1981) was an attempt at a comprehensive overview of the different perspectives within which we were conducting our debates. It distinguished three main approaches within the cross-national study of organizations – 'contingency, culture and capitalism' (institutional) – discussing the problems attaching to each.

The plight of first-line managers and inferior industrial performance compared to Germany were symptoms of the so-called 'British disease'. Much of British manufacturing was then characterized by low productivity, appalling quality, resistance to technological change and bad industrial relations. This reinforced the view of many scholars that the time had come to refocus our interest in organization back onto the workplace. We at Aston agreed, especially in the historical context of the work undertaken there during the previous twenty years. At the end of the 1960s, Tom Lupton fresh from his shop-floor studies had brought in the funding that established the Aston research programme. At the time, Tom felt that the priority was to conduct more precise investigations into the factors like organization and technology that formed the *context* for shop-floor behavior. After a long period of research largely focused on organization structure in the broad, it now appeared timely to return to how work itself was organized. Apart from the problems of first-line supervision, there were other pressing issues at the time, including a poor record of applied innovation, and the challenge of the new information technologies then becoming available.

Reflecting this general view, the British Economic and Social Research Council [ESRC] announced a national competition to establish and house a new centre of excellence in the field of work organization. Our bid was selected, and the Work Organization Research Centre was established at Aston in 1981 for a period of five years. WORC had a rotating directorate of Peter Clark, Ray Loveridge and myself. Its principal researchers included Margaret Greico, Alan McKinlay, Chris Smith, Ken Starkey, and Richard Whipp, all of whom went on to become full-fledged professors. The Centre spawned several lines of research. For example, Peter Clark and Richard Whipp, working with Neil Staunton, initiated a long line of studies into innovation. Chris Smith and I researched the ambitious 10-year programme of capital investment and work restructuring that Cadbury Limited, the chocolate company, had launched in the late 1970s. We were joined by Mick Rowlinson, whose Ph.D. researched the history of work organization in the company. Cadbury's had established a work organization department as early as 1910 but, as befits a Quaker-led firm, it had always insisted that scientific management be applied with regard to the well-being of employees. McKinlay and Starkey focused on restructuring in the motor industry. Ray Loveridge and I joined with teams from five other European countries to conduct comparisons of the introduction of information technology into European services.

This last project went by the somewhat doubtful acronym of MESS [Microelectonics in the Service Sector]. It examined 36 cases. There were six cases from each participating country, two from each of three services: retail banking, hospital biochemistry laboratories, and retailing. Close attention was paid to specific situations through methods such as direct observation, in addition to interviews. This project drew together several of the emerging strands in my work. It focused on the processes of organizational change, whereby new IT based technologies were introduced and applied to the organization of work. It closely investigated how the design of new socio-technical systems emerged and who participated in the process. It was also internationally comparative. The comparison across six countries was motivated by an interest in whether outcomes would vary between countries and whether such variance could be accounted for by contrasting national institutions and cultures, such as their industrial relations systems and attitudes towards the improvement of working life.

The MESS project produced many fruitful insights, such as how the premises for organizational learning were a political issue between different organizational interest groups ('contested learning'), and how what we termed 'organizational conservatism' impacted on the process of introducing technological change. The findings clearly indicated that there could be choice and equifinality in the use of IT. The extent to which that choice was realized depended importantly on the extent of participation in the design and decision process, and this is where institutions and embedded tradition had a major influence. The study was published in the book, co-authored with Ray Loveridge, titled *New Technology in European Services* (1990).

There were two further international extensions of the MESS Project. Both confirmed that the same new technology could be interpreted quite differently depending on the context. Suzana Rodrigues from the Federal University of Minas Gerais replicated the project in Brazil. This showed how the importance in Brazilian culture of personal communication and relations led to the mediation of IT being regarded with great suspicion. Suzana is a neo-Astonian in-so-far as she had studied for her Ph.D. under David Hickson's supervision. Her work with the MESS project was the beginning of a long and continuing collaboration.

The second extension, in 1986, was to China. I undertook a case study in the biochemistry laboratory of the Chinese Academy of Medical Sciences central teaching hospital in Beijing. This also pointed to the relevance of context including, in this instance, recent history. The laboratory in China had the same automated analysers as many of its European counterparts, supplied under a World Health Organization development program. Yet in contrast to most technicians in European laboratories, who (apart from Sweden) generally regarded the application of IT-based automation as deskilling, those in the Beijing hospital took a very positive view of it. There seemed to be two prime contextual reasons for this. First, they had missed out on a proper training because of the Cultural Revolution. The machines could perform a wide range of blood and urine analyses, and they displayed each step of every programme on their monitors. This provided the technicians with important knowledge that was new for them, though it would not have been for their fully trained European counterparts. Second, the equipment in their laboratory was the most advanced in the whole of China; this was a source of great pride and status in their eyes.

The bulk of this research had been completed when WORC's funding ran out in 1986, though the work on innovation continued in a newly-formed centre on industrial design and operations management [IDOM]. I had to relinquish much of my active research work for three years from the start of 1986, when I was elected Dean of the Aston Management Centre. Much of my time was taken up with trying to get permission to recruit new faculty in a context where the University was coping with a budget deficit by milking areas like management studies. At one time, the Aston Management Centre was maintaining a load equivalent to 91 faculty members with just 67 in post. This was a common problem in the U.K. at the time which, as a member of the University Grants Committee's sub-committee on business and management studies, I encountered on almost every site visit. The Vice-Chancellor at Aston was pursuing this policy to an extreme, so much so that in 1988 the UGC told him publicly that he was to allow new appointments in management or have the university's budget cut. On the whole, these were a grim three years. We did make some progress, including the establishment of the Aston Business School, the launch of its executive programme and the upgrading of its residential facilities. Later, once the brakes had been taken off, some excellent new appointments were also made. On reflection, I think that the experience of managing a business school strongly confirmed the need for networking, persuasion and patience in order to introduce any improvements. Nevertheless, the context was sufficiently discouraging that I have to admit there were times when I began to doubt the existence of strategic choice!

CHINA (1989–1991)

Back in 1984, I had responded to an advert in *The Economist* inviting applications for two-month teaching appointments in the about-to-be-established China-European Community Management Programme. This was a two-year MBA programme established through the vision and energy of Max Boisot, funded by the EC and located in Beijing. Its partner was the division of the Chinese government's economic reform commission concerned with management education. I taught OB to the first cohort of MBAs in September–October 1985 and returned to teach or conduct research for short periods in each of the following three years. The EC programme was pioneering in several respects. Apart from the U.S. Department of Commerce/State University of New York Buffalo MBA programme at Dalian, it was the first in China. One of its innovative features lay in the nine months of project work the students had to complete in Chinese enterprises. During their two years on the programme, they progressed from conducting basic descriptive research, through to a consulting project and finished by writing a case study together with teaching notes. For the students, the projects provided a means of learning how to collect and analyse relevant information and then how to apply or adapt western management to the Chinese context. For the faculty, supervising the students provided an insight into Chinese factories that was rare for foreigners at the time.

Two events coincided in 1988, providing a further major intervention of serendipity. Max Boisot decided not to renew his contract as Dean and Director of the European Community programme. Second, my elected deanship at Aston was drawing to a close. I was invited to succeed Max with the prospect of a four-year term. My good friend Eugene McKenna, a professor of psychology, had for some time detected a certain urge in me to change direction as we talked during many shared walks along the glorious, and also changeable, coast of South Devon. Engagement with China was becoming ever more attractive as the country's reform gathered pace. Obviously, there were some major domestic adjustments to be made, but Liz with the insight of another psychologist, encouraged me to take the plunge.

The Vice-Chancellor of Aston University, Sir Frederick Crawford, was only prepared to grant me a one-year secondment from Aston in the first instance. I also had to complete my term as Dean. At first, I therefore worked part-time on the new assignment and from a distance, only arriving in Beijing on April 26, 1989. This happened to be the date of the first large-scale demonstration in what grew into an emerging democracy movement. I had already decided to keep a daily diary because I knew full well that I was facing a daunting learning experience and thought that a record of events might assist reflection. What events they turned out to be. The diary ran to well over 100 pages and I am still contemplating using the material as a backdrop to a novel for which there is no lack of real-life characters.

By mid-May, virtually every section of Beijing society had joined the demonstrations including government departments and Party offices. Naturally, the MBA students wanted to add their support, but I found myself criticising the way they went about this. We were flying in faculty from major European business schools for eight-week teaching assignments. The weekly timetable was full and ran from Monday morning to midday Saturday. One afternoon the class disappeared to join the daily demonstration which generally built up during the afternoon and evening, moving in the direction of Tiananmen Square where the student occupation was centred. The next morning I called the class together and said that while I did not wish to make a political statement, as director of the programme I could not accept its disruption without the courtesy of prior consultation. I discovered later that what I said had been reported to our Chinese partner as John Child criticising the students for joining the anti-government movement.

In those days, I had long and intense debates with the MBA students around the canteen table. This was a new experience for them and it took me back to my own student days. They wanted to enjoy the democratic freedoms we already had in the 'West', without delay. I reminded them that in the U.K. these had taken 800 years to secure, required several revolutions and faced violent acts of military suppression, as at Peterloo in 1819. I recall arguing that even under the most favourable circumstances it was likely to take several generations in China until universal literacy and education could provide sufficient competence and confidence for the population to exercise its democratic rights responsibly. Otherwise, there was the risk that the democratic process would be subverted by chaos and demagogy, as had happened all too often elsewhere in the developing world and indeed not long before in parts of Europe.

1989 is an unforgettable (and not to be forgotten) year, both in China and Eastern Europe. In Beijing during the period April to early June, there was an uplift of the human spirit that it was impossible not to share, even for a foreigner. As hope gathered that political reform would come, and with it an end to the tyranny of corruption and petty officialdom, so people's attitudes towards each other changed. Quite spontaneously, politeness, consideration and honesty shone through. For example, previously it was a scrum to get onto one of the Beijing buses, which were normally grossly overcrowded because fares were so heavily subsidized. Then, all of a sudden people formed queues. The generosity of ordinary people towards the demonstrators was legion: food, drink, shelter and monetary support were all offered. The crime rate dropped sharply and there were many stories of people returning purses and other property lost in the street. Nobody told this people, so accustomed to receiving instructions from government and Party, to do any of these things. It was simply the Spring sprit of Beijing that everyone shared. Each evening as May wore on and passed into June, literally millions were on the streets, moving towards Tiananmen Square or listening to the information broadcast through loudspeakers outside the universities by student radio, yet there was no disturbance. Each time a truck with a new relay of student protestors passed, or an ambulance came though with exhausted hunger strikers, the crown somehow parted in the middle, made room and then came together again. I marvelled at what this same collective spirit and self-organization could achieve if translated into the world of everyday work. Would we need managers? I had, of course, seen some glimmers of the same on the Rolls-Royce shop floor, but this had been compromised by managerial indifference and the underlying conflict of interest over the effort-bargain.

After June 4, those of our MBA students who came from Beijing stayed at home with their families. The others wanted to get away to their families as soon as they could. We had two weeks of the semester left with three courses running. So we photocopied all the remaining materials and officially sent all the students back home saying, with some bravado, that we would be back two weeks early in mid-August to retrieve the lost classes. We did come back two weeks early.

Having got both students and faculty off to what they perceived as a safer place, our main task was now to think about the future of the programme. It soon became clear that the post-Tiananmen Chinese policy of 'defeating bourgeois liberalization' (i.e. suppressing dangerous western values) translated into closing all foreign educational programmes. There were also serious doubts at the European Commission in Brussels as to whether the programme should continue. Our argument from Beijing was that this would only penalize the students. Well, to cut a long story short, our programme was the only one that did survive. Fortunately, with the unfailing guidance of my PA, Yanni Yan, I had managed to build up considerable goodwill through engaging with my Chinese partners socially and listening patiently to their point of view. I am convinced that this approach helped to save the programme from being closed down by the Chinese authorities, and the subsequent benefits were consider-able. We began to expand from the core MBA programme, initiating both research and executive programmes. This led us to become the China-Europe Management Institute [CEMI]. Eventually in 1994, the organization moved to

Shanghai to become the China-Europe International Business School [CEIBS], with Jiaotong University as its local partner.

China has made a profound impression on both my work and life. One reason is that it was the source of my collaboration with Max Boisot. We discovered that we had usefully complementary abilities. Max has a fertile imagination and reads widely well outside the social sciences into biology, physics, information theory and complexity. I was able to contribute my own perspective from organizational theory, backed by an accumulating knowledge of Chinese enterprises and the progress of the economic reform within them. I was the net beneficiary from this partnership because it introduced perspectives that were entirely new to me and state-of-the-art in themselves. Our collaboration continues, when time and travel permit. Its products have appeared in the *Administrative Science Quarterly* and *Organization Science*, where we have been able to interplay constructively between new conceptual schemes and evidence grounded in China. CEMI also introduced me to talented students and staff, Derong Chen, Yuan Lu and Yanni Yan, who later went on to complete their doctorates in the U.K. and to become colleagues.

Benefiting both from interaction with these friends and the projects undertaken by the MBA students at CEMI, I was able to pull together some of the emerging material and insights in the book *Management in China During the Age of Reform*, published by Cambridge University Press in 1994. This book provided an opportunity to reflect on my encounters with the implementation of China's economic reform within enterprises. It also enabled me to explore wider issues such as the extent to which management in China could be accounted for by Western concepts and theories. Most of my Chinese colleagues were convinced it was a case of *sui generis*, requiring its own theory, but then few Chinese are prepared to admit that foreigners can really understand their country!

I have debated many times with western colleagues who maintain that my interest in China has diverted me away from more mainstream work. My response is that business schools and universities generally should bring China squarely into the mainstream. As I have tried to show in my book and various articles, China is both too important in the world and too challenging intellectually to ignore. It is on course to become the world's largest economy by the third decade of this century and, inevitably, the other superpower. It has achieved this remarkable feat due to the most profound and extensive economic and social revolution a nation has ever undertaken. China's path to reform has been pragmatic and experimental, rather than driven by dogma. In other words, it has been a massive learning process. These are of themselves powerful reasons for choosing it as one's subject of study. In addition, China's clearly distinctive path of economic and organizational development presents a challenge to any assumed universality of western theories. To take a topical example, we in the West look for new e-commerce technologies to extend the arena of transactions largely on the basis of the codified information they can readily carry. I perceive that the Chinese tend to regard the same technologies as an opportunity to extend the arena of transactions (or to decrease their risk within a given arena) on the basis of the closer personal interaction they can bring via e-mail and video-conferencing. The western perspective tends to take categorical rationality as its main criterion, whereas a theory for China would have to accord greater weight to relational rationality. At the practical level, I firmly believe that the facility Chinese people have with business and social networking can offer lessons from which organizations from other countries can benefit, especially as a basis for retaining attributes such as loyalty and trust within the context of large, extended business systems. In my book and in various articles, I have tried to draw attention to such issues.

The Vice-Chancellor of Aston University had agreed reluctantly to extend my leave in China to October 1990, but this was to be the limit. In the same year, 1990, the University of Cambridge announced that it was establishing a Chair of Management funded by an endowment from the Guinness Company. I had always harboured a deep wish to return to my *alma mater*, especially to St. John's College. My obligation to return to Aston in the autumn of 1990 coincided with the interview for the Guinness Chair. I was extremely rusty as an interviewee, having become much more accustomed to asking difficult questions than answering them. Eugene McKenna and Liz both took me in hand with the help of a video recorder, first to expose my appalling interviewee manner and then to permit some self-learning through practice and feedback. Well, it seemed to work, because I was offered the position and moved to Cambridge in July 1991. Sir Frederick Crawford wrote me a generous congratulatory letter, and my departure from Aston after 18 years was on a pleasant note.

CAMBRIDGE (1991–2000)

The school I joined at Cambridge had been established in the previous year, 1990. It was given the label 'Institute' of Management Studies to indicate that this new departure was to be both research-led (and hence academically respectable) and small (and so not a serious competitor to other faculties). There were many in the ancient University of Cambridge who harboured a deep suspicion about the academic respectability of management studies, because it was not a single discipline subject and had a commercial taint about it. There were others, especially in my old faculty Economics, who feared the loss of undergraduate students to the new school. Later in 1990, Sir Paul and Lady Ann Judge made a significant gift towards the funding of a new building, and the school therefore took on its present name: the Judge Institute of Management Studies. Unfortunately, Judge Institute or JIMS inadvertently confused the identity of the school, and so it is now subtitled 'Cambridge's Business School'.

It was a thrill to return to Cambridge after 25 years, especially when my former college, St. John's, elected me to a Fellowship. The Oxbridge colleges provide an ideal working environment. They combine tranquillity and everyday contact with extremely gifted intellectual minds. Coming from other subject areas and being members of a very traditional college, many of the other Fellows took a delight in challenging what I was 'professing', a process which could be both humbling and a source of new insights at a tangent to one's own. As I was continuing to research on China, it was a particular pleasure to find that David McMullen, the Professor of Chinese studies and an undergraduate contemporary, and Joe McDermott a lecturer in Chinese studies, were both Fellows of the College.

The early days of the Judge Institute were, of course, extremely busy, not least because the other Professor of Management and the Institute's Director, Stephen Watson, had suffered a serious road accident just two weeks after the start of my appointment and was out of action for a considerable time. The fond images I had nurtured of professorial life at Cambridge, extrapolating from the discourses over a glass of sherry during undergraduate supervisions, proved to be quite illusory. They overlooked the fact that beyond the protective walls of the college, departmental activities and responsibilities at Cambridge are actually very much like those in any other university, though with the extra dimension of taken-for-granted tradition to master. And it all landed on the new boy's plate. I had hoped that the move to Cambridge would enable me to catch up with some of the backlog of academic reading, following five years of mainly administrative duties at Aston and in China. In the event, the time and energies of our little band were taken up with establishing the Institute's identity and strategy, launching two new Masters' courses, and matching growth with additional facilities and staff. Although the Judge Institute did not come under the aegis of a faculty, these and many other matters had still to be presented and discussed in committee. The fact that our final year under-graduate programme in management was the responsibility of the Engineering Faculty and that some of our staff were officially members of that faculty just added to the meetings and general complexity. Nevertheless, the University was unflinching in its support of its new offspring and, looking back, much was achieved quickly though it did not always appear so at the time.

If I had hoped to relax just a little, a further surprise was about to unfold in Vienna. Given the momentous events in Europe of the previous two years, the focus of the 1991 Colloquium of the European Group for Organization Studies [EGOS] in Vienna was on societal change between market and organization. Michel Crozier, Renate Mayntz and I were invited to present keynote speeches to the meeting. I gave the opening keynote on the subject of 'Society and Enterprise Between Hierarchy and Market'. With the intellectual excitement of transition in the air, it was a memorable meeting, but also for another reason. It became apparent from the frequent disappearance of members of the *Organization Studies* advisory board and editorial team that something was up. Then, on the last afternoon of the meeting, David Hickson, chair of the advisory board, asked me to join him for a chat outside the conference building. To my amazement he said that the board would like me to become Editor-in-Chief. He said that the workload on the current Editor had created problems and a change was needed. Even though at this point I had not become fully immersed in the Judge Institute, I could see that this was rather ironic. The last thing I wanted was to take on another responsibility. Also, although I had published in OS and reviewed for it, I had not had any formal connection with the journal. I therefore said that I had to decline the offer, high honour though it was. It is a tribute to David's dogged persuasiveness, as well as his sheer likeability, that he ended up getting me to agree to think the matter over and not come to a decision right away. So, the outcome was probably inevitable. With considerable misgiving, but buoyed up by the feeling of being needed, the intriguing challenge of taking the helm of a great journal, and the realization that it would be good for the image of the new Judge Institute, I became editor of OS in January 1992.

The first vital step was to find an editorial assistant. In addition to the usual management of submissions and reviews, the editorial assistant had to ensure that communication and co-operation were maintained with the rest of the scattered OS operational network: the co-editors in Germany, USA, U.K. and later on Italy; the managing editor in the Netherlands, and the publisher in Berlin. On the day we interviewed, Mary Beveridge, the Judge Institute's very experienced administrator, and I had one more candidate to see at the end of a somewhat depressing autumnal afternoon. In came Sally Heavens who soon lifted our spirits with the way she joked irreverently through the proceedings. We could see that Sally had the ability and experience to do the job, she seemed highly motivated, and we guessed that she was actually not so zany as she pretended: so why not go for someone who could liven things up as well? Sally came on board and as she says in her poem in the journal's 20th birthday special issue (Vol. 21, issue 0, 2000), 'OS filled my life with tears, and stress, and strife'. She was in the front line chasing reviewers, placating waiting authors, keeping the network wires humming, and always making sure the editor was up to speed. After I handed over to Arndt Sorge in April 1996 and immediately sank into a long sleep in his garden (captured by an OS paparazzo on the last page of the special issue), Sally with her Masters in Linguistics and racy style stayed on as language editor. I think the sleep was actually well deserved because during the previous four years the journal had expanded from four to six issues a year, increased the number of submissions, tightened quality in terms of using more reviewers and reducing acceptance rates, and jumped up in the citation indices.

By 1993, with Stephen Watson back in the saddle, I was able to return to my originally designated role, namely Director of Research. This involved an encouragement of faculty research, the organization of a regular research seminar programme and direct responsibility for the doctoral programme. The latter rapidly built up to a stock of over 70 Ph.D. students by the mid-1990s. It gained formal recognition by the ESRC as a programme of excellence and this provided additional scholarships for students from the U.K. and EU. By this time, I was also able to resume a more active personal involvement in research. This now concentrated on the international dimension. Following my 1991 presentation on transition, several doctoral students with an interest in Eastern Europe enrolled with the Judge Institute. One of them, Livia Markoczy, who is now on the faculty at UC Riverside, was the first Institute student to be awarded a Ph.D. Another, Noreena Hertz, carried out pioneering case studies into how Russian enterprises were coping with a disintegrating system. After writing these up in a scholarly book; Noreena went on to claim greater fame with her controversial best-seller, *The Silent Takover* (2001). I had the opportunity to work on several projects concerning the management of foreign joint ventures in Brazil and China, working with colleagues in those countries and doctoral students at Cambridge. In 1994, we hosted an international workshop at St. John's College on 'Management Issues for China in the 1990s', which led to two edited books of papers. The following year, we hosted another international workshop on 'Managerial Learning in the Transformation of Eastern Europe'. A selection of papers from this workshop was published in a special issue of *Organization Studies* (Vol. 17, 1996). With David Faulkner and Robert Pitkethly, both now at the Said Business School in Oxford, I also initiated a project comparing the changes brought about in U.K. companies following acquisition by firms from the USA, Japan, France and Germany. The findings were recently published in a book, *The Management of International Acquisitions* (2001).

This was a hectic, but heady time. It looks at first sight as though we were branching out in all directions, but in reality all these projects had a common focus on strategic choice and social embeddedness in international business. Each study was concerned with the processes of adaptation and transfer of practice across borders and the extent to which national styles of management are preserved in the context of globalization. On the side of choice, the research was exploring the possibilities for equifinality by which organizations of different nationalities can perform similar tasks and achieve similar goals in different ways. On the contextual side, we were conscious of the competition between high and low context explanations for organization. The essay on 'Theorizing about organization cross-nationally' in *Advances in International Comparative Management* (Vol. 13, 2000) incorporates some of my thinking on these issues in suggesting an approach towards achieving greater theoretical and operational synthesis between different perspectives.

I am wholly convinced of the enormous contribution that internationally comparative research can make to our understanding of organization. Such research indicates that organizations can adopt different means to perform similar tasks and achieve similar goals. So it obliges us to face up to the possibilities of choice and equifinality, even though these open-ended and dynamic notions are very difficult to model. The extent of choice depends on the extent to which viable organizational practices are necessarily situation-specific, as well as on our criteria of viability. Here international comparison can encourage us to take careful account of the context. The way that the internationalisation of firms has led to new organizational forms, such as alliances, networks and transnational corporations, also challenges existing theory and obliges it to take better account of emerging realities.

With considerable activity building up on international business and management, we decided in 1995 to form the Centre for International Business and Management. This brought together faculty with interests ranging from reform in China (Peter Nolan and Malcolm Warner), through contrasting cultures of capitalism (Charles Hampden-Turner), to economic development in Eastern Europe (Christos Pitelis). CIBAM also offered an intellectual home for many doctoral students. The establishment of centres like CIBAM at the Judge Institute greatly enhanced the intellectual culture and collegial contact within which doctoral students could thrive, and it was one of the features leading to official national recognition of our programme. I served as CIBAM's founding director until going on leave to the University of Hong Kong in January 1998, when Christos Pitelis took over the role.

With the determined encouragement of Dr. Sek Hong Ng, I had accepted an appointment as a Distinguished Visiting Professor in the School of Business at the University of Hong Kong. This position is locally called "Star Professor", which is the nearest I have ever come to Hollywood! One of my main objectives was to help found a sister centre to CIBAM, though of necessity one primarily concerned with Chinese business and management. During 1998 we worked on this plan and the Chinese Management Centre [CMC] was officially inaugurated in December of that year with a splendid opening ceremony. This was held in the University's new downtown teaching facility with many toasts and hundred of photographs in a setting bedecked with richly coloured backcloths, banners and flowers, all in the best Chinese tradition. Dr. David Li, Chairman of the Bank of East Asia, and Mr. Qin Xiao, President of CITIC in Beijing, both gave very considered opening addresses, and the Centre is fortunate to be able to have them among its distinguished group of senior advisors.

One of the projects colleagues and I conducted through the CMC was a survey of 615 Hong Kong firms concerning their experience of doing business in China. This project was conducted in collaboration with the HK General Chamber of Commerce. It has thrown up some fascinating insights into factors bearing upon the performance of China-based operations, which we are still digesting as I write. It is a tribute to the speed at which things get done in Hong Kong that a large number of relevant firms were identified (with only limited guidance from published directories), their co-operation solicited, 615 of them visited personally, and the data collated, all within the space of seven months. This was achieved through the co-ordination provided by Leanne Chung who has gone on to study for her Ph.D. at Cambridge. Three former Ph.D. students of mine now work in Hong Kong universities, Yuan Lu, Yanni Yan and Terence Tsai, and it was a great please to renew their acquaintance and to resume working with them.

When it was finally time to leave Hong Kong in April 2000, at least on a full time basis, Professor David Tse took over as the Chinese Management Centre's Director. I always feel at home when I return to that unique territory. I say 'territory' rather than city because there are many visitors who do not realize that not far away from the noisy bustle of downtown there is truly magnificent scenery waiting to be enjoyed in peace and quiet in the New Territories or on some of the outlying islands. I continue to work with colleagues there on several aspects of Chinese management, including the internationalisation of Chinese firms with Christine Wong, and strategy and management in China's hotel sector with Yanni Yan.

Living in a different environment for a while helps one to take stock and consider one's situation in the wider perspective that distance literally brings. Liz had by now developed her work and the network on which it depended for 20 years. She did not want to up sticks and start again in a new environment, be this Cambridge or elsewhere. And she was accomplishing some really marvellous healing, both mental and physical. So I had become a weekend commuter between Cambridge and our home just south of Birmingham. This was not satisfactory either in terms of the limited family time it provided or the increasing strain that travelling on ever more heavily trafficked roads created. Was this really worthwhile? Eventually it became clear that I should make a move to work closer to home within the U.K.

Again serendipity intervened. Towards the end of 1999, the University of Birmingham advertised a vacancy for its Chair of Commerce, now located in its Business School. This chair has a distinguished lineage. You may recall from my December 1959 industrial visit that Professor Sargant Florence had been one of its incumbents. I was aware that the Business School was now embarking on a major programme of development, based on further integrating its long-standing departments of Commerce (founded back in 1902) and Finance and Accounting, and expanding other areas such as international business and organization. The University is also a leading member of Universitas 21, a group of 18 major universities around the world, including the University of Hong Kong and Peking and Fudan Universities in Mainland China. Part of the Universitas 21 secretariat is housed at Birmingham. It made perfect sense to apply.

BACK TO BIRMINGHAM (2000 AND THE FUTURE)

Since September 2000 I have been Professor of Commerce at the University of Birmingham. This has both reunited me with former colleagues such as Peter Clark and spawned new plans. With the support of the Birmingham Business School, I am planning to develop the International Management and Organization Studies Group that I head. Our intention is to focus on the international dimension, nourished through continuing links with both Brazil and Hong Kong. So the award made to me in August 2000 by the Academy of Management as a 'distinguished scholar' in the field of international management was a great encouragement. A further significant development has been Suzana Rodrigues's decision to join the Group. Over the years her philosophical approach to the social sciences coupled with a deep under-standing of Latin America have blended well with my own mix of pragmatism and knowledge of transition economies. As well as participating in much of our research during the past fifteen years, Suzana was instrumental in building her school at the Federal University of Minas Gerais into a position where it is officially ranked as Brazil's No. 1 business school in postgraduate programmes and doctoral research. Her experience will be invaluable. So far, so good. We are extremely busy, bright new doctoral students are knocking at the door, and we are already looking for more space.

My more personal academic goals for the next few years are to consolidate and build upon an experience accumulated over some 40 years, and to pass this on through books, teaching and doctoral supervision. The more I reflect, the more I become aware that certain key issues run through the apparently disparate streams of research and writing that others and I have undertaken. It seems to me that there is a latent theory of human organization still awaiting articulation and recognition. It remains my dream to facilitate this process, and though a dream does not necessarily come true, it can provide a guide. I also appreciate that it is a Herculean task and any younger scholars reading this are most welcome to come and support the project!

CONCLUSION

Writing this account has sharpened my awareness of how the continuities in my work betray a theoretical eclecticism, a sense of history, and a deep belief that organization is fundamentally a political matter. Theoretical eclecticism is a frame of mind that encourages a search for integration between competing but partial perspectives. There are many valuable insights available to inform the study of management and organization, but they are too often kept in isolation from each other. As some recent papers indicate, I am now searching for paths towards synthesis, such as that between action and context in terms of the dynamics of learning and structuration, and between high and low context perspectives. It is quite common to deplore the theoretical and disciplinary fragmentation of our field, but less usual to find anything being done about it.

A sense of history applies both to how we approach a particular subject under study and to the view we adopt of our own field. I feel very strongly about the latter. Given the pressures upon younger faculty to publish with ever increasing frequency, and to demonstrate novelty with each new paper, they are in danger of overlooking the fact that we have so much already to build on. I hear with utter incomprehension, and no little anger, stories about professors who chide students or junior faculty for citing references that are more than three or four years old. How can this give new members of the profession any encouragement to appreciate the fundamentals of the subject, most of which were uncovered many years ago? It is therefore salutary to note how leading figures in business and management studies have attested their debt to Mary Parker Follett, who both came from outside the field and did so some 80 years ago (Graham, 1995).

As Ray Loveridge has correctly noted in *The Handbook of Management Thinking* (1998), I have never forsaken my interest in opening up the explanation of organization to the incorporation of political processes and hence of choice. This stems from my belief that this is the only way we come to regard organization as a tool for us to use rather than as an oppressive instrument to be used on us. I firmly believe that the more we can understand organization, the easier it will be to demystify it and open it up to a truly informed participative process. Similarly, the more we can appreciate the source and nature of international differences in organization, the more we place ourselves in a position both to value the cultural identities these may express and judiciously to weigh up any trade off between their preservation and the pursuit of greater efficiency. These are fundamental issues of human self-expression and wellbeing, and the part that organization plays in them can never be understated. I therefore have no regrets that it became my chosen field of work, albeit by fortunate circumstance. Rather, my concern remains how to do sufficient justice to its challenge.

John Child
Birmingham and Hong Kong
September 2001

PUBLICATIONS

1964

Quaker Employers and Industrial Relations. *Sociological Review, 12*(3), 292–315.
The Teaching of Management Principles. *Scientific Business*, November.

1967

With S. R. Parker et al. *The Sociology of Industry* (revised editions 1972, 1977, 1981). Allen & Unwin.
The Comparative Study of Organizations. *Association of Teachers in Management Bulletin*, December.

1968

British Management Thought as a Case Study within the Sociology of Knowledge. *Sociological Review, 16*(2), 217–239.

1969

British Management Thought – A Critical Analysis. London: Allen & Unwin.
The Business Enterprise in Modern Industrial Society. London: Collier-Macmillan.

1970

More Myths of Management Organization? *Journal of Management Studies*, 7(3), 376–390.
With Derek Pugh. How to Measure Organization. *Management Today*, February: 127–129.

1971

The Organization of Innovation. *Metron*, 3(2), 27–32.

1972

Organizational Structure, Environment and Performance – the Role of Strategic Choice. *Sociology*, 6(1), 1–22.
With Brenda Macmillan. Managerial Leisure in British and American Contexts. *Journal of Management Studies*, 9(2), 182–195.
Organization Structure and Strategies of Control. *Administrative Science Quarterly*, 17(2), 163–177.
With Roger Mansfield. Technology, Size and Organization Structure. *Sociology*, 6(3), 369–393.
With Robert Ashall. Employee Services – People or Profits or "Parkinson"? *Personnel Management*, 4(8), 18–22.

1973

Editor and contributor. *Man and Organization*. London: Allen & Unwin.
With R. J. Loveridge & M. Warner. Towards an Organizational Study of Trade Unions. *Sociology*, 7(1), 71–91.
Strategies of Control and Organizational Behaviour. *Administrative Science Quarterly*, 18(1), 1–17.
With Tony Ellis. Predictors of Variation in Managerial Roles. *Human Relations*, 26(2), 227–250.
Predicting and Understanding Organization Structure. *Administrative Science Quarterly*, 18(2), 168–185.
With Tony Ellis. Placing Stereotypes of the Manager into Perspective. *Journal of Management Studies*, 10(3), 233–255.
Parkinson's Progress: Accounting for the Number of Specialists in Organizations. *Administrative Science Quarterly*, 18(3), 328–348.
With Brenda Macmillan. Managers and their Leisure. In: M. A. Smith, S. R. Parker & C. Smith (Eds), *The Sociology of Leisure*. Allen Lane.
With Elizabeth Child. Children and Leisure: Towards a Sociology of Play. In: M. A. Smith, S. R. Parker & C. Smith (Eds), *The Sociology of Leisure*. Allen Lane.
Why Company "A" Manages Better. *Management Today*, November, 112–119.

1974

Managerial and Organizational Factors Associated with Company Performance – Part I. *Journal of Management Studies*, *11*(3), 175–189.

What Determines Organization Performance? The Universal vs. the It-All-Depends. *Organizational Dynamics*, Summer.

1975

Managerial and Organizational Factors Associated with Company Performance – Part II, A Contingency Analysis. *Journal of Management Studies*, *12*(1), 12–27.

With Lex Donaldson & Howard Aldrich. The Aston Findings on Centralisation: Further Discussion. *Administrative Science Quarterly*, *20*(3), 453–460.

The Literature of Organizational Behaviour. In: K. D. C. Vernon (Ed.), *Use of Management and Business Literature*. Butterworth.

Technical Progress. In: B. Barrett et al. (Eds), *Industrial Relations and the Wider Society*. Collier-Macmillan.

The Industrial Supervisor. In: G. Esland et al. (Eds), *People and Work*. Holmes McDougall.

1976

Participation, Organization and Social Cohesion. *Human Relations*, *29*(5), 429–451.

With Betty Roderick. Designing Work: Educational Materials for Engineering Students, Dealing with Some Social and Psychological Aspects of the Industrial Working Environment. *General Education in Engineering*. Nuffield Foundation.

1977

Organization: A Guide to Problems and Practice (2nd ed., 1984). London: Harper & Row.

Organizational Design and Performance – Contingency Theory and Beyond. *Organization and Administrative Studies*, Special Issue on Organizational Design, August: 169–183.

With Arthur Francis. Strategy Formulation as a Structured Process. *International Studies of Management and Organization*, *7*(2), 110–126.

1978

Quality of Life at Work: Problems and Approaches. In: A. Negandhi & B. Wilpert (Eds), *Work Organization Research: European and American Perspectives*. Kent State University Press.

The Myth at Lordstown. *Management Today*, October, 80–83.

The 'Non-Productive' Component within the Productive Sector. In: M. Fores et al. (Eds), *Manufacturing and Management*. HMSO.

1979

With Alfred Kieser. Organization and Managerial Roles in British and German Companies – An Examination of the Culture-Free Thesis. In: C. J. Lammers & D. J. Hickson (Eds), *Organizations: Like and Unlike*. Routledge and Kegan Paul.

Organizational Growth. In: S. Kerr (Ed.), *Organizational Behavior*. Grid Publishing Company.

With David Walker. The Development of Professionalism as an Issue in British Marketing, *European Journal of Marketing*, *13*(1), 27–54.

1980

With Lisa King & Sandra Pearce. Class Perceptions and Social Identification of Industrial Supervisors. *Sociology*, *14*(3), 363–399.

Factors Associated with the Managerial Rating of Supervisory Performance. *Journal of Management Studies*, *17*(3), 275–302.

1981

Culture, Contingency and Capitalism in the Cross-National Study of Organizations. In: L. L. Cummings & B. M. Staw (Eds), *Research in Organizational Behavior*, Vol. 3. JAI Press.

Comment on Kochan: An American Perspective on the Integration of the Behavioural Sciences into Industrial Relations. In: A. Thomson & M. Warner (Eds), *The Behavioural Sciences and Industrial Relations*. Gower.

With Alfred Kieser. The Development of Organizations Over Time. In: P. Nystrom & W. H. Starbuck (Eds), *Handbook of Organizational Design*, Vol. 1. Oxford University Press.

1982

With Bruce Partridge. *Lost Managers: Supervisors in Industry and Society*. Cambridge: Cambridge University Press.

With Janet Fulk. Maintenance of Occupational Control: the Case of Professions. *Work and Occupations*, *9*(2), 155–192.

With Andreas Budde, Arthur Francis & Alfred Kieser. Corporate Goals, Managerial Objectives and Organizational Structures in British and West German Companies. *Organization Studies*, *3*(1), 1–32.

Divisionalisation and Size: a Comment on the Donaldson/ Grinyer Debate. *Organization Studies*, *3*(4), 351–353.

Professionals in the Corporate World: Values, Interests and Control. In: D. Dunkerley & G. Salaman (Eds), *International Yearbook of Organization Studies 1981*. Routledge & Kegan Paul.

1983

With Michael Fores, Ian Glover & Peter Lawrence. A Price to Pay? Professionalism and Work Organization in Britain and West Germany. *Sociology*, *17*(1), 63–78.

With Monir Tayeb. Theoretical Perspectives in Cross-National Organizational Research. *International Studies of Management and Organization*, Winter 1982/3: 23–70.

With R. J. Loveridge. Capital Formation and Job Creation within the Firm in the U.K. In: *Relations Between Technology, Capital and Labour.* Brussels, EEC.

1984

New Technology and Developments in Management Organization. *Omega, 12*(3), 211–223.
With R. J. Loveridge, J. Harvey & A. Spencer. Micro-electronics and the Quality of Employment in Services. In: P. Marstrand (Ed.), *New Technology and the Future of Work and Skills.* Frances Pinter.
New Technology and Managerial Strategies Towards the Labour Process. In: P. Koistinen & K. Urponen (Eds), *New Technologies and Societal Development.* University of Joensuu, Finland, Research Reports in Social Policy and Sociology.
The Literature of Organization Studies. In: K. D. C. Vernon (Ed.), *Information Sources in Management and Business.* Butterworth.

1985

With Marion Tarbuck. The Introduction of New Technologies: Managerial Initiative and Union Response in British Banks. *Industrial Relations Journal, 16*(3), 19–33.
Managerial Strategies, New Technology and the Labour Process. In: D. Knights et al. (Eds), *Job Redesign: Critical Perspectives on the Labour Process.* Gower.
Effetti e Conseguenze dell' introduzione della nuove tecnologie nelle filiali delle aziende di Credito Inglesi. In: Emanuele Invernizzi (Ed.), *Organizzazione del Lavoro in Banca e Automazione.* Milan: Franco Angeli, Chap. 2.
The Role of Supervisors in the Paper and Board Industry. London: National Economic Development Office, December.

1986

With Michael Fores, Ian Glover & Peter Lawrence. Professionalism and Work Organization: Reply to McCormick. *Sociology,* November, *20*(4), 607–613.
Information Technology and the "Service Class." In: K. Purcell, S. Wood, A. Waton & S. Allen (Eds.), *The Changing Experience of Employment.* Macmillan.
New Technology and Developments in Management Organisation. In: T. Lupton (Ed.), *Human Factors.* Bedford: IFS.
Technology and Work: an outline of theory and research in the Western social sciences. In: P. Grootings (Ed.), *Technology and Work: East-West Comparison.* Croom Helm.
Work and the Transformation of the City. In: *Crisis and Planning: The Transformation of the City and of Work.* City of Genoa.

1987

With Paul Bate: editor and contributor. *Organisation of Innovation: East-West Perspectives,* Berlin: De Gruyter.
Information Technology, Organization and the Response to Strategic Challenges. *California Management Review, XXX*(1), 33–50.

With Chris Smith. The Context and Process of Organizational Transformation. *Journal of Management Studies*, 24(6), November, 565–593.
With A. Kieser & D. Ganter. Technological Innovation and Organizational Conservatism. In: J. M. Pennings & A. Buitendam (Eds), *New Technology as Organizational Innovation*. Ballinger.
Organizational Design for Advanced Manufacturing Technology. In: T. D.Wall, C. W. Clegg & N. J. Kemp (Eds), *The Human Side of Advanced Manufacturing Technology*. Wiley.
Enterprise Reform in China – Progress and Problems. In: M. Warner (Ed.), *China's Management Reforms*. Pinter.
With Penny David. *Technology and the Organisation of Work: The Move Towards Millwide Systems*. London: National Economic Development Office.
The Future of Management Chinese Style: The Long March Ahead. *Issues*, 3/3.
Commentary on a Process Model of Strategic Redirection in Large Complex Firms. In: A. Pettigrew (Ed.), *The Management of Strategic Change*. Blackwell.

1988

With Kuniyoshi Urabe (deceased): Editor and Contributor. *Innovation and Management: Its International Comparison*. Berlin: De Gruyter.
On Organizations in their Sectors. *Organization Studies*, 9(1), 13–19.
With M. Boisot. The Iron Law of Fiefs: Bureaucratic Failure and the Problem of Governance in the Chinese System Reforms. *Administrative Science Quarterly*, 33(4), 507–527.
Participacion en la Introduccion de las Nuevas Tecnologias en las Empresas. In: J. L. Gayarre (Ed.), *Cambio Social Actual y Estructura de las Empresas: Participacion-Nuevas Tecnologias*. Ediciones Deusto.
Informaciotechnologia, Szervezet Struktura es Valasz a Strategiai Kihivasokra. In: *Korszeru Vezetesi-zervezeti Formak es Modszerek*. Budapest: MKKE.
With Max Boisot. The Future of Management: Chinese Style. *Gestion* 2000, 4, 139–150.

1990

With Martin Lockett: editor and contributor. *Reform Policy and the Chinese Enterprise*. Greenwich, CN: JAI Press.
With Chris Smith & Michael Rowlinson. *Innovations in Work Organization*. Cambridge: Cambridge University Press.
With Ray Loveridge. *New Technology in European Services*. Oxford: Blackwell.
With Yuan Lu. Industrial Decision Making under China's Reform 1985–1988. *Organization Studies*, 11(3), 321–351.
With Max Boisot, Jill Ireland, Z. Li & Jane Watts. *The Management of Equity Joint Ventures in China*. Beijing: China-EC Management Institute.
With Ray Loveridge & Janet Harvey. New Technologies in Banking, Retailing and Health Services: the British Case. In: F. J. Dy (Ed.), *Advanced Technology in Commerce, Offices and Health Services*. Aldershot: Avebury for I.L.O.
With Max Boisot. Efficiency, Ideology and Tradition in the Choice of Transactions Governance Structures: The Case of China as a Modernizing Society. In: S. R. Clegg & S. G. Redding (Eds), *Capitalism in Contrasting Cultures*. Berlin: De Gruyter.

1991

A Foreign Perspective on the Management of People in China. *International Journal of Human Resource Management, 2*(1), 93–107.

With Xu Xinzhong. The Communist Party's Role in Enterprise Leadership at the High-Water of China's Economic Reform. *Advances in Chinese Industrial Studies, 2,* 69–95.

1993

With Michel Crozier, Renate Mayntz et al. *Societal Change Between Market and Organization.* Aldershot: Avebury.

With Livia Markoczy. Host-Country Managerial Behaviour and Learning in Chinese and Hungarian Joint Ventures. *Journal of Management Studies, 30*(4), 611–631.

Society and Enterprise Between Hierarchy and Market. In: John Child, Michel Crozier, Renate Mayntz et al. *Societal Change Between Market and Organization.* Aldershot: Avebury.

With Livia Markoczy. Host country managerial behaviour in Chinese and Hungarian joint ventures: assessment of competing explanations. In: M. Boisot (Ed.), *East-West Business Collaboration.* London: Routledge.

1994

Management in China During the Age of Reform. Cambridge: Cambridge University Press.

1995

With Livia Markoczy & Tony Cheung. Managerial Adaptation in Chinese and Hungarian Strategic Alliances with Culturally Distinct Foreign Partners. *Advances in Chinese Industrial Studies, 4,* 211–231.

Changes in the Structure and Prediction of Earnings in Chinese State Enterprises during the Reform. *International Journal of Human Resource Management, 6*(1), 1–30.

Follett on Constructive Conflict. In: Pauline Graham (Ed.), *Mary Parker Follett – Prophet of Management: Writings from the 1920s.* Boston: Harvard Business School Press.

With Livia Markoczy. International Mixed Management Organizations and Economic Liberalization in Hungary: From State Bureaucracy to New Paternalism. In: H. Thomas, D. O'Neal & J. Kelly (Eds), *Strategic Renaissance and Business Transformation.* New York: Wiley.

With Yuan Lu. Fuhrung in China. In: A. Kieser et al. (Eds), *Handworterbuch der Fuhrung.* Stuggart: Schaffer-Poeschel.

1996

With Lu Yuan (Ed.), *Management in China during the 1990s: International Enterprises.* London: Routledge.

With André Czeglédy. Managerial Learning in the Transformation of Eastern Europe: Some Key Issues. *Organization Studies, 17*(2), 167–179.

With Yuan Lu. Institutional Constraints on Economic Reform: The Case of Investment Decisions in China. *Organization Science, 7*(1), 60–77.

With Max Boisot. From Fiefs to Clans: Explaining China's Emerging Economic Order. *Administrative Science Quarterly*, *41*(4), 600–628.

With Suzana Rodrigues. The Role of Social Identity in the International Transfer of Knowledge through Joint Ventures. In: Stewart Clegg & Gill Palmer (Eds), *Producing Management Knowledge*. London: Sage.

With Max Boisot. The Institutional Nature of China's Emerging Economic Order. In: David Brown & Robin Porter (Eds), *Management Issues in China: Domestic Enterprises*. London: Routledge.

With Yuan Lu. Decentralization of Decision Making in China's State Enterprises. In: David Brown & Robin Porter (Eds), *Management Issues in China: Domestic Enterprises*. London: Routledge.

1997

Strategic Choice in the Analysis of Action, Structure, Organizations and Environment: Retrospect and Prospect. *Organization Studies*, *18*(1), 43–76.

With Yuan Lu & Yanni Yan. Adventuring in New Terrain: Managing International Joint Ventures in China. *Advances in Chinese Industrial Studies*, *5*, 103–123.

With Terence Tsai. Strategic Responses of Multinational Corporations to Environmental Demands. *Journal of General Management*, *23*(1), 1–22.

With Sally Stewart. Regional Differences in China and their Implications for Sino-Foreign Joint Ventures. *Journal of General Management*, *23*(2), 65–86.

With Y. Yan & Y. Lu. Ownership and Control in Sino-Foreign Joint Ventures. In: P. W. Beamish & J. Peter Killing (Eds), *Cooperative Strategies: Asia-Pacific Perspectives*. San Francisco, CA: New Lexington Press.

From the Aston Programme to Strategic Choice: A Journey from Concepts to Theory. In: T. Clark (Ed.), *Advancement in Organizational Behaviour*. Aldershot: Ashgate.

1998

With David Faulkner. *Strategies of Co-operation*. Oxford: Oxford University Press.

Trust and International Strategic Alliances: The Case of Sino-Foreign Joint Ventures. In: Christel Lane & Reinhard Backmann (Eds), *Trust Within and Between Organizations*. Oxford: Oxford University Press.

PRC Investment Control: Exploding the Myths. *China Direct Investor*, *3*, 10–15.

Seeking Greater Investment Control: Foreign Firms in China. *FT Mastering Management Review*, *18*, 36–39.

1999

With Max Boisot. Organizations as Adaptive Systems in Complex Environments: The Case of China. *Organization Science*, *10*(3), 237–252.

With Yanni Yan. Investment and Control in International Joint Ventures – the Case of China. *Journal of World Business*, *34*(1), 3–15.

With Sally Heavens. Managing Corporate Networks from America to China. *Asia Pacific Business Review*, *5*(3/4), 147–180.

With David Faulkner & Robert Pitkethly. Changes in Management Practice and the Post-Acquisition Performance Achieved by Direct Investors in the U.K. *British Journal of Management*, *10*(3), 185–198.

Management in China. In: Peter J. Buckley & Pervez N. Ghauri (Eds), *The Global Challenge for Multinational Enterprises* (pp. 444–466). Amsterdam: Pergamon.

2000

Theorizing about Organization Cross-Nationally. *Advances in Comparative International Management*, *13*, 27–75.

With David Faulkner & Robert Pitkethly. Foreign Direct Investment in the U.K. 1985–1994: The Impact on Domestic Management Practice. *Journal of Management Studies*, *37*(1), 141–166.

Management and Organizations in China: Key Trends and Issues. In: J. T. Li, Anne S. Tsui & Elizabeth Weldon (Eds), *Management and Organizations in China*. London: Macmillan.

Occupying the Managerial Workforce in Sino-Foreign Joint Ventures: A Strategy for Control and Development? In: Malcolm Warner (Ed.), *Changing Workplace Relations in the Chinese Economy* (pp. 139–162). London: Macmillan.

With David Faulkner & Robert Pitkethly. National Differences in Acquisition Integration. In: David Faulkner and Mark de Rond (Eds), *Cooperative Strategy* (pp. 283–306). Oxford: Oxford University Press.

With Yanni Yan. Effects of the Value Chain in International Joint Ventures: The Case of the Electronic and FMCG Sectors. *Journal of Global Marketing*, *14*, 37–56.

2001

With David Faulkner & Robert Pitkethly. *The Management of International Acquisitions*. Oxford: Oxford University Press.

Co-editor and contributor. *Handbook of Organizational Learning and Knowledge*. Oxford: Oxford University Press.

With Yanni Yan. National and Transnational Effects in International Business: Indications from Sino-Foreign Joint Ventures. *Management International Review*, *41*(1), 53–75.

With David Tse. China's Transition and its Implications for International Business. *Journal of International Business Studies*, *32*(1), 5–21.

Trust: the fundamental bond in global collaboration. *Organizational Dynamics*, *29*(4), 274–288.

With Rita McGrath. Editor and Contributor, Special Research Forum on New and Evolving Organizational Forms. *Academy of Management Journal*, *44*(6).

2002

With Yanni Yan. Predicting the Performance of International Joint Ventures, *Journal of Management Studies* (forthcoming).

A Configurational Analysis of International Joint Ventures Drawing upon Experience in China, *Organization Studies* (forthcoming)

Organizational Learning. In: John Kay & David Faulkner (Eds), *Handbook of Strategy*. Oxford: Oxford University Press (forthcoming).

ACKNOWLEDGMENTS

In writing this essay, a number of friends have helped me with comments and reminiscences. I am grateful to Peter Clark, Leanne Chung, Sally Heavens, Eugene McKenna, Suzana Rodrigues and Christine Wong. Art Bedeian also kindly lent me the benefit of his editorial skills. I am grateful to my wife, Liz, for her comments too, and more importantly for her lifelong support without which much of what you read would not have happened.

REFERENCES

Child, J. (1997). From the Aston Programme to Strategic Choice: a Journey from Concepts to Theory. In: T. Clark (Ed.), *Advancement in Organizational Behaviour: Essays in Honour of Derek S. Pugh* (pp. 45–71). Aldershot: Ashgate.

Graham, P. (Ed.) (1995). *Mary Parker Follett: Prophet of Management*. Boston, MA: Harvard Business School Press.

Loveridge, R. (1998). John Child 1940–. In: M. Warner (Ed.), *The Handbook of Management Thinking* (pp. 114–121). London: International Thomson Business Press.

George B. Graus

"IT'S ALL ABOUT LMXs, STUPID": COLLECT HIGH-QUALITY DATA, FOLLOW IT, TRUST LMXs, AND ALWAYS SEEK SERENDIPITY

George B. Graen

My career as a "retrospective construction" is, as I hope to show, a nonlinear human story of different kinds of interpersonal relationship-making processes, sprinkled with serendipity at many of my life's choice points. That's a mouthful, but please forgive me because I have just read Karl Weick's[1] autobiographical essay in Volume III of the *Management Laureates* (1993) series. I admire the way Karl writes, but I am more impressed with the way he thinks, because he is even more nonlinear than I am. I had fun following Karl's "bouncing ball" and "all that jazz."

Art Bedeian sent me two exemplars of autobiographical essays: Karl Weick's and his. Although I know that Art was just being helpful, he set the standard at the top rung and my Pygmalion tendencies could not resist the challenge. I, like Karl and Art, will be as honest and insightful as I can with the hope that whatever lessons I have learned may help someone sometime. I am a history buff and I believe in the lessons from the past.

My career clearly is a product of multiple forces converging on my life space over time. This Lewian conceptualization seems inescapable to me. From this multitude of forces, I've chosen to focus on the impact of numerous interpersonal relationships on my career and the wondrous outcomes that flowed therefrom. As the title of this essay suggests, based on former President

Management Laureates, Volume 6, pages 53–81.
Copyright © 2002 by Elsevier Science Ltd.
All rights of reproduction in any form reserved.
ISBN: 0-7623-0487-1

Clinton's 1992 campaign slogan, "It's all about LMXs" at so-called "defining moments" in my life and career.

EARLY SOCIALIZATION (1937–1956)

Mary Graen, my mother, a young third-generation German-American farm girl from Foley, Minnesota, brought me into this world in Minneapolis, Minnesota, on August 7, 1937. She was my first contact with another human and she was awesome in her motherly love. What a lucky guy! My father, Clarence (Kelly) Graen, a disabled vet from the "Great War" (World War I), did what he could for his brood of four sons and a daughter. We were his second family, and much too active for him and his chosen trade, home-watch repair. He struggled to cope, but we often were too much for even an able-bodied person. Growing up in the Great Depression, in a working class neighborhood in North Minneapolis, I failed to realize how dirt poor we were, because all of our neighbors were equally poor. Only after I was at the University of Minnesota, in the company of my friends from the middle-class suburbs, did I recognize the grinding poverty of my homestead. I gathered this from the pictures my folks took and the recollections of our family's economic circumstance. We always had good food. We went without new clothes, a hot water heater, a phone, an automobile, vacations, and an allowance, but we had lots of motherly love. Mom had to work two jobs outside of the home just to make ends meet. In the early years, we lived with my paternal grandparents. Annie, a Canadian-Irish lass, and Louie, a German-immigrant jeweler. My older brother Jim, two years my senior, latched on to Grandad Louie and I, being the second born attached myself to Grandma Annie. My sister Betty, only a year younger than me, was left to catch Mom between jobs. My brother John, was left with Dad. Finally, my brother Rich, ten-years younger than Jim, was truly Mom's baby boy.

We all went to the neighborhood parish Catholic school, St. Bridget.[2] It was an Irish-American elementary 1–8 grade school, operated by the nuns of the Benedictine Order out of Duluth, Minnesota. Nuns, with the aid of a few lay special-topics teachers, taught all classes. Because the church/school was self-supporting and poor, almost all grades were double classes (i.e. first and second grade in one room with one nun). The parish was ruled by an autocratic and rightfully feared priest, Father Donahue, a fiery Irishman from Prince Edward Island, Canada. The prevailing advice was that if you needed to see Father, you were to throw your hat into his room and, if he didn't throw it back at you, it was okay to enter.

Graen boys acquired quite a reputation in the neighborhood as an extremely athletic and tough clan who would protect each other regardless of the personal sacrifice. This reputation was hard earned in a tough neighborhood. No one dared eat a Graen's lunch or take anything from a Graen kid. We were a close sibling group. Mom was always our righteous defender. She told anyone who would listen and once told a juvenile court judge, "All my boys are good boys." The infamous gangster matriarch Ma Barker couldn't be more convincing. Unfortunately, without a mother at home, I went to St. Bridget School completely unprepared. I had no idea what school was all about and I acted accordingly. I was such a poor and ignorant student that the nuns kept me back in the first grade, and rightfully so. I had no clue about school. I thought it was play school before its time. I recall that the class periods were boring intervals between recess, lunch, and class dismissal. Attention-deficit disorder might be the diagnosis, but it was simply ignorance.

It wasn't until I reached the third- and fourth-grade classroom of Sister Janet, as a third grader, that I experienced my first non-family mentor. Sister Janet sunk her hooks into little George at the beginning of the year and didn't let me go until I was forced to learn what school was all about and, by the end of fourth grade had become the very best student that I could. She taught me how to learn. Sister Janet's intense interest in my life was not welcomed. I resisted her advances in every way I could, but she just came at me longer and stronger. She escalated from my mother, to Father Donahue, to the supreme authority, Sister Superior Gregory. After several months of resistance, my defenses were overrun and I listened for the first time to the wisdom of a very bright woman who was neither my mother nor grandmother. Sister Janet[3] changed my life's direction and set me on a path that I eagerly follow still. I can never repay her, but I have tried to pay back her kindness by becoming a mentor (and dissertation advisor) of researchers-in-training who need to see life's dimly-lighted path. I have done this 26 times thus far, but even this is not enough to repay Sister Janet's kindness.

I graduated from St. Bridget's eighth grade and went to St. Philip for both ninth and tenth grades. It was there in a Polish-American Catholic grade 1–10 school, run by the Sisters of Notre Dame, that I met Joni Melchior, my life-long wife, partner, and mother of our two sons, Mike, now an Information Systems Director at Procter and Gamble, and Marty, a General Manager and Chief Marketing Officer at Kodak.[4] Joni was also from the wrong side of the city and we were on our way out. After St. Philip, I moved on to Patrick Henry, a 9–12 city high school. Here I excelled at both academics and athletics. I was most fortunate that I played football (quarterback and outside linebacker) for the Twin City High School Champions in 1956, my senior year. I had played ball since early grade school and enjoyed the competition a good deal, but now it was time for college and I had no time for sports. The same was true for our sons, who excelled at playing ball 3–12, but also retired their cleats upon entering college.

UNIVERSITY OF MINNESOTA (1956–1967)

I was accepted at the University of Minnesota and told my high-school counselor that I intended to enroll in the fall. I'd saved my money from my newspaper route and odd jobs during the summers and I intended to work my way through to the Bachelors degree. He said "Why bother, you'll only flunk out." I responded appropriately for a street kid and left. I was the only member of my extended family to go to college and I sure didn't intend to flunk out. In fact, Minnesota was so good that I stayed for all three degrees!

At the University, I majored in psychology because a high-school teacher had taught a psychology course with such enthusiasm. Later, the content affirmed my choice. It was interesting, but (of course) so were history, humanities, sociology, political science, economics, and religion. Professors at Minnesota all taught very large classes and were forced to use objective, multiple-choice exams. Because my high-school preparation was that of city school quality, and clearly inferior to that of my suburban classmates, I had to find an "edge." On the street those without an "edge" didn't last very long. My edge was mastering multiple-choice exams. I studied them inside and out and learned the secrets of their construction. I learned how to prepare for them and how to take them. I got so proficient at them that I estimated that I had a 10%–15% advantage over my classmates. This was confirmed again and again by scoring 10%–15% above the next highest scorer on numerous exams. I also needed this edge, because I was working full- or part-time during my undergraduate years, whereas my suburban classmates were full-time students. To make matters worse, at Minnesota, the work ethic was strong among nearly all of my classmates, and the competition was challenging. Fortunately, I graduated *cum laude* in 1961 with a major in psychology and minors in history and sociology.[5]

My last quarter, senior year, I took an industrial relations course from Jack Rhode, an instructor and doctoral student in the University's Industrial Relations Center (IRC) graduate program. Jack's enthusiasm for industrial relations convinced me to enroll in the IRC program for a Master's degree. When I told Joni and Mike (my oldest son) of my desire to go for the Master's they were supportive. I became a graduate research assistant (GRA) for the first time and really loved being paid for my hobby, namely, my own research.

Whatever research I worked on became mine regardless of who was called the Principal Investigator. Self-efficacy theory worked in my case.

The IRC was a blast. Herb Heneman and Dale Yoder started the IRC in a charming old World War II wooden building. While I was there the IRC moved to the new West Bank Business School building. My mentors on the faculty, in addition to Herb and Dale were Marv Dunnette, Rene' Dawes, Bill England, Tom Mahoney, and Karl Weick.[6] As I was preparing to graduate from the IRC program in 1963, Marv Dunnette, who I first met by foolishly enrolling in his doctoral seminar during the middle quarter and who in spite of this helped me get my MA thesis data from Remington Rand Univac, asked me to go on for a Ph.D. in Industrial Psychology. When I asked why I should do that, he simply said, "Because you'll never regret it," and I never have.[7]

I enrolled in the Industrial Psychology doctoral program, and found new mentors: Dave Campbell, Jack Darley, Paul Meehl, Milt Trapold, and Elaine Walster. I also found a lively peer group: Merle Ace, John Campbell, Milt Hakel, Bob Opshal, Bob Pritchard, and Paul Wernimont. It was the best of times. I was doing what I really enjoyed and was doing it with the best people in the field. I remember that Lyman Porter and Victor Vroom came to visit Dunnette's shop to pay homage to the great man, my surrogate father. I did my Masters thesis, which was published in the *Journal of Applied Psychology* (*JAP*) in 1966, on Fred Herzberg's two-factor motivation theory (1959). I also reanalyzed data from another study by Pat Smith and her associates on Herzberg's theory and published it also in *JAP* the same year. My first two publications were back to back in *JAP*. I was delighted to get these published before I graduated, because it was common knowledge at Minnesota that the best predictor of career research productivity was a single item: whether or not one published in a decent journal before receiving one's doctorate. This meant that I made the cut.

For my dissertation, I decided to conduct a field experiment to test Vroom's Valence-Instrumentality-Expectancy (VIE) theory of work motivation. With Marv Dunnette's and National Science Foundation's (NSF) help I founded a temporary, part-time organization, paid my "employees" and tested VIE over time using three separate conditions: (a) Contingent Reward, (b) Rewarding A while hoping for B, and (c) Control. This before-after, true field experiment was published as a *JAP Monograph* in 1969. Its results convinced me in a rather dramatic fashion, that the problem with worker job satisfaction, job involvement, and performance were due less to motivation than to failures of leadership, and I switched my research appropriately. I was delighted that my dissertation also won an award from the American Institutes for Research Creative Talents program (1967). I was especially proud of this achievement because Marv was my dissertation advisor and he let me "do my thing." As I was doing my dissertation research, I took time to write a leadership entry for the new American Psychological Association James McKeen Cattell competition for original research designs. I was amazed that, in the second year (Bob Guion won it the first year) of the competition, I entered and won first prize for 1967, edging out my mentor Marv, and his doctoral student partner, Bob Opshal, my senior peer at Minnesota, John Campbell, and other senior researchers, including Bernie Bass, Arnold Tannebaum, and Vic Vroom. This was heady stuff for a lowly doctoral student.[8] I received second place in this competition in 1968 and the American Psychological Association's Industrial and Organizational Division passed a rule that "Graen could not compete in this competition again." Winning two-years in a row disqualified me I am flattered to report. I guess I just have a knack for research design in addition to being "over-trained" in it at Minnesota.

After I enrolled in Marv's doctoral program and our youngest son Marty was born, Joni, Mike, Marty and I moved into the University's St. Paul Agricultural campus married student housing complex. We were eligible for a two-bedroom apartment because we had two children. During this time, I really got to know my father, Kelly. At least once every week or two I would go over to the homestead in North Minneapolis and just sit down with Dad and we would talk about anything and everything. It was a great seminar for a doctoral student, because it was totally honest, open, and caring. I learned many things at my father's knee including the secrets of my political world before they were discovered and reported by my contemporaries and my scholarship was improved thereby. I recall that, during this time, one of my friends in the doctoral program in Labor Economics was devastated to learn about the "power elite" and its implications. He lamented that his power elite father never told him about this. I told him that I had learned about the power elite at my father's knee. I still remember the feeling of pride in my father's teachings. I'm grateful that I got to know him before he took his own life. He was a casualty of World War I and was buried with full military honors at Fort Snelling.[9]

UNIVERSITY OF ILLINOIS (1967–1977)

Upon graduating with my doctorate in 1967, I receive two solid offers, a rebuff, and a protest. My solid offers were from two of the top Psychology Departments in the country: the University of California at Berkeley, and the University of Illinois at Champaign-Urbana. The rebuff came from the Graduate School of Industrial Administration (GSIA) at the Carnegie Institute of Technology in Pittsburgh, Pennsylvania (later Carnegie-Mellon University), and the protest came from Yale University in New Haven, Connecticut. The rebuff came when various GSIA faculty members attempted to intimidate a Minneapolis "street kid" and got their feelings hurt. Later, they got more than their feelings hurt by GSIA Dean Dick Cyert for the same inappropriate, bullying behavior of young faculty recruits during their later campus visits. The protest came from Chris Argyris when I decided against visiting Yale for an interview. I decided, with the help of Marv, to join the University of Illinois faculty and I have never regretted the decision.

Mentors at Illinois were numerous in psychology and labor and industrial relations (LIR), where I had a joint appointment. These included Lloyd Humphreys (Head), Jack Adams, Don Delaney, Milt Derber, Bill Form, Walt Franke, Joe McGrath, Mel Rothbaum, Ivan Stiener, Koji Taira, Harry Triandis, and Martin Wagner. My peers who also helped me develop academically included Jim Davis, Fred Fiedler, Marty Fishbein, Dick Hackman, Chuck Hulin, John Kimberly, Greg Oldham, Jeff Pfeffer, Ken Rowland, Jerry Salancik, Barry Staw, and David Whetten. In psychology, it was great to chat with so many former APA presidents. They always made time for my chatter.

Doctoral students at Illinois were as eager and hard working as they had been at Minnesota. Students that I had the pleasure to mentor during their doctoral studies included Ken Alvares, Milt Blood, Dan Brass, Jim Cashman, Hans Peter Dachler, Fred Dansereau, Bill Davidson, Jerry Ferris, Cindi Fukami, Steve Ginsburgh, Bill Haga, Jeanne Herman, Ginny Ingersol, Dan Ilgen, Tom Johnson, Takao Minami, Dean Orris, Chuck Parsons, Bill Schiemann, Lee Stepina, Eric Thomanek, Bob Vecchio, Mitsuru Wakabayashi, and Mary Zalesny. They worked hard on our joint projects and many have gone on to be famous researchers. I am proud to have known and worked with all of them.

My Leader-Member Exchange (LMX) theory, which began at Minnesota was extended and enriched in many ways at Illinois. My James McKeen Cattell award paper, which contained the LMX perspective, was delivered in San Francisco at the Society of Industrial and Organizational Psychology (SIOP) meeting in 1968.[10] I was told later a slight but uncomfortable earthquake occurred during my paper presentation. At the time I was too involved to notice! The LMX perspective is to focus on the career development of managers employing longitudinal hypotheses about the contributions of leadership, followership, and their interactions over time. This theoretical bent was unexpected for a Minnesota trained "Dustbowl Empiricist", but I was uncomfortable with much empiricism and too little theory. At Minnesota I came to believe that the functional interplay between theory and data over a series of longitudinal, rigorously designed studies would improve our understanding more efficiently than a single focus on either theoretical or empirical activity. For a review of these early years of LMX theory and research see Graen and Uhl-Bien (1995, 2002).

In 1970, Professor Katsu Sano, Vice President of Keio University in Tokyo, Japan, visited Illinois looking for someone to teach modern research methods in applied psychology at Keio. I got to know him quite well as he had a visitor's office in the Institute of Labor and Industrial Relations (ILIR) where I had a second office. Sano asked to sit in on my graduate research methods course in Applied Psychology. I, of course, was flattered and said okay. Sano sat in the back of the class and said nothing, but one day he told me that he had to return to Keio and asked me if he could send his best doctoral student to study with me. Again I was flattered, and once more said okay. About six-months later, Takao Minami arrived on campus, but no one could understand his English. After a semester of intensive instruction he spoke conversational English clearly. He became my first Japanese Ph.D. student at Illinois. Mitsuru Wakabayashi was my second. Minami and Wakabayashi are now professors at Keio University and Nagoya University, respectively.

In 1972 my young family, together with Minami, went to Keio University for one year. We lived in a traditional landowners compound in a house built half Japanese and half Western. Among our neighbors, only the landowner's daughter and her husband, a professor at Keio University, spoke English. Joni, Mike, Marty, and I were confronted with culture shock from the first day. For this story, see Graen, Hui, Wakabayashi and Wang (1997).

My primary reason for going to Keio University (the Harvard of Japan) was to collaborate with Professor Sano and his colleagues to do a normally impossible research project. We called this project the Japanese Management Progress Study (JMPS; after Doug Bray's (1974) classic study at American Telephone and Telegraph). The JMPS was to include four top-tier Japanese corporations, including Honda Motors, Nomura Securities, and last from the hiring of new college graduates in 1972 until their retirement some 35 years later. It was also to gather information on entry test scores, promotability, and performance appraisals, as well as detailed salary information. We successfully received all of these data over time, plus we surveyed all of the new 1972 hires and their immediate supervisors in all four corporations every six months for their first three years together (dyadically). This was made possible by the fact that Sano had been the professor of the key personnel managers in all four corporations and they trusted him implicitly as part of their LMXs with him. Sano's former students had convinced their executives that our study was desirable for the corporations. After what seemed like an endless series of meetings between Sano, Minami, and me and the personnel managers, all four corporations gave us the okay. During the negotiations, I learned three things:

(a) how to drink endless cups of green tea, (b) how to sit quietly as my LMX partners negotiated in Japanese, and (c) how to answer English questions emerging abruptly from a sea of Japanese. Sano was teaching me to act like a proper Japanese (see Graen et al., 1997).

We did well on this longitudinal study in that retirees in one of the four corporations are still under study. Wakabayashi and I will be collecting data about the retirement when I travel to Tokyo in the near future. For the latest 22-year follow-up see Graen, Dharwadkar, Grewal, Hui and Wakabayashi (2002).

Returning back to Illinois, I was granted an appointment to the Center for Advanced Study and also received a James McKeen Cattell Fellowship from the American Institute for Research to do LMX research. In 1976, I was elected to be an APA Fellow in Industrial and Organizational Psychology and was invited to become one of the founding members of the Society of Organizational Behavior (SOB). I am humbly proud of both of these recognitions. I am equally proud of the accomplishments of my doctoral advisees including: (a) Bill Haga's Geissert Award for best dissertation proposal in the University of Illinois Sociology Department in 1971, (b) Jim Cashman's 1976 award in the Society of Industrial and Organizational Psychology S. Rains Wallace dissertation competition, (c) Bill Schiemann's 1977 S. Rains Wallace Award for best dissertation, (d) Wakabayashi's 1979 dissertation, which was selected for publication by the University of Michigan, (e) Min Basadur's 1980 S. Rains Wallace Award for best dissertation, (f) John Weitzel's 1983 Richard D. Irwin Foundation Award for dissertation research, (g) Terri Scandura's 1986 American Association of Collegiate Schools of Business Fellowship for dissertation research, (h) Mary Uhl-Bien's 1990 Richard D. Irwin Foundation Award for dissertation research, and (i) Lisa Bell's 1995 American Society of Training Directors Award for best dissertation.

UNIVERSITY OF CINCINNATI (1977–1997)

Illinois was a great place to do research and teach, but I needed a new environment in which to further blossom. After some searching, I found it at the University of Cincinnati. Being river city kids, Joni, Mike, Marty and I welcomed the metropolitan scene of Cincinnati. It wasn't the Mississippi River, but it was the Ohio and not the Mackinaw. Also, it was the College of Business and I was the Head of the Management Department. The Dean, Al Simone, asked me to build the department into a center of excellence. Thus, in 1977, we moved to what would be our home for the next 20 years. Cincinnati was always a work in progress. Hal Angle, Norm Baker, Caroline Boyer, Reg Bruce, Jim Dean, Jim Evans, Gail Fairhurst, George Gore, Steve Green, Rajan Kamath, Ralph Katerberg, Yong Kim, Chuck Matthews, Amit Raturi, Fritz Russ, Joe Steger, Tom Taber and Ann Welch were on the College of Business faculty.

While at Cincinnati, in 1985, I was named the first Johnson Wax Fulbright Senior Scholar to Japan. This was the first Fulbright Senior Scholarship funded fully by the Japanese government. It was quite a ceremony in Japan as I traveled to Johnson's Japanese headquarters, outside of Tokyo, with the Senior USA Fulbright Officer, to be wined and dined in a major celebration of Japan's initial Fulbright reciprocation. After the official ceremony, Joni and I and my graduate assistant, Terri Scandura, settled in at Nagoya University with Wakabayashi to write a few theory papers and collect data.

While on the Fulbright, Joni and I visited Hong Kong, and I visited Mainland China for the first of over a dozen visits. My first visit was on a 24-hour visa to Guangzhou. Later, in 1994, and again in 1996, I taught at the Department of the Management of Organisations at the University of Science and Technology in Hong Kong. Starting in 1993, I began studying the modern People's Republic of China, and continue to do so. For the last two years, my Chinese research partners at East China University in Shanghai, Professors Ge, WenLei, Gu, WenLei, Pan, Jin and Wu, Yongyi, at Chinese University in Hong Kong, Chun Hui, and at Nagoya University, Mitsuru Wakabayashi have been conducting a study to understand cross-cultural and "third culture" (Graen et al., 1997) factors that contribute to the job mobility of young Chinese managers working in Shanghai-area Sino-foreign joint ventures. We collected data for our predictor variables two-years ago and now we are collecting data on criterion variables. After eight years of concentrated study, I humbly admit that I understand precious little about coastal China. The country is so vast and complex that a "China expert" is in danger of being an oxymoron. I often feel this way about my mastery of a culture that I've admired intensely ever since I read Pearl Buck's *The Good Earth* as my first adult book in high school.

Cincinnati also encouraged me to follow my interests in strategic management and I founded the Center for Strategic Management Studies (CSMS) in 1985, which continues to the present. The Center focuses on strategic issues in leadership including a 5-year study of the USA electric power industry. Later, in 1989, with the aid of Rajan Kamath, Yong Kim, and Amit Raturi, I founded the Center for the Enhancement of International Competitiveness. This Center did competitiveness studies of major industries including a 10-year study of the major machine tool industry and how from 1980 to 1985 the United States went from first to fourth in the world.

My doctoral students at Cincinnati were as talented and eager as those at Illinois. They were Gayle Baugh, Lisa Bell, Pamela Brandes, Ravi Dwardkar, Bob Liden, Terry Moore, Michael Novak, Lisa Phillips, Anson Seers, Tim Serey, Pat Sommerkamp, Pam Tierney, Mary Uhl-Bien, Damayanti Vasudevan, Kathy Verderber and John Weitzel. They had been introduced to LMX theory at a more developed stage than their Illinois counterparts and have benefited thereby. Many have produced their own LMX scholars. I feel ancient when I must admit that I am talking to an LMX researcher who is a student of a student of a student of mine. Time flies in LMX years!

LMX Theory and Research

As mentioned, I first described the beginnings of what has become in later years the LMX leadership theory in my 1968 James McKeen Cattell paper. This paper proposed a research plan and a research design to provide a scientific understanding of the early development of managers. It employed longitudinal designs and focused on leadership, followership, and their interactions over time. At about the same time (1969), I created my own laboratory organization for the purpose of testing Vroom's (1964) VIE theory in an ecologically valid, true experiment. As said above, I concluded from this field experiment that the problems of follower job dissatisfaction, lack of job involvement, and ineffectiveness were due more to failures of leadership than to failures of a follower's ability or work motivation and that a "follower's focus" on leadership was needed. This insight placed the action camera directly on follower and leader interactions as related to followers' performance and commitments. The question of what leader-follower (i.e. dyadic) interactions contributed to leader-follower communication, coordination, cooperation, and symbiotic benefits was the primary focus of my Cattell paper. I later found creative support for this work in Ed Hollander's research (1978) on "Idio-syncrasy Credits", in Jacobs's (1971) work on exchange as a style of leadership, and in Homan's (1961) theory on interpersonal social exchanges. Clearly, social as well as economic exchanges were early LMX themes.

In our first study of dyadic interactions (Graen, Orris & Johnson, 1973), we found that dyadic follower-leader communications over the early workplace assimilation of new hires was critical to job survival. Inaccuracy in dyadic communications strongly contributed to new hire turnover. This early study supported the critical hypothesis derived from LMX theory that variance in leader-follower interactions could contribute to relevant follower outcomes. Results showed that, *within* groups, dyadic follower-leader communications were significantly related to new hire turnover. This was true even after other communications were partialled out using a generic *within* and *between* group analysis (WABGA). Turnover was not influenced by the average communication style of leaders but by their dyadic style. We were disappointed in the former and delighted in the latter effects, because we had hoped for both. In our next study (Haga, Graen & Dansereau, 1974) we focused on followers' professionalism and found that it was a strong contributor to follower and leader behavior. This study was about follower-leader dyads (*within* work groups), and also about the professional composition of each leader's unit (*between* groups). In generic WABGA terms, desired outcomes were a function of the professionalism of the people for both a dyad (within) effect and a group (between) effect. Follower professionalism contributed to dyadic level outcomes. We should note that follower professionalism was never considered dependent on a group for definition. Rather, relevant reference for followers was their national profession not their organizational unit (*between* groups). We (Graen & Cashman, 1975) later found that follower-leader LMX was a contributor at the dyadic level (*within* effect), but not the work-group level (*between* effect). Its contributions were found on work outcomes such as performing extra-role behavior and collaborating with a leader on critical decisions and projects. This was similar to what was later called Organizational Citizenship Behavior (Organ, 1988). Supporting results were found in other studies (Dansereau, Graen & Haga, 1975; Gerstner & Day, 1997; Graen & Schiemann, 1978; Liden & Graen, 1980; Graen, Novak & Sommerkamp, 1982; Graen, Scandura & Graen, 1986).

It wasn't until 1982 however, that we (Graen, Liden & Hoel, 1982) published a study that we considered a "Strong Inference critical" test (Dunnette, 1996) of LMX theory. Based on the Graen, Orris and Johnson (1973) study, this investigation was completed employing an experimentally independent, criterion variable, which was measured by a different method of assessment, namely, turnover. We were delighted that the results of this study showed that within group dyadic leadership (LMX), in contrast to between group leadership (average unit LMX), contributed to follower turnover. Moreover, *within* LMX contributed more strongly to predicting turnover than competing job satisfaction scales. Three years later, I was overjoyed by the "critical" support of our findings provided by an independent replication published in the *Journal of Applied Psychology* (Ferris, 1985). The results were virtually identical to the Graen, Liden and Hoel (1982) study. I was relieved, because few things are more embarrassing than unreplicated findings.

These rigorous tests strongly supported the proposition that leadership (LMX) at the dyad level can contain valid variance. In short, leadership also lives at the dyadic (two-person) level, as well as the group (all members of a unit including its superior) level. This *within* group effect held even after partialling out a large amount of potentially valid variance from LMX scores by removing all between group variance. Let us be clear, this did not mean that leadership (LMX) at the group level could not also be valid. This has been demonstrated before on experimentally independent criterion variables (Stogdill, 1948). Thus, LMX theory maintains that leadership can exist at either or both levels, depending on the situation: (a) leaders can develop varying LMX relations with different followers; and (b) different leaders can develop varying LMX relations within their groups. This can happen at the same time for the same people. Also LMX dyads can be independent of any group: LMX dyads can operate in several different groups and may even briefly reverse follower and leader roles in some groups. This is the so-called "free LMX dyad."

LMX: DISTINGUISHING BETWEEN THEORIES (1976–1995)

Building on my work (Graen, 1976), and that of Jim Burns (1978), and Bob House (1977), Bernie Bass (1985) proposed his version of a leader-based (Graen & Uhl-Bien, 1995) model he called "transformational leadership." In the process, he attempted to reduce LMX leadership to the lowly status of a "transactional model of expected performance" far below that of his "transformational model of performance beyond expectations." Bob House later (1991) joined Bernie making the same claims as Bernie and also committing the same misinterpretation of LMX theory. In 1995 we reviewed the 25 years of LMX research (Graen & Uhl-Bien, 1995) and such misinterpretations were corrected – employing the three domain approaches to leadership meta-theory. According to this theoretical taxonomy, both the Bass (1985) and the House (1991) theories were residents of the leader-based domain. In contrast, LMX theory was a resident of the relationship-based domain. In addition, we made it crystal clear that the LMX theory was about "performance beyond expectations" as are all true leadership theories. We emphasized that those theories not about performance beyond expectations were theories of managership only. In addition, we emphasized that leaderfollower dyads usually begin at transaction stage, but quickly move to transformational level within a developmental process. The term "Transformational" leadership is redundant, in that, all leadership is about transformations to performance beyond expectations.

We have struggled to get the idea across that LMX theory is most concerned with a purely dyadic perspective independent of groups (Graen & Uhl-Bien,

1995). It should be understood (Graen & Wakabayashi, 1994; Graen & Uhl-Bien, 1995) that LMX theory is about developing dyadic leadership relationships independent of groups (free LMX dyads). Let us try to clarify this. The only reason that we used dyads *within* groups was to determine whether it was valid to consider leadership variance outside of a group's mean value. As described above, this has been tested and replicated conclusively (Graen, et al., 1982; Ferris, 1985). LMX theory focuses on dyads independent of the groups in which they occur. When Yammarino and his associates (Yammarino, Spangler & Dubinsky, 1998) suggest that the dyad level appears to be first suggested by Bass's theory (1985), they were mistaken. On the contrary, it is correct to state that we first proposed it in 1976 and restated it several times before 1985 (Graen & Cashman, 1975; Graen & Scandura, 1987; Graen & Wakabayashi, 1994; Uhl-Bien & Graen, 2000, 1995; Zalesney & Graen, 1987).

A "dyads-independent-of-groups" (free LMX dyads) approach is what I have been proposing since the early days of LMX theory. It has evolved into a very sophisticated view of dyads as not leader and followers with fixed roles, but leader and followers with mutually negotiated and often interchangeable roles. This means that LMX relations are also independent of who's on top and who's on the bottom. Employees may belong to several groups at the same time and also may have dyadic LMX relations with several individuals. As dyads move from one group to another, they can change positions vis-à-vis who leads and who follows. Typically, in project team organizations, which we have studied *within* dyads, the person who has the idea and initiates it becomes the leader and other dyad members become the led. Moreover, these dyads are assembled into larger networks, as well as multiple project groups. The older organizational concept of fixed-and single-group membership does not explain much variance in team organizations. Professionals may have many different unrelated leaders with which to form LMX relationships. No single group is needed to define the quality of these LMX relations. LMX dyads usually are defined independent of groups, and we suggest that they be used to define several significant dimensions of groups.

Let me get off my soapbox by stating that theoretically Bernie Bass's transformational and Bob House's charismatic leadership are leader-based models and should focus on a leader's average leadership style (ALS) using Bales-type methods (Bales, 1949), not on his dyadic relationship building behavior employing dyadic differentiation methods (Graen & Uhl-Bien, 2002). These models belong at the group level of operation and not at the dyadic level *within* groups or the dyadic level *without* groups. We've tried to tell them several times that they are researching in the wrong place, but they say that the data are richer at the dyadic level.

UNIVERSITY OF LOUISIANA (1997–PRESENT)

Leaving Cincinnati after 20 years was difficult because so much of our lives were spent in this wonderful place. Our sons went through the University of Cincinnati from freshman to MBAs, Mike and Ruthie's children, Stephanie (Dollfin) and Andy (Andy-Man), and Marty and Donna's children Lauren (Little Angel), Jessica (Jessie), and Joseph (Joey), were born in the greater Cincinnati area. Joni and I were happy there and there we did some of our best scholarly work.[11] I have always seen program development as one way to "give back" in return for all the good fortune I've received throughout my career. It was time to once again broaden my horizons and extend my work as program developer.

The University of Louisiana (UL) approached me with the plea that they were struggling to pull their College of Business Administration up by its "bootstraps" and they needed an established management scholar with program development experience to help bring them to the next level – the Ph.D. level. For the first time in its history, the college had put together a team of faculty and administrators who were committed to going beyond the MBA. This team was headed by Dean Jan Duggar, Associate Dean Bill Roe and the Gene Brauns Endowed Chair committee: Kerry Carson (Head), Ray Authement, Paula Carson, Lewis Gale, Ron Heady and Cary Heath. After a campus visit to Lafayette, they convinced me that I could do some good by making a contribution to the UL program. It would be a challenge, but I accepted the Gene Brauns Endowed Chair in International Leadership and in 1997 we moved to the heart of Cajun country.

To date, with the enthusiastic assistance of my new colleagues, we've made good progress. We proposed a new MBA concentration in International Business (IBUS) and won a Louisiana Board of Regents grant to establish this new IBUS MBA and to create a high technology, "Louisiana's International Business Clearinghouse." The plan was to make UL the state of Louisiana's premier graduate-level international business program with a MBA, the Clearinghouse and, one day, a Ph.D. program. This is our work in progress.

I continue my LMX theory development and research, mainly in partnership with Ravi Dwardkar, WenLei Gu, Chun Hui, Mary Uhl-Bien and Mitsuru Wakabayashi, and others (Graen & Uhl-Bien, 2002; Uhl-Bien, Graen & Scandura, 2000). Likewise, I continue my annual visits to China and Japan and my research into "third culture" organizations continues.

CONCLUSION

This is my opportunity to write my own epitaph. So, I'll take it: He was a stern mentor, a demanding teacher, a caring friend, and a loving family member who sought to advance LMX relationships with whomever he worked whether similar to or different from him, but the different had the advantage.

One lesson that I have learned after 42-years of studying face-to-face leadership is that we all need LMXs to survive and prosper. Without a doubt, we are social creatures who achieve less than our full potential without adequate social relationships. LMX is how we work best. For example, in my LMX with Wakabayashi, my best friend, whoever has the superior expertise is the leader and the other is the follower. In LMXs, leadership is less about position than about expertise.

In 1999 at the SIOP meetings in Atlanta, Milt Hakel and I organized a testimonial program to our mentor Marv Dunnette. It was well attended and a revelation to many outside of the Minnesota experience. I only hope that I can approach the heights of mentorship of this great man. Marv taught me to always end on the upswing. Here goes. The one thing that I learned early about research is that you must collect the highest quality data, follow it wherever it goes, trust your research partners, and always seek serendipity. This recipe has seldom failed. Now, I recommend it to you. Go forth with it and prosper.[12]

PUBLICATIONS

1965

With T. E. Carroll, R. V. Dawis & D. J. Weiss. Items analysis of the development pool of items for the Youth Opinion Questionnaire. *Minnesota studies in work attitudes, 1.* Industrial Relations Center, University of Minnesota: Minneapolis.

1966

Motivator and hygiene dimensions for research and development engineers. *Journal of Applied Psychology, 50,* 563–566.
Addendum to "An empirical test of the Herzberg two-factor theory." *Journal of Applied Psychology, 50,* 551–555.

1967

With R. V. Dawis. Development and administration of the Youth Opinion Questionnaire. *Minnesota studies in work attitudes, 2.* Industrial Relations Center, University of Minnesota: Minneapolis.

1968

Testing traditional and two-factor hypothesis concerning job satisfaction. *Journal of Applied Psychology, 52*, 366–371.

Review of Martin Fishbein, Reading in attitude theory and measurement. *Psychometrika, 33*, 387–389.

Review of Felician F. Foltman, White-and-Blue collars in a mill shutdown: A case study of relative redundancy. *Personnel Psychology, 21*, 69–72.

With R. V. Dawis & D. J. Weiss. Need type and job satisfaction among industrial research scientists. *Journal of Applied Psychology, 52*, 286–289.

With C. L. Hulin. Addendum to "An empirical investigation of two implications of the two factor theory of job satisfaction." *Journal of Applied Psychology, 52*, 341–342.

1969

Instrumentality theory of work motivation: Some experimental results and suggested modifications. *Journal of Applied Psychology Monograph, 53* (Whole No. 2, Part 2).

Review of Educational Testing Service, Motivation of managers. *Personnel Psychology, 22*, 91–94.

Review of Ray C. Hackman. The motivated working adult. *Personnel Psychology, 22*, 352–355.

Work motivation: The behavioral effects of job-content and job-context factors in an employment situation. *Creative Talents Award Program.* Pittsburgh: American Institutes for Research.

Review of Robert N. Ford, Motivation through the work itself. *Contemporary Psychology, 15*, 291–294.

1970

With K. Alvares, D. Orris, & J. Martella. The contingency model of leadership effectiveness: Antecedent and evidential results. *Psychological Bulletin, 74*, 285–296.

1971

With R. V. Dawis. A measure of work attitudes for high-school-age-youth. *Journal of Vocational Behavior, 1*, 343–353.

With D. Orris & K. Alvares. The contingency model of leadership effectiveness: Some experimental results. *Journal of Applied Psychology, 55*, 196–201.

With D. Orris & K. Alvares. The contingency model of leadership effectiveness: Some experimental results. *Journal of Applied Psychology, 55*, 205–210.

1972

With M. Ace & R. Dawis. Biographical correlates of work attitudes. *Journal of Vocational Behavior, 2*, 191–199.

With F. Dansereau, Jr. & T. Minami. Dysfunctional leadership styles. *Organizational Behavior and Human Performance, 7*, 216–236.

With F. Dansereau, Jr. & T. Minami. An empirical test of the man-in-the-middle hypothesis among executives in a hierarchical organization employing a unit set analysis. *Organizational Behavior and Human Performance, 8*, 262–285.

1973

Review of M. Scott Myers, Every employee a manager: More meaningful work through job enrichment. *Contemporary Psychology, 18*, 13–14.

With F. Dansereau, T. Minami & J. Cashman. Leadership behaviors as cues to performance evaluation. *Academy of Management Journal, 16*, 611–623.

With F. Dansereau, Jr. & J. Cashman. Instrumentality theory and equity theory as complementary approaches in predicting leadership and turnover among managers. *Organizational Behavior and Human Performance, 10*, 194–200.

With T. Johnson. Organization assimilation and role rejection. *Organizational Behavior and Human Performance, 10*, 72–87.

With D. Orris & T. Johnson. Role assimilation processes in a complex organization. *Journal of Vocational Behavior, 3*, 395–420.

1974

Review of Duane P. Schultz, Psychology and Industry Today. *Contemporary Psychology, 19* 474.

With F. Dansereau, Jr. & J. Cashman. Expectancy as a moderator of the relationship between job attitudes and turnover. *Journal of Applied Psychology, 59*, 228–229.

With W. Haga & F. Dansereau. Professionalism and role making within a service organization: A longitudinal investigation. *American Sociological Review, 39*, 122–133.

1975

Review of Siegel and Lane, Psychology in Industrial Organization. *Contemporary Psychology, 20*, 669.

With J. Cashman. A role making model of leadership in formal organizations: A development approach. *Organization and Administrative Sciences, 6*, 143–165.

With F. Dansereau & W. Haga. A vertical dyad linkage approach to leadership within formal organizations; a longitudinal investigation of the role making process. *Organizational Behavior and Human Performance, 13*, 46–78.

1976

Role making processes within complex organizations. In: M. D. Dunnette (Ed.), *Handbook of Industrial and Organizational Psychology* (pp. 1201–1245). Chicago: Rand McNally.

With J. Cashman, F. Dansereau & W. Haga. Organizational understructure and leadership: A longitudinal investigation of the managerial role-making process. *Organizational Behavior and Human Performance, 15*, 278–296.

With J. Cashman, S. Ginsburgh & W. Schiemann. Effects of linking-pin quality upon the quality of working life of lower participants: A longitudinal investigation of the managerial understructure. *Administrative Science Quarterly, 22*, 491–504.

1977

With S. Ginsburgh. Job resignation as a function of role orientation and leader acceptance: A longitudinal investigation of organizational assimilation. *Organizational Behavior and Human Performance, 19*, 1–17.

With K. Sano, M. Wakabayashi & T. Minami. Japanese private university as a socialization system for future leaders in business and industry. *International Journal of Intercultural Relations, 2*, 269–289.

1978

With W. Schiemann. Leader-member agreement: A vertical dyad linkage approach. *Journal of Applied Psychology, 63*, 206–212.

1980

With R. Liden. Generalizability of the vertical dyad linkage model of leadership. *Academy of Management Journal, 23*, 451–465.

With E. McCracken. *Evaluation of current residential energy conservation programs and implications for future RCS, multifamily and small commercial energy conservation programs.* Center for Strategic Management Studies, University of Cincinnati, Cincinnati, Ohio.

With E. McCracken. *Electric utility options for the 1980s.* Center for Strategic Management Studies, University of Cincinnati, Cincinnati, Ohio.

1981

With M. Wakabayashi, T. Minami, M. Hashimoto, K. Sano & M. Novak. Managerial career development: Japanese style. *International Journal of Intercultural Relations, 4*, 391–420.

1982

With M. Basadur & S. G. Green. Training in creative problem solving: Effects on ideation and problem finding and solving in an industrial research organization. *Organizational Behavior and Human Performance, 30*, 41–70.

With R. Liden & W. Hoel. The role of leadership in the employee withdrawal process. *Journal of Applied Psychology, 67*, 868–872.

With M. Novak & P. Sommerkamp. The effects of leader-member exchange and job design on productivity and satisfaction: Testing a dual attachment model. *Organizational Behavior and Human Performance, 30*(1), 109–131.

1983

Bias in management research: A defense. *Business Horizons*, June, 42–50.

Where management research is needed: Transitional management. *Business Horizons*, June, *26*, 44–50.

With A. Seers, G. W. McGee & T. T. Serey. The interaction of job stress and social support: A strong inference investigation. *Academy of Management Journal, 26,* 273–284.

1984

With T. A. Scandura. The moderating effects of initial leader-member exchange status on the effects of a leadership intervention. *Journal of Applied Psychology, 69,* 428–436.

With A. Seers. A dual attachment concept: A longitudinal investigation of the combination of task characteristics and leader-member exchange. *Organizational Behavior and Human Performance, 33,* 283–306.

With M. Wakabayashi. The Japanese career progress study: A seven-year follow up. *Journal of Applied Psychology, 69,* 603–614.

1985

Some challenges of Japanese management. *Cincinnati Business Courier,* November.

1986

Review of Worker capitalism and worker participation. *Contemporary Psychology, 31,* 885–886.

With M. Basadur & T. Scandura. Training effects on attitude toward divergent thinking among manufacturing engineers. *Journal of Applied Psychology, 71*(4), 612–617.

With T. A. Scandura & M. R. Graen. A field experimental test of the moderating effects of growth need strength on productivity. *Journal of Applied Psychology, 71,* 484–491.

With T. A. Scandura. A theory of dyadic career reality, In: G. Ferris & K. Rowland (Eds), *Research in Personnel and Human Resources Management* (pp. 147–181). Greenwich, CT: JAI Press.

With T. A. Scandura & M. Novak. When managers decide not to decide autocratically. An investigation of decision influence in managerial dyads. *Journal of Applied Psychology, 71,* 579–584.

With W. Schiemann. Agreement in dyadic leadership. In: F. Landy (Ed.), *Readings in Industrial and Organizational Psychology.* Englewood Cliffs, NJ: Prentice Hall.

With T. A. Scandura. Vertical dyad linkage theory of leadership. In: A. Kieser, G. Reber & R. Wunderer (Eds), *Handbook of Leadership* (pp. 377–389). C. E. Paeschel Verlag: Stuttgart.

1987

With T. A. Scandura. Toward a psychology of dyadic organizing. In: B. Staw & L. L. Cummings (Eds), *Research in Organizational Behavior* (pp. 175–208). Greenwich, CT: JAI Press.

With M. Zalesny. Exchange theories of leadership. In: A. Kieser, G. Reber & R. Wunderer (Eds), *Handbook of Leadership* (pp. 714–727). C. E. Paeschel Verlag: Stuttgart.

1988

Readings in Modern Japanese Management: Theory and Practice (Ed.). Cincinnati: Little Professor Publishing.

With M. Wakabayashi. Human resource development of Japanese managers: Leadership and career investment. In: K. Rowland & G. Ferris (Eds), *Research on International Human Resource Management*. Greenwich, CT: JAI Press.

With M. Wakabayashi & M. R. Graen. Japanese management progress: Mobility into middle management. *Journal of Applied Psychology, 73*, 217–227.

1989

Unwritten Rules For Your Career: Fifteen Secrets For Fast-Track Success. New York: John Wiley and Sons, Inc., October.

Readings in Organizational Effectiveness (Ed.). Cincinnati: Little Professor Publishing.

Graen's Seminar Looks at Japanese Management (Ed.). Cincinnati: Little Professor Publishing.

With M. Basadur & M. Wakabayashi. Comparing attitudes toward divergent thinking of managers and non-managers before and after training. *Japanese Journal of Administrative Behavior, 4*, 19–27.

With M. Wakabayashi & D. Gallagher. Career development under the lifetime employment system of Japanese organizations. *Journal of Organizational Research*.

With J. R. Weitzel. System development project effectiveness: Problem-solving competence as a moderator variable. *Decision Sciences, 20*, 507–531.

1990

Unwritten rules are on-ramp to fast track. *Cincinnati Enquirer*, February 26.

Designing productive leadership systems to improve both work motivation and organizational effectiveness. In: U. Kleinbeck et al. (Ed.), *International Work Motivation* (pp. 200–233). New York: Erlbaum.

With M. Basadur & M. Wakabayashi. Identifying individual differences in creative problem solving styles. *Journal of Creative Behavior, 24*(2), 111–131.

With T. Scandura. A theory of dyadic career reality. In: K. Rowland & G. Ferris (Eds), *Career and Human Resources Development* (pp. 147–181). New York: JAI Press.

With M. Uhl-Bien, P. Tierney & M. Wakabayashi. Belief in paternalism as an indicant of the "right type" of manager for the Japanese corporation. *Group and Organization Studies, 15*, 414–430.

With M. Uhl-Bien & M. Wakabayashi. Generalizability of the hidden investment hypothesis among line managers in five leading Japanese corporations. *Human Relations, 43*, 1099–1116.

With M. Wakabayashi. Japanese transplants in the united states: Problems in domestic management assimilation. In: B. Shaw & K. Rowland (Eds), *International Human Resources Management, 2*, New York: JAI Press.

With M. Wakabayashi & M. Basadur. Attitudes toward divergent thinking before and after training. Focusing upon the effects of individual problem-solving styles. *Creativity Research Journal, 3*, 22–32.

With M. Wakabayashi, M. R. Graen & M. G. Graen. International generalizability of American hypotheses about Japanese management progress: A strong inference investigation. *The Leadership Quarterly, 1* 1–23.

1991

With M. Uhl-Bien. Transformation of work group professionals into self-managing and partially self-designing teams: Toward a theory of leadership-making. *Journal of Management Systems*, January, 34–48.

With M. Uhl-Bien. Leadership-making applies equally well to teammate – sponsor, teammate – competence network, and teammate – teammate relationships. *Journal of Management Systems*, 49–54.

With M. Uhl-Bien. Job redesign: Managing for high performance. *Productivity Press Proceedings*. Cambridge, MA.

With M. Uhl-Bien. The transformation of professionals: Toward a theory of leadership-making. *Technology Management Research, 3*(3), 33–48.

With M. Wakabayashi. Cross-cultural human resource development for transfer of management technology. In: M. Trevor (Ed.), *International Business and the Management of Change* (pp. 147–169). Worchester GB: Avebury Publishing.

1992

Self-management and team-making in cross functional work teams: Discovering the keys to becoming an integrated team. *Journal of High Technology Management, 3*, 225–241.

With M. Basadur & M. Wakabayashi. Identifying differences in creative problem solving style. In: S. J. Parnes (Ed.), *Source Book for Creative Problem Solving*, Chapter 18. Buffalo, N.Y.: Creative Education Foundation Press.

With M. Wakabayashi. Adapting Japanese leadership techniques to their transplants in the united states: Focusing on manufacturing. In: M. Serapio (Ed.), *Research in International Business and International Relations, 5*, 259–278.

1993

A Psychology of cross-cultural partnership between Japanese and American colleagues. In: A. Bird (Ed.), *Best Paper Proceedings in Association of Japanese Business Studies*. New York.

With M. Uhl-Bien. Leadership-making in self-managing professional work teams: An empirical investigation, In: K. E. Clark, M. B. Clark & D. P. Campbell (Eds), *The Impact of Leadership*. West Orange, NJ: Leadership Library of America.

1994

With M. Uhl-Bien. Team leadership-making theory: From mature dyads grow higher performance teams. In: A. Kieser, G. Reber & R. Wunderer (Eds), *Handbook of Leadership* (2nd ed., pp. 177–389). Poeschl Verlag: Stuttgart.

With M. Wakabayashi. Cross-cultural leadership-making: Bridging American and Japanese diversity for team advantage. In: M. D. Dunnette, M. Hough & H. Triandis (Eds), *Handbook of Industrial and Organizational Psychology* (*4*, pp. 415–446).Consulting New York: Psychologists Press.

With M. Zalesny. Exchange theory in leadership revisited: Same actors, different plot and location. In: A. Kieser, G. Reber & R. Wunderer (Eds), *Handbook of Leadership* (2nd ed., pp. 714–727). Poeschl Verlag: Stuttgart.

1995

Leadership of people in your firm, a chapter in M. J. Dollinger *Entrepreneurship: Strategies and Resources*. Flossmor, IL: Austen Press.

With C. Hui. Finally a production system that works and allows everyone to be an insider. *International Journal of Applied Psychology, 45*(2), 130–135.

With M. Uhl-Bien. Development of leader-member exchange (LMX) theory of leadership over 25 years: applying a multi-level-multi-domain perspective. *Leadership Quarterly, 6*(2), 219–247.

With Z. M. Wang. Third culture training for joint ventures in China. *Chinese Journal of Applied Psychology*, Cross-cultural partnership-making in action.

1996

Who's the Boss? *Wall Street Journal*. Panel of 11 top experts in International Business Ventures, September 26.

Review of *Japanese Industry in the American South* by Choong Soon Kim. *New Asian Review*.

With C. Hui. Managing changes in globalizing business: How to manage cross-cultural business partners. *Journal of Organizational Change Management, 9(3), 62–72.*

1997

With G. Baugh. Effects of team gender and racial composition on perceptions of team performance in cross-functional teams. *Group and Organization Management, 22*(3), 366–384.

With C. Hui, M. Wakabayashi & Z. M. Wang. Cross-cultural research alliances in organizational research. In: C. Earley & M. Erez (Eds), *Cross-Cultural Research in Industrial and Organizational Psychology* (pp. 160–189). San Francisco, CA, Jossey-Bass.

With C. Hui. Guanxi and professional leadership in contemporary Sino-American joint ventures in mainland China. *Leadership Quarterly*, Winter, *8*(4), 451–465.

1998

With C. Hui. When to use which approach of leadership: Building towards a complete contingent model of leadership. In: M. Erez, U. Kleinbeck & H. Theirry (Eds), *Work Motivation in the context of a Globalizing Economy*. Mah Wah, NJ: Lawrence Erlbaum Associates, Inc. Publishers.

With C. Hui. U.S. army leadership in the twenty-first century: Challenges and implications for training. In: J. G. Hunt, G. E. Dodge & L. Wong, (Eds), *Out-of-the-Box Leadership: Transforming the Twenty-First-Century Army and Other Top-Performing Organizations* (pp. 239–252).

With M. Uhl-Bien. Individual self-management: Analysis of professionals' self-managing activities in functional and cross-functional work teams. *Academy of Management Journal*, June, *41*(3), 340–351.

1999

Sino-foreign joint ventures in coastal china. *American Council of Learned Societies.*

With C. Hui. Transcultural Global Leadership in the twenty-first century: Challenges and implications for development. In: W. H. Mobley, V. Arnold & M. Gessner (Eds), *Advances in Global Leadership* (*1*, pp. 9–26). Stamford, CT: JAI Press.

With P. Tierney & S. Farmer. An examination of leadership and employee creativity: The relevance of traits and relationships. *Personnel Psychology,* Autumn *52*(3), pp. 591–620.

2000

With M. Wakabayashi & C. Hui. Third culture management issues in two-culture business ventures in the United States and the People's Republic of China. *Japanese Journal of Administrative Science, 13*(2), 87–98,

With M. Uhl-Bien & T. Scandura. Implication of leader-member exchange (LMX) for strategic human resource management systems: Relationships as social capital for competitive advantage. In: G. Ferris (Ed.), *Research in Personnel and Human Resources Management* (*18*, pp. 137–185). Information Age Publishing, (formerly JAI Press).

With Wu, Nengquan. *Gaining and Growing Guanxi in American Companies*, Guangzhou, China: Zhongshan University Press.

2001

With C. Hui. Approaches to leadership: Toward a complete contingency model of face-to-face leadership. In: M. Erez & P. C. Earley (Eds), *Work Motivation to Clinical Language Problems* (pp. 203–217). New York: Erlbaum.

2002

With M. Uhl-Bien. Thirty-five years of LMX theory and research: Programmatic functional theory building using the strong inference approach. *Leadership Quarterly.*

In Press

With R. Dharwadkar, R. Grewall, C. Hui & M. Wakabayashi. Long-term prediction of career success: First promotion or early job experience? *International Journal of Human Resource Management Education.*

Leadership and followership making via a third culture: So You Want Success? LMX Leadership, Volume 1. Greenwich, CT: Information Age Publishing, Inc.

NOTES

1. Karl should move to South Louisiana if he wants to enjoy real jazz where it was invented, e.g. Clifton Chenier, the King of Zydeco's band, consisting of his son (bandleader), Stanley Duval Jr., Robert St. Julien (master of double-cluchin), Sonny

Landreth (first white member and slide guitarist), Harry "Big Daddy" Hypolite (blue's guitarist) and John Hart (blind saxophonist) recently played their brains out here in Lafayette, LA at the Festival International.

2. St. Bridget School still operates, but lay teachers have replaced most of the nuns.

3. I lost touch with Sister Janet because I did not understand her wondrous gift, but I support the "Pathway" sisters of St. Benedict for their great work. Perhaps, what Sister Janet saw was from my paternal lineage which I recently discovered, and notably highlighted by University of Berlin graduate Baron, Georg Von Graen, Justice of the Brakel District of Prussia (1798–1853).

4. Mike and Marty were wise enough to find career paths different from their father's. Moreover, they have always made Joni and me proud parents. They struggled through the usual difficult events as children but, the culture shock they experienced both socially and educationally in Japan (to be discussed) was particularly hard. They were both strong young men and I hope profited from their cross-cultural experiences. The enjoyment Joni and I had "growing up again" with them was endless. Clearly, their hard work, education and, we hope, their genes, have brought them both to very rewarding positions. Mike and Marty both have wonderful families – they are the greatest. Joni and I are extremely proud of our two sons. They, as well as their families, remain my truly motivating factors.

5. My Bachelor's thesis was a library study on "Accident proneness: The J-curve." It was advised by Professor Howard Longstaff, a student of Donald G. Patterson, the founder of Applied Psychology at Minnesota.

6. René Dawes became my transcultural mentor. He was amazingly bicultural and could think in both European (Western) and Asian (Eastern) logic. More dissertation topics came out of his seminars than anyone else's at Minnesota. Karl Weick became my social psychology and theory building mentor. Karl once became so exasperated by my "dust bowl" empiricism that he asked me if I had a "clinical soul." I had yet to discover it.

7. Marv Dunnette, also a student of Donald G. Patterson, became my super mentor and much more over time. His numerous doctoral advisees have added to his academic family.

8. The Cattell award came with $500 and a trip to the conference in San Francisco from the Society of Industrial and Organizational Psychology (SIOP). The money was welcome and the trip to far off California was mind-boggling. I had seldom been out of Minnesota.

9. After my father's suicide, Marv became my surrogate father. I would drop into his office every week or two for a chat. He would always find time for his young street kid student.

10. Because of the San Francisco paper, I had to leave Joni, Mike and Marty to move us into our new house in Champaign, Illinois. Due to the timing of our move to Champaign/Urbana, Lloyd Humphreys picked up my James McKeen Award at the SIOP meeting the year before.

11. Joni would never allow me to put her name on the author's line of any publication. She deserves to be a co-author on all of my publications. Many of my publications would not have been possible without her never-give-up attitude. More than once my colleagues have suggested that she be canonized for her life and work with me over 42 years of marriage and research partnership.

12. I wish to thank Art Bedeian for asking me to write this autobiographical essay. It was a joyful and tearful jaunt down memory lane.

ACKNOWLEDGMENTS

I thank Joni Graen, Mike Graen, Marty Graen and my siblings for checking a draft manuscript against their recollections, and Joni Graen and Mary Uhl-Bien for checking my research history. Finally, editorial assistance of Joni Graen is likewise gratefully acknowledged. Correspondence concerning this manuscript should be addressed to the author at lmxlotus@aol.com

REFERENCES

Bales, R. F. (1949). *Interaction process analysis*. New York, Reading Press.

Bass, B. M. (1985). *Leadership and performance beyond expectations*. New York: Free Press.

Bedeian, A. G. (1998). And fate walked in. In: A. G. Bedeian (Ed.), *Management Laureates* (Vol. 5, pp. 1–40). Greenwich, Connecticut, JAI Press Inc.

Bray D. W., Campbell, R. J., & Grant (1974). *Formative years in business: A long-term AT&T study of managerial lives*. New York: Wiley.

Burns, J. M. (1978). *Leadership*. New York: Harper & Row.

Dunnette, M. D. (1966). Fad, fashions and folderol in psychology. *American Psychologist, 21*, 343–352.

Eden, D. (1993). Leadership expectations: Pygmalion effects and self-fulfilling prophecies in organizations. *Leadership Quarterly, 56*, 215–239.

Ferris, G. R. (1985). Role of leadership in the employee withdrawal process: A constructive replication. *Journal of Applied Psychology, 70*, 777–781.

Gerstner, C. R., & Day, D. V. (1997). Meta-analytic review of leader-member exchange theory: correlates and construct issues. *Journal of Applied Psychology, 82*, 827–844.

Herzberg, F., Mausner, B., & Snyderman, B. B. (1959). *The Motivation to Work* (2nd ed.). New York: Wiley.

Hollander, E. P. (1978). *Leadership Dynamics: A Practical Guide to Effective Relationships*. New York: Free Press/Macmillan.

Homans, G. C. (1961). *Social Behavior: Its Elementary Forms*. New York: Harcourt, Brace and World.

House, R. J. (1977). A 1976 theory of charismatic leadership. In: J. G. Hunt & L. L. Larson (Eds), *Leadership: The Cutting Edge* (pp. 189–207). Carbondale, IL: Southern Illinois University Press.

House, R. J. (1991). The distribution and exercise of power in complex organizations: A meso theory. *Leadership Quarterly, 2*, 23–58.

Jacobs, T. (1971). *Leadership and Exchange in Formal Organizations*. Alexandria, VA: Human Resources Research Organization.

Organ, D. W. (1988). *Organizational citizenship behavior: The "good soldier" syndrome*. Lexington, MA: Lexington Books.

Stogdill, R. M. (1948). Personal factors associated with leadership: A survey of the literature. *Journal of Psychology, 25*, 35–71.

Yammarino, F. J., Spangler, W. D., & Dubinsky, A. J. (1998). Transformational and contingent reward leadership: Individual, dyad, and group levels of analysis. *Leadership Quarterly,* *9*(1), 27–54.

Vroom, V. H. (1964). *Work and motivation.* New York: Wiley.

Weick, K. E. (1993). Turning context into text: An academic life as data. In: A. G. Bedeian (Ed.), *Management Laureates* (Vol. 3, pp. 285–323). Greenwich, Connecticut: JAI Press Inc.

Donald C. Hambrick

STRATEGIST WITHOUT A PLAN:
AN ACADEMIC LIFE CONSIDERED

Donald C. Hambrick

It's weird. Even though I fashion myself as a strategist and am seen by others as almost comically deliberate, my life has been full of ironic twists and turns. An earnest newspaper boy, A student, and Eagle Scout, I fathered a child at age 16. As a college senior who had spent all my years in the West, I signed up to meet with an itinerant admissions interviewer for Columbia's MBA program, which I assumed was located close to the Columbia River. I never got to Columbia as a student but eventually spent 23 years on its faculty. Following my MBA, I went to Penn State for an administrative post, but eventually got lured into the Ph.D. program there. Soon after arriving at Penn State, my first wife met another woman, Peg Rzetelny, at a newcomers' reception; at the end of the evening, she said to Peg, "You have to meet my husband; you'd really like him." Four years later I was married to Peg. The first term paper I wrote as a doctoral student elicited a ho-hum reaction from my professor; it later became my most highly-cited work by far. A mid-'80s sabbatical back at Penn State caused me to swear off the insularity of small-town life; but now I'm eagerly anticipating my return to Penn State's faculty, where I plan to spend the rest of my career. And so it goes.

THE EARLY YEARS (1946–1964)

Ina Winburn and Richard Hambrick met and married in South Carolina, where he was stationed at the end of the War. They stayed there a few months, until Ina finished high school, and then moved to Dick's hometown, Pueblo,

Management Laureates, Volume 6, pages 83–121.
© 2002 Published by Elsevier Science Ltd.
ISBN: 0-7623-0487-1

Colorado, where he enrolled at Pueblo Junior College. I was born soon after, November 27, 1946, delivered by the same doctor who had delivered my dad.

With their new baby in tow, Ina and Dick moved to Denver. They didn't have anything in particular lined up, but were eager and resourceful. Dad went to night school at the University of Denver, majoring in accounting. By day, he worked a series of jobs, including as hospital orderly, janitor, and bookkeeper. Ina watched the baby, made their small upstairs apartment a home, and pinched pennies. The hard work and sacrifice paid off with a triple-win in 1950: Dad graduated; he got an entry-level accounting job at the Denver and Rio Grande Western Railroad ("Main Line Through the Rockies"); and we moved to a $9000 two-bedroom dream house in the suburb of Aurora.

My childhood in Aurora was a caricature of 1950s suburban life. There was Little League, swim lessons, Cub Scouts (Mom was Den Mother), then Boy Scouts (Dad was Scoutmaster), and biannual car vacations to Yellowstone, Mount Rushmore, Dodge City and other Western high spots. Dad took the bus to work and back. He arrived home every evening at 5:25, and we sat down to eat promptly at 5:30. We even had the requisite second kid, brother Dan, who was born five years after me.

One might say that it was just like the Cleavers (as in "Beaver") or the Nelsons (think "Ozzie"). But there were differences. For one thing, the Cleavers and the Nelsons had a lot of big trees in their yards. We were in a new subdivision, looking out toward Kansas. We had no significant trees for several blocks in any direction; instead we had tumbleweeds, which would pile up to our roofline from the prairie winds each spring. For another, the Cleavers and the Nelsons were always engaged in casual banter, a lot of good-natured verbal give-and-take. We didn't banter. Our discussions were primarily utilitarian. "Did you mow the lawn today? Do you know where the pliers are? How'd you do on your math exam?"

Both of my parents were products of attentive but sternly Calvinist upbringing, and this predictably carried over to our own family. Hard work, sacrifice, thrift, and accomplishment – these would define the Hambricks of Aurora. There was love but little warmth, purpose but little passion.

My mother especially was a bastion of parsimony. She gave us our haircuts, canned and froze vegetables in ludicrous quantities, and regularly sent Dan and me with our red wagon to the local Piggly-Wiggly to load up on such deals as ground beef for 19¢ a pound or bread for 15¢ a loaf, which we piled in our gargantuan freezer.

There was a lot of emphasis on achievement and hard work. Any acts of sloth would cause Dad to ask, "Do you want to grow up to be a ditch digger?" Less than a full effort – at anything – would elicit his other favorite: "Anything worth doing is worth doing well." Being a mere kid, I didn't realize Dad was spouting clichés. Instead, I thought he had developed these pearls specifically with me and my life challenges in mind, and that I'd better heed them closely. So, by the time I was 16, I wasn't just a pretty good student, but an A student; not just a Boy Scout, but an Eagle Scout; not just a tennis player, but winning tournaments; not just a drummer, but in All-State band and orchestra.

And I was always earning money. I was never told I had to work, but my allowance was modest and my parents perpetually talked about how I needed to save for college, even when I had little idea what college was. I started with the typical boyhood money-makers: selling greeting cards and mowing lawns. But eventually I sold eggs door-to-door (from the same wagon that made the trips to Piggly-Wiggly), worked as a night receptionist at a mortuary, delivered newspapers (and thus became accustomed to waking up at 4:30 a.m.), played the drums in a dorky Dixieland band which we incongruously named "The Beachcombers"; then played in a much cooler rock band; and taught tennis.

I was a work and achievement junkie. My parents praised my accomplishments, spurring me on to even more, and I basked in my self-discipline. Hmmm. Something has to give here. A kid in this situation has to rebel somehow. That's where a girl – I'll call her Elaine – comes in. Elaine played oboe in the high-school band. She was great-looking, sweet, and smart. Most notably, though, Elaine expressed interest in me. I melted, and we had an intense relationship starting at the end of our junior year.

Naturally, Elaine didn't fit into my parents' picture. She was distracting me from serious work; and, because I was clearly swept up in her charms, I now see that my parents were terrified that I would get married way too early and face the same struggles they had worked so hard to surmount. We had many arguments at home about Elaine. Inexperienced as we were with emotional exchanges, the arguments invariably spiralled into screamfests. My parents tried to ban me from seeing Elaine. Of course, that didn't work. Among other stratagems, I learned how to disconnect the odometer on the family car so I could make the five-mile drive to Elaine's undetected.

All Americans beyond a certain age remember where they were when President Kennedy was shot. I was home with mononucleosis and the accompanying stress from falling behind in my senior-year studies. The day is also indelibly memorable because of Elaine's call. "I'm pregnant," she sobbed. After the inevitable questions about whether she was 100% sure, I asked, "What are we going to do?", terrified to hear the answer – any answer. She said she wanted to have the baby and give it up for adoption. We didn't discuss any other alternatives. I hung up the phone and spent the rest of the day in bed staring at the ceiling. I can't begin to imagine how Elaine spent the rest of her day.

I was soon back in school, getting ready to apply to colleges. I came very close to accepting a full scholarship, based on my musical promise, at Colorado State College, in Greeley. But I decided instead to attend the academically stronger University of Colorado at Boulder. Without a scholarship, CU would cost a lot more, but this is what I had been saving for for years. My plans were to major in political science and then attend law school.

Elaine finished her senior year at a newly-opened high school across town. No one but the two of us and her family knew she was pregnant, least of all my parents. The baby, whom Elaine named Marie Christine, was born in July after we had graduated. The extent of my sense of duty was to go to the hospital to see mother and daughter. Astoundingly, Elaine and I continued our relationship for another year or so; then she moved to San Francisco to be part of the Haight-Ashbury scene.

I told no one about my daughter for over 30 years, burying this life event every way I could. Now I cannot look back on it with anything but guilt and sadness.

BOULDER (1964–1968)

The University of Colorado at Boulder is a charmed place. Nestled at the base of the Rockies, the red-tile roofs perched on graceful Italianate architecture create the sensation of a Renaissance Oz. In the 1960s, the University was arguably the premiere educational institution between the Mississippi River and the West Coast. I thrived there in every way.

By the end of my sophomore year, my interest in political science had given way to an interest in business. Although I greatly enjoyed my liberal arts courses (especially English, history, psychology and sociology), I liked even more an introductory business course I took on a whim. I liked the practicality of business studies, the here-and-now, and the fact that I'd have a possibly useful credential without needing to go to graduate school.

Once I transferred to business, I was pulled in all sorts of directions, drawn to the appeal of several fields of study. My answer to this nice problem was to have three majors: accounting, finance, and marketing. I liked the precision of accounting and the fact that it had served my Dad well. (By this time, he had become Controller at the Rio Grande.) I liked the Big Money image associated with finance, as well as the feeling that it was complicated and somehow exotic. But I loved marketing.

Marketing involved both analysis and creativity. It particularly catered to my growing interest in human and social behavior. I'm sure my fondness for marketing also was enhanced by the extraordinary talent on CU's marketing faculty at the time. The group consisted of a veritable Who's Who in the field – William Stanton, Richard Buskirk, Philip Cateora, Morris Massey, and other fabulous teacher-scholars. I took every marketing course I could and became convinced that I was destined to be a Madison Avenue advertising executive.

My extracurricular life was varied and enriching. I played intramural tennis as a freshman and varsity tennis as a sophomore. As an upperclassman, I took on more professionally-related activities – as president of the business fraternity Delta Sigma Pi, president of the Marketing Club, and chairman of the Business Student Council. Music was about the only endeavor I turned my back on. I had originally intended to play in the University band, but inexplicably lost interest after a couple of practices.

In the finest Hambrick tradition, I was always on the prowl for money. I played briefly in a rock band in Boulder, but we dissolved after a few months. Then, in one of the all-time colossal cases of downward job movement, I went from rock band drummer to pizza delivery boy. My efficiency as a delivery boy was hampered by a certain annoying quirk of my 1958 Renault, which I had purchased for $250 expressly for this job. After I got the car home from the used car lot, the engine would only start if the car was already moving. Whenever the car came to a halt, the engine came to a halt. So, with each pizza delivery, I had to carefully station the car in such a way that I could then run alongside and push it for 20 or 30 feet to get it going again. Needless to say, this arrangement didn't last too long. My Renault quickly gave way to a much hipper motorcycle, and my delivery job was replaced, in a truly upward move, by a job as dormitory cook.

I specialized in breakfasts, because I was the only 19-year old they could find who would start cracking eggs at 5:00 a.m. each day. Actually, this job was great for me. For 15 hours of work each week, I received room and board and some cash. Then, as a senior, my pay-per-hour shot up even more when I landed a job as dormitory resident advisor. This job only paid room and board but involved next to no work. Of course I also worked summers, as a counselor at a mountain camp for troubled boys and as a tennis pro at a private club.

In my senior year, I had no idea what I wanted to do after college. I received offers from a couple of large California banks. My marketing professors, however, encouraged me to apply to Ph.D. programs; so I applied to and got accepted by Northwestern and a few other places. I also applied to the MBA programs at Harvard and Columbia. Before I started preparing to talk to the Columbia recruiter, however, I had literally never heard of it and guessed from its name that maybe it was in Idaho or Oregon. After a bit of research, however, I learned that it was located near my still-dreamy Madison Avenue. Harvard turned me down, but Columbia accepted me. I sent Columbia my tuition deposit, started reading everything I could about New York City, and got set for my move East. I was about to become a man of the world.

Yes, but not the way I thought. When my family and I arrived home from my commencement in Boulder, there was a piece of mail waiting for me. It was from the U.S. Selective Service, announcing that my draft status had been switched to classification 1A – eligible for induction and, it being 1968, pretty much a shoo-in for Vietnam.

U.S. ARMY (1968–1970)

With the Vietnam War raging in 1968, the Army needed many more draftees. As a way to help out, the Selective Service took an action which caught all of America by surprise: they did away with draft deferments for graduate school. So, basically all single, healthy male college graduates of the class of 1968 were eligible for service. I knew this noisome change had occurred, so the letter from the authorities was not completely unexpected. Still, I was hoping that my draft board had maybe lost my file or had singled me out for a special exception, because, after all, I was going to study to be an advertising executive.

But they hadn't lost my file, and they weren't impressed by my lofty plans. They were now after me. Over the next few weeks, I half-heartedly flirted with several possible escapes. I tried unsuccessfully to convince a doctor that my childhood asthma had returned with a mighty vengeance. I looked into a last-minute application to medical school, which would have gotten me a deferment (future doctors being seen as societally more desirable than future ad execs). Unfortunately, a quick perusal of medical school catalogs confirmed that my one puny college science course would not carry my application very far. I also considered joining an increasing number of draft resistors in Canada. Such a move, though, seemed way too extreme and irreversible. So, resigned that I was about to get drafted, I signed-up for Army officers' candidate school (OCS). Even though being an officer meant an extra year of service, it seemed like the fitting avenue for an achievement-minded college graduate. If I couldn't avoid Vietnam, I reasoned, at least I could develop and test my leadership skills there. What a dope.

Almost every man in my basic training company was in the same situation as me – a college graduate signed up for OCS. We drove the drill sergeants crazy with our unrelenting, "Why?" Many of us quickly concluded that we absolutely hated the Army and that our new main objective was to get it over with as soon as possible. I was the first to go to the company commander's office to say that I was dropping my plan for OCS and that he should file the paperwork for me to make the switch to be a regular enlisted man. By the end of the fourth week of basic training, almost half the men in the company had done the same. We knew we were going to Vietnam one way or the other; our goal now was to get the Army behind us as fast as possible.

After advanced infantry training, I was assigned to the Fourth Infantry Division in the Central Highlands of Vietnam. My battalion was responsible for conducting reconnaissance of the Ho Chi Minh trail and its many tributaries. This work took us into Laos and Cambodia well before the American public knew about it. Since our mission was to observe the North Vietnamese without being detected ourselves, we worked primarily in three-man patrols deep in the jungle for three days at a time. Of course, our efforts didn't always escape the notice of the North Vietnamese. Our patrols often came under intense fire, and we had several three-man groups wiped out by overpowering force.

The most horrendous action I saw, though, was when our entire company was helicoptered to the Plei Trap Valley near the tri-border area, with the plan of establishing a temporary new base from which we would start fanning out in our three-man patrols. As soon as our helicopters left, the jungle erupted on every side with the unmistakable crack of AK-47 fire and North Vietnamese mortars. By hideously bad luck, we had been dropped amidst a North Vietnamese unit at least as big as ours. We were surrounded. They were so close that calling in artillery or air fire would have certainly taken a huge toll on us. (Incidentally, about a third of all the American deaths I witnessed in Vietnam were due to friendly fire or other accidents.) After being pinned down for several hours, we were instructed to form two wedge-shaped formations and to move forward as quickly as possible through the dense jungle, firing steadily. The aim was to penetrate the North Vietnamese circle at two points, try to get behind them, and hope that our position would somehow improve. Our desperate maneuver drew intense counter-fire. Coming on top of the deafening sound and acrid smell of gunfire were the screams and moans of men on both sides. After half an hour of this terror, the North Vietnamese began retreating. We then turned to our wounded and counted our dead. We had lost almost a quarter of our men. When we started our patrols the next day, we passed the bodies of young North Vietnamese soldiers. We left them where they lay and morosely carried on.

After eight months in the jungle as a lowly foot soldier and infantry squad leader, I caught someone's attention – I have no idea whom – and was made Protocol Director for the entire Fourth Infantry Division. Reporting to the

Division Chief of Staff, I was responsible primarily for hosting dignitaries. I found myself ordering specially requested wines for elaborate dinner parties, making sure we had the right VIPs in the right billets (it was seen as a grave mistake to mix-up the rooms intended for a Deputy Secretary of Defense and a mere three-star general), and – always, it seemed – arranging for fleets of chauffeured sedans to be at the ready to sweep our visiting potentates from one spot to another. So, I had gone from the merely ridiculous in the jungle to the supremely ridiculous at base camp.

After my year in Vietnam, I still had six months left in the Army. Because I had been hanging out with bigwigs, I was given my choice of stateside locations. I picked Fort Carson, just outside of Colorado Springs. My first day there, the commanding general called me to his office and explained that he was a West Point classmate and a good friend of the general I had worked for in Vietnam. Then, in an act without precedent in all of military history, he asked me what I'd like to do at Fort Carson. Utterly amazed by this fairy-tale meeting, I was unable to speak. The general then rattled-off a few possibilities. I jumped at the job that seemed most likely to help me get back on my track toward professional achievement – as a budget analyst. I was still planning to go to business school, and I thought that a brush-up on financial stuff, statistical analysis, and computers would help propel me. I shared an office with the civilian budget director and a secretary. When I was introduced to the secretary, a fiery redhead named Judy, she exhaled a sultry, "Hi, Sarge," looking and sounding just like Lauren Bacall in *To Have and Have Not*. These are going to be six fabulous months, I said to myself.

And they were. Judy and I started our inevitable romantic relationship. I produced several complex budget analyses, which, even though completely uninsightful, provided more mental stimulation than I'd had for a while. I also worked on my graduate school applications. Once again, I applied to the Harvard and Columbia MBA programs. Still schizoid about my goals, I also applied again to Northwestern's Ph.D. program in marketing. I was readmitted to Columbia and Northwestern. And now Harvard concluded that my time with Uncle Sam had made me worthy. So, I was off to Harvard.

Before I went into the Army, I had what could only be described as a vague unease about U.S. involvement in Vietnam. When I finished my year there, I was vehement in my opposition and took my sentiments on the road, speaking at churches about the folly and horror of our policies. I was still in the Army, so I sometimes worried that my crusade amounted to some sort of serious military offense, perhaps even treason. But I gave the talks anyway and felt better for it.

I wish I could say with clarity how my military service affected me. But I can't. I am sure I have a mélange of hopes, fears, resentments, and fortitude that are traceable to my time in Vietnam. I do recognize that, of those who were there, I was one of the luckier ones.

HARVARD (1970–1972)

As a middle-class kid from out West, with no connections to the Ivy League whatsoever, I had long viewed Harvard as mystical. When I arrived there in September 1970, the gauze was stripped away and I had to see the place for what it was. I was not disappointed.

The campus of the Harvard Business School was stunning, with dozens of stately buildings, sweeping lawns, world-renowned Baker Library, and the richly paneled classrooms of Aldrich Hall. The students were drawn from all corners of the world and the U.S., but with an intimidatingly large number who had attended the elite boarding schools and colleges of the Northeast. I never felt as though I was out of my league, but I quickly concluded that I couldn't match the dazzling repartée and cosmopolitan glibness that many of the students issued forth during our thrice-daily case discussions. I concluded that to perform well, I would have to excel at my written work.

The greatest asset of HBS, of course, was its faculty. A steady stream of remarkably effective instructors demonstrated why the place is known for its teaching excellence. There are jokes about a cookie-cutter teaching style at HBS (sleeves rolled up, pacing the aisles of the tiered classroom and exaggerated gestures). But I saw numerous styles, from the quiet to the bellicose, from the warm to the stern, from the abstract to the concrete. Without knowing I'd ever need it, I collected at Harvard an immense mental scrapbook full of images of great teachers at work.

Judy and I got married midway through my first year at Harvard. All the married-student housing was taken by then, so we rented an apartment in a refurbished landmark hotel in downtown Boston. The front of the building looked over Boston Commons. The rear of the building – which of course is where we were situated – looked out over "The Combat Zone," Boston's legalized enclave of porno shops and strip joints. We never felt threatened by our environs, but Saturday nights were often raucous. The good news was that we were within walking distance of all of historic Boston, great shopping, and Judy's work as a secretary at a large bank.

Like most MBAs, my second year at Harvard was largely devoted to getting a job. But, unlike most MBAs, I had no idea what I wanted to do. I knew, however, what I *didn't* want to do: be in a big mill with a bunch of other MBAs.

Therefore, product management, consulting, and investment banking were out of the question. They were too obvious, too vanilla. I wanted to stand out and quickly make a difference. I had also cooled to a career in advertising, now seeing it as somehow sleazy. My iconoclastic streak drew me to the offbeat, one-of-a-kind job leads that were posted in a three-ring binder located in the placement office. These "correspondence opportunities" – so-called because the employers couldn't justify any more recruiting expense than a mere letter – came primarily from small and distant companies, along with not-for-profit organizations. I was in heaven with this book, both because it held exactly the kinds of jobs that interested me, and, as far as I knew, I had it all to myself. I never encountered any classmates who had the faintest idea about this book's existence, intent as they were on more mainstream endeavors.

One job listing especially caught my attention. It was from the Pennsylvania State University for a newly-created position as Director of the MBA Program. Hmmm, I thought. I like being around universities; I know a thing or two about MBA programs; and I like that this is described as a "general management position," where I can do my own thing. The only problem was that I'd never heard of the Pennsylvania State University (I had vaguely heard of "Penn State" but was uncertain as to whether they were one and the same). Although I could guess what state it was in, I had no more precise idea about its location. But since I had never been anywhere in Pennsylvania, that was of little matter.

I also applied – once again – to marketing Ph.D. programs, including Northwestern. (If you're counting, we're up to three.) But again I balked. Getting a Ph.D. seemed like a huge undertaking, and for what? I still had no real idea whether I would like being an academic. The job at Penn State seemed like a perfect hybrid. It drew upon my managerial training and aptitudes, but it would keep me in a university and allow me to learn more about academic life before making the Ph.D. plunge. So, Judy and I were off to Penn State.

PENN STATE (1972–1978)

I was hired for the Penn State job by Max Richards, the dean of graduate programs in business, who had crafted the idea of having a managerial type devoted to advancing the quality and reputation of the Penn State MBA Program. An irascible, cigar-smoking curmudgeon, referred to by students as "Max The Ax," he was a fabulous boss. With a Harvard MBA himself, along with an almost innate mastery of organizations and management, Max gave me a lot of room to do my thing.

Influenced heavily by "open systems theory" while at Harvard, I quickly concluded that our challenge was to simultaneously improve the MBA

Program's inputs, throughputs, and outputs. Advances on just one of these fronts, without progress on the other two, would quickly crumble. So, we worked hard on improving student quality, through an aggressive recruitment and promotional program, as well as tighter admissions standards. We significantly revised the curriculum, to allow better integration among courses; instituted formal course and instructor evaluations; and built up our extra-curricular and student life activities. We created a dedicated MBA placement operation; worked hard at getting top companies to look at our students; and supported on-campus recruiters everyway we could. Overall, we made decent strides in getting the Penn State MBA Program on the map. When *MBA* magazine published the first-ever rankings of MBA programs in 1976, we came in at a respectable 19th.

None of this was smooth or easy. I was always jostling with faculty members and department heads about turf, priorities, and academic freedom. In the midst of our curriculum revision, I had all the departments feeling as though they had come out the losers. To this, I opined to Max, "Well, that means we must be on exactly the right track." I forget his exact response, but the essence of it was, "You idiot." I obviously had a thing or two to learn about leading an organizational change.

After a year or so at Penn State I was drawn into teaching. Bob Pitts, who coordinated the undergraduate policy course, asked whether I would be willing to teach one section of 40 students. I remember working very hard at it but enjoying it immensely. The students showed a gratifying level of interest, and the course evaluations were favorable. Bob, a superb teacher himself, made a point of telling me I had done extremely well. I was hooked. I liked teaching, and it looked as if I might be able to become adept at it. I also became involved in a research project with Bob, and I became captivated by that side of scholarship too.

So in 1975 my applications to Ph.D. programs went out once again (including to Northwestern, of course) – for the fourth and final time. My interest was now in strategy, where I had done my little bit of teaching. Strategy also seemed like a fitting catch-all area for someone with a catch-all background like mine – undergraduate majors in accounting, finance, and marketing; and MBA concentrations in marketing, planning, and control.

I decided to stay at Penn State for my studies, and not just out of inertia. Penn State had assembled an extraordinary management group – Max Richards, John Slocum, Bob Pitts, Chuck Snow, Don Hellriegel, and others – that I thought would be difficult to beat anyplace else. That proved to be correct. I learned a great deal from these Penn State mentors, not only about theories, analytic methods, the craft of research, and teaching, but also about the ethos of scholarship – responsibility to one's field, to one's colleagues, to one's students, and to one's institution.

In my first semester as a Ph.D. student, I took a strategy seminar from Max Richards (who was no longer my boss). The first readings on the syllabus were books by Cyert and March, March and Simon, and Mintzberg. Here I was, all set to learn about grand plans and brilliant strategies, only to be abruptly confronted with the human realities of top executive work – bounded rationality, limited search, information overload, biases, and coalitional dynamics. These works had a big influence on me. I went on to write a term paper for that course, in which I proposed that executives' background characteristics (such as tenure, education, and functional backgrounds) serve to filter and distort the stimuli that the executives confront, and that those background characteristics could be used to predict strategic choices. Max gave me an A for the paper but clearly lacked enthusiasm about my ideas. Deflated, I set the paper aside. The paper lay dormant for several years but proved to be the precursor to my most highly-cited work by far, the 1984 Hambrick and Mason article, "Upper Echelons: The Organization as a Reflection of Its Top Managers" (*Academy of Management Review*). I now have this fun hypothesis that doctoral students are very heavily influenced, or "imprinted," by the first readings they encounter in their studies.

My decision to stay at Penn State was also influenced by the business school dean, Eugene Kelley, who in 1975 offered me a new, attractive post, as Director of External Relations. This was another newly-created position, where I could once again conceive of the job in whatever way that suited me. With overall responsibilities for alumni relations, corporate relations, fund-raising, and external communications, I worked long and hard hours. Between my administrative job and my Ph.D. studies, 80-hour weeks were common.

We achieved a lot of fund-raising successes but also encountered plenty of frustrations along the way. An episode with one wealthy alumnus will always stick in my mind. Gene Kelley and I had this guy targeted for very big bucks, even though he had never given to Penn State (except, predictably, to the football program). So, one day Mr. Big Bucks calls me from his Florida getaway, saying, "I have something for you and Dean Kelley, and I'd like to come to campus next week to give it to you." On the appointed day, Gene and I were rubbing our hands together and exchanging high-fives. In comes the guy, proudly carrying two big mesh bags of Florida grapefruit. "These are for you," he says. "You'll love'em." Gene and I were too slack-jawed to say anything except a mumbled "thank you". After the guy left, Gene and I cut open the bags, looking for –you guessed it – a check. There was no check, only endless grapefruit. When Mr. Big Bucks showed up the following year with two decks of Bicentennial playing cards for Gene and me, we didn't even bother looking inside for real loot. To this day, I have no idea whether this person was intentionally out to get us or was simply loony. This episode and many others during my three years in fundraising left me with a profound respect for those who do it as a career.

By late 1974, Judy and I had parted ways. There was no acrimony in our marriage, just a malaise. With no kids, no pets, and no property to speak of, our divorce was practically a non-event. I repressed it in my typical way, refusing to think or talk about it. My work became my sanctuary, with sporadic, half-hearted dating as a diversion.

In the spring of 1975, I fell in love like never before. I had known Peg Rzetelny, assistant director of admissions for the graduate school, a bit through our related work. Now she was directly responsible for processing my application for the Ph.D. Program, and I needed to deliver some paperwork to her. Little did I know that a mutual friend had alerted her to my divorce and availability, allowing her to lay all sorts of traps. As if she needed to. With her vivaciousness, good looks, sense of humor, intelligence, and warmth, I was instantly hooked. We dated for about a year and got married at the Penn State chapel in June 1976. We bought a tidy little Cape Cod house within walking distance of campus and commenced a long, wonderful marriage.

By mid-1977, I was starting my dissertation and had become absolutely convinced that I wanted to be a regular faculty member rather than continue in university administration. Gene Kelley tried to lure me with a bigger administrative job and a bigger salary. But I was committed. I just wanted to do research and teach.

Like most management Ph.D. students, I launched my job search at the annual Academy of Management meetings. In August 1977, the meetings were at a sprawling hotel complex in Kissimmee, Florida, near Orlando. The temperature and humidity were both in the 90s, and I was in my suit running between far-flung buildings to my various job interviews. I was soaking wet and out of breath for three solid days. But it paid off. I received four invitations for job trips, and by Christmas had offers from all four schools – Indiana, Tennessee, Kansas, and my undergraduate *alma mater*, Colorado.

In January, Peg and I were in the throes of our decision making, when Max Richards came by to say that he had just gotten off the phone with Bill Newman at Columbia and learned that Columbia was hiring in the strategy area and that he had told Bill about me. I thought nothing more about it.

A few days later, I got a call from Ian MacMillan, who was heading Columbia's search, asking if I'd like to come in for an interview. I said I'd think about it. Considering that I was once devoted to the idea of being a big deal in

New York City, this was an unusual response. But my years in State College had given me a taste of the comforts of a small university town, and I no longer aspired to have an urban edge. Also, at the time, New York City was at its nadir, widely seen as a hell-hole unlikely ever to be redeemed.

Peg and I mulled over the Columbia invitation at a restaurant one evening. We started the discussion dismissively: "Even if by remote chance they made me an offer, we wouldn't want to go there, would we?" "No way." By the end of dinner, we were saying, "Well, it wouldn't hurt to make the trip."

I made the trip. They made me an offer. I accepted and went on to prosper immensely at Columbia for 23 years.

EARLY YEARS AT COLUMBIA (1979–1984)

During its nearly 250-year history, Columbia has changed its location on the island of Manhattan several times. Still, the current Morningside Heights campus conveys the majesty of an institution that was known as King's College back when we still had a king. Walking across campus conjures up a Vivaldi overture: The massive McKim, Mead and White buildings boom out the bass chords; the lush lawns and manicured hedges provide the melody; and the liberally sprinkled names of early alumni – Jay, Hamilton, and Livingston – are the grace notes. The place has to be taken seriously. And it is. There is nothing fun-loving or laid back about Columbia. Even the undergraduates have furrowed brows.

The first thing that hit me about the climate at Columbia Business School was the total preoccupation with tenure, both by those who had it and those who didn't. This wasn't totally surprising, inasmuch as only about 10% of new assistant professors at Columbia eventually got tenure; and the process – if you were willing to submit to it – was labyrinthine and fraught with peril. In the Management Division, there was a particularly dark mood about tenure; no one had gotten the nod for about fifteen years, and the previous five years had been especially bloody.

My own attitude was mixed. On the one hand, I fully understood the odds at Columbia and was prepared to view the place simply as a springboard to something else. On the other hand, I cannot stand to fail. In fact, I have an immense fear of failure, traceable no doubt to how I was raised. So, I was as swept up by the preoccupation with tenure as anyone, while trying to keep my sanity by throwing myself into my research and teaching.

But I worried about failure on another front too. As a member of the first significant cohort of strategy Ph.D.s, outside those trained in the Harvard case tradition, I felt a responsibility to help the newly christened field of "strategic management" survive its infancy. The groundwork had been laid by those before us who saw the need for systematic, theory-based, rigorous work on general management problems – Ned Bowman, Arnie Cooper, John Grant, Bill Guth, Chuck Hofer, Bill Newman, Max Richards, Dan Schendel, Charlie Summer and others. Now, the responsibility to keep the fledgling enterprise going fell to those of us who had been the first to sign up specifically to do duty in this new field – such people as Dave Jemison, Tom Lenz, Ken Hatten, Kathy Harrigan, Jay Bourgeois, Rich Bettis, Kurt Christensen and me. Thus, I viewed the stakes as larger than simply my career or Columbia's stature. Lest I sound presumptuous, let me note that within a couple years, my friends and I were all scooped by a young scholar at Harvard who had been largely unknown to all of us – Michael Porter. It was because of Mike's stunningly influential book on competitive strategy that the future of the field of strategic management became assured.

Even though Columbia wasn't a fun-loving place, at least it wasn't cutthroat. Colleagues were generous and collaborative. I learned an immense amount about teaching MBAs from Mel Anshen, John O'Shaughnessy, and Kirby Warren. I enhanced my theoretical and methodological repertoires, and learned how to craft journal articles, through the help of Mike Tushman, Dave Nadler, Ian MacMillan, and Hans Pennings.

At the outset, I was committed to producing refereed articles from my dissertation. I also resolved to avoid the biggest pitfall facing young management professors at Columbia, by being very sparing and selective in doing any consulting or executive education. I adopted as my rule that I would only do as many days of outside work per year as I had refereed articles on my CV.

Within 18 months of arriving at Columbia, I had acceptances for two articles in *Academy of Management Review*, two articles in *Strategic Management Journal*, and one piece in *Administrative Science Quarterly* (*ASQ*). My CV now had some stuff on it; and I had earned the right to do a bit of outside work. Most importantly, though, I had a hearty confidence in my ability to do refereed research. Looking back now, and thinking about the countless young professors I've watched struggle to get just one early hit, I realize just how lucky I had been.

Peg and I felt financially strapped when we moved to Columbia. My salary was appreciably lower than it had been as an administrator at Penn State, and Peg did not have a job lined up. Housing prices terrified us. Because we had sold our State College house, we had to buy another one to avoid a hefty capital gains tax. Comparable houses cost about twice as much in the New York area as in Central Pennsylvania. A New York cooperative apartment would require a large up-front cash payment that was out of the question. We settled in upper Bergen County, New Jersey, in the town of Demarest, a sterile bedroom community that we barely tolerated. As the crow flies, our house was just eleven miles from Columbia. Unfortunately, the crow wasn't flying, and it took me an hour on a lousy combination of bus and two subways to reach campus. Within a few weeks of arriving at Columbia, Peg got a job as manager of recruiting for a major consulting firm headquartered in midtown. This provided a nice financial relief but meant that Peg too was schlepping on the bus (a different one) for over an hour each way daily. We were both stressed and grumpy.

It's amazing, then, that we were able to make a baby. But we did, and in early 1981, our daughter Claire was born. I still joke with Claire that her delivery caused my only classroom absence in my entire teaching career and that I wouldn't have done it for just anyone.

About the time Claire was born, Peg took a new job with Exxon, further west in Morris County, New Jersey, and we moved to be close to her work. It resulted in a 40-mile commute for me, but only about three days a week, as I did all my writing at home. Our overall quality of life improved considerably.

Even though my dissertation work had focused squarely on strategic processes (environmental scanning and power within top management teams), my long-standing interest in marketing and my MBA teaching made me hungry to do research on the content of strategy. A chance meeting in 1981 allowed this to happen in a big way. After teaching an executive program session at Columbia's executive campus, Arden House, I met the speaker who was to follow me, Sidney Schoeffler, the executive director of the Strategic Planning Institute (SPI). While an executive at GE, Sid had masterminded the idea of establishing a large database full of quantified information about the environmental context, strategic characteristics, and performance of hundreds of individual business units of numerous corporations. His unit was spun off from GE, turned into a member-run corporate cooperative endeavor, and the database was named Profit Impact of Market Strategies (PIMS). I was aware of the PIMS data through some *Harvard Business Review* articles by Sid and others, but I had never seen them used in a rigorous, theory-driven way. After hearing Sid talk about the scale and scope of the sample, the array of variables collected, and the exceptional safeguards for data reliability (Members were provided consulting assistance in quantifying all aspects of their businesses, and the key reports they received were only meaningful if their own data were correct), I asked Sid if I could have access to this treasure trove, and he said yes.

A data junkie, I was like a kid in a candy store for the next three years. I started with some very specific research questions about the performance implications of competing through product/market innovation vs. competing through efficiency – based upon my prior work with the Miles and Snow strategy typology. But one project led to another and another and another. Over the next three years, I teamed up with several fabulous collaborators – including Diana Day, David Lei, Ian MacMillan, Hans Pennings, and Steve Schecter – to produce 11 refereed articles based on the PIMS database. We conducted the first empirical test of the Boston Consulting Group's product-portfolio matrix, we studied business turnarounds, determinants and effectiveness of R&D spending, vertical integration, and particularly attempted to contribute to development of a contingency theory of business strategy. My PIMS research exposed me to a wide array of multivariate analyses and helped to reinforce a way of thinking about context, strategy, and performance that went on to be of central importance to my teaching, subsequent research and consulting.

Eventually, though, I yearned to return to my abiding interest in the human side of strategy. In some casual conversations with a Columbia doctoral student, Phyllis Mason, I was reminded of the first term paper I had ever written in my Ph.D. program – the one that produced a yawn from Max Richards. As we talked, we refined and extended the ideas and submitted our upper echelons paper to the *Academy of Management Review.* For the first and only time in my career, the paper was accepted without revision. It went on to spawn a major stream of inquiry over the nearly 20 years since.

In 1983, my good friend, Ian MacMillan, abruptly accepted an offer of an endowed chair at New York University. This was a huge loss for Columbia and a personal loss for me, but it posed an additional complication. Mac was supposed to be the one who would demonstrate whether it was possible for a good strategy person to get tenure at Columbia. I was counting on Mac's tenure case to help me decide whether it was worthwhile for me to stay or not. Now he had robbed me of my data point.

I was feeling adrift and unsure when I went to the Academy meetings in Dallas that August. Here I was, with a decent CV, lots of citations by others, and seminar invitations galore; but I had no idea whether I could get tenure at Columbia. Indeed, there was still no evidence that anyone could get tenure in strategy at a top business school other than Harvard. It was at a reception at John Slocum's house, in the Dallas suburbs, that things suddenly looked better.

With the gin and tonics flowing, I found myself jostled up against Larry Cummings, who was then at Northwestern. We introduced ourselves, and then he said, "Oh, you're the one everybody's talking about and wants to hire." I thought it would be tacky to ask him to elaborate, so I simply blushed and demurred. Larry turned to talk to someone else, and I floated through the rest of my time in Dallas.

A few weeks later, Larry's Northwestern colleague, Bob Duncan, called to ask if I would come interview for an endowed chair with tenure. Soon after that, I was called about a tenured post at Wharton. Needless to say, I was now emboldened enough to force the tenure issue at Columbia. Even though my five years at Columbia was well shy of the customary seven years for a tenure review, I asked my dean to set the elaborate Columbia machinery into motion. By March 1984, I had tenured offers from Columbia, Northwestern, and Wharton. I came exceedingly close to going to Northwestern, even resolving at one point to make the move. Ultimately the inertial tug of Columbia, the appeal of the New York City area (which we had come to savor), and Peg's work caused us to stay. But my days of worrying about getting tenure were over.

MIDDLE YEARS AT COLUMBIA (1984–1995)

In 1985, I was eligible for a sabbatical. In trying to decide how to spend this precious time, I was driven by two insights I had garnered in my short academic career. First, I had seen many sabbaticals squandered, and I was not going to let it happen to me. I was going to put this time to use. I wasn't sure how, but I was going to come back a year later refreshed, smarter, better looking, or something. This bonanza of time was not going to slip through my fingers.

My second insight was that I had seen a woeful number of professors experience a post-tenure letdown, losing their bearings, their drive, their momentum. They would typically claim, while puttering around, that they were readying themselves for the transition to a grander research agenda. But they were often left with a three- or four-year hole in their CVs, or even CVs that trailed off for good. This too was not going to happen to me.

These two insights led me to the perverse conclusion that I had to use this valuable year to produce more than ever. I had to get away from the hassles of Columbia, while incurring minimal transition costs or disorientation. Exotic places like London, Paris, or Palo Alto were therefore clearly out of the question. I needed a place I could slide right into and start working without distraction. That place, of course, was Penn State.

We rented Bob Pitts' house, a magnificent stone colonial just three blocks from the business school, while he and his family were on leave in Boise. Peg taught an undergraduate human resources course, Claire was in pre-school, and

I worked hard, as planned. The year was OK but bland. We missed the stimulation of New York and felt dislocated. My zeal for productivity, I'm sure, stood in the way of our enjoyment and relaxation.

My number one research priority for that year was to make progress on my first empirical study based on the upper echelons perspective. In collaboration with Richard D'Aveni, an immensely creative Columbia Ph.D. student, we were interested in how different top management team (TMT) characteristics affect company performance. As a way of finessing the inevitable difficulties in gauging performance, we decided to examine major bankruptcies – instances where performance was unequivocally bad. We generated a sample of 60 large bankruptcies (companies at least large enough that we could obtain archival information about their executives) and 60 carefully matched companies of the same size and industry. Richard conducted a prodigious amount of data analysis at Columbia and conveyed everything to me at Penn State via the mid-80s precursor to the Internet, known as "Bitnet." We generated two jointly-authored papers, in which we invoked the metaphor of a "downward spiral" to describe how troubled firms tend to take actions that mostly make things worse. The first piece, published in *ASQ*, observed that troubled firms flail around, engaging in extreme and vacillating strategic actions, which the companies lack the competences for and which chew up their already-dwindling resources. The second paper, published in *Management Science*, examined how failing companies, in their final years, suffer various forms of deterioration in the composition of their top management teams, severely impairing their ability to formulate and execute their needed turnarounds. Richard published additional papers on other aspects of organizational failure and executive prestige from our sample, and he won the Business Policy and Strategy Division's (of the Academy of Management) prize for the best dissertation.

Our *ASQ* paper taught me a memorable lesson about dealing with journal editors. The three reviewers generally liked the paper and asked for relatively minor modifications. The editor, John Freeman, said as much; but he still decided to reject the paper based upon what he saw as a fatal methodological flaw – sampling on the dependent variable. For a population ecologist such as John, our's was an egregious problem. In his view, one must study whole populations or large random samples, but one never, never generates a sample based on outcome conditions. I hit the roof and called Richard to tell him the bad news. After stewing for a few days, I decided to write John and tell him why, in this case, he was wrong. I explained that large corporate bankruptcies are so exceedingly rare that in order to generate a viable sample of them, as part of a random sample, we'd be talking about a sample size in the thousands, maybe even tens of thousands. (I had a bunch of good statistics.) If we ever want to learn anything systematic about the failure of large companies, I said, we must resort to a matched-pair design such as ours. Researchers in the medical sciences learned this long ago in their efforts to study the causes of rare diseases. John wrote back saying that he saw my logic and that if I could include the same explanation in a revision, he would be optimistic about acceptance. This episode taught me three things: (1) a "no" from an editor isn't always final; (2) editors, like reviewers, can be persuaded by a strong argument; and (3) John Freeman is a good guy.

It was with Richard D'Aveni that I really hit my stride in working with Ph.D. students. Over the next few years, I benefited from fruitful collaborations and close friendships with several more students, including Syd Finkelstein, John Michel, Bert Cannella, Sylvia Black and Marta Geletkanycz. Not only did they teach me leading-edge theories and methods, but they also greatly influenced my basic thinking.

My collaboration with Syd was to become the most enduring of my scholarly partnerships. Our work started with our 1987 chapter in *Research in Organization Behavior*, "Managerial Discretion: A Bridge Between Polar Views of Organizational Outcomes". This paper attempted to reconcile two, then antagonistic, polar views: managers don't matter very much to organizational outcomes vs. managers matter immensely. Our idea was that sometimes managers matter a great deal, sometimes not at all, and often are somewhere in between, depending on how much discretion – or latitude of action – they possess. Discretion exists when there is an absence of constraint and when means-ends ambiguity is great, that is, when there are a lot of plausible alternatives. Discretion, we argued, emanates from the environment, the organization, and from the executive himself or herself. We asserted that discretion has widespread implications, affecting executive behavior, compensation, succession, staffing, and symbolism. Accordingly, our chapter stimulated research by others on a wide array of topics.

Typical of my career, Syd and I hit upon the concept of managerial discretion in a roundabout way. We were actually working on CEO compensation, searching for an explanation as to why executives in different industries are paid such wildly different amounts. For instance, after controlling for company size and profitability, CEOs in fashion, cosmetics, entertainment, and high-tech are paid a lot, whereas (at least when we were doing our research) CEOs in insurance, utilities, and commodity industries are paid much less. Our first explanation – that some industries are simply more flamboyant and outrageous than others – was not conceptually too appealing. We eventually identified the concept of discretion as the underlying driver: In some industries, managers are frequently making very big choices, and the economic difference between the best managers and the worst managers is huge; boards and shareholders will be inclined to pay a lot in an effort to get one of the golden managers. In other industries, where managers are more constrained and hemmed-in, the economic difference between the best and worst managers is not so great, and boards can be more sparing in what they pay. This vignette is just an example of the twists and turns I've taken on my various intellectual journeys.

In 1987, I was named the Samuel Bronfman Professor of Democratic Business Enterprise, the oldest and most visible chair at the School. The Bronfman Professorship had added meaning because of my great admiration for my two predecessors in the chair. Bill Newman, one of the leading management thinkers of the twentieth century, as well as a co-founder and early president of the Academy of Management, held the chair from its inception in 1951 until 1978. He was followed by Kirby Warren, a legendary Columbia teacher and world-recognized executive educator, who was my most important mentor at Arden House.

The same year, 1987, Peg decided she wanted to spend more time at home, especially with Claire, and so quit her job at Exxon. This meant there was no reason for us to stay in the Morristown area, and we could move wherever we wanted. We settled in Englewood, New Jersey, a vibrant, diverse suburb with large properties and big, lush trees, located close to the George Washington Bridge. Now my drive to Columbia would only take about 15 minutes, and getting to the Broadway theatre district would take less than half an hour. As a result, we further increased our enjoyment of New York, frequently going in for theatre, restaurants, cabaret shows, and shopping. We also savored Englewood itself, with its charming downtown, full of great restaurants, galleries, and boutiques. We joined the 100-year old Englewood Field Club, where Claire would go on to learn to ice skate, swim, and play tennis and squash. We felt connected to our community like never before; we felt connected to New York City like never before; and I was about to feel more connected to Columbia than ever before, primarily because of the energy of a new dean.

By 1988, Columbia Business School was stagnant. There had been no MBA curriculum review since 1960, almost 30 years; there was uneven commitment to teaching quality and student needs; fund-raising was lackluster; and there was a general malaise at the place. We shouldn't have been surprised, therefore, when the first *Business Week* MBA rankings placed us at number fourteen, well below where our collective self-concept put us.

It was into this context that Meyer Feldberg arrived as our new dean in 1989. Meyer was an MBA alumnus of the School, who returned to his home country of South Africa for a Ph.D., and then came back to the States for a series of progressively impressive administrative posts – including as dean of Tulane's business school and as president of the Illinois Institute of Technology. He had a reputation as a prodigious fund-raiser with a knack for making things happen.

In my own early meetings with Meyer, I was impressed by his energy, high standards, and insights about the place and its people. I was frankly thrilled he was at Columbia and quickly resolved that I would help his campaign for change every way I reasonably could – every way, that is, except taking on an administrative job, which I resolutely avoided. But I did take on my share of committee assignments – on the Curriculum Review Committee (and as chair of one of its subcommittees), on the School's Executive Committee, on the Promotion and Tenure Committee, on an executive education committee, as chairman of a Ph.D. program review committee, and as chairman of a committee to reform our faculty governance processes.

It was this latter task that tested and stretched my political skills like never before. I personally believed that a lot of our governance procedures were creaky and ineffective, but a number of faculty members (especially old-timers) thought they were fine. I envisioned more power for the faculty on some matters than Meyer, our dean, thought was right; I envisioned more power for the dean's office on other matters than some of my faculty colleagues thought was right. And, most difficult of all, I saw a need for more strenuous review of senior faculty, with the possibility that individual faculty members could elect to take on different portfolios of teaching, research, and service, depending on their evolving interests and track records. These were all exceedingly contentious issues, and I remember having a number of very difficult conversations with Meyer on the one hand and with faculty colleagues on the other. Through an exhausting process of engagement, compromise, cajoling, and cooptation – a process which, if I say so myself, verged at times on artful – we developed a comprehensive proposal that the faculty unanimously approved.

It was during this same time – the late '80s and early '90s – that I was intensively involved in the leadership of the Academy of Management. Those of us who have been through the presidential succession stages of the Academy frequently joke and commiserate about how long the commitment is: assistant program chair, program chair, president-elect, president, and (just when you think it's over) past-president (which actually carries duties). The most time-consuming of these tasks is being program chair. This is a massive logistical undertaking, which requires juggling the allocation of 40 to 50 hotel meeting rooms to 20 division program chairs and numerous pre-convention activity organizers; as well as composing, proofing, proofing again, and mailing the printed program to 10,000 members in the U.S. and abroad. The potential for slip-ups and hurt feelings is limitless. I thought I had managed to come through the process unscathed, when, on the final day of the meetings, a prominent professor caught me in the hotel elevator and vehemently accused me of personally relegating his presentation to a room that was smaller than he thought was his due. I just smiled and, with my hands hidden in my pockets, saluted him with the universal gesture of ill will.

The scariest part of being in the presidential chairs of the Academy – as agreed by all of us who have done it – is giving the Presidential Address. The idea of speaking formally to a ballroom full of several thousand colleagues – people who are there primarily to get the lunch that's included for their meeting fee – without sounding trite, preachy, or stale is enough to rivet one's thoughts and emotions for months beforehand.

In my 1993 speech, "What If the Academy Actually Mattered?," I decided to go out on a limb by criticizing the Academy for being irrelevant. Mind you, this was an organization I cared for dearly. I asserted that the Academy of Management had a "minimalist ethos: minimal programming, minimal dues, minimal staff, minimal innovation, minimal visibility, and minimal impact." In a twist on the Frank Capra movie classic, *It's a Wonderful Life*, I argued that the academic field of management and the practice of management might have been better off if another, more ambitious, activist organization had taken the Academy's place. I went on to propose several concrete initiatives that could move the Academy in the right direction. The speech was published in the *Academy of Management Review* and came to be frequently invoked by those who agreed with my message. Of course, there were some colleagues who disagreed with my thrust. By and large, though, the Academy has moved in the direction I encouraged, and I'm not sure I could mount the same criticism today.

In February 1995, my personal life was upended. I received a call at home from a lawyer in Chicago who said he represented a woman who believed I was her father. My heart stopped. Then I stammered that I had no idea what he was talking about. "She was born in July 1964," he said. "Her mother was . . ." He gave Elaine's name. "Are you sure you're not her father?" Shamefully, I repeated that he had the wrong man, and I hung up.

Peg called me to dinner, but I couldn't get up from my desk chair. I was frozen, catatonic. I, of course, knew that some adopted children seek to locate their biological parents, but never in my wildest thoughts did I think about this happening. Over the prior 30 years, not a week had gone by that I didn't think abstractly about Marie Christine (even picturing that I was probably by now a grandfather); but I still had never told anyone about her existence. I had kept a 30-year secret, and now presented with a chance to deal with it, I was intent on further perpetuating it. I prayed that the lawyer and his client would drop the issue.

Nothing happened for several weeks. Then I received an envelope in the mail from the Chicago lawyer, with a small note-size envelope inside. I opened the inner packet and re-read the handwritten letter several times. It was beautiful and moved me to tears. Her name was now Jennifer, no longer Marie Christine. She had already located and met Elaine. Now she wanted to meet me, as a way to bring closure to her life. Her letter was tender and conveyed her sensitivity to the anxiety and distress this would be causing me.

I had to see her. I called her, and we arranged to meet for lunch when she would be in New York on business. On the day of our lunch, I was a wreck. But our meeting was supremely meaningful and memorable. Physically, Jennifer was an exact mix of Elaine and me. She was raised in a loving home along with an adopted brother and sister. She was now a successful 30-year old consultant, healthy, happy, once married and now single; and, no, I was not a grandfather.

It was about a month after our lunch that I got the courage to finally tell Peg about Jennifer. She initially expressed empathy and understanding, but went on to feel deep hurt. Peg and I had always had a very close marriage, and she understandably found it unforgivable that I had kept this from her. I count as the biggest mistake of my life not telling Peg about my daughter before our marriage.

Shortly after telling Peg about Jennifer, I told our daughter Claire, my parents, my brother, and a few friends. Jennifer has visited our home a few times. She and I try to see each other two or three times a year. Our relationship has no particular agenda; it rests on long-overdue love and acknowledgement; and it is exceedingly important to both of us.

LATER YEARS AT COLUMBIA (1995–2000)

In 1995, I finally agreed to take on an administrative position, as chair of the Management Division of the School. Kirby Warren, a Columbian since his undergraduate days, had been our chair for about 20 years, and now it was only fair that someone else should take the job. We were blessed with a highly capable, solid core of tenured faculty: Joel Brockner, Kathy Harrigan, Ray Horton, Casey Ichniowski, Mike Tushman and Kirby Warren, along with a group of very talented junior faculty. The terrific horsepower and good cheer of this group made my job easier, but other factors conspired to make me miserable.

I was my biggest problem. In my usual fashion, I took the chairmanship far too seriously and, in turn, took every challenge and setback personally. The occasional management course that bombed I took to be a reflection on my leadership. The departure of promising young faculty members became my personal catastrophe. Lost tenure cases were the worst. Peg reached the point where she dreaded my arrival home each evening, anticipating that I would be in a deep funk about some new mini-tragedy. After a few comforting words, she would politely say, "Grow up." What I'm acknowledging here, of course, is that I am a lousy manager. I'm good at thinking about being a manager and advising managers, but I am temperamentally ill-suited for the role. I have the technical ability to do the work, but not the stomach.

Shepherding tenure cases through the Columbia process probably took years off my life – well, maybe not years. As I noted earlier, getting tenure at Columbia Business School was extraordinarily difficult. Unfortunately, many business academics across the country – in management, but also finance, marketing, and accounting – saw the Columbia tenure process not just as stringent, but as opaque, bizarre, even random. Various features of the process could easily lead to that conclusion.

A Columbia tenure case started with the endorsement of the candidate's academic division in the School. It then proceeded to the Promotion and Tenure Committee where a vote was taken as to whether the case had enough merit to warrant seeking outside letters. The Committee's vote was an advisory input at a meeting of the entire School tenured faculty. If the vote there was overwhelmingly positive, letters from leading figures in the field were sought – not the customary eight or ten people that most schools find sufficient, but as many as 24. Twelve were senior leaders in the field, and twelve were in the candidate's "cohort" – those prominent scholars who received their Ph.D.s about the same time as the candidate, with a strong bias for those who had recently been granted tenure at other top schools. There was inevitably a lot of jockeying and posturing that went into the composition of these referee lists. A particularly odd feature of the process was that if a vocal faculty member from another field wanted to propose that a name be added – say a former colleague at another school or someone whose research interests were tangential to the candidate's – the name, as often as not, was added. As a result, if you tried to draw a social network diagram of the people on these lists, you would end up with an exceedingly elongated picture, with loose linkages among the referees' names, and often exceedingly tenuous linkages to the candidate, the candidate's field, and the candidate's particular research domain.

The Promotion and Tenure Committee then met to assess the letters, and again the Committee's vote was advisory at a tenured faculty meeting. One or two negative letters would provide enough grist for nay-sayers to shoot down the case, even if all the other 20 or so letters were glowing in their praise. Two or three lukewarm or mixed letters would have the same result, yielding less than the 75% positive vote the dean needed to proceed.

But, most astoundingly, a Columbia tenure case could accumulate 24 effusively positive letters from the leading lights in the field, receive a unanimous vote of support from the tenured Business School faculty, the enthusiastic endorsement of the dean, but still be turned down at the University level. I saw it happen.

It was because of Columbia's system of *ad hoc* tenure review committees. For each case that survived to his level, the Provost selected a committee consisting of four tenured faculty from various departments of the University (but outside the Business School) and one person from the candidate's field who was at another university. The result, predictably, was, well, unpredictable. No two committees had the same composition, so there was no comparability of cases and no uniformity of standards. A committee member who was selected by the Provost expressly because of the closeness of his research interests to the candidate's could easily be dogmatic or jealous about what the candidate was doing. The Provost had notorious difficulty getting the requisite outsiders from other universities to serve. This was not surprising, since he was asking people to give up the better part of a day for an activity that was not a conventional professional obligation (unlike writing tenure letters). Indeed, I was always puzzled by the judgement, if not the motives, of those who agreed to do it. The cherry on top of this system was that each *ad hoc* committee's composition and deliberations were completely secret.

It was in this forbidding context that I served as divisional chair, trying to recruit talented young people, hold on to them, and help the best of them get tenure. I certainly came to understand why tenured faculty at Columbia Business School were almost as preoccupied by tenure as those who didn't have it. It was an arduous process for both groups. I disagreed with various elements of this process in every civil way I could – in discussions with our deans, at tenured faculty meetings, and in meetings directly with the Provost. My efforts were to no avail. An external review committee, established by the Provost to review the overall health of the Business School, and consisting of distinguished professors from other top schools, also raised serious criticisms of the tenure process. Their critique, too, whizzed right by the Provost, who was highly satisfied, even proud, of this process. The arts and sciences faculty endorsed the process as a way to keep close reins on the professional schools (though, intriguingly, Columbia's renowned law school had long been exempt from University-level tenure reviews, thanks to the initiative of a former president who had come from the law faculty). Some of my colleagues in the Business School supported the process. But I believed, as I still do, that the Columbia tenure process was harmful to the interests of the Business School; through its direct and indirect effects, the process amounted to the chief obstacle that kept the School from rising to the top five in the rankings.

Fortunately, in contrast to my administrative headaches, I was still having great fun with my research. My work with three doctoral students especially provided exhilaration.

In 1996, our student Theresa Cho teamed up with Ming-Jer Chen and me on an *ASQ* paper that examined the effects of TMT heterogeneity on competitive moves and countermoves in the airline industry. Ming-Jer brought to the study his unrivalled understanding of competitive dynamics; I brought my understanding of TMTs; and Theresa brought a host of fresh theoretical and analytic insights, along with a fabulous capacity to get things done. Theresa went on to write a superb dissertation on the changes in TMT composition and compensation that were engendered by airline deregulation, and how those TMT changes affected executive attention, strategy, and performance.

In 1997, Mathew Hayward and I published a piece (in *ASQ*) on CEO hubris as an explanation for large acquisition premiums. Not only was the paper widely noted by scholars interested in strategy and acquisitions, but micro-organizational researchers also liked to use it as an example of decision-maker biases in real, large-stakes situations. The business press was also drawn to the paper. That's probably because the press was implicated, when we found that, for every highly favorable article about a CEO that had appeared in major periodicals in the prior two years, he or she would pay 6% more for a major acquisition. Mathew went on to write an award-winning dissertation that explored how companies benefit from experience in making acquisitions.

Eric Jackson joined me in my first foray into the study of boards of directors. I had always been skeptical about the significance of boards and so had pretty much omitted them from my research scope. But when McKinsey and Company, the consultants, asked me in 1998 to sign on for a study of corporate boards, as part of their Project Evergreen, I couldn't resist. Project Evergreen derived its name from the sample of companies generated by McKinsey: 40 firms that significantly outperformed their business sectors (in shareholder returns) over a 10-year period (Stars) and a matched sample of companies that underperformed their sectors during the same period (Laggards). In our analysis, Eric and I couldn't find any differences between the boards of the Stars and Laggards on the dimensions usually considered by governance researchers – not in board size, director age, percentage of outsiders, or whether the CEO was also the chairman. What we did find was that at the outset of the 10-year period – before their performance diverged – the outside directors of the Star companies held substantially more equity (about six times more) than did the directors of the Laggard companies. Our findings strongly suggested that directors with a meaningful stake are a pivotal factor in improved governance. The paper was published by *California Management Review* and received a great deal of attention from the press. Journalists thought our results were noteworthy, but they also seemed to like our prescription for getting stock into outside director's hands. We proposed that, instead of their existing stock and option grant programs, companies should establish a fund, perhaps about $200,000, for each director, which would be used to match the director's own voluntary purchases of company stock. In addition to this matching program, annual retainers would be paid one-half in cash and one-half in stock.

Some companies started adopting variations of this plan, but our paper certainly didn't create a stampede. Institutional investors liked our approach as a way to make outside directors more vigilant. But outside directors themselves were not wild about our proposal, because it required them to put some skin in the game, instead of just being handed wads of stock or options, as was typical. And CEOs really disliked our plan because it would cause their outside directors to be personally invested, hence nosey and assertive.

After almost two decades of studying top executives, I became sensitive to criticism that my area of research put too much weight on the importance of executives and contributed to the glorification and hero-worship of elites. Critics went on to say that there are many, many people throughout organizations who affect results, and they are all worthy of scholarly attention. I never disputed this latter point, and I hoped and assumed that researchers would maintain interest in human endeavor at all organizational levels. But the criticism about glorifying executives was ironic in the extreme. After all, upper echelons research was entirely premised on the flaws and human limits of executives. We poked holes in the mythology of the all-knowing economic optimizer at the top of the firm. This was the antithesis of glorification.

When I would present my research results to executives – say my project on CEO hubris or work I had done on the seasons of a CEO's tenure – they certainly didn't feel glorified. In fact they often reacted by saying that they were smarter, more level-headed, more utterly capable than I gave them credit for. So, I got it from both sides.

No, I wasn't glorifying executives at all. But neither was I trying to demean them. Being an executive is exceedingly demanding. I greatly admire those who do it well, and I'm deeply troubled by those who don't. Part of our job as management scholars is to develop insights that will improve executive effectiveness. But no matter how clever our insights, we will not be able to surmount or escape the fact that executives have the same human foibles as the rest of us.

In a departure from my primary focus on top executives, and in an effort to apply my interest in teams to an international context, during the mid-to-late-1990s I joined with two sets of colleagues to study multinational groups. One project, with Penn State friends Chuck Snow and Scott Snell, and Sue Davidson of the London Business School, focused on the organizational challenges in relying on various kinds of groups of mixed nationalities. The second project, with Anne Tsui, J. T. Li and Katherine Xin (all of Hong Kong University of Science and Technology), took a new tack in trying to understand why so many international joint ventures fail, by examining the management groups that head up these ventures. Across both projects, we published a series of conceptual, empirical, and applied papers on the topic of international teams. These projects were exceedingly helpful in enhancing my understanding of cross-cultural dynamics, an important topic that had previously escaped my attention.

In 1997, I won the Dean's Award for outstanding teaching in the MBA core. I had previously won the School's other two major teaching prizes, but this new honor was especially gratifying. For one thing, teaching quality at Columbia Business School had increased dramatically by the mid-90s, so there were now an unprecedented number of highly effective instructors who could have warranted this honor. I was also pleased that the award was for core course teaching. All business school professors who have taught both MBA core courses and MBA electives know which is tougher – by far. As a former infantryman, I've come to think of teaching electives as being at base camp. It's not surprising that so many faculty – especially senior faculty – only want to be there, with the academic equivalent of hot meals, showers, and U.S.O shows. I've never understood why deans don't seem to comprehend the immense workload differential in teaching core courses as opposed to electives. At least our dean had established this nice award, and I was honored to receive it.

By the late 1990s, I was doing an extraordinary amount of consulting and executive education. I had always tried to be careful not to let this work get out of hand; but at the same time, I found it valuable. In addition to the obvious financial rewards, I obtained innumerable insights, examples, and contacts from companies that were helpful in my research and teaching. I did some of this work independently, and some through Columbia's well-established executive programs, including as director of the two-week Business Strategy Program. Columbia's custom executive programs accounted for a great deal of my involvement in the late 1990s.

My biggest commitment was as faculty director of a major multi-phase program for the British conglomerate GKN plc. The good news about this project was that the CEO was fully invested in our program, viewing it as the centerpiece for his corporate change effort. The attendees were intact business leadership teams working on issues of major strategic importance, so we were able to witness real business progress while learning a great deal about some thorny contemporary business issues. The bad news was that the GKN program required me to go to Europe about six times a year, typically for a week at a time, over a two-year period. It was thus pulling me away from my two dearest loves: my family and my research.

In fact, things on the home front were not smooth. Peg and I were spending less and less quality time together. Claire was experiencing typical teenage challenges, and my response – modeled upon how I was raised – was to lay down rules, get strict, and above all, avoid talking about any difficult subjects. When Claire asked to go away to boarding school, all I could think of was how much I would have liked boarding school and what a great opportunity it would be for her. Peg, on the other hand, was devastated. She correctly saw that Claire wanted to get away from us.

Claire went to the elite St. George's School in Newport for her sophomore year and half of her junior year. It proved to be a disaster, qualifying as the second-biggest mistake I've ever made. Surrounded by kids from wealthy but often dysfunctional families, Claire was lonely but didn't, or couldn't, tell us so. Eventually she developed a severe sleep disorder and agreed to come home to finish her junior year. She then completed high school at a local private school. Her sleep problems abated and she went on to be a happy, successful college student.

At the same time Claire was starting college, in 1999, I was entitled to a sabbatical. Peg and I decided to visit Dartmouth, as a way to bring maximum change to our surroundings. Here, I could be with several good friends: my former students Syd Finkelstein, Rich D'Aveni, and Phil Anderson, as well as Vijay Govindarajan and Connie Helfat. But the big agenda item was for Peg and me to reconnect. We resolved to relax like never before, talk like never before, and stay off airplanes like never before. We rented an exquisite 200-year old farmhouse, on 100 acres, deep in the woods. We had a fabulous time, and the seeds were sown for even more contemplation and change.

FROM MORNINGSIDE HEIGHTS TO HAPPY VALLEY (2000–2002)

Upon returning from sabbatical in summer 2000, I re-immersed myself in life at Columbia. I took a leadership role in the total redesign of our MBA strategy core course, taught two sections of the new course, and chaired the Management Division's faculty search committee. But by December, I knew something was wrong. The walls in my lucky-numbered office, 711 Uris Hall, seemed to be closing in on me. Everything seemed repetitive. My closest Columbia friends had trickled away over the years – Ian MacMillan, Jim Fredrickson, Warren Boeker, Ming-Jer Chen, and most recently, Mike Tushman. I had nothing left to prove at Columbia.

Over the Christmas season, I contemplated all sorts of possible changes. I thought about becoming a dean – bad idea. I thought briefly about leaving academe entirely for the world of consulting – another bad idea. I thought of going to another Top 10 business school, but it wasn't at all clear what that would accomplish.

It was in mid-January that I received an e-mail from my friend Barbara Gray at Penn State. She was responding to a research question; then, in a P.S., she wrote: "We're still conducting our search for the Smeal Chair in Management, and we would be delighted if you would reconsider." They had asked me about this chair two years before. But now they were catching me in the right mood. I went home and told Peg about Barbara's note, and she said, "Why not?"

One thing led to another. I had lunch in New York with Penn State's new business school dean, Judy Olian. I was exceedingly impressed by her vision, energy, and values. Peg and I made a hurried, unannounced trip to State College to see if we could envision ourselves there. It felt fabulous. Then we made a formal visit, and then another. Each visit, each communication, each exchange made us feel better about this move. From the time Barbara Gray contacted me until I accepted the offer was about six weeks. It felt exactly right and I never had second thoughts.

As I write this, Peg, Claire, and I are house-hunting in State College, getting ready for our move in several months. Peg and I have glorious feelings about "going home" – where we met, married, bought our first house, and made many lasting relationships. As importantly, Smeal College is on the move, and I am excited about playing a role in its continued progress. The Management and Organization Department houses some of my long-time friends and collaborators, and my research interests intersect with a large number of folks there.

Leaving Columbia is not an easy thing to do. It's a fabulous university, a fabulous business school, and we have a terrific management group. I could not have hoped for more. But after 23 years I very much want a change.

Of course, one of the wonderful things about a life of scholarship is that I will be able to carry a lot of Columbia with me in the form of continuing collaborations. Right now I have research projects underway with my long-term friends Bert Cannella, Theresa Cho, Danny Miller, Syd Finkelstein, Jim Fredrickson, Marta Geletkanycz, Andy Henderson and Phyllis Siegel. I am also working with a brand-new set of colleagues: Ann Mooney, Atul Nerkar, Srikanth Paruchuri, and Kurt Wurthmann. Columbia's influence on my research – whether I am physically at Morningside Heights or somewhere else – will still be felt for years to come.

But I am also heavily influenced by whatever environment I'm in. So I am sure I will savor and benefit from many collaborative adventures with Penn State colleagues and students.

CONCLUDING THOUGHTS

If you've stuck with me this long, you know that my life has been full of good fortune. I've had my share of tribulations and missteps, but I've mostly been blessed. I was lucky to be raised by loving parents who passed their eminently decent values on to me. I benefited from mentors and role models at every stage of my life – most memorably in graduate school and at Columbia, but most certainly in earlier settings as well. I have had many stupendously supportive, invigorating colleagues and students. As I glance back through this manuscript, I am embarrassed by how many of their names go unmentioned, and I can only hope that they know how much I appreciate them. Above all, of course, providence smiled on me in giving me Peg and Claire. They've spurred me on, supported me in every possible way, and kept me humble.

I can't imagine that I will be as lucky in the future. But I hope I am, because I still don't have a plan.

PUBLICATIONS

1980

With C. C. Snow. Measuring organizational strategies: Some theoretical and methodological problems. *Academy of Management Review, 6,* 253–276.

Operationalizing the concept of business-level strategy in research. *Academy of Management Review,* 5(4), 567–575.

1981

Environment, strategy and power within top management teams. *Administrative Science Quarterly, 1*, 253–276.
Strategic awareness within top management teams. *Strategic Management Journal, 2*, 263–279.

1982

Environmental scanning and organizational strategy. *Strategic Management Journal, 3*, 159–174.
With I. C. MacMillan & D. L. Day. Strategic attributes and performance in the four cells of the BCG matrix – A PIMS-based empirical analysis. *Academy of Management Journal, 25*(2), 370–385.
With I. C. MacMillan & D. L. Day. The association between strategic attributes and profitability in the four cells of the BCG matrix – A PIMS-based empirical analysis of industrial-product businesses. *Academy of Management Journal, 25*(3), 510–531.
With I. C. MacMillan. The product portfolio and man's best friend. *California Management Review, 25*(1), 84–95.

1983

Some tests of the effectiveness and functional attributes of Mile's and Snow's strategic types. *Academy of Management Journal, 26*(1), 5–26.
An empirical typology of mature industrial-product environments. *Academy of Management Journal, 26*(2), 213–230.
With S. M. Schecter. Turnaround strategies for mature industrial product business units. *Academy of Management Journal, 26*(2), 231–248.
With I. C. MacMillan & R. Barbosa. Business unit strategy and changes in the product R&D budget. *Management Science, 29*(7), 757–769.
High-profit strategies in mature capital goods industries: A contingency approach. *Academy of Management Journal, 26*(4), 687–707.

1984

With P. A. Mason. Upper echelons: The organization as a reflection of its top managers. *Academy of Management Review, 9*(2), 193–206.
With J. M. Pennings & I. C. MacMillan. Interorganizational dependence and forward integration. *Organization Studies, 5*(4), 307–326.
Taxonomic approaches to studying strategy: Some conceptual and methodological issues. *Journal of Management, 10*(1), 27–41.
With I. C. MacMillan. Asset parsimony: Manage assets to manage profits. *Sloan Management Review, 25*(2), 67–74.
Turnaround strategies. In: W. Guth (Ed.), *Handbook of Strategic Management* (pp. 480–513). New York: Warren, Gorham, and Lamont.

1985

With I. C. MacMillan. Efficiency of product R&D in business units: The role of strategic context. *Academy of Management Journal, 28*(3), 527–547.

With D. Lei. Toward an empirical prioritization of contingency variables for business strategy. *Academy of Management Journal, 28*(4), 763–788.

1986

With L. Cozier. Stumblers and stars in the management of rapid growth. *Journal of Business Venturing, 2*(1), 19–38.

With I. C. MacMillan & J. M. Pennings. Uncertainty reduction and the threat of supplier retaliation: Two views of the backward integration decision. *Organization Studies, 7*(3), 263–277.

1987

The top management team: Key to strategic success. *California Management Review, 30*(1), 1–20.

With S. Finkelstein. Managerial discretion: A bridge between polar views of organizational outcomes. In: B. Staw & L. L. Cummings (Eds), *Research in Organizational Behavior* (9, pp. 369–406).

1988

With J. W. Fredrickson & S. Baumrin. A model of CEO dismissal. *Academy of Management Review, 13*(2), 255–270.

With R. A. D'Aveni. Large corporate failures as downward spirals. *Administrative Science Quarterly, 33*, 1–23.

With S. Finkelstein. Chief executive compensation: A synthesis and reconciliation. *Strategic Management Journal, 9*, 543–558.

The executive effect: Concepts and methods for studying top managers. Greenwich, CT: JAI Press.

With I. C. MacMillan. Capital intensity, market share instability, and profits – The case for asset parsimony. In: R. Lamb & P. Shrivastava (Eds), *Advances in Strategic Mangement* (pp. 207–222). Greenwich, CT: JAI Press.

With G. Brandon. Executive values. In: D. C. Hambrick (Ed.), *The Executive Effect: Concepts and Methods for Studying Top Managers* (pp. 3–34). Greenwich, CT: JAI Press.

Strategies for mature industrial-product businesses: A two-tier taxonomic approach. In: J. H. Grant (Ed.), *Strategic Management Frontiers* (pp. 107–146). Greenwich, CT: JAI Press.

1989

With S. Finkelstein. Chief executive compensation: A study of the intersection of markets and political processes. *Strategic Management Journal, 10*, 121–134.

With J. Vasconcellos. Key success factors: Test of a general theory in the mature industrial-product sector. *Strategic Management Journal, 10*, 367–382.

Reinventing the CEO: 21st century report. New York: Korn/Ferry International and Columbia Business School.

Putting top managers back into the strategy picture. *Strategic Management Journal, 10,* 5–15.

With A. A. Cannella, Jr. Strategy implementation as substance and selling. *Academy of Management Executive, 3*(4), 278–285.

With C. C. Snow. Strategic reward systems. In: C. C. Snow (Ed.), *Strategy, Organization Design, and Human Resource Management* (pp. 333–368). Greenwich, CT: JAI Press.

1990

With C. A. Summer, R. A. Bettis, I. H. Duhaime, J. H. Grant, C. C. Snow & C. P. Zeithaml. Doctoral education in the field of business policy and strategy. *Journal of Management, 16*(2), 361–398.

With S. Finkelstein. Top management team tenure and organizational outcomes; The moderating role of managerial discretion. *Administrative Science Quarterly, 35,* 484–503.

The adolescence of strategic management, 1980–1985: Critical perceptions and reality. In: J. W. Fredrickson (Ed.), *Perspectives on Strategic Management* (pp. 237–261). New York: Harper and Row.

1991

With G. Fukutomi. The seasons of a CEO's tenure. *Academy of Management Review, 16*(4), 719–742.

1992

With J. Michel. Diversification posture and the characteristics of the top management team. *Academy of Management Journal, 35*(1), 9–37.

With R. A. D'Aveni. Top team deterioration as part of the downward spiral of large bankruptcies. *Management Science, 38*(10), 1445–1466.

With D. F. Raskas. Multifunctional managerial development: Practical options and complications. *Organizational Dynamics, 21*(2), 5–17.

With S. Black & J. W. Fredrickson. Executive leadership of the high-technology firm: What's special about it? In: L. R. Gomez-Meija & M. W. Lawless (Eds), *Top Management and Effective Leadership in High Technology* (pp. 3–18). Greenwich, CT: JAI Press.

Commentary on Jackson's "Consequences of group composition for the interpersonal dynamics of strategic Issue Processing." *Advances in Strategic Management, 8,* 383–389.

1993

With A. A. Cannella, Jr. Effects of executive departures on the performance of acquired firms. *Strategic Management Journal, 14,* 137–152

With A. A. Cannella, Jr. Relative standing: A framework for understanding departures of acquired executives. *Academy of Management Journal, 36*(4), 733–762.

With M. A. Geletkancyz & J. W. Fredrickson. Top executive commitment to the status quo. *Strategic Management Journal, 14,* 401–418.

1994

1993 Presidential address: What if the academy actually mattered? *Academy of Management Review*, *19*(1), 11–16.

Top management groups: A conceptual integration and reconsideration of the 'Team' label. *Research in Organizational Behavior*, *16*, 171–213.

1995

With S. Finkelstein. The effects of ownership structure on conditions at the top: The case of CEO pay raises. *Strategic Management Journal*, *16*, 175–193.

With M-J. Chen. Speed, stealth, and selective attack: How small firms differ from large firms in competitive behavior. *Academy of Management Journal*, *2*, 453–482.

Fragmentation and the other problems CEOs have with their top management teams. *California Management Review*, *37*(3), 110–126.

With E. Abrahamson. Assessing the amount of managerial discretion in different industries. *Academy of Management Journal*, *38*(5), 1427–1441.

1996

With C. C. Snow S. C. Davison & S. A. Snell. Use transnational teams to globalize your company. *Organization Dynamics*, *24*(3), 50–67.

With T. S. Cho & M-J. Chen. The influence of top management team heterogeneity on firms' competitive moves. *Administrative Science Quarterly*, *41*, 659–684.

With S. Finkelstein. *Strategic Leadership: Top executives and their effects on organizations*. St. Paul, MN: West.

With P. A. Siegel. Business strategy and the social psychology of top management teams. *Advances in Strategic Management*, *13*, 91–119.

1997

With M. L. A. Hayward. Explaining the premiums paid for large acquisitions: Evidence of CEO hubris. *Administrative Science Quarterly*, *42*, 103–127.

With E. Abrahamson. Attentional homogeneity in industries: The effect of discretion. *Journal of Organizational Behavior*, *18*, 513–532.

With M. A. Geletkanycz. The external ties of top executives: Implications for strategic choice and performance. *Administrative Science Quarterly*, *42*, 654–681.

Teaching as leading. In: R. Andre & P. Frost (Eds), *Researchers Hooked On Teaching* (pp. 242–254). Thousand Oaks, CA: Sage.

1998

With S. C. Davison S. A. Snell & C. C. Snow. When groups consist of multiple nationalities: Toward an understanding of the implications. *Organization Studies*, *19*(2), 181–205.

With S. A. Snell C. C. Snow & S. C. Davison. Designing and supporting transnational teams: The human resource agenda. *Human Resource Management Journal*, *37*(2), 147–158.

With D. A. Nadler & M. L. Tushman (Eds). *Navigating change: How CEOs, top teams, and boards steer transformation.* Boston: Harvard Business School Press.

With K. Stucker. Breaking away: Executive leadership of corporate spinoffs. In: J. Conger, G. Spreitzer & E. Lawler (Eds), *The Leader's Change Handbook* (pp. 100–124). CA: Jossey-Bass.

Corporate coherence and the top management team. In: D. C. Hambrick, D. A. Nadler & M. L. Tushman (Eds), *Navigating Change: How CEOs, Top Teams, and Boards Steer Transformation* (pp. 123–140). Boston: Harvard Business School Press.

1999

With J. T. Li, K. Xin & A. Tsui. Building effective international joint venture leadership teams in China. *Journal of World Business, 34*(1), 52–67.

2000

With E. M. Jackson. Outside directors with a *stake:* The Linchpin in improving governance. *California Management Review, 42*(4), 108–127.

Putting the team into top management. *Financial Times* (Mastering Management Series), October 9.

2001

Better boards: The equity answer. *Chief Executive*, March.

Donald Hambrick on executives and strategy (Crosstalk interview series) *Academy of Management Executive* (Crosstalk interview series), *15*(3), 36–47.

With J. T. Li, K. Xin & A. Tsui. Compositional gaps and downward spirals in international joint venture management groups. Forthcoming in *Strategic Management Journal*.

ACKNOWLEDGMENTS

In preparing this essay, I benefited greatly from encouragement, guidance, and suggestions from the following individuals: Bert Cannella, Syd Finkelstein, Jim Fredrickson, Claire Hambrick, Peg Hambrick, Chuck Snow and Mike Tushman.

RIDING INTO THE SUNSET ON A THOROUGHBRED

Michael A. Hitt

Contrary to popular opinion, all children who grow to adulthood in Texas do not know how to ride a horse. I was born and spent most of my early life in a small to medium-size city in west Texas and I did not learn how to ride a horse. However, I knew that if I ever rode a horse, it would be a thoroughbred.

Most of this story is about my professional development and career. However, you should know that I am married and have two children and a daughter-in-law of whom I am very proud. I also have a wonderful young grandson. I married my wife while still in college and she worked to support us until I finished. Later, she completed her degree after I began my academic career. My two children obtained college degrees and are professionals, one as owner manager of a business and the other working for a large advertising firm. They are both highly independent in thought and all other ways. While this was difficult at times as they grew up, I am proud that they can hold their own with anyone.

My wife and I have a partnership and have been married for almost 35 years now. Like any marriage, there have been stresses and strains but no breaks. Our partnership is stronger now than it has ever been. Whatever success I have achieved is attributable to the wonderful family I have. I thank God for my family and the many blessings I have received over the years. I am a fortunate man. I begin with my education and the early career interests.

Management Laureates, Volume 6, pages 123–159.
Copyright © 2002 by Elsevier Science Ltd.
All rights of reproduction in any form reserved.
ISBN: 0-7623-0487-1

THE DAWN OF A CAREER DESIRE

When I entered college, (I started at a junior college in my home town for financial reasons), my long-term goal was to become a corporate executive. Thus, my major was business management. While a sophomore in college, I enrolled in two different English literature courses. In these courses, we not only had to read many different works, but also we were expected to write. It was my first opportunity to compose papers, and I found it an interesting and satisfying activity. Of course, it helped that I received positive feedback from the two separate professors and encouragement to continue writing. It was at this time that I developed an interest in writing and a desire to publish my work. Of course, I did not have the skills to write for publication at that time. The two English literature professors however planted a seed and instilled a desire. Little did I know that this would lead to the professional career I eventually selected.

As I entered upper division classes at Texas Tech University, I continued to enjoy academic success and received encouragement to attend graduate school from several professors in my major field. I contemplated this possibility, but also had a desire to go into business (which was my major). However, my educational process occurred during the 1960s and the Vietnam War. I was classified as 1A (high probability of being drafted) and assumed that upon graduation with a Bachelor's degree, I would be drafted into the military. In response, along with some friends, I joined the Army Reserves and spent six months on active duty training and five-and-one-half years thereafter in the active Reserves. After the military training, I entered the Master of Business Administration program at Texas Tech. While I was in the program, some of the professors encouraged me to consider obtaining a Ph.D. and entering an academic career. I considered this strongly and to test the waters, I requested and received permission to take a Ph.D. seminar while completing my MBA degree. I found the Ph.D. seminar to be interesting and challenging and strongly considered entering a Ph.D. program. However, as a student with little income for several years, and a wife who was pregnant with our first child, I felt the need to enter the business world and earn an income for at least a period of time. Doing so would allow me the opportunity to gain some business experience as well as to test my interest in a managerial career versus an academic career.

Therefore, I interviewed with several companies and received some interesting opportunities. However, I accepted a position with Samsonite Corporation headquartered in Denver, CO. I chose this company because it was medium-size, family owned and controlled in the process of professionalizing its management. As such, several senior managers were hired from other major corporations, and I was one of a number of young MBAs brought into the organization to provide future managerial talent. During my time with the company, I was assigned a major project to develop and helped implement an executive incentive compensation program. I worked with another newly minted MBA and reported directly to the vice-president of finance (who had a Ph.D. in finance from the University of Chicago). We developed a rather sophisticated incentive compensation program. I was afforded the opportunity to make presentations on this program to the Executive Committee of the Corporation (president and CEO, and two executive vice-presidents) and to the Board of Directors. Furthermore, I met with all the top executives in the Corporation to help explain this program. Thus, for a young 24-year old new MBA, I had opportunities that I probably would not have had at almost any other corporation at the time. Development of this program spurred my interest in corporate strategy and governance.

Although this was an interesting and exciting project and I did have opportunities that were quite unique for someone so young in business, I still found my business activities to be constraining and at times boring. I wanted more challenge and more flexibility to pursue ideas in which I was interested. Furthermore, I was fascinated by the opportunity to teach. As a result, I applied for entrance into several Ph.D. programs. I was accepted at all programs to which I applied, but I chose to enter the program at the University of Colorado. CU had hired several new faculty from top academic programs in recent years and was in the process of building its Ph.D. program. While in the program I worked most closely with Cy Morgan, Dale Meyer, and Dick Beatty. My major was Organizations (primary interest in organization theory) and had a minor field in what was then called Business Policy. Business Policy was in a separate department within the College and staffed largely by business economists. While in the program, I developed a strong interest in integrating work in Organization Theory and Business Policy. I graduated with my Ph.D. at the age of 28 in 1974.

THE EARLY MORNING OF THE CAREER

When I graduated with my Ph.D., the market was tight and not many opportunities were available. I accepted an offer to join the faculty at Oklahoma State University, primarily to teach Business Policy. My early years at Oklahoma State were ones of intense learning and development as I grew as a teacher and researcher. The first major challenge I encountered however was related to a dean's intent to make the Business Policy course required for all students wishing to obtain a Bachelor of Science degree in business administration. While this has been relatively common for the last 20 or so years, it was not common at the time. The American Assembly of Collegiate Schools of Business (AACSB) had recently implemented a recommendation for a terminal-integrating course, which was interpreted as a requirement. Many thought the Business Policy course would be the best to satisfy this requirement. Our dean, a former finance professor, strongly believed that the Business Policy course should be required. He pushed this recommendation while being confronted by faculty opposition from most departments. He somehow was able to gain approval and implement this requirement. Meanwhile, I remember a highly contentious faculty meeting in which a senior professor from another department asked where we would obtain this "renaissance person" to teach such a course integrating the various disciplines of business. When I came to work the next morning I had a large sign on my door titled "Renaissance Man". I carried that title for several years among my colleagues. This was an uncomfortable time being an untenured assistant professor teaching a course that was highly unpopular among faculty and administrators in other departments. In fact, the dean was forced to resign the next year, primarily by those who were opposed to implementing this course as a requirement. The dean left, but the course requirement remained.

When hired at Oklahoma State University, there were two senior faculty members in Management who had been productive researchers. Unfortunately, one of them died suddenly (in his late 30s) and the other, who was a close friend, became disillusioned and took a leave of absence but never returned. Therefore, those of us who were hired as untenured assistant professors virtually had no senior faculty in our areas to provide guidance and support. Over a period of about three years, seven young professors in Management were hired. All were talented young scholars and have gone on to successful careers on their own. We largely learned the craft of research and publication together.

As a young assistant professor, I developed two manuscripts from my dissertation that were submitted to top scholarly journals and rejected. The feedback was not very kind and certainly was not positive. After reading the feedback from the reviewers and the editor, I decided that I did not want to embarrass myself by submitting poor work. As a result, I placed these manuscripts on the shelf and never resubmitted them. Later, I realized this was a major mistake as I could have used that feedback to develop the manuscripts and publish them in good quality journals. Without senior guidance and experience however, I made a poor decision. Still, I was able to publish three other manuscripts from the dissertation in scholarly journals, one of those in the *Academy of Management Journal* (my first *AMJ* article). I also started new research projects with some of my colleagues at OSU. My early work was not in strategy because in the first two years I had no colleagues in this area. My first colleague in strategy, Duane Ireland, was hired in my third year on the faculty. Thus, my early research was in areas of particular interest to my colleagues and me. For example, Dennis Middlemist and I designed a major study to measure organizational effectiveness in unique ways. Additionally, I began a study on sex and race discrimination in employment practices with another colleague, Bill Zikmund, who was a faculty member in Marketing. Because of my early life growing up in a small town in Texas and my parents' values, I developed an unusual but strong belief in the importance of equity, treating everyone fairly. I lived next door to an African-American family, and my best friend as a youth was a young African-American boy. When we entered the public school system however, we went to separate schools. This along with other events created a strong interest in discrimination. One of the advantages of an academic career is to pursue ideas and research topics of your own choosing. Thus, I chose to study discrimination in employment, even though my primary teaching and research interests were in organization theory and business policy (later called strategic management). Fortunately, Bill and I completed a study that was eventually published in the *Journal of Applied Psychology*. Our research showed blatant sex and race discrimination in the employment of young business school graduates. The work that Dennis Middlemist and I completed on organizational effectiveness was published in the *Academy of Management Journal* and another part of the research was published in the *Journal of Management*. Therefore, although this research did not focus in the business policy area, I was learning how to design studies and craft manuscripts that could be published in top scholarly journals.

Our department head at the time had the right value set and emphasized the importance of research and publication. However, his methods of trying to promote more research were, at times, counterproductive. Essentially, he attempted to create a competitive atmosphere among the young professors in the department. He did so by going to each individual's office and announcing the manuscripts accepted by one's colleagues. His intent was obviously to provoke competition and encourage more research productivity. However, the competition became unhealthy and created conflict. When we realized this, the group of young professors met and decided that we would work together more closely and would avoid dysfunctional competitiveness among us. Our approach worked quite well and over time, we developed a strong cadre of good young faculty and a collegial group of researchers all of whom were mutually supportive. Therefore, OSU became a good environment to develop one's research skills and a positive environment in which to work.

When I began my teaching career at Oklahoma State, the normal teaching load was three sections per semester, or eighteen semester hours per year. However, in a relatively short time, new policies were developed to reduce the teaching load for active researchers to six semester hours or twelve hours per year. Additionally, in my first year, I taught two courses in summer school for the income I needed to support my family. My wife and I now had two children; the second was born in the last year of my Ph.D. program. I found summer teaching however to be highly challenging and unsatisfying. I vowed then to do whatever possible to avoid summer teaching in the future. As a result, I've only taught during three summers since my career began in 1974.

I also learned a lot about teaching during these early years. Overall, I thought that I was a reasonably good teacher. I received very good student evaluations, but most of my classes were relatively small (e.g. 30–40 students) and I taught them in an interactive fashion. However, when I was asked to teach a large introductory class, I encountered my first negative reactions from students. Out of naiveté based on a lack of experience, I attempted to teach the large class in much the same way as I taught smaller classes. Needless to say, I did not obtain appropriate participation from the students and my lack of structure created problems for the students' preparation. While most people know this today, I learned that I had to adapt my style of teaching for each course that I taught. Therefore, over time, I have become more flexible in my approach to teaching and continue to learn and innovate in the classroom. Thus, my current teaching approaches had their origins from my early years in the profession. But, they have been highly refined over time.

I spent nine years on the faculty at Oklahoma State and advanced from assistant professor to full professor before I moved to another university. I worked on a number of different research projects, some more behavioral, others focused in human resource management (e.g. published in *Personnel Psychology, Journal of Applied Behavioral Science*) and some focused more in macro areas such as organization theory, but I only published a few works in business policy prior to 1982. I had the opportunity to work with and serve as chair of three Ph.D. students' committees while at OSU, Joe Cox, who joined the faculty at Baylor University, Kyamas Palia, who went back to his native India and worked for his former firm as its controller, and Barbara Keats, who is my colleague at Arizona State University. My major strategy research first began as I worked with Kyamas and Barbara. I worked with Barbara on several research projects that culminated in publications in good scholarly journals. In both cases (Palia and Keats), we worked on articles that were eventually published in the *Academy of Management Journal* (Hitt, Ireland & Palia, 1982; Keats & Hitt, 1988).

I also became reasonably active in executive development programs as well as external consulting while on the faculty at OSU. I found both activities gave me an opportunity to grow professionally, and in some cases provided sites and contacts for my research projects. Thus, the executive development work was often synergistic with my research. It also afforded me experiences, contacts, and helped me further develop my teaching and instructional skills.

Therefore, the first nine years of my career at Oklahoma State University were a time of growth, the chance to work with other top young scholars, and the opportunity to enjoy the profession. Although we had developed a good faculty, we recognized there were limitations on the ability to develop further at OSU. This was partly due to resource constraints, but also to other evident constraints such as limitations on the growth and development of the College of Business as an important unit within the University. Thus, several of us decided to examine other opportunities. In 1983, three of us accepted positions at other universities. Kirk Downey became the Chair of the Management Department at TCU, Duane Ireland accepted a faculty position at Baylor University, and I accepted the position as Chair of the Management Department at the University of Texas at Arlington.

EARLY IN THE AFTERNOON – ADMINISTRATION

My administrative experience actually began while I was on the faculty at Oklahoma State University. Early in my career I had the good fortune of working on several research grants, mostly as a co-investigator. When I was an associate professor, the position of Director of the Office of Business and Economic Research came open. The Dean asked me to take on this role. Given my desire to continue my research program and become a full professor, I politely declined his offer. A few weeks later he came to my office and asked me again to take on the position. I thanked him, but politely declined. He then responded, "Mike, you do not understand. I am making you an offer that you cannot refuse." As a result, I became the Interim Director of the Office of Business and Economic Research. I supervised several professionals (individuals who held Ph.D.s in Economics and largely oversaw the development and application of a state econometric model). There were also several staff members who provided support for the office and for faculty who developed proposals to obtain research grants. Hence, this was my first opportunity to gain experience in managing and evaluating professional employees. In this role, I had the responsibility of encouraging faculty to seek research grants and to support those who received such grants. Additionally, my responsibilities included marketing the state econometric model to external parties for funding to continue its operation. One of the most valuable activities in which I engaged during my time in this role was spending time in Washington, D.C. visiting various agencies and learning about the formal and "less formal" means of obtaining research grants. This knowledge was helpful in my later research grant activities. While I was in an interim capacity, I was asked by the Dean to submit my credentials for the permanent position. Once again I politely declined. Fortunately, thirteen months after I stepped into this position, a candidate for the position was hired from another university.

My second administrative opportunity was at the University of Texas at Arlington as Chair of the Management Department. This was a positive opportunity because there were several faculty who were active researchers. Additionally, the Dean promised to help develop the department with proper leadership, and the department was not overly large (originally about 14 tenure track faculty). There were several adjunct faculty members however who helped teach a fairly large student body. As an urban institution, UTA had both an active day and night program.

I developed a good relationship with the Dean and generally liked his approaches for promoting and supporting research. For example, when he received merit dollars, he separated those into a flat percentage that was given to each department and held a portion of the monies out to reward those departments that had the most active and productive research programs. Essentially, he used this money to provide differential merit monies, allocating them to the most productive researchers. While this was not popular with all departments, particularly those that were less productive in research, I particularly liked the program and found it useful to encourage the faculty in our department to continue and/or to increase their research productivity.

The Dean also allocated some new faculty positions to our department, which allowed us to begin recruiting some new faculty. We recruited and hired two excellent new faculty members, one out of the Ph.D. Program at Cornell, and the other out of the Ph.D. Program at Michigan State University. Additionally, there were two other significant activities in which I was involved as Chair of the Department. First, we developed, proposed, and obtained permission to begin a new Master of Science Program in Human Resource Management. Second, we developed a new center to build relationships with industry and obtain monies to support our ongoing research program.

In general, I found my time at the University of Texas at Arlington to be productive and positive. I enjoyed the faculty, which became cohesive, and we had a number of successes. Additionally, I was able to continue my research program, while at a slightly reduced level. As a whole, I was happy at UTA and in my position. However, during my second year, I was contacted by Texas A&M University and asked to apply for the position as Head of the Management Department. The Management Department at Texas A&M University was quite strong and was developing a national and international reputation for research productivity. It was a much larger department (approximately 34 tenure track faculty) than at UTA. Therefore, I was attracted to the opportunity, but had some misgivings, primarily because I was quite happy in my current position.

I interviewed at Texas A&M and realized it would be a highly challenging position, because of the strong personalities, highly active researchers, and a group of quite competitive faculty. I was impressed with the Dean who had formerly been the Management Department Head and was a recognized scholar, primarily for his research on employee turnover. I was offered the position at TAMU and gave it strong consideration. However, I did not want to leave the Department at UTA, partly because the tasks I had started were not complete. After strong consideration, I turned down the offer from Texas A&M.

After several weeks, I was contacted again by the Dean at Texas A&M and he strongly encouraged me to reconsider my decision. In addition, he improved the offer, primarily by promising me the opportunity for an endowed position. This was very attractive. After careful and thorough consideration, I made a decision to accept the offer and move to TAMU. In 1985, I became Head of the Management Department at Texas A&M University.

I found the position as Department Head at Texas A&M to be both highly challenging and quite interesting. The College operated on a highly decentralized model so that each department received a budget and the head of the department administered that budget. With 34 tenure track faculty, several non-tenure track faculty, a large Ph.D. Program (approximately 25 students) and a cadre of staff and other graduate assistants, I had somewhere between 90 and 100 people at any one time who largely reported to me. Of course, this is an excessive span of control. Also, during my first year, the state of Texas experienced a weak economy and funds to the University were reduced. As a result, all of the colleges' and departments' budgets were reduced. This was a particularly difficult situation with a group of highly active, competitive and visible researchers. I had to undertake several activities to increase the cohesion in the department, as it had become somewhat fractured in recent years.

Another issue dealt with recruiting for which they had not had significant success in the last few years, particularly in the strategic management area, a difficult market at the time. However, we embarked on an active recruiting program, which over the first couple of years resulted in hiring some outstanding faculty to complement the already strong faculty in the department.

During my first year at Texas A&M, because of the budget cuts, the Dean had a meeting of the department heads and strongly encouraged them to begin seeking external monies to make up for the budget reductions. He implored us to do so because of the concern of losing quality faculty. Of course, he was also quite active in external fund raising. While some departments, particularly Accounting, already had strong external relationships developed from which they obtained financial support, the Department of Management at Texas A&M, like many other management departments, did not have a natural constituency and had few strong external ties. As such, I embarked on several activities. Simultaneously I began developing executive advisory boards, one for the department and one specifically focused on our new Master of Science in Human Resource Management Program. We were successful in gaining agreement from 35 executives to participate in these boards. Over my term as head of the department, we built a group of advisory board members who began to provide support, often through their companies, for the department. For example, we obtained financial support from such companies as Southwestern Bell, Kraft Foods, Exxon, and others. Companies on the HRM Board such as Texas Instruments and organizations such as NASA provided internship opportunities for students as well as scholarship and fellowship monies used to attract top students into the program. I was pleased with the success of these advisory boards.

Though it was difficult, I continued to be active in research. I began collaborating with a new colleague, Bob Hoskisson, and continued my work with Duane Ireland and a few others with whom I had been previously active in joint research. This meant working many extra hours at nights and on weekends because the Head of the Management Department was a full-time (and more) job. However, my largest challenges in this role were ahead of me.

A NEW DEAN

At the end of my first year as Head of the Management Department, the Dean received a promotion to Vice Chancellor of the Texas A&M University system. The Dean was an excellent administrator and leader, a person with vision, and an ambition to become a university president. Therefore, it is not surprising to see his rapid movement into higher administration after only three years as Dean of the College of Business. Unfortunately, it left a big hole. During the next year, Don Hellriegel, one of the faculty members in Management, took over the job as Interim Dean. Overall, he also did an excellent job. However, he had no interest in doing the job long term. Therefore, the College conducted an active search for a new Dean. There were several candidates brought to campus for interviews and one was eventually hired. The new Dean's style of management was quite different from the previous Dean's and Don Hellriegel's. Therefore, his first year at Texas A&M was quite difficult. In fact, the next two years of my term as Department Head under his Deanship were exceptionally difficult and challenging. When coupled with a highly bureaucratic university, with vestiges of an old military style of operation in the central administration, I experienced many frustrations.

The major problem I encountered was the new Dean's desire to have a much more centralized decision and control system. He was less open and did not communicate. Because the Management faculty was a strong group, they were quite vocal about their desires, and several openly expressed concerns about the lack of vision from the Dean's office. Part of the problem was a contrast with the previous Dean who was a visionary and was an exceptional communicator. The new Dean became aggravated with several faculty members in my department and during a meeting, told me that I needed to more effectively control my faculty. My response was that we don't operate that way. We operate in a collegial system where faculty members have a right to express their opinions and while I may not always agree with those opinions, I believed they had the right to do so and I would defend that right. This did not please the Dean.

Additionally, the Dean was unhappy with the system of funding faculty in the summer, wanted to control those monies and reduce the annual compensation paid to faculty by one month. I fought this proposal vigorously. I told the Dean and my colleagues on the committee that our department would lose a number of faculty members if we reduced their income by one month. Frankly, all of them would have lost faculty as well, but I believe most of them were afraid to tell the Dean.

There was a third area in which I disagreed with the Dean. Near the end of the previous Dean's term, he asked me to chair a committee to explore the establishment of a new Center for Entrepreneurship and New Venture Management in the College of Business Administration. It was his belief that entrepreneurship was a newly developing field and one for which substantial external support could be developed. Our committee examined this opportunity closely and, while observing that the entrepreneurship field was not strong in scholarship, it had much potential. We developed a proposal for the establishment of a Center that was eventually approved by the Board of

Regents. The Regent's approval for this Center came shortly before the new Dean's arrival.

During his first year, the Dean asked me to change the Center from entrepreneurship to something else because he felt it would better fit the faculty. On the one hand, he was correct in that we had few faculty with entrepreneurship interests. However, his request ignored the fact that this Center was strongly supported by the previous Dean who was in higher administration and had a high potential to become a major player in the University. Additionally, it overlooked the potential for external funding. One of the Dean's suggestions was to focus the Center on strategic management that probably had much lower probability of external funding. For these reasons, I did not accept his proposals and moved forward with the establishment of the Center for Entrepreneurship and New Venture Management. Unfortunately, this Center became a point of contention for the rest of my tenure as a Department Head. Members of the Management Advisory Board that we had established helped provide some funding for this Center so that it was operational for several years. This Center eventually failed due to lack of funding and was placed in an inactive status a few years after I left the Department Head's position.

In many ways, the last two years of my term as Department Head were successful with two highly active advisory boards, and we continued to hire some excellent new young faculty. Thanks to the strong support of the faculty in the department, the Dean asked me to remain in the position for another four-year term. However, I was tired after six years in this role and the last two years were stressful because of my strained relationship with the Dean. Additionally, I was concerned that the Dean was likely to reduce the budget for our Department and felt that possibly a new Department Head would have a higher probability of forestalling such an action. As a result, I declined the opportunity for a new appointment and Don Hellriegel accepted the position as Department Head. I felt that this was a positive outcome for the Department and for all involved.

During my years as Department Head, I continued to be active in my research and writing as I had two textbooks and several journal articles published (*AMJ*, *SMJ*, *JAP*, and other good quality journals). I was on the editorial review board of the *Academy of Management Journal* and became consulting editor for *AMJ* during the time period of 1988–1990.

Because of my administrative experience at TAMU, my preference was not only to step out of the position of Department Head but also to leave Texas A&M University. Thus, when I was approached about the Dean's position in the College of Business at the University of Missouri, I gave it strong consideration. I was not certain that I wanted to give up my research activities, but also found this position attractive. I submitted my credentials and eventually was offered the position. At this time, I had to make a decision as to whether to pursue an administrative career or move back into a primary faculty role and continue to develop my research program. This was not an easy decision. There was an additional complicating factor in that my family strongly opposed moving as they were happy in College Station. I was quite torn because of my strong desire to leave. However, I finally made a decision to remain for the sake of my family and to allow me to move back into a full-time faculty role.

However, the first couple of years after I moved out of the Department Head's role were some of the lowest periods in my professional life. I had strong negative feelings and I was concerned about possible retribution on me personally by the dean. As a result, I made several decisions. First, I made a decision to be extremely active in research and build a strong and productive research program. I broadened my research program to include international strategy, as I believed this was an important area requiring more theoretical development and empirical work. Additionally, I made a decision to seek the editorship of the *Academy of Management Journal* upon the completion of my role as consulting editor. Fortunately, I was successful in achieving both of these goals.

THE EDITOR'S ROLE

I became Editor of the *Academy of Management Journal* for the 1991–1993 period. This was a highly significant activity in my professional life for a number of reasons. A minor and short-term benefit was that the Dean respected this position and the tension between us began to lessen. At one social function, he commented to me that being a journal editor entailed real power. I did not desire the position for power, nor was this important to me. However, the Dean respected people who had power. More importantly, this position afforded me an opportunity for significant learning, as well as an opportunity to have an impact on the management field.

One of my goals as Editor was to ensure thorough and fast reviews and an equitable process, to the extent possible. I was determined to give authors constructive feedback, but attempt to do so in a humane way. Additionally, because my own experiences suggested that editors oftentimes made publication decisions without reading a manuscript, I committed to reading every manuscript submitted to *AMJ*. This became a substantial task because of the large number of manuscripts submitted. I read almost 2,000 manuscripts during my term as Editor. One outcome of this activity was the requirement to change from simple reading glasses to bifocals.

My interest in a broad set of research activities, both micro and macro, actually helped me as Editor. Although I was not an expert on all of the methods used in the empirical research submitted to *AMJ*, I did have a reasonable understanding of many of the methodologies and approaches used by micro and macro scholars. During my term as Editor, we increased the number of annual issues from 4 to 6 and implemented special research forums focused on important topics. I am pleased that both of these innovations have remained with *AMJ* since their implementation. As Editor of *AMJ*, I had never worked longer or harder. Most of my workweeks were 80–90 hours in length. I must admit that I was pleased to see the end of my term as Editor. However, I also should emphasize that I learned a great deal by reading all those manuscripts. I learned a lot about different methodologies and theories as well as about writing. What I learned as Editor has continued to benefit my own research productivity.

THE LATE AFTERNOON – PROFESSIONAL SERVICE AND CONTINUED RESEARCH ACTIVITY

During my last year as Editor of *AMJ*, I was nominated to be a candidate for the position of Vice President and Program Chair of the Academy of Management. I gave this opportunity due consideration because it came so quickly after my *AMJ* editorship. My original plan was to return my focus to research. In particular, I was interested in furthering my research on international strategy and continuing to work on corporate strategy, particularly on mergers and acquisitions. I decided it was an honor to be nominated for this position and would be an even greater honor if I were to be elected. Thus, I allowed my name to be placed on the ballot and to my delight; I was elected to the position.

With the election, I continued my service on the Board of Governors of the Academy of Management, this time as an officer in the presidential succession. As such, I spent five more years on the Board moving through each of the five positions, Vice President and Program Chair Elect, Vice President and Program Chair, President Elect, President, and Past President. Thus, I spent eight consecutive years on the Academy's Board of Governors. I met many outstanding colleagues, several of whom served with me on the Board and others who worked in and for the Academy in a variety of capacities.

The most challenging of the officer positions were the Vice President and Program Chair and President. At the time, the Academy had approximately

4,000 members attending its annual meeting. I was responsible for the 1995 annual meeting held in Vancouver, British Columbia, Canada. I was fortunate to have an exceptional Local Arrangements Chair, Steve Havlovic, who was on the faculty at Simon Frazer University and other first-rate members of the Local Arrangements Committee. This particular program was a challenge organizationally, because all of the hotels were small and it was the first time that we had used a convention center for the meetings. We had to use the convention center and several of the hotels to have enough meeting rooms for the program. Overall, while the program was a substantial challenge, it was a success largely due to the efforts of many people managing the divisional programs, as well as those facilitating my efforts.

There were a few major policy issues considered by the Board of Governors during my service in officer roles. First, a major issue was the continuing growth, size and complexity of the Academy. After considerable discussion and debate, the Board decided to hire a professional manager to help operate the home office of the Academy of Management. This decision was controversial but, in retrospect, was completely necessary and has been an unqualified success. We were fortunate to hire an experienced manager of professional organizations, Nancy Urbanowicz. During my term as officer, the Academy continued to grow to approximately 10,000 members. Today, the Academy's size exceeds 12,000 members. Consequently, we needed a permanent home office and professional management and staff to help manage the Academy and serve the members in an effective and efficient way.

A second issue of great magnitude was the internationalization of the Academy. Previous officers and Board members had made such efforts, but most of the efforts had relatively minor impact. In a strategic planning exercise, while I was President of the Academy, a decision was made to increase efforts to internationalize the Academy. Of particular importance, was the support for two new affiliate organizations, the Iberoamerican Academy of Management and the Asia Academy of Management. Our intent was not to control but to facilitate and support the development of these organizations so that they could grow and serve their members as well as to participate in the Academy, thus helping it to globalize. This action was also controversial with some, particularly those who had been actively involved in the International Federation of Scholarly Associations of Management (IFSAM), because they believed that in fostering these organizations, the Academy of Management represented a threat to IFSAM. But, we continued to participate actively in IFSAM, while at the same time continuing to facilitate and encourage more members from outside North America to join and participate in our Academy of Management. Much of the growth the Academy has experienced in the last several years has come from outside the United States. I believe that our international members represented slightly over 15% of the total Academy of Management membership at the time we made this decision, but are now approximately 25%. Therefore, I conclude that these efforts have been successful.

Another policy issue considered was how to more actively create a dialogue between Academy members and practicing managers. We debated this on the Board of Governors with significant differences of opinion. I established a committee to examine ways in which we could encourage this dialogue, but the committee was unable to develop any useful recommendations. Some favored starting a research organization as an affiliate, but we were unable to bring this to fruition as well. I was disappointed with the lack of progress in this area during my term as an officer of the Academy.

During this time, I emphasized research and began to develop several streams with renewed vigor. In particular, I continued the work on corporate strategy and corporate governance, but also strongly emphasized work on international strategy. I was fortunate enough to work with a number of very bright and talented Ph.D. students from whom I learned much. My philosophy with Ph.D. students however is to encourage them to follow their own research stream (or dream), thus their dissertations were largely not a part of my research streams. Many of them participated in projects related to my streams of research, however. It is hoped that they learned by participating in this process. Certainly, my research was facilitated by their work and by the excellent colleagues with whom I worked on these projects, to include Bob Hoskisson, Duane Ireland (both of whom I had worked with for a number of years) and others.

The decade of the 1990s was a period of editorial work, professional service, and intensive research. After completing my service on the Board of Governors and the officer roles at the Academy of Management, I served two years as representative of the Academy on the IFSAM Board and began working for the Strategic Management Society as Director/Editor of the Strategic Management Book Series and overseeing the Society's mini-conference programs. I was also elected to the Strategic Management Society Board. I continue in these roles today. In 1995 I edited a special issue of the *Strategic Management Journal* with Rich Bettis on the New Competitive Landscape. Doing so initiated a new research thrust for me. Additionally, I co-authored a textbook on strategic management with Duane and Bob. We did this partly because we were displeased with available textbooks in this area and hoped to make a contribution to the teaching of strategic management. Our book was well received and in the fourth edition as we entered the new century, became the market leader.

SEARCHING FOR THE NEXT CHALLENGE

I had reached a time in my career where I had accomplished a number of professional goals. First, I had served as Editor of *AMJ*. I also completed my terms as President and Past President of the Academy of Management. Additionally, I was fortunate enough to have co-authored several books and have an active research program resulting in a number of journal articles. Finally, earlier in my career I had set a goal of having an endowed position. In 1987 I was named to my first endowed professorship at Texas A&M. In 1991 I was named as a chair holder.

In my professional life, I primarily work with a set of goals. Once those goals are achieved, I develop a new set. At this point in my career, I began trying to decide what my next set of goals would entail. For several years, I had been contacted by schools about potential dean positions. Most of these contacts stemmed from my earlier work as an administrator and receiving the offer to be dean at the University of Missouri (although I ultimately turned down this opportunity). I decided that I had two different potential paths to follow. One was to become an administrator, and dean was the next logical step on that path. Or, I could remain in a professorial role but work toward making important contributions to the field. Here, my desire would be to not only make contributions of a scholarly nature but to translate the work being done in our field for the practice of management, as well. I had difficulty in deciding on one of these two paths as both had some attraction for me. I decided to continue my professional work and see what opportunities arose.

I was contacted about several dean positions and received offers to become dean in a few of those. The first was at the University of South Carolina. Later I also received offers to be Dean at the University of Colorado and Georgia Tech. Each of these positions provided attractions. Both South Carolina and Colorado had major budget problems that could not be resolved easily. There were other concerns about higher administration support. They had unique but serious problems that a new Dean was unlikely to resolve. Thus, I decided not to accept the positions.

Alternatively, the opportunity at Georgia Tech was very attractive to me. I found the higher administration to be progressive and visionary. The College had much opportunity and with the right leadership, I felt, it could develop. I came very close to accepting this offer. However, over the years, I developed a strong affinity for Texas A&M University. In general, I was treated well. More importantly, I developed strong friendships with a number of alumni, and former students. Both of my children received degrees from that University. Essentially, because of a loss of important faculty over several years in the Management Department and in the College, our Department Head, representing others, made a special plea for me to not to leave Texas A&M. He said that it would cause major harm to the Department and to the College if I were to leave. Hence, I was faced with an opportunity that I found very attractive, but to accept that opportunity, I had to take an action that harmed an institution for which I had developed a strong positive feeling. In the end, I was torn with this decision, but out of loyalty remained at Texas A&M. Simultaneously, I made two other decisions. One was that I would pursue my efforts to make important contributions to the field. Second, I would likely remain at Texas A&M for the rest of my career.

As a result of these decisions, I began to develop and implement a number of projects that would result in books along with a renewed and enthusiastic emphasis on my research program. I also began teaching the core Strategic Management course in the MBA Program. These new goals entailed a significant commitment of time and effort. I continued my thrust in international strategy research, with a particular focus on international strategic alliances. I, along with several colleagues, collected data in ten different countries. I also continued my research in corporate strategy and governance. In particular, I decided to write a book on mergers and acquisitions as a culmination of a research stream for a number of years. Additionally, partly through serendipity, I began to develop an interest in, and research program, focused on entrepreneurship.

Whereas this interest grew partly out of my prior work on corporate innovation, sometimes referred to as corporate entrepreneurship, Dale Meyer, a mentor from the University of Colorado, also introduced me into the entrepreneurship area. Additionally, I was invited to a small special purpose conference at Rensselaer Polytechnic to speak about my research and how it related to entrepreneurship. This forced me to think about my various research streams and how they related to the field of entrepreneurship. I delineated six separate domains of research and shaped a presentation around those domains. Later, I was invited to write a chapter for the *Handbook of Entrepreneurship*, co-authored with my good friend and colleague, Duane Ireland, integrating work from strategy and entrepreneurship. I agreed to do so only if I could use the prior presentation as a basis for the chapter and the co-editors agreed.

A third element involved invitations from the Kauffman Foundation to become more actively involved in entrepreneurship research. They offered small research grants to facilitate that work. So, I began to work on research projects, primarily with Duane Ireland, but also with others, like Shaker Zahra, that focused more on new ventures and entrepreneurial firms. This activity eventually culminated in a new research stream that we referred to as strategic entrepreneurship. Consequently, I was working on a number of research projects and research streams, as well as several books simultaneously. I believed that a number of these projects had high potential to help me fulfill my goals. As a result, I was quite excited and energized by these opportunities.

Ph.D. STUDENTS AND FRIENDS

I was very fortunate to work with some excellent Ph.D. students over the years I was at Texas A&M. I learned from them and many have become my friends as well. Among them are Ken Cory, Barbara Bartkus, Parthiban David, Amy Hillman, Rahul Kochhar, Ho-uk Lee, Ed Levitas, Doug Lyon, Rick Martinez, Doug Moesel, Bert Morrow, Robert Nixon, Scott Sherman, Katsu Shimiju, Dennis Smart, and Doug Thomas. I had the honor of chairing the dissertations of these people. I also worked with several other Ph.D. students on research projects, serving on their committees or frequently interacting with them in some of the administrative roles I had (e.g. Ph.D. Program Coordinator, Department Head). Among them were Jon Beard, Aleta Best, Lowell Busenitz, Jim Fiet, Bob Hill, Rick Johnson, Micki Kacmar, Hicheon Kim, Yangmin Kim, Daewoo Park, Tim Peterson, Glen Rowe, Matt Semadeni, Wei Shen, Linda Trevino, Beverly Tyler and Margaret White. I also had the opportunity to work with some Ph.D. students at other universities. Among those are Sam DeMarie (Arizona State University – before I joined the ASU faculty), Debra Nelson (University of Texas at Arlington – when I was on the faculty at UTA), and Tim Reed (University of Colorado). It has been a pleasure to watch each of these persons develop into an independent scholar and to work with them. Each of them has touched my life and I am a better person for it.

While space precludes reviewing my work with each individual, a few events and projects warrant emphasis. For example, Bob Hoskisson and I designed and obtained external funding for a major research project examining the effects of significant corporate strategies (e.g. mergers and acquisitions) on firm innovation and performance. The National Science Foundation and a competitive research program funded by the state of Texas funded this project. We involved several Ph.D. students in this project to help collect and interpret the data. The two who were the most actively involved were Rick Johnson and Doug Moesel. All of us invested many hours in this project but it has paid off handsomely in the publications (and hopefully the contributions) resulting from it. Doug Moesel has two outstanding traits. He is a perfectionist with outstanding quantitative skills. I remember that we sometimes had to "wrest the statistical results" from him because he kept wanting to check them out one more time. Doug often conducted special classes for the other Ph.D. students on particular statistical tools (e.g. EQS). Rick Johnson is also an excellent methodologist and his dissertation was based on data from this project. He continues to work with Bob and myself on research projects today.

Barbara Bartkus worked with me on the Academy of Management program when I was the vice president and program chair for the Academy in 1995. She probably saved my life several times over because of her outstanding organization skills and ability to help me coordinate activities with many groups and individuals. She was unflappable and had a calming influence on me. Additionally, she developed one of the richest data sets I have ever observed for her dissertation. This data set alone would probably afford ten or more years of study.

Amy Hillman deserves special mention because of her tenacity and motivation, not to mention her other excellent professional attributes. Amy had a strong interest in research on the business government interface. It is not an area of my expertise and I was concerned because it is not a major area of emphasis in strategic management. So, against my advice, she focused her dissertation on this topic. And, in the first four years after completing her Ph.D., she published two articles in AMR and three in SMJ along with several other journal articles. In addition, she now serves on the editorial review Board of AMJ and wants to be a journal editor someday. Given her success to date, I suspect she will realize her goal.

Robert Nixon came to the Ph.D. program without a masters degree (although he had graduate work), and substantial experience as a manager and entre-preneur. Robert was of significant help in our research, particularly in gaining executives' agreement to participate in our survey work. Robert has excellent interpersonal skills, is mature and is a kind person as well. He also worked with me to produce several edited books for the Strategic Management series sponsored by the Strategic Management Society. Our last book is currently in production for publication by Blackwell Publishers.

The last person I will mention is Rahul Kochhar. Rahul had more heart than anyone I know. He completed an excellent dissertation but the market was poor when he finished his degree. He had trouble finding a job and he wanted badly to go to a top research university. Unfortunately, this was not "in the cards" for him. He accepted a position at a small teaching-oriented university. He was determined, however, to reach his goal. Thus, while teaching 12 hours per semester often involving three preparations, he also had a highly active research program. He had several articles published in *SMJ* and *AMJ*. When the labor market improved, Rahul went on the market and accepted a position at Purdue University, one of the best strategic management faculties in the U.S. I was so proud of Rahul and happy for him. He and I continued our research collaboration. Then one day, I received a phone call from Dan Schendel, a senior faculty member at Purdue. He communicated that Rahul had not shown up for his classes and had not come to his office for a couple of days. So, they went to his home to check on him. They found him in his bed where he had passed away during his sleep. They were unable to determine the cause of his death. This came as a major shock. The blessing is that Rahul made it to "the mountain top" for him before he passed away. After a couple of months languishing, I was determined to have our last joint research project published in a major journal. Thanks to other important colleagues working with me as coauthors, Len Bierman and Katsu Shimizu, and significant work in theory development and collecting additional data, it was published by *AMJ* in 2001. Rahul remained a coauthor and we dedicated the article to him.

Each of the others has touched my life in important ways (e.g. in addition to being a good friend, Margaret White brought me one of the most challenging human resource problems with which I had to deal as a an administrator). I continue to be active in working with Ph.D. students today. While I find it a challenge and much work, it also invigorates me and helps me achieve my goals as well. Thus, I have had many opportunities through the years, several of which have come through my Ph.D. students. I continue working toward my ultimate goals and my work with Ph.D. students is a work in progress. However, as often is the case, I have encountered some unexpected problems along the way.

BUMPS IN THE ROAD TO ACHIEVE MY GOALS

As noted earlier, my primary goals at this stage were to make a contribution to the management field, both in the scholarly dimension and to the practice of management. As such, I took on a number of different projects. For example, Duane Ireland and I, as a pair and in conjunction with others, agreed to and/or proposed to co-edit four separate special issues for different journals. The journals included the *Journal of Engineering and Technology Management*, *Academy of Management Review*, *Academy of Management Executive*, and *Strategic Management Journal*. Further, I became involved in several book projects and the revision of our strategic management textbook was on a two-year cycle. All of these activities were in addition to the several scholarly research streams in which I was involved. As noted earlier, at this time, I also began teaching the core Strategic Management course for the MBA Program.

I continued to serve on the Board of the Strategic Management Society along with fulfilling other responsibilities for the Society. One might conclude that my plate was not only full, but 'it runneth over'.

During this time, I was asked to play a leadership role in a major service activity for the University. The President of Texas A&M University developed a large and vital activity referred to as "Vision 2020". Essentially, this was a strategic planning exercise designed to make Texas A&M University a top ten public university by the year 2020. There were several hundred people involved in this effort, drawing on all the University's important constituencies. I was asked to co-chair, with a prominent alumnus, one of the major groups comprising this effort. I did so and after a year of development, a formal plan was developed describing twelve major areas of needing development for the University to reach its goal by 2020. Surprisingly, I was then asked by the President to co-chair, with a major alumnus, the Vision 2020 Advisory Committee that would oversee and advise the President on the implementation of this plan. This was a highly visible activity within the University and among its constituencies.

Although important to the University, there were complications. The Dean of the College of Business had become involved in a substantial conflict with the Vice President and Provost and the President of the University. This conflict also involved several members of the TAMU Board of Regents. Part of the conflict related to the Vision 2020 Plan, as the Dean in the College of Business felt that it was too heavily weighted toward the Liberal Arts and Sciences and was biased against the University's professional schools, particularly the College of Business. Thus, he was a vocal critic of this plan. I believe that the Dean was partly correct about the support needed for the College of Business, but the conflict was unfortunately dysfunctional. The plan was weighted toward the development of the Liberal Arts and Sciences, but this was necessary to develop the breadth and depth in the University to become a top ten public university. However, I had argued as a member of the Committee that it could only become a member of the top ten if it accomplished these goals while simultaneously maintaining the University's strengths in its professional schools. In other words, I believe that with proper management and commitments, all parties' requirements could be satisfied. Again, I performed the leadership role as a service to the University and hopefully to represent the College's interests on this Committee.

During this time, the College of Business decided to develop and implement an Executive MBA Program to be offered in the north part of Houston. For competitive as well as revenue enhancement reasons, this move had been needed for some time. I supported this strategic action. I was asked to help develop and participate in the program as an instructor for the strategic management content. The program was to be designed around modules rather than courses, making it unique but challenging to develop and implement. I agreed to participate on the premise that I would not teach in it as an overload, but as a part of my regular teaching load. I invested considerable time in helping to develop the strategic management module outlines, helping to integrate this content with the modules from other business disciplines and developing the specific content for the modules I was asked to teach. Unfortunately, even though the administration had originally agreed to substitute my teaching in the EMBA for a course in my regular teaching load, the administration decided that the hours scheduled for my modules were inadequate for a course release. I was not pleased with this decision, as I felt a trust had been broken, but I fulfilled my part of the informal contract. Thus, I taught my modules, and I was pleased to receive highly positive feedback from the students. I enjoyed the time with them, even though it was very demanding. The biggest problem for me was the time involved. Teaching this course as an overload detracted from my ability to achieve my goals.

During the same period of time, the College administration had obtained a commitment from an external party to provide funds to revive the Center for Entrepreneurship and New Venture Management. I was approached to serve as Director of the Center. I politely declined the opportunity. There were several reasons for my decision. First, it would take considerable time to build this Center, as it should be developed. To take on this responsibility would detract from the pursuit of my goals. Second, this Center had been a point of conflict between the Dean and myself a number of years earlier. Unfortunately, the Department Head and the College's Executive Associate Dean expressed a strong desire for me to accept the role. Thus, I finally agreed to do it, but with some release time from teaching. By the end of the first year, I had built an external Advisory Board for the Center and we had developed and implemented a new award for an outstanding new venture leader. Unfortunately, I was asked to teach an overload the next year, as well, which caused me grave concern. I was teaching an overload with the Executive MBA program and now there were questions about the release time promised for managing the center as well. I considered my schedule of commitments on books, journal special issues, and as co-director of mini-conferences for the Strategic Management Society. Many of these commitments were made with the premise that I would have release time from teaching. I strongly suspected that they simply did not want to substitute someone else into the courses that I taught. Therefore, I felt that I was being penalized for doing a good job.

To say that I was upset and displeased with this situation is an understatement. I had made a decision that I would not leave Texas A&M University. I cared about the university and I had taken on a number of activities above and beyond those expected of others. I had turned down positions that were highly attractive to avoid harming the institution. I also had been treated well in other ways. I held an endowed chair and had been named as a Distinguished Professor by the University. However, I became concerned about the pattern of decisions and the lack of time and energy to focus on achieving my research goals. Largely, these goals and my accomplishment of them defined my professional life and my career. Within a few days, I received a phone call from Bill Glick, Chair of the Department of Management, at Arizona State University. The offer I received to join the faculty at Arizona State University was attractive in many ways. But, I was impressed with the development of the Faculty (I have a number of excellent colleagues at ASU), and with the Dean's goals and willingness to take calculated but necessary risks. And, my overall teaching and administrative load would be lighter than at TAMU. I was recruited aggressively and made an excellent offer on multiple dimensions. However, these were only part of the reasons I was attracted to ASU. No place is perfect and ASU has its challenges. I like my colleagues here. They work hard and there is little or no arrogance. I have several highly productive colleagues (across the business disciplines) for whom I have a great deal of respect. I assessed that the College of Business at ASU had significant potential and that I could contribute, along with many others, to the realization of that potential. I also felt that ASU would afford me a better opportunity to reach my own professional goals and that if I did so, they would recognize and rejoice in them. Therefore, I accepted the offer and joined the ASU faculty in August 2000.

RIDING INTO THE SUNSET

I truly care about the students whom I have taught, many of the colleagues with whom I have worked and the institutions that I have served. I want them all to succeed. I have gained much from them all and have received many blessings in return.

I remember two specific comments that were made to me by others related to my career and background. The first was made by a dean at an institution trying to recruit me. He commented that he was impressed with my scholarly productivity, but did not believe that I would ever be highly successful in the profession, because I worked in so many diverse areas. In some ways, his comment is accurate in that it is difficult to establish a reputation publishing in micro and macro areas and multiple separate journals which tend to be read by specialists rather than generalists (e.g. *Journal of Applied Psychology, Strategic Management Journal*). However, I decided this fact would not change my research activities or career path. One of the major benefits of this profession is the opportunity to work on any research question that I find of interest. My goal has been to conduct high quality research, to the extent of my abilities, and let "the chips fall where they may."

The president of a prominent institution where I was being recruited for an endowed position made the second comment. This occurred relatively early in my career; I was a new full professor at the time. The president said that I had come a long way, given the institutions where I received my education (this is a paraphrase). In other words, he was not impressed with the universities from which I received my degrees, but seemingly was impressed with my productivity. While, in general, I understood his comment, I also decided that I did not want to be at an institution where that type of attitude prevailed. Therefore, upon arriving home after my visit, I promptly wrote a letter withdrawing my name from candidacy for this position. I don't know whether my work at this point would satisfy that dean or that president. And, I don't particularly care. I continue to do the research that I want to do, and enjoy my profession.

If I'm fortunate, I hope to have approximately ten more years until I end my career. I do not intend to ride into the sunset on just any horse. I still have major goals and I intend to be riding a thoroughbred racehorse toward the achievement of those goals, until I dismount and retire. My career decisions and activities will be directed toward this end. To date, it has been a great ride. I hope that when I dismount, others will say that I made a difference.

PUBLICATIONS

1975

The Creative Organization: Tomorrow's Survivor. *Journal of Creative Behavior, 9*, 283–290.
Technology: An Intervening Variable in the Relationship Between Organizational Climate and Work-Unit Effectiveness. *Proceedings Academy of Management*, August, 209–211.

1976

Technology, Organizational Climate and Effectiveness. *Journal of Business Research, 4*, 383–399.
With R. H. Thomas. The Development of an Inventory to Measure Classroom Climate. *The Teaching of Organization Behavior*, January, 2, 37–39.

1977

With W. G. Zikmund. Organizational Climate: An Empirical Approach to the Perceptual Consensus Question. *Review of Business and Economic Research, 13*, 59–67.

With C. P. Morgan. Organizational Climate as a Predictor of Organizational Practices. *Psychological Reports, 40*, 1191–1199.

With R. D.Middlemist & C. R. Greer. Sunset Legislation and the Measurement of Effectiveness. *Public Personnel Management, 6*, 188–193.

With D. R. Thomas. The Rights of Business. *Journal of General Management,* Winter *4*, 68–79.

With C. P. Morgan. Validity and Factor Structure of House and Rizzo's Effectiveness Scales. *Academy of Management Journal, 20*, 37–39.

1978

With R. D.Middlemist. The Measurement of Technology Within Organizations. *Journal of Management, 4*, 47–67.

With R. D. Middlemist & C. R. Greer. Evaluating the Public Organizations. *Atlanta Economic Review, 28*(2), 54–58.

With W. G. Zikmund & B. A. Pickens. Influence of Sex and Scholastic Performance on Reactions to Job-Applicant Resumes. *Journal of Applied Psychology, 63*, 252–254.

With J. A. Cox & W. W. Stanton. An Examination of the Relationship of Boundary Relevance to Hierarchical Level, Perceived Environmental Uncertainty and Role Stress Variables. *Proceedings Academy of Management*, August, 175–179.

1979

With R. D. Middlemist. A Methodology to Develop the Criteria and Criteria Weightings for Assessing Subunit Effectiveness in Organizations. *Academy of Management Journal*, June, *22*, 356–374.

With R. D. Middlemist & R. L. Mathis. *Effective Management*. St. Paul: West Publishing Co.

1980

With R. D. Middlemist. The Role of Technology in the Relationship Between Perceived Work Environment and Subunit Effectiveness. *Proceedings Academy of Management*, August, 241–245.

1981

With R. D. Middlemist. Technology as a Moderator of the Relationship Between Perceived Work Environment and Subunit Effectiveness. *Human Relations, 34*, 517–532.

With R. D. Middlemist. *Organizational Behavior: Applied Concepts*. Chicago: Science Research Associates.

1982

With R. D. Ireland & G. Stadter. Functional Importance and Company Performance: Moderating Effects of Grand Strategy and Industry Type. *Strategic Management Journal, 3,* 315–330.

With O. M. Amos & L. Warner. Life Satisfaction and Regional Development: A Case of Oklahoma. *Social Indicators Research, 11,* 319–331.

With R. D. Allen & C. R. Greer. Occupational Stress and Perceived Organizational Effectiveness in Formal Groups: An Examination of Stress Level and Stress Type. *Personnel Psychology, 35,* 359–370.

With W. G. Zikmund & B. A. Pickens. Discrimination in Industrial Employment: Investigation of Race and Sex Bias Among Professionals. *Work and Occupations, 9,* 217–231.

With R. D. Ireland & K. A. Palia, Industrial Firms' Grand Strategy and Functional Importance: Moderating Effects of Technology and Uncertainty. *Academy of Management Journal, 25,* 265–298.

With D. R. Cash, Task Technology, Individual Differences and Satisfaction. *Review of Business and Economic Research, 17,* 28–36.

With R. D. Ireland. Strategy, Industry, Structure and Performance. *American Institute for Decision Sciences Proceedings,* November, *2,* 26–28.

With K. A. Palia, R. D, Ireland & Y. H. Godiwalla. *Grand Corporate Strategy and Critical Functions: Interactive Effects of Organizational Dimensions.* New York: Praeger Publishing Co.

1983

With M. R. Fusilier. Effects of Age, Race, Sex and Employment Experience on Students' Perceptions of Job Applications. *Perceptual and Motor Skills, 57,* 1127–1134.

With O. M. Amos & L. Warner. Social Factors and Company Location Decisions: Technology, Quality of Life and Quality of Work Life Concerns. *Journal of Business Ethics, 2,* 89–98.

With B. W. Keats & S. Purdum. Affirmative Action Effectiveness Criteria in Institutions of Higher Education. *Research in Higher Education, 18,* 391–408.

With R. D. Ireland, B. W. Keats & A. Vianna. Measuring Subunit Effectiveness. *Decision Sciences, 14,* 87–102.

With R. L. Mathis. Perspectives on Personnel and Organization Development (OD): Survey Results Shed Light Upon Important Developmental Tools. *Personnel Administrator,* February, 87–97.

With R. D. Middlemist & R. L. Mathis. *Management: Concepts and Effective Practice.* St. Paul: West Publishing Co.

With R. D, Middlemist & C. R. Greer. *Personnel Management: Jobs, People, Logic.* Englewood Cliffs, NJ: Prentice-Hall.

1984

With R. D. Ireland. Corporate Distinctive Competence and Performance: Effects of Perceived Environmental Uncertainty (PEU), Size, and Technology. *Decision Sciences, 15,* 324–349.

With B. W. Keats. Empirical Identification of the Criteria for Effective Affirmative Action Programs. *The Journal of Applied Behavioral Science, 20,* 203–222.

1985

With R. D. Ireland. Strategy, Contextual Factors and Performance. *Human Relations, 38,* 793–812.

With R. D. Ireland. Corporate Distinctive Competence, Strategy, Industry and Performance. *Strategic Management Journal, 6,* 273–293.

With W. G. Zikmund. Forewarned is Forearmed: Potential Between and Within Sex Discrimination. *Sex Roles, 12,* 807–812. Abstracted in *Psychology Today.*

With B. W. Keats. Linkages Among Environmental Dimensions and Macro-Organizational Characteristics: A Causal Modeling Approach. *Proceedings Academy of Management,* August, 171–175.

1986

With R. D. Ireland. Relationships Among Corporate Level Distinctive Competencies, Diversification Strategy, Corporate Structure and Performance. *Journal of Management Studies, 23,* 401–416.

With S. H. Barr. A Comparison of Selection Decision Models in Manager vs. Student Samples. *Personnel Psychology, 39,* 599–617.

With J. Rosenstein. Experimental Research on Race and Sex Discrimination: The Record and the Prospects. *Journal of Occupational Behavior, 7,* 215–226.

With R. D. Middlemist & R. L. Mathis. *Management: Concepts and Effective Practice* (2nd ed.). St. Paul: West Publishing Co.

1987

With R. D. Ireland, R. A. Bettis & D. A. de Porras. Strategy Formulation Processes: Differences in Perception of Strength and Weaknesses Indicators and Environmental Uncertainty by Managerial Level. *Strategic Management Journal, 8,* 469–486.

With R. D. Ireland. Peters and Waterman Revisited: The Unended Quest for Excellence. *Academy of Management Executive, 1,* 91–97.

With R. D. Ireland. The Executive Search for Excellence Through Quick Fixes: Advocacy Versus Science. *Business Education, 8,* 28–35.

With R. D. Ireland. Developing Competitive Strength in International Markets. *Long Range Planning,* February, *20,* 115–122.

With R. E. Hoskisson. Strategic Control and Innovation in Large Multiproduct Firms. *Proceedings Academy of Management,* August, 323–327.

1988

With R. E. Hoskisson. Strategic Control Systems and Relative R&D Investment in Large Multiproduct Firms. *Strategic Management Journal, 9,* 605–621.

With B. W. Keats. A Causal Model of Linkages Among Environmental Dimensions, Macro Organizational Characteristics and Performance, *Academy of Management Journal, 31,* 570–598.

The Measuring of Organizational Effectiveness: Multiple Domains and Constituencies. *Management International Review*, *28*, 28–40. Reprinted in R. M. S. Wilson, *Management Accounting*, Volume II. Hampshire, England: Dartmouth Publishing Co., 1997

With C. W. L. Hill & R. E. Hoskisson. Declining United States Competitiveness: Reflections on a Crisis. *Academy of Management Executive*, *2*, 51–60.

With R. D. Ireland & I. Goryunov. The Context of Innovation: Investment in R&D and Firm Performance. In: U. Gattiker & L. Larwood (Eds), *Technological Innovations and Human Resources* (pp. 75–92). New York: Walter DeGruyter.

With R. D. Middlemist. *Organizational Behavior: Managerial Strategies for Performance*. St. Paul: West Publishing Co.

1989

With D. L. Nelson & J. C. Quick. Men and Women of the Personnel Profession: Some Differences and Similarities in their Stress. *Stress Medicine*, *5*, 145–152.

With S. H. Barr. Managerial Selection Decision Models: An Examination of Configural Cue Processing. *Journal of Applied Psychology*, *74*, 53–61.

With R. E. Hoskisson, T. Turk and B. Tyler. Balancing Corporate Strategy and Executive Compensation: Agency Theory and Corporate Governance. In: G. Ferris & K. Rowland (Eds), *Research in Personnel and Human Resources Management* (pp. 25–57). Greenwich, CT: JAI Press.

With R. E. Hoskisson, R. D. Ireland and J. Harrison. Acquisitive Growth Strategy and Relative R&D Intensity: The Effects of Leverage, Diversification and Size. *Proceedings Academy of Management*, August. 22–26.

With R. D. Middlemist & R. L. Mathis. *Management: Concepts and Effective Practice* (3rd ed.). St. Paul: West Publishing Co.

1990

With D. L. Nelson, J. C. Quick & D. Moesel. Politics, Lack of Career Progress, and Work/Home Conflict: Stress and Strain for Working Women. *Sex Roles*, *23*, 169–185.

With R. E. Hoskisson. Antecedents and Performance Outcomes of Diversification: Review and Critique of Theoretical Perspectives. *Journal of Management*, *16*, 461–509.

With R. E. Hoskisson & R. D. Ireland. Mergers and Acquisitions and Managerial Commitment to Innovation. *Strategic Management Journal*, Special Issue, *11*, 29–47.

With R. D. Ireland & J. Skivington. Managing R&D in Diversified Companies. *Research-Technology Management*, *33*, 37–42.

With D. L. Nelson & J. C. Quick. Stress and Strain in the Personnel Profession. *Personnel*, August. 36–39.

With G. G. Dess & R. D. Ireland. Industry Effects and Strategic Management Research. *Journal of Management*, *16*, 7–27.

With B. B. Tyler & D. Park. A Cross Cultural Examination of Strategic Decision Making: Comparison of Korean and U.S. Executives. *Proceedings Academy of Management*, August. 111–115.

1991

With R. E. Hoskisson, R. D. Ireland & J. S. Harrison. Are Acquisitions a Poison Pill for Innovation? *Academy of Management Executive, 5*(4), 22–34.

With R. E. Hoskisson, R. D. Ireland & J. S. Harrison. The Effects of Acquisitions on R & D Inputs and Outputs. *Academy of Management Journal, 34*, 693–706.

With B. B. Tyler. Strategic Decision Models: Integrating Different Perspectives. *Strategic Management Journal, 12*, 327–351.

With R. E. Hoskisson & C. W. L. Hill. Managerial Risk Taking in Diversified Firms: An Evolutionary Perspective. *Organization Science, 2*, 296–314.

With R. E. Hoskisson & J. S. Harrison. Strategic Competitiveness in the 1990s: Challenges and Opportunities for U.S. Executives. *Academy of Management Executive, 5*(2), 7–22.

With J. S. Harrison, R. E. Hoskisson & R. D. Ireland. Synergies and Post Acquisition Performance: Similarities Versus Differences in Resource Allocations. *Journal of Management, 17*, 173–190.

With R. E. Hoskisson. Strategic Competitiveness. In: L. W. Foster (Ed.), *Advances in Applied Business Strategy* (Vol. 2, pp. 1–36). Greenwich, CT: JAI Press.

1992

With C. W. L. Hill & R. E. Hoskisson. Cooperative Versus Competitive Structures in Related and Unrelated Diversified Firms. *Organization Science, 3*, 501–521.

With C. W. L. Hill, P. C. Kelley, B. Agle, & R. E. Hoskisson. An Empirical Examination of the Causes of Corporate Wrongdoing. *Human Relations, 45*, 1055–1076.

With R. Duane Ireland. Mission Statements: Importance, Challenge and Recommendations for Development. *Business Horizons, 35*(3), 34–42. Reprinted in A. A. Thompson, Jr., A. J. Strickland III & T. R. Kramer (Eds), *Readings in Strategic Management*, Homewood, Illinois: R. D. Irwin.

With R. D. Ireland & J. C. Williams. Self-Confidence and Decisiveness: Prerequisites for Effective Management in the 1990s. *Business Horizons, 35*(1), 36–43.

With B. W. Keats. Strategic Leadership and Restructuring: A Reciprocal Interdependence. In: R. L. Phillips & J. G. Hunt (Eds), *Strategic Leadership: A Multi-organization Level Perspective* (pp. 45–61). New York: Quorum Books.

With D. L. Nelson. Working Women and Stress: Implications for Enhancing Women's Mental Health in the Workplace. In: J. C. Quick, J. J. Hurrell, Jr. & L. R. Murphy (Eds), *Work and Well-Being: Assessments and Interventions for Occupational Mental Health* (pp. 164–177). Washington, D.C.: American Psychological Association.

1993

With R. E. Hoskisson & R. D. Nixon. A Mid-Range Theory of Interfunctional Integration: Its Antecedents and Outcomes. *Journal of Engineering and Technology Management*, 161–185.

With R. A. Johnson & R. E. Hoskisson. Board of Director Involvement in Restructuring: The Effects of Board Versus Managerial Controls and Characteristics. *Strategic Management Journal, 14*, Special Issue, 33–50.

With R. E. Hoskisson & C. W. L. Hill. Managerial Incentives and Investment in R&D in Large Multiproduct Firms. *Organization Science, 4,* 325–341.

With R. E. Hoskisson, R. A. Johnson & D. D.Moesel. Construct Validity of an Objective (Entropy) Categorical Measure of Diversification Strategy. *Strategic Management Journal, 14,* 215–235.

With R. D. Ireland & V. D. Gray. Relationships Among Competitive Strategies, Core Competences and Innovation in Small Manufacturing Firms. In: L. R. Gomez-Mejia & M. W. Lawless (Eds), *High Technology Venturing* (pp. 61–77). Greenwich, CT: JAI Press.

1994

With B. W. Keats, H. F. Harback & R. D. Nixon. Rightsizing: Building and Maintaining Strategic Leadership and Long-term Competitiveness. *Organizational Dynamics,* Autumn. 18–32.

With R. E. Hoskisson & R. D. Ireland. A Mid-Range Theory of the Interactive Effects of International and Product Diversification on Innovation and Performance. *Journal of Management, 20,* 297–326.

With D. L. Smart. Debt: A Disciplining Force for Managers or a Debilitating Force for Organizations. *Journal of Management Inquiry, 3,* 144–152.

With R. E. Hoskisson, J. S. Harrison & T. P. Summers. Human Capital and Strategic Competitiveness in the 1990s. *Journal of Management Development, 13*(1), 35–46.

With D. L. Smart. A Mid-Range Theory Regarding the Antecedents of Restructuring Types: An Integration of Agency, Upper Echelon and Resource Based Perspectives. In: P. Shrivastava, A. Huff & J. Dutton (Eds), *Advances in Strategic Management* (Vol. 10b, pp. 159–186). Greenwich, CT: JAI Press.

With R. E. Hoskisson & R. D. Ireland. The Effects of Acquisitions and Restructuring (Strategic Refocusing) Strategies on Innovation. In: G. von Krogh, A. Sinatra & H. Singh (Eds), *Managing Corporate Acquisitions* (pp. 144–169). London: MacMillan Press.

With R. E. Hoskisson. *Downscoping: How to Tame the Diversified Firm.* New York: Oxford University Press.

1995

With D. Lei. Strategic Restructuring and Outsourcing: The Effect of Mergers and Acquisitions and LBOs on Building Firm Skills and Capabilities. *Journal of Management, 21,* 835–859.

With R. Bettis. The New Competitive Landscape. *Strategic Management Journal,* Special Issue, 7–19.

With B. B. Tyler, C. Hardee & D. Park. Understanding Strategic Intent in the Global Marketplace. *Academy of Management Executive, 9,* 12–19.

With R. Kochhar. Toward an Integrative Model of International Diversification. *Journal of International Management, 1,* 33–73.

Academic Research in Management/Organizations: Is It Dead or Alive? *Journal of Management Inquiry, 4,* 52–56.

With D. Park. Understanding the Strategic Intent of Korean Executives: A Competitor Analysis. In J. Doukas & L. Lang (Eds), *Research in International Business and Finance* (Vol. 12, pp. 261–284). Greenwich, CT: JAI Press.

With R. D. Ireland & R. E. Hoskisson. *Strategic Management: Competitiveness and Globalization.* St. Paul: West Publishing Co.

1996

Problems and Potential Solutions to Strategic Competitiveness in Global Markets. *Advances in Competitiveness Research, 4,* 4–23.

With R. E. Hoskisson, R. A. Johnson & D. D. Moesel. The Market for Corporate Control and Firm Innovation. *Academy of Management Journal, 39,* 1084–1119.

With D. Lei & R. Bettis. Dynamic Core Competences Through Meta-Learning and Strategic Context. *Journal of Management, 4,* 547–567.

With D. Lei & J. Goldhar. Advanced Manufacturing Technology: The Impact on Organization Design and Strategic Flexibility. *Organization Studies, 17,* 501–523.

With W. S. Sherman. Creating Corporate Value: Integrating Quality and Innovation Programs. In: S. Ghosh & D. Fedor (Eds), *Advances in the Management of Organizational Quality* (pp. 221–244). Greenwich, CT: JAI Press.

With P. David & J. Gimeno. The Role of Activism by Institutional Investors in Influencing Corporate Innovation. *Proceedings Academy of Management,* August. 378–382.

1997

With R. E. Hoskisson & H. Kim. International Diversification: Effects on Innovation and Firm Performance in Product Diversified Firms. *Academy of Management Journal, 40,* 767–798.

With E. Levitas & M. T. Dacin. Competitive Intelligence and Tacit Knowledge Development in Strategic Alliances. *Competitive Intelligence Review, 8,* 20–27.

With M. T. Dacin & E. Levitas. Selecting Partners for Successful International Alliances: Examination of U.S. and Korean Firms. *Journal of World Business, 32,* 3–16.

With M. T. Dacin, B. B. Tyler & D. Park. Understanding the Differences in Korean and U.S. Executives' Strategic Orientations. *Strategic Management Journal, 18,* 159–167.

The Maturation of the *Academy of Management Journal. Academy of Management Journal, 40,* 1451–1456.

With R. D. Ireland. Strategy-as-Story: Clarifications and Enhancements to the Barry and Elmes Arguments. *Academy of Management Review, 22,* 844–847.

With R. Serpa. Bullish on Karate, Bearish on Corporate Judo as a New Paradigm for Competitive Strategy. *Journal of Management Inquiry, 6,* 31–34.

With B. Bartkus. International Entrepreneurship. In: J. A. Katz & R. H. Brockhaus, Sr. (Eds), *Advances in Entrepreneurship, Firm Emergence, and Growth* (pp. 7–30). Greenwich, CT: JAI Press.

The Evolution of Multinational Corporations: Integration of International Diversification and Strategic Management. In: B. Toyne & D. Nigh (Eds), *International Business Inquiry: An Emerging Vision* (pp. 506–513). Columbia, SC: University of South Carolina Press.

With R. D. Ireland. Performance Strategies for High-Growth Entrepreneurial Firms. *Frontiers of Entrepreneurial Research.* Babson Park, MA: Babson College. 90–104.

With R. D. Ireland & R. E. Hoskisson. *Strategic Management: Competitiveness and Globalization* (2nd ed.). St. Paul: West Publishing Co.

1998

With B. W. Keats & S. DeMarie. Navigating in the New Competitive Landscape: Building Strategic Flexibility and Competitive Advantage in the 21st Century. *Academy of Management Executive, 12*(4), 22–42.

With J. S. Harrison, R. D. Ireland & A. Best. Attributes of Successful and Unsuccessful Acquisitions of U.S. Firms. *British Journal of Management, 9,* 91–114.

With R. Kochhar. Linking Corporate Strategy to Capital Structure: Diversification Strategy, Type and Source of Financing. *Strategic Management Journal, 19,* 601–610.

With J. Gimeno & R. E. Hoskisson. Current and Future Research Methods in Strategic Management. *Organizational Research Methods, 1,* 6–44.

Twenty-First Century Organizations: Business Firms, Business Schools and The Academy. *Academy of Management Review, 23,* 218–224.

With R. D.Nixon & J. E. Ricart. New Managerial Mindsets and Strategic Change in the New Frontier. In: M. A. Hitt, J. E. Ricart & R. D. Nixon (Eds), *New Managerial Mindsets: Organizational Transformation and Strategy Implementation* (pp. 1–12). Chichester, U.K.: John Wiley & Sons.

With J. E. Ricart & R. D. Nixon. The New Frontier. In: M. A. Hitt, R. E. Ricart & R. D. Nixon (Eds), *Managing Strategically in an Interconnected World* (pp. 1–12). Chichester, U.K.: John Wiley & Sons.

With J. E. Ricart & R. D. Nixon (Co-Editors). *New Managerial Mindsets: Organizational Transformation and Strategy Implementation.* Chichester, U.K.: John Wiley & Sons.

With J. E. Ricart & R. D.Nixon (Co-Editors). *Managing Strategically in an Interconnected World.* Chichester, U.K.: John Wiley & Sons.

1999

With A. J. Hillman. Corporate Political Strategy Formulation: A Model of Approach, Participation and Strategy Decisions. *Academy of Management Review, 24,* 825–842.

With R. E. Hoskisson, H. Kim & D. E. Thomas. Global Markets and the International Diversification of Firms: Motives and Outcomes. *Global Focus: An International Journal of Business, Economics and Social Policy, 11*(3), 1–11.

With R. E. Hoskisson, W. P. Wan & D. W. Yiu. Swings of a Pendulum: Theory and Research in Strategic Management. *Journal of Management, 25,* 417–456.

With R. D. Ireland. Achieving and Maintaining Strategic Competitiveness in the 21st Century: The Role of Strategic Leadership. *Academy of Management Executive, 13*(1), 43–57. Selected as the Best Paper published in AME in 1999.

With R. D.Nixon, R. E. Hoskisson & R. Kochhar. Corporate Entrepreneurship and Cross-Functional Fertilization: Activation, Process and Disintegration of a New Product Design Team. *Entrepreneurship Theory and Practice, 23,* 145–167.

With R. D. Nixon, P. G. Clifford & K. P. Coyne. The Development and Use of Strategic Resources. In: M. A. Hitt, P. G. Clifford, R. D. Nixon & K. P. Coyne (Eds), *Dynamic Strategic Resources: Development, Diffusion and Integration* (pp. 1–14). Chichester, U.K.: John Wiley & Sons.

With W. S. Sherman, B. W. Keats & S. M. DeMarie. Organizational Morphing: The Challenges of Leading Perpetually-changing Organizations in the Twenty-first Century. In: J. G. Hunt, G. E. Dodge & L. Wong (Eds), *Out-of-the-Box Leadership: Transforming the Twenty-first*

Century Army and Other Top Performing Organizations (pp. 43–62). Westport, CT: JAI Press.

With K. W. Artz & R. D. Ireland. International Expansion by Entrepreneurial Firms: Competitive Strategy, Core Competencies and Financial Performance. *Frontiers of Entrepreneurial Research*. Babson Park, MA: Babson College. 15–29. Kauffman Foundation Award for Best Paper.

With P. G. Clifford, R. D. Nixon & K. P. Coyne (Co-Editors). *Dynamic Strategic Resources: Development, Diffusion and Integration*. Chichester, U.K.: John Wiley & Sons.

With R. D. Ireland & R. E. Hoskisson. *Strategic Management: Competitiveness and Globalization* (3rd ed.). Cincinnati: ITP Southwestern Publishing Co.

2000

With R. D. Ireland & H. Lee. Technological Learning, Knowledge Management, Firm Growth and Performance. *Journal of Engineering and Technology Management, 17*, 231–246.

With S. M. DeMarie. Strategic Implications of the Information Age. *Journal of Labor Research, 21*, 419–429.

With S. A. Zahra & R. D. Ireland. International Expansion by New Venture Firms: International Diversity, Mode of Market Entry, Technological Learning and Performance. *Academy of Management Journal, 43*, 925–950. Selected as the Best Paper published in AMJ in 2000.

With S. A. Zahra, R. D. Ireland & I. Gutierrez. Privatization and Entrepreneurial Transformation: Emerging Issues and a Future Research Agenda. *Academy of Management Review, 25*, 509–524.

With M. T. Dacin, E. Levitas, J-L. Arregle & A. Borza. Partner Selection in Emerging and Developed Market Contexts: Resource-based and Organizational Learning Perspectives. *Academy of Management Journal*, 448–667.

The New Frontier: Transformation of Management for the New Millennium. *Organizational Dynamics, 28*, 6–17.

With J. L. Morrow, Jr. Rational and Political Models of Strategic Decision Making: Understanding the Role of Firm Performance and Stakeholder Political Pressure. In: G. J. Miller, J. Rabin & B. Hildreth (Eds), *Handbook of Strategic Management* (pp. 165–179). New York: Marcel Dekker.

With T. Reed. Entrepreneurship in the New Competitive Landscape. In: G. D.Meyer and K. Heppard (Eds), *Entrepreneurial Strategies* (pp. 23–47). Newbury Park, CA: Sage Publications.

With R. D. Ireland. The Intersection of Entrepreneurship and Strategic Management Research. In: D. Sexton & H. Lanstrom (Eds), *Handbook of Entrepreneurship* (pp. 45–63). Oxford, U.K.: Blackwell.

With R. Bresser, R. Nixon & D. Heuskel (Co-Editors). *Winning Strategies in a Deconstructing Environment*. Chichester, U.K.: John Wiley & Sons.

2001

With R. D. Ireland, S. M. Camp & D. L. Sexton. Strategic Entrepreneurship: Entrepreneurial Strategies for Creating Wealth. *Strategic Management Journal, 22*, special issue. 479–491.

With R. D. Ireland, S. M. Camp & D. L. Sexton. Integrating Entrepreneurship and Strategic Management Actions to Create Firm Wealth. *Academy of Management Executive, 15*(1). 49–63.

With L. Bierman, K. Shimizu & R. Kochhar. Direct and Moderating Effects of Human Capital on Strategy and Performance in Professional Service Firms: A Resource-Based Perspective. *Academy of Management Journal, 44,* 13–28.

With P. David & J. Gimeno. The Role of Activism by Institutional Investors in Influencing R&D. *Academy of Management Journal, 44,* 144–157.

With R. D. Ireland & J. S. Harrison, Mergers and Acquisitions: A Value Creating or Value Destroying Strategy? In: M. A. Hitt, E. Freeman and J. S. Harrison (Eds), *Handbook of Strategic Management* (pp. 384–408). Oxford, U.K.: Blackwell.

Mastering the Intellectual Challenge of Conducting International Research. In: B. Toyne, A. Martinez & R. Menger (Eds), *Mastering the International Research Dimension for Business Scholars.* New York: Quorum Books.

With E. Freeman & J. S. Harrison (Co-Editors). *Handbook of Strategic Management.* Oxford, U.K.: Blackwell Publishers.

With J. S. Harrison & R. D. Ireland. *Mergers and Acquisitions: A Guide to Creating Value for Stakeholders.* New York: Oxford University Press.

With R. D. Ireland & R. E. Hoskisson. *Strategic Management: Competitiveness and Globalization* (4th ed.). Cincinnati: ITP Southwestern Publishing Co.

2002

With R. E. Hoskisson, R. A. Johnson & W. Grossman. Conflicting Voices: The Effects of Institutional Ownership Heterogeneity and Internal Governance on Corporate Innovation Strategies. *Academy of Management Journal,* in press.

With K. Uhlenbruck & K. Meyer. Organizational Transformation in Transition Economies: Resource-Based and Organizational Learning Perspectives. *Journal of Management Studies,* in press.

With R. D. Ireland & D. Vaidyanath. Managing Strategic Alliances to Achieve a Competitive Advantage. *Journal of Management,* in press.

With J. S. Harrison, R E. Hoskisson & R. D.Ireland. Resource Complementarity in Business Combinations: Extending the Logic to Organizational Alliances. *Journal of Management,* in press.

With R. Amit, C. Lucier & R. D. Nixon. Strategies for the Entrepreneurial Millennium. In: M. A. Hitt, R. Amit, C. Lucier & R. D. Nixon (Eds), *Creating Value: Winners in the New Business Environment.* Oxford, U.K.: Blackwell Publishers, in press.

With R. D. Ireland, S. M. Camp & D. L. Sexton. Strategic Entrepreneurship: Integrating Entrepreneurial and Strategic Management Perspectives. In: M. A. Hitt, R. D. Ireland, S. M. Camp & D. L. Sexton (Eds), *Strategic Entrepreneurship: Creating New Integrated Mindset.* Oxford, U.K.: Blackwell Publishers, in press.

With R. Amit, C. Lucier & R. D. Nixon (Co-Editors). *Creating Value: Winners in the New Business Environment.* Oxford, U.K.: Blackwell Publishers, in press.

With R. D.Ireland, S. M. Camp & D. L. Sexton (Co-Editors). *Strategic Entrepreneurship: Creating a New Integrated Mindset.* Oxford, U.K.: Blackwell Publishers, in press.

Jerry Hunt

BORN TO BE AN EDITOR: TALES OF A RIGHT BRAIN, DEFROCKED ENGINEER

James G. (Jerry) Hunt

As I look back at my earlier years, four stories set the tone for my career and life. When I was five, I had a second bout with pneumonia that almost did me in. This bout, following an earlier attack when I was 18 months old, was in both lungs, before Sulfa or antibiotics, in general, were developed. I was put in an oxygen tent and I can well believe I almost cashed it in, given the seriousness of this disease to this very day. This was the bad news. The good news was that I survived. I remember being in my hospital room and a maroon pedal car I received as a gift. I believe it was a 1937 or 1938 Chrysler Airflow replica, actually. As an aside, the full-size car had one of the ugliest designs ever created. At the same time, the design was among the most advanced. Regardless, as a five-year old, I was excited beyond wonder at the car, my parents' visits, and all the attention I remember the nurses lavishing upon me. For me, then, this was a bad news, good news, worst of times and best of times scenario.

Now let's move along to my earliest college years at Michigan College of Mining and Technology in the far North nuzzled against the Canadian border and some 600 miles from downstate Detroit. Although the college still had "mining" as part of its title, it had other strong programs, including mechanical engineering, of which automotive engineering was of special interest to me. Perhaps my interest stemmed from receiving a pedal car in the hospital. Regardless, I was so interested in cars, especially car body design, that my high school yearbook predicted that I would become an automotive tycoon.

Management Laureates, Volume 6, pages 161–198.
Copyright © 2002 by Elsevier Science Ltd.
All rights of reproduction in any form reserved.
ISBN: 0-7623-0487-1

All of this leads up to my second story and the first of what some might euphemistically call "character building". Besides the solid technical education I received, this story epitomized Michigan Tech experiences for me and set the tone for much in my life that followed. Picture if you will, a technical drawing course. Nowadays, this course would be taught with personal computers – then we used special, high-quality paper and India ink. This course became increasingly sophisticated and demanding throughout my entire freshman year. The course called for using a special pen with two steel nibs, that could widen or narrow with a small thumbscrew. The width determined the thickness of the lines in a drawing. The space between the nibs was filled with India ink. Lettering was done with another pen that was also used with India ink.

As you might imagine, both drawing and lettering were prone to catching large drops of misplaced ink. And, of course, these ink blots tended to come very close to completion of a drawing, done with additional carefully crafted drafting instruments. For these drawings, regardless of complexity, all lines were to be of uniform width and when intersecting were required to touch without overlapping or leaving a space, no matter how small. Some readers may remember the days of Saturday morning classes and, quite often, I had one. Thus, it was common for me to spend Friday nights completing an assigned drawing.

Then, off I would go to an early Saturday class. Of course, as I remember it, the class was always at 8 A.M. Quite often the drawing instructor would be sitting on a high drafting school and would give our work an initial evaluation as we turned it in. And, the instructor always looked for the kinds of things previously mentioned, especially ink blots that had been scraped off using a razor blade. I thought, momentarily, that I was quite proficient in scraping with such a blade. That is until my first contact with the drawing instructor. All the while, as the drawings were being turned in, the instructor was circling various offenses in red, writing short red notes, and marking –2.5, or –5 or even –10% wherever he discovered uneven lines, ink blots, lines that did not match, and lettering that was not to his liking. Thus, I too often faced an initial score of 75 or so, for a long Friday night's work, where 78 to 86 was required for a C.

A third story, that even a silver stake will not kill, involves the grading system used for physics and related analytical mechanics examinations, of which there were too many or not enough, depending on one's viewpoint. Regardless, these were multiple choice exams, but with a couple of twists. First, to discourage guessing, they were scored right minus wrong. Along with this, the test designers had diabolically included a number of wrong answers that looked right, if test takers did not really know what the course involved. Exams typically were 20 questions, and the class median out of 20 was a middle C. The first of these I took had a class average of 4 or 5. As I remember, I received something like a minus one. I could have done better by missing the exam. You better believe exams such as these had a big impact on me.

A final story, involving a couple of separate but related activities, took place in our machine shop courses. Along with drawing, and various heavy-duty chemistry, physics and mathematics courses, we spent two or three quarters in a machine shop. These courses, believe it or not, required a stint in a blacksmith shop. These stints included bellows, red-hot metal, and everything but a spreading chestnut tree. The shop was run by an old (he really was) blacksmith. We were assigned to make chain links and other related projects out of red-hot metal. Of course, if the temperature was too hot or too cold, the links would either burn or not be welded together where they were supposed to be. The old smithie would let each of us flounder for an appropriate length of time, by his reckoning, and then when we were not looking, or sometimes even when we were, he would drop off completed links, which we would turn in for a grade. I understand he retired shortly after I left and the smithing activities were no more.

Accompanying these smithing activities, but in another part of the machine shop, was the "block squaring" project. It consisted of a cast iron block that had been rough cast and was far from square. Our job was to smooth and square it using a hammer, a chisel, a file, and an L-shaped square – and do it within specifications. This time there was no smithing fairy – we were on our own. If the block got too small from chiseling and filing, then we received a new block, started the process again and, of course, our grade suffered. Ultimately, we turned in an acceptable block and moved on to another project.

How might we interpret these experiences and their impact on me? They indeed were "character building" and reinforced dormant characteristics that sometimes had earlier emerged and would re-emerge again. My interest in cars and car design was one side of these experiences. The other side is reflected in the old saying, "That which does not kill you, strengthens you", and I believe that was the case with me. Am I a better person, I am unsure but I certainly have a much better appreciation for the high skills and hard work required of our blue-collar workers, and I learned perseverance, as I believe this essay will demonstrate. Also, for better or worse, I picked up or had reinforced the philosophy of "no pain, no gain".

Interestingly, lest one think I did not complete my undergraduate degree or barely graduated, I ended up graduating with "Honors" and was in the upper third of my class. As this essay also will show, however, I was not really cut out to be an engineer and, thus, defrocked myself fairly early and switched careers. Nevertheless, the discipline required in engineering and way of approaching problems continue to have a deep impact on me to this very day, in spite of my strong right-brain orientation. As a final note, casual conversations with engineering students, or recent graduates, suggest that they resonate with these stories and could tell similar tales of their own.

GROWING UP

I was born in Aurora, a suburb of Denver on Groundhog's Day, February 2, 1932, at Fitzsimmons Army Hospital. My father was a career Army non-commissioned officer. Except for being sick a lot, my childhood was pretty typical for that time. The Great Depression loomed large, but my family felt it less than many.

When I was eight, my life suddenly changed – we began the first of many family moves. I was, indeed, an "Army Brat". So, I attended a succession of schools in Texas, California, Missouri (twice), Colorado (between various moves), and Oregon, before settling down for three years in Washington state during my junior high years, and then three years in Kentucky while in high school.

My clearest memories are of my junior high years at Ft. Lewis, Washington and high school years at Ft. Knox, Kentucky. I remember becoming much more mature during my junior-high years. I became an Eagle Scout and student body president and was interested in track and football. Because of an early growth spurt I did well in both, though it was only sandlot football. All along, I maintained my interest in cars, mostly body design, and for three years competed and did well in a design contest sponsored by General Motor's Fisher Body Division. My high-school years were logical continuations, where once again I spent a lot of time thinking about car design. And I was class president for three years. I was also very influenced, as were many students, by my high school English instructor and activities teacher, Miss Jasper Schlinker.

All along, it was my parents' expectation that I would go to college. This was one of their supreme gifts to me. As I look back, I am more and more impressed by this driving force – it was not whether I would go, but where and what I would study. In some families, with a history of college education, this strong encouragement would be natural. Here, neither parent had this experience. I was the first generation of our immediate family to attend college, and my younger sister, Phyllis, followed afterwards.

A key question in all this was how my interest in cars would play out. I did not have a car of my own but was in car heaven with my father's 1949 and 1950 Fords – breakthrough post war designs if there ever were. I doodled car pictures constantly in class – yet besides my writing and social science classes, which were of special interest, I took engineering and natural science-oriented classes. These involved physics, mathematics, biology and the like, but were all offered at a small high school with limited course specialization and not much career counseling. In hindsight, what I might have done was taken more right brain-oriented courses and considered attending a design school for an advanced degree. Whether I would have been admitted, of course, will never be known.

Be this as it may, I qualified for a number of engineering schools. I decided on Michigan Tech because its automotive engineering option was part of a BS in mechanical engineering, it was in Michigan, the center of the 1950s car universe, and I could express my independence from my parents by being away from home. As it turned out, my father was almost shipped to Korea near the beginning of that "police action", narrowly missing being in a unit where virtually everyone was killed. Shortly thereafter, however, he was shipped to Germany. In the meantime, I had enrolled at Michigan Tech and stayed until graduation in 1954.

As previously mentioned, besides the strong education I received in engineering and science-based subjects at Michigan Tech, I picked up a way of thinking that remains with me for better or worse. In addition to technical courses, and need it be said, the storied ones that had such an impact on my future, I got a strong dose of English and a reasonable dose of the social sciences. I also had the opportunity to take elective courses in business and management, which were part of a fifth-year engineering administration offering. I did not take the offering, and had room only for a limited number of courses, but this option might well be considered a precursor to today's techno MBA programs.

At any rate, I took as many non-engineering courses as possible and otherwise prepared for an entry-level position with one of the Big 3 U.S. car firms. I chose a job with what was called the "power development department" of the General Motors Pontiac Motor Division. My key duties were to help design engine components and test cars with different components for performance, fuel economy, and the like.

These duties were a long way from body design and right-brain thinking, but were exciting because of their testing ground aspects. Once this excitement had worn off, which took a while, it became more and more obvious that designing engine components was not a long-term career for me. I began to wonder about going back to school for graduate study in business or management. I also flirted briefly with attending design school, but had no portfolio or related materials. With career counseling and interest tests beyond those in my small high school, I finally opted to consider an MBA or industrial relations program.

In the meantime, I had met my future wife Donna Rose, while participating in a church group and another social group that had an overlap in membership. She became a crucial partner in my decision making and together we chose the University of Illinois at Urbana-Champaign, where I would study for an MA degree.

GRADUATE SCHOOL (1956–1957, 1961–1966)

Whereas moving to the University of Illinois Institute of Labor and Industrial Relations was a big step for me, it was a bigger move yet for Donna. She had just turned 19 and had lived all her life in Detroit in the same house. She was, indeed, adventuresome and her administrative and secretarial skills helped me through graduate school and have remained very handy to this day.

Actually, as I look back at it, the move was probably bigger than I anticipated. I had a new bride and was enrolled in a demanding graduate program in a world-class university that was, by choice, largely different from my undergraduate program. I was very apprehensive, especially once we actually moved into our Champaign apartment. Things went well, however, and I particularly enjoyed writing the many required papers. Interestingly, and perhaps surprising to some, I had also written lots of papers in engineering school. Many were, of course, technical – but not all. Again, my right brain was allowed to function. I suspect that with current engineering school demands, such functioning and the number of "soft" electives would be far less, or maybe even non-existent.

The MA program took nine months plus, what now might be called a summer internship, where I worked for a division of Stewart-Warner in Chicago. My job involved a low-level production activity in which I was in contact with workers as I was preparing a "Plan B" paper in lieu of a master's thesis. Building on an in-depth study by the sociologist, Ely Chinoy, I was studying the extent to which the workers in my department saw the American Dream (of getting ahead) operating for them. I didn't simply interview them, I did the interviews as part of my production job, where I moved around the department working on various assignments. The job was a real eye-opener, as once again I was exposed to blue-collar work, this time of a low-skilled variety. Not surprisingly, few of the workers saw the American Dream as real.

Donna and I spent our first anniversary moving back to Detroit, where we stayed temporarily with her parents, while I wrote my Plan B paper, replete with a literature review and all the other accouterments of a comprehensive research report. While in Detroit, I looked for an HR/IR position. Also, while there, our first born, a son named Doug, was born literally when I was in Champaign taking the required exam on my completed paper.

Ultimately, I obtained a position with the Michigan Limestone Division of what was then United States Steel. That job, where I again wrote a number of reports, worked on policy manuals and the like, and engaged in much soul searching, whetted my appetite for seriously considering college teaching as a career. Again, Donna was ready. Of course, to really be a college or university professor one needs a Ph.D. The opportunity, however, came up to be an instructor at a, you guessed it, small engineering school. This time in West Virginia at West Virginia Institute of Technology, which had a separate business administration division that bordered on being a small college or large department, replete with a division head. A key difference here, as compared with my undergraduate experience, was that the course offerings were much more extensive and several undergraduate business degrees were offered.

This seemed like a good entry-level job. Donna and I thought I should give it a try and if I liked it, go back for a doctorate and prepare for a long-term career. West Virginia Tech is located in Montgomery, then and now a really, really small town about 30 miles southeast of Charleston and nestled in a smog-infested valley. Because of my work, I didn't mind it as much as Donna did, tending a very young child. But this was not the highpoint of our lives.

I found the work to be challenging. By today's standards, the teaching load was quite heavy – five classes, typically with five preparations each semester – but I did not know the difference. Some of the subjects I taught I had never taken. Over the three years I was there, I taught 13 different courses, in addition to being chair of a one-person department, advising students and serving as advisor to a couple of student organizations. For me, it was an adventure and certainly kept me off the streets at night. For Donna with young Doug, it was less enjoyable and not the least bit adventuresome.

One of the very important things I did, at least for me, was to revise the Tech curriculum for the undergraduate business program. The opportunity came when the well known Gordon and Howell (1959) and Pierson (1959) reports were published with recommendations for strengthening business school programs.

Both reports recommended a very thorough keelhauling and the inclusion of behavioral science and quantitative requirements for the curricula thus envisioned. I was asked by Reed Davis, division head, to undertake a project to make recommendations for what should be done at West Virginia Tech. I may have suggested it, or it may have been his idea, but I was instructed to get the project done – not as a committee member or a committee chair, but me personally. This was an advantage or disadvantage, depending on one's viewpoint, of a small school such as West Virginia Tech. I left before the recommendations were implemented, but I understand most of them were, and they were substantial. So far, my research efforts beyond earlier engineering reports had been modest, but I was certainly getting heavy exposure to writing, documentation, and to some important projects.

After three years at West Virginia Tech, Donna and I were convinced that "professoring" was worth pursuing, so it was back to graduate school. Once again we considered a number of options. The University of Illinois business school, however, had just introduced a new curriculum that looked as if it reflected the kinds of new wave b-school changes on which I had been working. I was especially excited and was encouraged by Earl Planty, one of my former professors. So, once again, we were off to Urbana-Champaign.

I found a split faculty. What I had originally heard about the U. of I. business school's embracement of the new-wave recommendations included in the Gordon and Howell and Pierson reports was true, as far as it went. I did not realize, however, the full significance of the split faculty. Superimposed on top of the traditional Ph.D. in Business program was a new DBA program staffed by young, hotshot professors with elite business degrees. Many had just completed their own programs, with all the new emphases.

I found the new curriculum interesting and challenging, moving through the coursework pretty quickly. Like many students, however, I got hung up on my dissertation. I flayed around with three or four topics and finally developed a leadership proposal. Given the breadth of the DBA program, it might almost have been in any number of areas. Since then, of course, the U of I and most other graduate business schools have become more specialized.

Regardless, when I defended my dissertation proposal, the new young faculty members, virtually none of whom I had had for class, made mincemeat of my proposal and of me. Nor did I get one-on-one encouragement from anyone but my chair, who unfortunately for me was unable to fend off faculty colleagues who smelled blood. I had flashbacks of the stories spun at the beginning of this essay, but this time the stakes were higher.

I faced a real dilemma. It was clear that, by and large, the faculty did not value the kind of research I was proposing, or at least the way I proposed it. I debated dropping out, but Donna and I had a lot invested and the perseverance part of my personality was activated, even though I was perhaps violating the sunk cost doctrine so dear to decision theorists.

I decided to investigate switching into the traditional five-field Ph.D. in Business program that had not yet been dislodged by the new DBA. I was able to obtain credit for much of my previous work, but had to take some additional courses in economics, political science, and psychology. The big stumbling block, aside from the ever-present dissertation requirement, was that two languages were required – typically French and German. I struggled with German, but squeezed out a "B" in the second semester and fulfilled that requirement. French was easier for me, and I passed the departmental exam by translating material about the "Father of Scientific Management", Frederick Taylor.

With these two language barriers out of the way, my former dissertation chair, Joe Litterer, who was on the faculty of both the new and old doctoral programs, recommended I do leadership work with Fred Fiedler in psychology. I did not have to shift gears too far to prepare a leadership proposal to test Fred's new leadership contingency model. He hired me to work in his group effectiveness research laboratory as a part-time research associate and the rest, as they say, is history.

In this case, the history was that I tested Fred's new model in a number of organizations across Illinois. Between being a part-time lecturer (in the business school, after doing a similar stint at Millikin University in close-by Decatur) and research associate (in psychology), however, I got paid relatively well and was able to complete the extra coursework, take my comprehensive examinations, and line up data sources after having my proposal readily approved. "Even a blind pig can stumble on an acorn", or however the saying goes.

At any rate, I spent about a year lining up my subject samples and about another year on data analysis and writing. All told, with the switch and extra work, plus the dissertation, it took me about five years to get my degree. Of course I couldn't have done it without the above-mentioned financial support and strong psychological support from Donna, my parents, and my in-laws. We now had Holly, a younger sister for Doug.

Additionally, I considered Joe Litterer and Fred Fiedler to be mentors. Joe spent many hours working with me on various dissertation chapters. I can still hear his response to my query on how I was doing – "You are inching along". And Fred helped instill real research norms, which were common in psychology, but far less so in business schools at that time. Both Joe and Fred also helped me line up research samples for my dissertation.

Working with the psychology doctoral students in Fred's lab was a real eye-opener for me. Many of these students, such as Doyle Bishop, Milt Blood, Marty Chemers, Richard Hackman, and others, including later ones such as Dan Ilgen, have gone on to distinguished careers. I was impressed just being around students such as these and I received critical help from some of them.

My stint in psychology changed me forever. Both Fiedler and his students gave me my first real taste of behavioral research. In addition to my dissertation, Fred helped me in conducting some pilot work with a laboratory experiment, a later version was ultimately published in *Administrative Science Quarterly* (*ASQ*). He didn't have to do any of this. With my lack of background in psychology, I would have been easy to reject. Rather than rejection, however, Fred encouraged me and changed me more than he knew. At that time, the U. of I. College of Commerce and Business Administration, and I suspect most other b-schools, simply did not provide comparable training. That is hard to believe today with so many strong b-school Ph.D. programs, but it was true in the early and mid-1960s.

Fiedler was extremely imaginative (the story was that he once spun a theory out of random numbers represented to him as real data) and a master writer. He also was a master at obtaining grants. He was both gruff and supportive at the same time. All these things made him a role model. Another extremely important contribution Fred made to my development was his telling me about the "after dinner test". He did this upon reading my write up of a paper based on my dissertation. After he mentioned the test, it was obvious that the paper had not passed it. Here, the argument is that most scholars, and others as well, tend to read articles after dinner, unless there is some compelling reason to do otherwise. The writer needs to grab the reader with a paper's title and first paragraph or two, or the reader loses interest and many even doze off. Likewise, a journal reviewer starts looking for reasons to reject a paper, rather than recommend its acceptance.

Two final points come to mind, one is the longevity of Fred's research and, borrowing the notion from Art Bedeian, I can say that Fiedler is into his seventh decade of research. Second is his mentoring of students so many of whom have gone on to successful research careers of their own.

Joe Litterer shared Fiedler's proclivity for clear writing – making difficult things appear easier than they are. Both also wrote interestingly and creatively. I was especially impressed with Joe because he was a former engineer – defrocked if you will. He also pushed me to clearer writing in my dissertation. Furthermore, he encouraged me greatly by inviting me to work on a book with him, which unfortunately never materialized. I can imagine it would have been a real pleasure working with Joe. During the later years of his life, we would make it a practice to share a breakfast at the annual Academy of Management meeting. We always had healthy discussions and he was always complimentary of my work.

As I noted earlier, it took me more than two years to complete my dissertation, closer to three if one includes my false starts before I switched programs. Of course, between the teaching and research positions I held, I was working nearly full time. Nevertheless, students who take a long time with their dissertation often are considered a little "slow" and the conventional wisdom is that they will likely not finish their degree. With my inauspicious dissertation start, were I an outsider, my bet would have been that I was someone in danger of not finishing. Ultimately, I defied conventional wisdom, and further upset the odds with five pretty quick publications from my dissertation. Needless to say, this helped launch my career.

SOUTHERN ILLINOIS UNIVERSITY AT CARBONDALE (1966–1981)

At the time I graduated, 1966, higher education was on the move. More and more students were enrolling in college and many institutions were undergoing very rapid growth. It was a "golden age" for higher education. Indeed, a number of former teachers' colleges and the like were becoming "universities". Whereas many of these had changed in name only, there was a university downstate in Carbondale that was undergoing an in-depth transformation – Southern Illinois University. I had heard rumors about this transformation and was able to obtain additional information from the Academy of Management Placement Office and preliminary information by mail and phone previous to an on-site visit.

Actually, the transformation included becoming a system with two branches and a medical school with campuses in Springfield and Carbondale. SIU was really on the move with a truly charismatic president and a key state legislator as a supporter – between the two, the SIU system was being provided increased funding from a high per capita income state. SIU was one of a relatively small number of universities that had the potential to become a major player, even given the world-class University of Illinois to the north.

The SIU business school appeared equally promising. The SIU management department, which would be my home, had a well-known scholar, Fremont ("Bud") Schull as department chair and the business school had a charismatic dean, Robert Hill. Both Bud and Bob were expecting to start a doctoral program, it seemed, almost as we spoke. All of this, and the natural attractions of the area with its lakes, forests, gently rolling hills, and mild winters, made SIU an easy sell for my family and me.

As it turned out, the potential was only partly realized and remains so to this day. For those who question whether or not leadership matters, SIU provides all the proof I need that it can have a big impact for good or ill. Although the charismatic university president remained for several years, the business school dean departed shortly after I came, the department chair also moved out of that position and a series of interim deans followed. The doctoral program became a will-o-the-wisp. I was becoming disenchanted.

Even so, the SIU business school was a good place to work and provided good travel and other support, and the teaching load was relatively light. I immediately began looking for research-oriented colleagues and, as with my earlier stint at U of I, discovered a strong research orientation in the psychology department, where there were faculty and Ph.D. students, some of whom were oriented toward industrial/organizational psychology and organizational behavior topics. I soon made contacts in psychology, in particular with Jim Hill who had just come to SIU as an assistant professor from Detroit, Michigan and who had a strong background in industry before receiving his Ph.D. in Industrial/Organizational Psychology from Wayne State University.

I also began writing grant proposals to follow up on some of the leadership work I had been doing at U. of I. Support facilities at SIU for grant seeking were just emerging, but I got enough support to obtain a three-year National Institute of Mental Health (NIMH) grant to study leadership in mental health organizations. At that time such organizations were undergoing transformation in many states, including Illinois. They were moving from custodial to much more open and supportive institutions, and many people who once would have been institutionalized were now exposed to very different treatment. All this had interesting leadership implications.

In the meantime, I was publishing off my dissertation and it was here that Fiedler's after dinner test became especially salient. My major dissertation publication went into *Organizational Behavior and Human Performance*, with other publications appearing in more practitioner-oriented outlets and a meeting proceedings. As was usual at the time, these were reprinted in various books of readings.

This work also laid the groundwork for my NIMH grant. At the same time, I was interested in doing some follow-up work to a lab study I had initiated while at Fiedler's lab. I was invited to a month-long Ford Foundation summer workshop at the University of California at Berkeley to develop this work further, and it ultimately led to my conducting a lab study at SIU in which the impact of leadership at two different organizational levels was investigated. That study was published in ASQ in 1971.

During this same period, Jim Hill and I began gathering multiple level leadership and related data in the Illinois mental health system. These works, along with other materials, culminated in my 1991 book, *Leadership: A New Synthesis*. This book reconceptualized leadership based on extensions of Elliott Jacque's work (1989) on organizational and leader complexity. Among other things, *New Synthesis* integrated current leadership, organizational and cultural aspects with demands at different hierarchical levels. Occasionally during this early career period, I also published other work on such topics as status congruence and motivation. Clearly, however, my major impetus was on leadership, as it has remained throughout my career.

In 1971 two events occurred that were especially important to me. The first involved obtaining funding from SIU to hold a leadership symposium as a part of the University's centennial celebration. The second was the hiring of Dick Osborn as an assistant professor out of Kent State's doctoral program. Such programs were reflections of the golden age for b-schools mentioned earlier. Dick and I spent a number of exciting years collaborating on a range of articles and projects.

The leadership symposium was originally conceived at a Midwest Academy of Management meeting in 1970 or so. I was talking with Paul Hersey and Ken Blanchard after a paper session. One thing led to another and we wondered why there could not be entire meetings devoted to leadership research – certainly not an original idea now, but an innovative notion at the time. That idea might have gone the way of many such ideas and sunk without a trace were it not for the funds provided as part of SIU's centennial celebration. I was able to put together a proposal that included funding for the symposium and also involved the Southern Illinois University Press as the publisher for a book based on the symposium. Thus were my editorial duties born and a previously unidentified passion for editing released.

The hiring of Dick Osborn took place at about the same time as the centennial symposium. He was in for a campus interview and, among other things, we discussed the upcoming symposium. Ultimately, the decision was made to offer him a job, he accepted, and I acquired a soul mate. Indeed, for the better part of the ten years we were colleagues, it was a glorious time for the two of us.

In terms of what shortly became the first of seven biennial symposia, I collaborated with a well-known figure – Ed Fleishman. Through his many contacts, Ed, helped attract people to the initial leadership symposium, which was held on the SIU campus. He then played a major role in the editing of the initial symposium volume, which we were determined would, indeed, be a book and not merely a proceedings. I learned much from Ed about putting on such events and even more about compiling and editing books. Given his stature and his professional contributions, it seemed fitting that he should be the senior editor. So Volume 1, of what turned out to be the Leadership Symposia Series, was a Fleishman and Hunt production.

In addition to papers by Fred Fiedler, Bob House, and a number of others, there were very strong commentaries by such noted contributors as Martin

Evans. Fleishman had a piece pulling together early Ohio State research, and Jim Hill and I had a piece examining leadership at different hierarchical levels, based on our early mental health grant research. Whereas books such as this are normally not large sellers, this volume sold out quickly and the SIU Press and I were happy. It seemed to have met a pent-up demand and pulled together some important areas of leadership research, including Bob House's path-goal leadership model.

Buoyed by the success of this first symposium, we (this time a small organizing committee and I) began to consider a second. Given the efforts involved in putting the first symposium together, and associated book editing, it looked like annual symposia would not be feasible (even if the leadership field developed that fast), so biennial symposia would be the way to go. Of course, with centennial funding no longer available, underwriting became a question. Fortuitously, in a visit I made to the Office of Naval Research to ask about other research funding, I stuck partial pay dirt. I was unable to get research funding for my initial interest, but was able to obtain some ONR funding through a special arrangement it had for conferences and symposia with the Smithsonian Institution. I was excited about having ONR and, especially, the prestigious Smithsonian involved with a second leadership symposium. That funding, together with a small amount from SIU and registration fees would provide the support we needed. Again, the SIU Press was on board and we were better organized to get a book out more quickly than Volume 1 of the symposium series, which did not come out until 1973.

The second symposium, "Contingency Approaches to Leadership", was held in 1973, and focused on extending approaches to contingency leadership, first explicitly labeled as such by Fiedler in his book, *A Theory of Leadership Effectiveness*, published in 1964. The symposium included papers by Bernie Bass and Enzo Valenzi, George Farris, and James Taylor, among others, and once again contained strong, well- constructed commentaries. A symposium volume of the same title was released in 1974. The volume was edited by Lars L. Larson with me as first editor. Lars was a recently hired SIU assistant professor in our department. Unlike Dick Osborn's macro background, Lars's training was similar to mine. He obtained his doctorate at U. of I. after its two doctoral programs in business were merged. Indeed, he may well have been one of the earlier graduates of that revamped degree program.

Once again, feedback suggested that the symposium was a success and we were encouraged to have another. I successfully tapped our previous funding agencies and also was able to obtain funding from the Army Research Institute (ARI). Thus, plans were put in place for a third symposium, "Leadership Frontiers". This time, the volume reporting the symposium was published by the Comparative Administration Research Institute and the Kent State University Press. A serendipitous feature was that Lars and I edited a special issue of *Organization and Administrative Science*, which also published the symposium's papers and commentaries. This was a reflection of the aggressiveness of the Kent State business school and our networking with Anant Negandhi, a well-known Kent State scholar.

The symposia were repeated on a biennial basis through 1985, with the last symposium volume published in 1988. Symposium volumes were all similar in their emphasis on cutting edge and off-beat leadership topics and a who's who of leadership authors. The editors varied somewhat, with me as a constant across the years. The most ambitious leadership symposium was held in 1982 at the Oxford Management Centre (now Templeton) in the United Kingdom, where Rosemary Stewart was a crucial player.

Again, there was a question about a book publisher and the choice, Pergamon, came about as we were visiting the renowned publisher, Robert Maxwell at his estate near Oxford. In chatting with Maxwell, I mentioned we did not yet have a publisher and he immediately volunteered. We later ran into some problems getting this arrangement implemented in the United States, because it was so informal. Once the word was out through the Pergamon bureaucracy, however, the name "Robert Maxwell" had an almost magical effect.

The 1985 leadership symposium was held at Lubbock after I moved to Texas Tech as Area Coordinator of Management. By then, however, I was getting tired of producing symposium volumes, even though there were co-editors and we split the work. I found the symposia wearing me down even with my strong editing tendencies. So after the 1985 symposium, and the 1988 symposium volume, *Emerging Leadership Vistas*, I decided I would take a sabbatical from hosting the biennial symposia.

Although I have not formally resurrected the symposium series per se, I have since been involved with variations on the series As an example, over more recent years, I have been involved in editing three leadership volumes with military themes, stronger in some volumes than others. These were published in 1985, 1992 and 1999, and with the exception of me, involved different co-editors. All these books had military support from the Army Research Institute, as well as a potpourri of other sources. As a whole, these volumes, in spite of their military heritage, were remarkably similar in spirit to those in the leadership symposia series. Most recently, another variation was conducted at the University of Mississippi as a part of my senior editor duties with *The Leadership Quarterly*'s Yearly Review of Leadership.

Also, during this period, serving on editorial review boards for such journals as the *Academy of Management Review* reinforced my editorial and writing focus. I still continue on some of these boards today and also do a fair amount of ad hoc reviewing.

At the same time as the leadership symposum series was developing, Dick Osborn and I picked up steam on our collaborative endeavors. Our research continued my leadership at multiple-levels work and extended into Dick's macro-organizational environment and structure forte. He also was involved in the final report which we prepared for NIMH. At about this time also, we extended the notion of discretionary leadership first suggested as "incremental influence" by Katz and Kahn (1978). That idea served as the basis for an Army Research Institute grant to test an approach we dubbed the "Multiple Influence Model of Leadership". Its precursor was our "Adaptive-Reactive Theory of Leadership" proposed in 1975. These approaches combined macro/micro and what would now be termed "meso" notions of leadership. They were accompanied by other related work throughout the late 1970s and 1981, when I left for Texas Tech, shortly after Dick left for the Battelle Institute in Seattle.

In 1980, I also spent a semester at the University of Aston in Birmingham, U.K., home of the renowned Aston studies. I was drawn there by John Child, but ended up working with Dian-Marie Hosking, on extensions to the Multiple Influence model. Although Dick and I had published scholarly chapters covering the model, we were unable to get the model accepted, as such, in a mainstream journal. A major reason, we suspect, for this was its emphasis on both micro and macro aspects, for which we typically got attacked by reviewers from both camps. I now think we were not persistent enough in continuing to push the model. Dick had departed for Seattle and I to Texas Tech, and apart from some conceptual treatment of the model, we let it drop, instead of championing it more aggressively.

Textbook Writing

In the late 1970s, Dick Osborn and I decided to try our hand at an organization theory (OT) text that blended macro with micro or organization theory with organization 21 behavior concepts. We thought the fields were converging, or at least should be converging, and this book would both reflect and help that convergence. Ultimately, John Wiley & Sons agreed to publish the book and it turned out to be such a major effort that we brought in our SIU colleague, Larry Jauch, as a third author. On the book's final revision we agreed with our Wiley editor to place less emphasis on micro material. The book was still an attempt at mating OT and OB, but did not go as far. It was a book with a message – that of blending the two areas in a systematic way. Actually, it was a risk for Wiley to publish. To few peoples' surprise, it did not sell a lot of copies, although another publisher later republished it. Regardless of its commercial success, or lack thereof, I believe this book reflects some of our best work. It included the Multiple Influence Model of Leadership and other related scholarly notions dear to our collective hearts.

Our OT/OB book was published in 1980. Shortly after, we became involved with a book that was much more student oriented. It was perhaps the first of the new-wave OB texts, with numerous examples and highly readable text. Dick and I co-authored the book with John Schermerhorn (then at SIU), a master at assessing the market and writing appropriately. The book has done well and we are now starting its eighth edition. I am pleased with it, but in a different way than our earlier OT book. Once again, Wiley was the publisher.

Hot Groups

I look back on my years at SIU with pleasure. Much of the time I was there we had what is now called a "hot group". Harold Leavitt describes groups as "hot" when they are "totally consuming places" (Leavitt, 1996, p. 289). In addition to teaching, our group was totally consumed with a steady outpouring of conference papers and proceedings, journal articles and special issues, book chapters, and books – both edited symposium volumes and texts. There also was a high level of professional activity and the beginnings of international contacts. Over the time I was at SIU, Jim Hill, Larry Jauch, Lars Larson, Tom Martin, John Schermerhorn and Uma Sekaran worked with Dick Osborn and me, and very frequently with each other.

This hot group also included ties with such international scholars as Peter Dachler, Dian Hosking, Timo Santalainen and Rosemary Stewart, as well as such domestic colleagues as Chet Schriesheim, now an eminent scholar and then just starting to come into his own. There also were a number of psychology doctoral and even business master's students involved, which included: Paul Duffy, Chris Liebscher, Harry Martin, Preston Newell, Joel Reaser, David Skaret, and Gary Yunker. These students have gone on to successful careers in business, academia and consulting and helped make our group the "hot" one that it was, even for such a short time in the grand scheme of things.

But all good things must come to an end and the magic went away – the group dissipated. Several members left, the students graduated and the magic was no more. I have occasionally thought about why the magic occurred and why it no longer exists. On its face, this question appears to provide an easy topic to analyze, but it seems more like the genie in the bottle – once it's out, analysis can't put it back in.

ONWARD TO TEXAS TECH (1981 – PRESENT)

As I mentioned earlier, SIU treated me well. Donna received a bachelor's degree from SIU, of which I am very proud. It took her many years going part time while our children were growing up. Our daughter, Robin, joined the family in 1967. Even so, I would periodically get restless while at SIU and would take a leave or sabbatical or sniff the employment winds. Finally a position at Texas Tech beckoned. In a short childhood stint at Ft. Sam Houston and my year at UT-Arlington as a visiting professor, I had developed a real affinity for Texas. I saw it, accurately I think, as a can-do state. It has since grown to number two in U.S. population and is certainly a national, even international, player.

A very attractive feature at that time was the state's oil money, which it was aggressively investing in higher education. Texas Tech had been expanded to university status in the 1960s and, besides a whole assemblage of colleges, had a law school and a medical school with four campuses. The position that I accepted was as Area Coordinator of Management, essentially a department chair in a business school with around 4500 undergraduates, 400 masters students (most of them MBAs) and 70 or 80 doctoral students. The business school was just coming off re-accreditation and the state and university were pouring (well, at least increasing) money into salaries and budgets.

This move presented an opportunity to build new programs and reinforce others. We tried many things, some worked and some did not, but we were able to instill strong research standards and strong norms for involvement in professional associations. Over time, and extending beyond my AC duties, we also were able to strengthen our Ph.D. program, make modest improvements in our undergraduate programs and were active players in a revamped MBA program, based on a report from the two committees that I chaired.

Our area also, with my colleague John Blair as the driving force, developed a very successful health-organization management MBA option, which has become increasingly well known. Finally, we were able to establish the Institute for Management and Leadership Research (IMLR), which was later split into separate units. I became the Director of the Institute for Leadership Research (ILR). This unit sponsors *The Leadership Quarterly* and the *Journal of Management Inquiry*, edited by associate ILR director, Kim Boal. In addition to these sponsorships, ILR has been involved in obtaining grants and contracts for research and symposia. The total for these, and earlier grants and contracts, with which I have been involved, now stands at more than one million dollars.

In 1981 Texas Tech was about the size of SIU and about as comprehensive (it was more like a land-grant than a narrow-gauged engineering school). Both were in the shadows of world-class universities and both were "betting on the come". Where SIU bottomed out, however, Texas Tech was temporarily infused with oil money, then stabilized and is now aggressively on the move again with a half billion dollar endowment raised over the last five years and spearheaded by a 25-million dollar business school endowment, spinning off real short-term dollars and accompanied by some 40-million longer term "when I die dollars". In my estimation, this is a rare window of b-school opportunity, with money, faculty and infrastructure just waiting to come together with aggressive leadership at the dean's level.

All of this discussion helps provide the context for my career since moving to Texas Tech. My career there has been quite different from SIU. Whether that's because of the differences in institutions, or in my career stage, is hard to say for sure – I suspect it is a bit of both. Also, I was AC for six years originally and then, after a reprieve, was called upon for another three-year stint from 1994–1997. For me, these years of service have made it more difficult to maintain my publishing, and even my professional activities, but have allowed for "institution building activities".

Be that as it may, a much higher proportion of my work has been editorial in nature and, indeed, the "born to edit" part of the title to this essay has been more than catchy phraseology. Since coming to TTU, I have edited two scholarly journals – the *Journal of Management* (4 years) and *The Leadership Quarterly* (where I started my editorship partway through 1997). I also have been senior co-editor of the last two *Leadership Symposia Series* volumes (1984 and 1988), as well as *Leadership on the Future Battlefield* (1985), *Strategic Leadership* (1991), and *Out-of-the-Box Leadership* (1999). Additionally, I have been co-editor of two special issues of *The Leadership Quarterly*, one on international aspects, and one covering charismatic/transformational work. Each has spanned two issues.

Additionally, I have edited *The Leadership Quarterly*'s newly developed Yearly Review of Leadership. In launching the inaugural 2000 Review, as mentioned earlier, we met at Ole Miss. There we had interactive feedback sessions to develop authors' manuscripts. These sessions were reminiscent of exchanges that characterized the previous leadership symposia.

The Leadership Quarterly's Yearly Review series follows in the footsteps of the *Journal of Management*'s Yearly Review of Management, the first two issues of which my TTU colleague John Blair and I edited. In between, I was editor of the *LQ* "Leadership Classics" series, before I became *LQ* senior editor. Finally, I continue to edit the Elsevier/Pergammon series, "Monographs in Leadership and Management".

All this is to say that, if I were not born to be an editor, I have surely experienced the next thing to it. It also is worth noting that much of this editorial work has been entrepreneurial in nature, involving contributions that have been either brand new or early in their intellectual development. Thus, they emphasize both right-brain, entrepreneurial orientations as well as the left-brain linear thinking required for scholarly editing.

Besides my administrative and editorial duties, my work reflects an increasing international emphasis. I made my first international trip in 1980, my last year at SIU. For that, as mentioned earlier, I spent a semester at the University of Aston in Birmingham. While there, besides conceptual work with Dian Hosking, I was able to obtain funding from ONR (London) and the North Atlantic Treaty Organization for the Oxford Leadership Symposium with which Rosemary Stewart was so heavily involved. Fortunately, I was able to network from both Aston and Oxford and attend European conferences in such countries as England, Scotland, and Spain, and to follow up sporadically after I returned to the United States. Most recently, in 1999, I taught a MBA leadership skills course in the Peoples' Republic of China.

In the middle 1980s, I became acquainted with Timo Santalainen, a high ranking fast-track Finnish banking official with a doctorate, who was also an adjunct professor at the Helsinki School of Economics and Business Administration. He was visiting at Carbondale and some time later he spent a year at TTU. It was Timo who initially invited me in 1989 to Finland. Given my strong interest in developments outside the United States, Donna and I jumped at the chance to go.

I took part in a series of symposia where I met Arja Ropo, who has since become a valued friend and colleague. At that time, she was well into her dissertation on leadership and change, tracking three stages of deregulation in the Finnish banking industry, the industry with which Timo also was involved.

She was using a grounded theory approach to track leadership and organization change across several years and considered deregulation to be a form of environmental jolt. I was fascinated with the setting and Arja's approach and agreed to serve as the "opponent" for her dissertation. This meant that I could grill Arja in public, in this case for up to four hours. The "public" really was in a medium-size auditorium that was filled and included Arja's family. She did well and we have worked together ever since.

Arja's dissertation provided the opportunity of bringing together my strong traditional U.S. interest in leadership with the broader contextual and organizational interests of European scholars. Thus, it picked up on some of the Multiple Influence Model notions that Dick Osborn and I were involved with in the late 1970s and early 1980s, but was less deterministic. The Finnish higher education system supports and encourages travel and extended stays outside Finland, and Arja and her immediate family have been able to spend a summer and a later follow-up year in Lubbock. Also, I was able to spend the summer of 1994 working with Arja in Finland.

Arja and I submitted articles based on her dissertation to the *Academy of Management Journal* and *Organization Science* and were encouraged by initial reviewer comments, but ultimately were unable to get acceptance from either. In looking over our efforts, we concluded that we had too many innovative ideas packed into a single piece, making our work too long and complex. First, there was a substantive innovation effort to describe and then reconceptualize leadership as a multiple-level organizational phenomenon accompanied by spiral configurations, across time. Additionally, the grounded theory method-ology that we used was then relatively unusual in leadership papers, and our detailed treatment made our manuscripts long and often hard to follow.

We concluded that we needed to prepare simpler, more highly focused manuscripts. We persevered and followed up by refocusing and recasting some of our data and then, in addition to some conference papers and proceedings, were able to get our work accepted. We have published in areas such as entrepreneurship and higher education, and have examined the decade-long tenure of the board chair of General Motors, during a period when the auto giant essentially went from riches to rags.

In a related effort, Susan Fox, a doctoral student of Kim Boal's and mine, completed a grounded theory dissertation covering the Federal Community Reinvestment Act, an important issue for United States Federal and State banks. Ultimately, the three of us got a paper from this dissertation published in ASQ. A little bit later, Arja and I were able to place a more highly focused version of Arja's dissertation-based paper. It went into a JAI series on qualitative methods. Fortunately, we did not let our interest wane the way Dick Osborn and I had done with our earlier Multiple Influence Model. Thus, my earlier perseverance lesson was reinforced.

Through all of this, Arja became very familiar with the U.S. publication system and I, particularly, could see the increasing difficulty of getting work published in top-tier outlets. There has been a large increase in the total number of outlets in the United States in recent years, while yet at the same time, top-tier outlets have become ever more demanding. All this is as it should be, although it can be carried to extremes (Bedeian, 1996). There are still individuals who complain about lack of quality. I am, however, not among them.

In spite of our very different training and background differences we worked together extremely well. As with Dick Osborn, on paper, our backgrounds would make us appear to be unlikely collaborators, but other things pulled us together, not the least of which was the above-mentioned conceptualization concerning the embedding of leadership. Thus, we continue to collaborate, though less frequently than we did earlier.

The above kinds of activities, along with my professional involvement (described below), have not gone unnoticed at Texas Tech. In 1984 I was honored with TTU's highest faculty position, the Paul Whitfield Horn Professor of Management and in 1991, I received the University wide Barnie E. Rushing, Jr. "Faculty Distinguished Research Award". Additionally, in 2000, I was made a Trinity Company Professor in Leadership. Once again, the "blind pig" saying appears appropriate.

Finally, I earlier touched on a number of hot-group graduate students at SIU. I also mentioned Susan Fox's (now Fox-Wolfgramm) dissertation at Texas Tech and the co-authored article emanating from it. I would be remiss if I did not also mention other Ph.D. students with whom I have been involved as a co-author or similar publishing role.

John Davis, George Dodge (recently deceased), Rao Korukonda, Joan Rivera, George Stelluto, and Jun Yan are from Texas Tech. Stan Granberg received a doctorate from the University of Oxford in the United Kingdom, where I was co-chair of his dissertation. I played a similar role for Lisa Valukangas in Finland, as I did for Arja Ropo much earlier. To all these students, and now colleagues, I owe much.

PROFESSIONAL ASSOCIATIONS

One of the things I picked up from my doctoral work was the importance of presenting papers and otherwise getting involved with professional associations. Joe Litterer was a role model here with his early Academy of Management activities. Despite my early involvement, I have never joined the American Psychological Association, although I have attended a meeting or two. I have found the Society for Industrial and Organizational Psychology (an APA division) more to my liking and have presented papers at its meetings over the last few years.

The Academy of Management, at both the national and regional levels, is where I have been most active. I attended my first Academy meeting while still a Ph.D. student. Not surprisingly, I was primarily interested in learning the job opportunities, but found the paper sessions interesting as well.

It is hard to imagine now, but the Academy was then a small organization – about the size of some of the current regionals, with perhaps less than a thousand members total, with a much smaller head count at the annual meetings. The regionals, of course, tended to be really tiny when compared with today.

I joined the Midwest Academy of Management shortly after moving to Carbondale and soon began to be active in both it and the national Academy. In 1973 or so, I was elected to the entry level position that ultimately led to my presidency of the Midwest in 1976. Similarly, when I moved to Texas Tech I became active in the Southern Management Association and went through various positions to become president in 1988. In 1983, I was appointed editor of the Journal of Management for a three-year term that stretched to four. I was president of the Allied Southern Business Association in 1988. At the national level, I was elected chair (equivalent to president) of the Organizational Behavior Division in 1978. I also was elected to a three-year term on the Academy Board of Governors in the late 1970s.

I have been fortunate to be honored by the national Academy, where I was elected a Fellow, in 1977. In 1991, I was honored with the Academy of Management Distinguished Service Award. In 1990, I was elected a Fellow and inaugural Dean of the newly instituted Southern Management Association Fellows Group.

All of this is just to say that I believe participation in professional associations helps the individual scholar and helps move the management discipline forward. This movement is reflected both content-wise, through paper presentations, and process-wise through facilitating knowledge dissemination.

SOCIOLOGY OF SCIENCE AND RELATED WORK

Although leadership research has certainly been my central career focus, I have also been interested in other thrusts. For example, I co-authored two papers with John Blair in 1986 and 1987 that dealt with the philosophy or sociology of science. The second article is of especial interest to me because of its emphasis on "process" and "content" aspects of scholarly careers. One day John and I were discussing our observations concerning career success. It was obvious to us that academics who published in "good" outlets were more successful in moving ahead than those who did not. Whereas on the surface this is a "duh" conclusion, there is really more to it than meets the eye.

Many people get caught up in, what I referred to above, as "process" activities. That is, they spend most of their time on facilitating the scholarly process through becoming active in various activities in professional associations. Thus, they may serve as track chairs, secretary-treasurers and the like, in various professional groups. In many cases, they engage in these activities soon after completing their doctorate and sometimes even before. Such activities, of course, can take considerable energy and usually lead to lots of "atta boys", but at most research-oriented universities they do not to lead to tenure and promotion. And quite often they are done in lieu of publishing and, thus, may be especially problematic early in one's career. I made the point above, however, that it is not this simple, and in our 1987 article, John and I hypothesized why this might be.

Based on the Matthew Effect (Merton, 1973), the argument is that people who co-author with well-known scholars get "Matthewed", that is, they receive less credit than they would otherwise and, perhaps, even less than they deserve. (This descriptor is based on a version of the Book of Matthew that says, in effect, that those who have much will receive even more, while those with little will have even that little taken away. In other words, the rich get richer.)

This effect is hypothesized to operate not just with publications, but with process and content activities, where the assumption is that content counts more than process. There are a couple of arguments at play: first, that background makes a difference (thus, for example, faculty with elite school backgrounds get more credit for process activities); second, faculty get more credit if they have emphasized content activities early in their career, before stressing process activities later. In other words, there is an assumed carry over from early publication.

Of course, not all activities are purely content or process. There are a number that are "mixed". Journal editing would be one of these and, given my proclivity for such editing, this reinforces my interest in understanding process and content activities. Indeed, over a period of time, Art Bedeian, Larry Jauch and I have been working on empirical testing of this notion. Across time, such work has the potential to contribute to a neglected area in the management field. I also have had an interest in pedagogical concerns. These concerns involve course and curriculum design, influences on teaching effectiveness, and so forth. Most recently, they have involved, primarily, faculty members, Gail Futoran and Ritch Sorenson, along with Joan Rivera, a Ph.D. student.

FAMILY, HOBBIES AND DIVERSIONS

Periodically, through this essay I have mentioned my parents, sister, and immediate family. I have been blessed with parents to whom I owe much, even beyond their educational emphasis. My father passed away at 93 and my mother is nearly 90 with all the frailties accompanying such a long and happy life. My sister, Phyllis, was born in 1941. She obtained a graduate degree from the University of Chicago and through a quirk of fate, is currently director of libraries at my alma mater, Michigan Tech.

I have written throughout this biography about Donna, my lovely wife. After successful family raising and human resource management careers, she currently works as a part-time editorial associate for *The Leadership Quarterly* and its associated book series mentioned earlier.

Doug, our oldest child (born during my master's report examination in 1957, as you may recall) is the real engineer in the family – left brain thinking is his middle name. He has a Ph.D. in electrical engineering from Duke University and is currently completing a masters degree in statistics, after an earlier career stint at McDonnell-Douglas in St. Louis. He is married to a physician and we have a 8-year-old granddaughter named Adrienne.

Holly, our older daughter, was born in Urbana and has a masters in social work from the University of Texas. She lives in San Antonio and works with abused family members. She is also a single parent, mother of our other grandchild, now 3-years-old, and adopted. His name is Hunter and, along with Adrienne, is a highpoint in our lives.

Robin, our youngest, was born in Carbondale, and lives in Dallas. She has a degree in technical writing from Texas Tech and has worked for several high-tech firms in the Dallas area. She has a number of interesting past-times, including analyzing animal feelings and interactions.

Finally, it is interesting to note that, just as Donna received a degree from SIU, Holly and Robin each received a bachelor's degree from Texas Tech. Where degrees from these two fine institutions are concerned, we are an equal opportunity family.

As for me, besides my interest in cars, I do some woodworking and am an avid Texas Tech Red Raider football and basketball fan. I also have been accused of impersonating a Texan – my reply is, "I got her as fast as I could". Our family diversions include considerable traveling in both this country and abroad. We also spend much time collecting artifacts from our travels to go with our very contemporary house.

COMING FULL CIRCLE AND A LAST HURRAH?: DYNAMIC SYSTEMS APPROACHES TO LEADERSHIP

Perhaps unexpectedly, given my linear training as an engineer, but maybe not given my right-brain orientation, I have been interested in leadership as a systems, or at least as a non-linear concept. Even as I was conducting a research project or two in Fiedler's lab, I really wished I could treat leadership non-linearly, and empirically recognize its complex relationships with other parts of the system with which it was involved. Hence, my resonation with Arja's work and with Dick Osborn's even earlier interests.

The problem for me was I had no idea how to empirically model systems' thinking. Later, as I became more knowledgeable and as empirical techniques evolved, I was impressed that structural equation modeling could get the field part way toward systems' notions. Grounded theory and related approaches have gone even further in emphasizing dynamism and process. Currently, I am most interested in learning more about various dynamic systems approaches, including computational modeling. For me, these approaches offer the potential of actualizing what I wanted to see happen when I was a Ph.D. student. Thus, as what could well be simultaneously the closing of a circle and a last hurrah, I hope to pursue work in this area aggressively. With that in mind, I have a manuscript in press on the topic.

CONCLUSIONS

As I look back on what I have written here, I am reminded once again of Karl Weick's (1979) well-known saying, "How can I know what I think until I see what I say?" My thinking, in turn, brings to mind some important points for me. First, my students constantly ask how they will use what I teach. In their minds, they already know what will be relevant for them and what will not. My life and career certainly would have been different had I restricted myself to engineering, believing I already knew what my career and life would be like.

Second, the persistence lesson, embodied in my opening stories, I have neglected at my peril. My work with Dick Osborn is an example. Persistence and serving as our own champions might well have pushed it forward. Even so, there is still the chance that it can be resurrected in a transmogrified form. In contrast, persistence paid off in my work with Arja.

Even though persistence is important, however, unlike the myriad self-help books, I do not believe that resoluteness triumphs over all. The old ability X motivation notion still lives. In looking back, I believe I was wise to move out of engineering and one could even make a case that I perhaps should not have completed the Michigan Tech program. Nevertheless, there's a "time to hold 'em and a time to fold 'em", as the saying goes. The trick, of course, is to know when these times are. As have all of us, I sometimes have called these times right and sometimes not – the results are reflected in my career.

I might also reiterate that I see the content and process work in which I have developed a great interest as being strongly related to my own career, although I did not plan it that way. Were I starting again, however, I would emphasize content aspects early and then piggyback on these with later process work, which come to think of it, was what I unknowingly did the first time around. Once again, the blind pig analogy rings true.

Finally, for a boy whose earliest thoughts were of pneumonia and a pedal car, how can I close without mentioning my first true interest? Though cars have not been a significant part of my career, they have been an important part of who I am. I say this as I slip into my BMW Z-3 roadster, currently one of the loves of my life!

PUBLICATIONS

1967

Breakthrough in leadership research. *Personnel Administration*, *30*(5), 38–44.
Fiedler's Leadership Contingency Model: An empirical test in three organizations. *Organizational Behavior and Human Performance*, *2*(3), 290–308.

1968

Another look at human relations training. *Training and Development Journal*, *22*(2), 2–10.
With J. O. Pecenka. The sad state of faculty recruitment. *Collegiate News and Views*, *22*(2), 1–4.
Organizational leadership: Some theoretical and empirical considerations. *Business Perspectives*, *4*(4), 16–24.

1969

College boards of trustees: A need for directive leadership – Some comments. *Academy of Management Journal*, *12*(1), 123–124.
Status congruence: An important organizational factor. *Personnel Administration*, *32*(1), 19–27.
With J. W. Hill. The new look in motivation theory for organizational research. *Human Organization*, *28*(3), 100–109.

1971

Leadership style effects at two managerial levels in a simulated organization. *Administrative Science Quarterly*, *16*(4), 476–481.

With P. F. Newell. Management in the 1980s revisited. *Personnel Journal, 50*(1), 35–43.
With J. O. Pecenka. An empirical study of business school faculty recruitment. *AACSB Bulletin,* 7(3), 55–68.

1972

Leadership in the media profession: Some vertical and lateral considerations. In: L. W. Cochran (Ed.), *Leadership development for the media profession.* Iowa City: Audio-Visual Center, University of Iowa.
With E. A. Fleishman (Ed.). *Current developments in the study of leadership.* Carbondale, IL: Southern Illinois University Press.
With J. W. Hill. Managerial level, leadership, and employee need satisfaction. In: E. A. Fleishman & J. G. Hunt (Eds), *Current developments in the study of leadership.* Carbondale, IL: Southern Illinois University Press.
With V. K. C. Liebscher. Leadership preference, leadership behavior, and employee satisfaction. *Organizational Behavior and Human Performance, 9*(1), 59–77.
With J. W. Hill & J. Reaser. Leadership behavior correlates at two managerial levels in a mental Institution. *Journal of Applied Social Psychology, 3*(2) 174–185.

1974

With L. L. Larson (Ed.). *Contingency approaches to leadership.* Carbondale, IL: Southern Illinois University Press.
With R. N. Osborn. An empirical investigation of lateral and vertical leadership at two organizational levels. *Journal of Business Research, 2,* 209–221.
With R. N. Osborn. Environment and oganizational effectiveness. *Administrative Science Quarterly, 19*(2), 231–246.
With L. L. Larson and R. N. Osborn. Correlates of leadership and demographic variables in three organizational settings. *Journal of Business Research, 2*(3), 335–348.

1975

With R. N. Osborn. An adaptive-reactive theory of leadership: The role of macro variables in leadership research. In: J. G. Hunt & L. L. Larson (Eds), *Leadership frontiers,* Kent, OH: Comparative Administration Research Institute and Kent State University Press, Kent State University.
With R. N. Osborn, Relations between leadership, size and subordinate satisfaction in a voluntary organization. *Journal of Applied Psychology, 60*(6), 730–735.
With L. L. Larson (Ed.). *Leadership frontiers,* Kent, OH: Comparative Administration Research Institute and Kent State University Press, Kent State University.
Guest Editor with L. L. Larson of a special leadership issue of *Organization and Administrative Sciences, 6*(2 & 3).
With R. N. Osborn & L. L. Larson. Upper level technical orientation and first-level leadership within a non-contingency and contingency framework. *Academy of Management Journal, 18*(3), 476–488.

1976

With G. W. Yunker. An empirical comparison of the Michigan Four Factor and Ohio State LBDQ scales. *Organizational Behavior and Human Performance*, *17*(1), 45–65.

With L. L. Larson & R. N. Osborn. The great hi-hi leader behavior myth: A lesson from Occam's Razor. *Academy of Management Journal*, *19*(4), 628–641.

With R. N. Osborn. Design implications for mechanistically structured systems in complex environments: Alterations in contextual variables. In: R. H. Kilmann, L. R. Pondy & D. P. Slevin (Eds), *The management of organizational design: research and methodology* (Vol. II). New York: American Elsevier.

1977

With L. L. Larson (Ed.). *Leadership: The cutting edge*. Carbondale, IL: Southern Illinois University Press.

With R. N. Osborn & D. J. Skaret. Managerial influence in a complex configuration with two unit heads. *Human Relations*, *30*(11), 1025–1038.

With R. N. Osborn & R. S. Bussom. On getting your own way in organizational design: An empirical investigation of requisite variety. *Organization and Administrative Sciences*, *8*(2 & 3), 295–310.

1978

With R. N. Osborn & R. S. Schuler. Relations of discretionary and non-discretionary leadership to performance and satisfaction in a complex organization. *Human Relations*, *31*(6), 507–523.

1979

With L. L. Larson (Ed.). *Crosscurrents in leadership*. Carbondale, IL: Southern Illinois University Press.

1980

With R. N. Osborn. A multiple influence approach to leadership for managers. In: J. Stinson & P. Hersey (Eds), *Perspectives in leader effectiveness*. Athens, OH: Center for Leadership Studies, Ohio University.

With R. N. Osborn & L. R. Jauch. *Organization theory: An integrated approach*. New York: Wiley.

1981

With T. N. Martin. A path-analytic influence process model of intent to leave. *Personnel Psychology*, *33*(3), 505–528.

With R. N. Osborn. Towards a macro-oriented model of leadership: An odyssey. In: J. G. Hunt, U. Sekaran & C. A. Schriesheim (Eds), *Leadership: Beyond establishment views*. Carbondale, IL: Southern Illinois University Press.

Book Review

Review of R. H. Miles, *Macro organizational behavior, Journal of Management Studies, 18*(1), 123–126

Case

With C. I. Cash. Uris hall dormitory kitchen. In: J. E. Dittrich & R. A. Zawacki (Eds), *People and Organizations: Cases in management and organizational behavior.* Dallas: Business Publications.

With D. McGill. The brown shoe and volar armies. In: J. E. Dittrich & R. A. Zawacki (Eds), *People and Organziations: Cases in management and organizational behavior.* Dallas: Business Publications.

With L. Neeley. Perfect pizzeria. In: J. E. Dittrich & R. A. Zawacki (Eds), *People and Organziations: Cases in management and organizational behavior.* Dallas: Business Publications.

With R. Ritter. Operation birthdate. In: J. E. Dittrich & R. A. Zawacki (Eds), *People and Organziations: Cases in management and organizational behavior.* Dallas: Business Publications.

1982

With U. Sekaran & C. A. Schriesheim (Eds). *Leadership: Beyond establishment views.* Carbondale, IL: Southern Illinois University Press.

With J. R. Schermerhorn, Jr. & R. N. Osborn. *Managing organizational behavior* and support materials. New York: Wiley.

1984

With R. N. Osborn & L. R. Jauch. *Organization theory: An integrated approach* (Revised ed.) and support material. Melbourne, FL: Krieger Publishing.

Managerial behavior and leadership. A monograph in the SRA MODMAN series. Chicago: Science Research Associates.

With D. M. Hosking, C. A. Schriesheim & R. Stewart (Eds). *Leaders and managers: International perspectives on managerial behavior and leadership.* Elmsford, NY and London: Pergamon Press.

1985

Leadership: The state-of-the-art and the future battlefield. In: J. G. Hunt & J. D. Blair (Eds), *Leadership on the future battlefield.* Washington: Pergamon-Brassey's.

Organizational leadership: The contingency paradigm and its challenges. In: B. Kellerman (Ed.), *Looking at leadership; Interdisciplinary perspectives.* Englewood Cliffs, NJ: Prentice-Hall.

With J. D. Blair. A research agenda for leadership on the future battlefield. In: J. G. Hunt & J. D. Blair (Eds), *Leadership on the future battlefield.* Washington: Pergamon-Brassey's.

With J. D. Blair (Ed.). *Leadership on the future battlefield.* Washington, D.C.: Pergamon-Brassey's.

With B. R. Baliga & J. D. Blair. A devil's advocate view of the future battlefield. In: J. G. Hunt & J. D. Blair (Eds), *Leadership on the future battlefield*. Washington: Pergamon-Brassey's.

With A. K. Ramaprosad, L. Jauch, & H. Wilson. Comparative outcomes of two policy course Structures. *Educational and Psychological Research, 4*(4).

With J. R. Schermerhorn, Jr. & R. N. Osborn. *Managing organizational behavior* (2nd ed.) and support materials. Wiley.

1986

With J. D. Blair. Getting inside the head of the management researcher one more time: Context-free and context-specific orientations in research. *1986 Yearly Review of Management of the Journal of Management, 12*(2), 147–166.

With J. D. Blair (Ed.). *1986 Yearly Review of Management of the Journal of Management, 12*(2).

Book Review

Review of L. L. Cummings & P. Frost (Eds). *Publishing in the organizational sciences, Administrative Science Quarterly. 31*(2), pp. 310–312.

1987

With J. D. Blair. Content, process and the Matthew Effect among management academics. *1987 Yearly Review of Management of the Journal of Management, 13*(2), 191–210.

With J. D. Blair (Ed.). *1987 Yearly Review of Management of the Journal of Management, 13*(2).

1988

With B. R. Baliga. An organizational life cycle approach to leadership. In: J. G. Hunt, B. R. Baliga, H. P. Dachler & C. A. Schriesheim (Eds), *Emerging leadership vistas*. Boston: Lexington Books.

With B. R. Baliga, H. P. Dachler, & C. A. Schriesheim (Eds). *Emerging leadership vistas*. Boston: Lexington Books.

With M. F. Peterson & B. R. Baliga. Strategic apex leader scripts and an organisational lifecycle approach to leadership and excellence. *Journal of Management Development, 7*(5), 61–83.

With T. M. Santalainen. Change differences from an action research, results-oriented OD program in high- and low-performing Finnish banks, *Group and Organization Studies, 13*, 413–440.

With J. R. Schermerhorn, Jr. & R. N. Osborn. *Managing organizational behavior* (3rd ed.) and support materials. New York: Wiley.

Book Review

Review of N. M. Tichy & M. A. Devanna, *The transformational leader, Administrative Science Quarterly, 33*(1), 132–135.

Cases

Written under the direction of and edited by J. G. Hunt. Let there by light corporation, M & M electric, Seventeenth national bank data processing department, student janitors at the big u. In: L. R. Jauch, S. Coltrin, A. G. Bedeian & W. F. Glueck (Eds), *The Managerial experience: Cases, exercises and readings* (5th ed.). Hinsdale, IL: Dryden.

1989

With A. R. Korukonda. Pat on the back vs. kick in the pants: An application of cognitive inference to the study of leader reward and punishment behaviors. *Group and Organization Studies, 14*, 299–334.

1990

With K. B. Boal & R. L. Sorenson. Top management leadership: Inside the black box. *The Leadership Quarterly, 1*(1), 41–65.

Book Review

Review of G. Little, *Strong leadership, Contemporary Psychology, 36*, 422–423.
Review of J. Kotter, *A force for change: How leadership differs from management, The Leadership Quarterly, 1*(4), 264–268.

1991

Leadership: A new synthesis. Newbury Park, CA: Sage.
With A. R. Korukonda. Premises and paradigms in leadership research. *Journal of Organizational Change Management, 4*(2), 19–33.
With A. R. Korukonda. Reward/punishment cues as sources of contextual bias in cognitive categorization: A laboratory investigation. In: J. R. Meindl, R. Cardy & S. Puffer (Eds), *Advances in information processing*, Vol. 4, Greenwich, CT: JAI Press.
With R. L. Phillips. Leadership in battle and garrison: A framework for understanding differences and preparing for both. In: R. Gal & D. Mangelsdorff (Eds), *Handbook of military psychology.* Chichester, U.K. and New York: Wiley.
With J. R. Schermerhorn, Jr. & R. N. Osborn. *Managing organizational behavior* (4th ed.) and support materials. New York: Wiley.

Book Review

Review of A modern classic, F. E. Fiedler, *A theory of leadership effectiveness, Journal of Management, 17*(20), 504–507.

1992

With Arja Ropo, Stratified systems theory and dynamic case study perspectives: A symbiosis. In: R. L. Phillips & J. G. Hunt (Eds), *Strategic leadership: A multiorganizational-level perspective.* Westport, CT: Quorum, 1992.

With Robert L. Phillips (Ed.), *Strategic leadership: A multiorganizational-level perspective.* Westport, CT: Quorum, 1992.

Book Review

With K. B. Boal, review of C. C. Manz & H. P. Sims, Jr., *Super-leadership: Leading others to lead themselves, The Leadership Quarterly, 3*(2), 159–163.

1993

Book Reviews

With Arja Ropo, review of A. Bryman, *Charisma and leadership in organizations, The Leadership Quarterly, 4*(4).
With K. B. Boal, review of Clarke & Clarke (Eds). Measures of leadership, *Contemporary Psychology, 38.*

1994

With J. R. Schermerhorn, Jr. & R. N. Osborn. *Managing organizational behavior* (5th ed.) and support materials. Wiley.

Case

With Arja Ropo. A fast track Finnish bank manager. In: J. R. Schermerhorn, Jr., J. G. Hunt & R. N. Osborn. *Managing organizational behavior.* (5th ed.). Wiley.

1995

Leadership. In: A. Kuper & J. Kuper (Eds), *Social science encyclopedia.* London: Routledge, 1995.
Ruminations on a continuum of leadership choices. *Journal of Management Inquiry, 4*(2), 207–208.
With Arja Ropo. Entrepreneurial processes as virtuous and vicious spirals in a changing opportunity structure: A paradoxical perspective. *Entrepreneurship Theory and Practice, 19*(3), 91–111.
With Arja Ropo. Multi-level leadership: Grounded theory and mainstream theory applied to the case of General Motors. *The Leadership Quarterly, 6*(3), 379–412.
With G. C. Futoran & J. B. Rivera. The temporal impact of management faculty style and course characteristics: Some theoretical and developmental implications. *Group and Organization Management, 20*(3), 310–336.

1996

Citation classics (Ed.). *The Leadership Quarterly, 7*(3), 303–352.
With Richard C. Thomson. Inside the black box of Alpha Beta, and Gamma change: Using a cognitive – processing model to assess attitude structure. *Academy of Management Review, 1996, 21*(3), 655–690.

With Arja Ropo and Paivi Eriksson, Three voices describing scholarly career journeys with international collaboration. In: P. Frost & S. Taylor (Eds), *Rhythms of academic life*. Thousand Oaks, CA: Sage, 1996.

1997

Leadership Classics (Ed.). *The Leadership Quarterly, 8*(2), 93–132.

With Robert Hooijberg & George E. Dodge. Leadership complexity and development of the Leaderplex Model. *Journal of Management, 23*(3), 375–408.

With Mark F. Peterson. International perspectives on international leadership. *The Leadership Quarterly, 8*(3), 203–231.

With Mark F. Peterson. Two scholars' views on some nooks and crannies in cross-cultural leadership. *The Leadership Quarterly, 8*(4), 343–354.

With Mark F. Peterson (Ed.). *The Leadership Quarterly, 8*(3 and 4). A two-part special issue on international leadership.

With Arja Ropo. Leadership and faculty motivation. In: J. L. Bess (Ed.), *Teaching well and liking it: Motivating faculty to teach effectively* (pp. 219–247). Baltimore: Johns Hopkins University Press.

With Richard C. Thomson. The Thomson/Hunt flight plan revisited. *Academy of Management Review, 22*(2), 333–334.

With A. Ropo & P.Eriksson (Eds). Processual approaches to organization studies. A special issue of the *Scandinavian Journal of Management, 13*(4).

With Arja Ropo & Pavi Eriksson. Reflections on conducting processual research on management and organizations. *Scandinavian Journal of Management, 13*(4), 331–335.

With J. R. Schermerhorn, Jr. & R. N. Osborn. *Organizational behavior* (6th ed.) and support materials. New York: Wiley.

1998

With Arja Ropo. Multi-level leadership: Grounded theory and mainstream theory applied to the case of General Motors. In: F. Dansereau & F. J. Yammarino (Eds), *Leadership: The multiple-level approaches* (pp. 289–328). Westport, CT: JAI Press.

With Arja Ropo. Appendix: Measures and assessments for the multi-level leadership approach. In: F. Dansereau & F. J. Yammarino (Eds), *Leadership: The multiple-level approaches* (pp. 329–340). Westport, CT: JAI Press.

With Susan J. Fox-Wolfgramm & Kimberly B. Boal. Organizational adaptation to institutional change: A comparative study of first-order change in prospector and defender banks. *Administrative Science Quarterly, 43*(1), 87–126.

With J. R. Schermerhorn & R. N. Osborn. *Basic organizational behavior* (2nd ed.). New York: Wiley.

1999

Leadership classics (Ed). *The Leadership Quarterly, 10*(1), 3–19.

Charisma and need for leadership revisited. *European Journal of Work and Organizational Psychology, 8*, 127–133.

Transformational/charismatic leadership's transformation of the field: An historical essay. *The Leadership Quarterly, 10*, 129–144.

With George E. Dodge & Robert L. Phillips. Out-of-the-box leadership for the twenty-first century: An introduction. In: J. G. Hunt, George E. Dodge, & Leonard Wong (Eds), *Out-of-the-box leadership: Transforming the 21st century army and other top performing organizations* (pp. 3–14). Westport, CT: JAI Press.

With George E. Dodge & Leonard Wong (Eds). *Out-of-the-box leadership: Transforming the 21st century army and other top performing organizations.* Westport, CT, JAI Press.

With Robert Hooijberg & R. Craig Bullis. Behavioral complexity and the development of military leadership for the twenty first-century. In: J. G. Hunt, George E. Dodge, & Leonard Wong (Eds), *Out-of-the-Box Leadership: Transforming the 21st century army and other top performing organizations* (pp. 111–130). Westport, CT: JAI Press.

2000

With George E. Dodge. Leadership déjà vu all over again. *Yearly Review of Leadership of The Leadership Quarterly, 11*(4), 435–458.

With George E. Dodge,. Organizational managers. In: A. E. Kazdin, (Ed.), *Encyclopedia of psychology.* Washington, D.C.: American Psychological Association Books

With J. R. Schermerhorn, Jr. & R. N. Osborn. *Managing organizational behavior* (7th ed.) and support materials. New York: Wiley, 2000.

2001

With Ritch Sorenson. A learned behavior approach to management skill development. *Journal of Management Education, 25*(2), 167–190.

In Press

With K. B. Boal & Stephen J. Jaros. Order is free: On the ontological status of organizations. In: Robert Westwood & Stewart Clegg (Eds), *Point/counterpoint: Central debates in organisation theory.* Oxford, U.K.: Blackwell.

With Arja Ropo. Longitudinal organizational research and the third scientific discipline. *Group and Organization Management.*

With J. R. Schermerhorn, Jr. & R. N. Osborn. *Organizational behavior* (8th ed.) and support materials. Wiley.

ACKNOWLEDGMENTS

I thank two friends and colleagues, Art Bedeian and Bill Vroman for a number of helpful suggestions in thinking about how to focus various aspects of this manuscript. I also thank my wife, Donna, for her help with the manuscript and cross checking my recollections. Correspondence concerning this manuscript should be addressed to J. G. Hunt, jhunt@ba.ttu.edu

REFERENCES

Bedeian, A. G. (1996). Improving the journal review process: The question of ghostwriting. *American Psychologist, 51*, 1189.

Gordon, R. A., & Howell, J. E. (1959). *Higher education for business.* New York: Columbia University Press.

Jaques, E. (1989). *Requisite organization.* Arlington, VA: Cason Hall.

Katz, D., & Kahn, R. L. (1978). *The social psychology of organizations* (2nd ed.). New York: Wiley.

Leavitt, H. J. (1996). The old days, hot groups, and managers' lib. *Administrative Science Quarterly, 41*, 288–300.

Merton, R. (1973). *The sociology of science.* Chicago: University of Chicago Press.

Pierson, F. C. (1959). *The education of American businessmen.* New York: McGraw-Hill.

Weick, K. E. (1979). *The social psychology of organizing* (2nd ed.). Redding, MA: Addison-Wesley.

CELEBRATING WORK:
A JOB UNFINISHED

Thomas A. Kochan

Growing up on a dairy farm in Wisconsin can be a pretty sheltered experience. I remember summer visits of cousins from Milwaukee and wondering if they weren't the exception – didn't most people live on farms like ours? Our farm was located about two miles from the Village of Francis Creek, ten miles from the blue-collar industrial town of Manitowoc and thirty miles south of Green Bay. For us, Francis Creek was the center of social and cultural life, consisting of our Catholic Church and grade school, three taverns, a bowling alley and dance hall for weddings, a bank, a feed mill and a few other little businesses. The church and school anchored the village and knit the community together. Baptisms, first communions, graduations, weddings, funerals, card parties, and parish picnics provided the venues for keeping in touch and sharing neighbors' ups and downs. For me the most important part of the village was our local baseball field where I both started and ended my brief flirtation with an alternative career as a left handed pitcher. What an MIT doctor diagnosed over thirty years later as a torn rotator cuff (at the time it was just a sore shoulder) eliminated that option at age 17.

But in case you are worried that what will follow will be some idyllic retrospective on the virtues of rural life and the family farm, rest assured. You will be spared of such selective recall. Indeed, one of my earliest and most lasting recollections is of a promise I repeatedly made to myself in the dark, cold Wisconsin winter mornings. I had no idea of what I wanted to do when I grew up, but I promised myself that it would be something that didn't require getting up in the dark, going out in the cold every morning to milk a herd of

Management Laureates, Volume 6, pages 199–242.
© 2002 Published by Elsevier Science Ltd.
ISBN: 0-7623-0487-1

cows! So now, when I find myself up before dawn sitting at my computer with a cup of coffee, I'm reminded that I got it about half right. At least it's warm in the house.

Perhaps, however, just a bit of reflection on what it was like to grow up in this setting in the 1950s (I was born in 1947) will help set the stage for the main point of this essay. It was our farm family and a cooperative, close-knit family and community that instilled several values that probably influenced my choice of occupations.

The first is the value of dignity, accomplishment, and service that one learned to associate with hard work, especially with a job recognized for being done well. From early on, my three older sisters and my older brother and I learned to work hard, helping with the "chores" morning and night. Farm families were tied to the "24 by 7" work and family life long before the term was invented.

The second is the value of independence and independent thinking that came from being given responsibilities early in life by parents who trusted, by necessity and by choice, their children to "do the right thing." I learned to drive a tractor by age eight and was expected to drive it slowly, carefully, and straight as we made hay the old fashioned way in the last years before transitioning to the modern baler.

The third value is a deep appreciation of a supportive community and the power of collective action. No individual farmer in our community could survive on his own. The entire family and neighborhood had to organize and work together. Neighborhood thrashing crews pooled their resources to purchase the machinery no individual farmer could afford. No individual family could provide the amount of labor needed to get the grain cut, thrashed, and in the granary in the short window of time when the grain was ripe for harvesting. So the neighborhood crew made the rounds from farm to farm. The day would come when the crew would be at our farm, working hard in the August heat, eating a gigantic noontime meal prepared by the wives also working together in hot kitchens with even the smaller children pitching in (my first job was to carry water and beer to men working in the fields). Later I graduated to the job of shoveling grain as it came off the thrash machine and into the granary. (I should have bargained to keep the first job. It was easier and more rewarding – at least the beer part).

So, these values of dignity associated with hard and productive work; independence and trust that a job would get done and done well without detailed instructions; and of organizing collective efforts for the common good were lessons from my early years that somehow may have made a lasting imprint and influenced by choice of vocations and style of work.

Another early memory is also very clear and telling – the urging of a father who was self taught and multi-skilled (he was a plumber and a carpenter, as well as a farmer) that his children should not stay on the farm but should aspire to something better – something that a good education might provide. Perhaps it was because his formal education ended after 8th grade. Perhaps because he recognized the marginal nature of family farming and wished for an easier and more prosperous future for his children. Or perhaps because he recognized his mechanical aptitudes had somehow not been passed on to his youngest son, and therefore, this kid better be encouraged to not try to make a living with his hands! But whatever the reason, it was instilled in us that we should stay in school, get as much education as we could, and use it to good advantage. That is probably why I stayed in school until there was nothing else left to do, but go to work after finishing my Ph.D. My sisters and brothers followed similar courses. My brother Jim became an economist, Mary and her husband run a dry cleaning business, Kathleen is a Catholic nun and school principal, and Carol is a nurse.

My parents sold the farm when I was fourteen both because it was at best marginally profitable and because my father was ailing from what turned out to be the cancer that would take his life two years later. My mother worked in a local department store, first part-time and then full-time, until it closed shortly before she was ready to retire. At some point before the stored closed it was unionized by the American Federation of State, County, and Municipal Employees (AFSCME) and to her delight and surprise she still gets a few dollars from the union pension fund each month into her now 88th year. I've always had a warm spot for AFSCME.

MULTIPLE INTERESTS-MULTIPLE LIVES

But back to the central theme of this essay. I want to trace some of my experiences as an industrial relations (IR) researcher and practitioner by stressing the rewards and frustrations, and sometimes the near schizophrenic worlds that can come with this territory. One of the most exciting and rewarding aspects of the IR field is it allows one to move between the world of research and the world of public policy and practice. But because our field is based on an acceptance of the legitimacy of the multiple interests of workers and employers, and views unions as legitimate and valued democratic institutions, I often find myself living multiple lives or taking positions that one or another of the field's constituent audiences opposes strongly. And because much of the work my colleagues and I have done over the years has proposed the need for changes that challenge prevailing ideas, institutions, and practices, opposition can sometimes be rather intense. That, too, makes this life, or multiple lives, interesting to say the least.

Rather than just recount the past, I also want to look to the future; hence the subtitle of this essay – a job far from done. We have much yet to do to complete the most important task facing my generation of industrial relations researchers. That task is to update our public policies, labor market institutions, and organizational practices to catch up with the changing nature of work and the changing workforce. That basic theme was introduced in three works that I'll use to describe both my personal work and the changing nature of the IR field. They are the publication of my first major book, *Collective Bargaining and Industrial Relations: From Theory to Policy and Practice* (Kochan, 1980), the publication of *The Transformation of American Industrial Relations* (Kochan, Katz & McKersie, 1986), and the more recent report of our Task Force on America's Labor Markets, *Working in America: A Blueprint for the Labor Market* (Osterman, Kochan, Locke & Piore, 2001).

THE UNIVERSITY OF WISCONSIN EXPERIENCE (1965–1973)

I was fortunate to grow up in a state that values education – from grade school right through one of the best public universities in the world. An early memory, perhaps my first participation in politics, was a campaign my father and others in our area led to include us in the Manitowoc high school district rather than another little district that had a high school mostly oriented toward producing the future farmers of America. We leafleted the local villages and farms and urged citizens to lobby their county commissioners so we would be able to attend Manitowoc's Lincoln High School. Our petition succeeded and Lincoln High served us very well.

It was, however, the experience of going to the University of Wisconsin that changed a pretty naïve and rather insecure kid into a questioning and challenging (some would say contrarian) student. There was never any question but that Wisconsin would be the school of choice. My brother went there; it was the best institution in the state; it was cheap, especially since I got a small scholarship to go there, and I could do my freshman and sophomore years at our local University Extension (junior college) Center and thereby save money by living at home.

During my junior year and first year on the Madison campus I got hooked on the industrial relations field by an accidental exposure to an awesome classroom performer, Jack Barbash. Jack would become one of my most influential mentors. It was accidental because, as an undergraduate, I was actually majoring more in drinking beer than in the mix of economics, business, and political science courses that now grace my transcript. So, after a long night of working on this major, between semesters, I found myself in a registration line in a stuffy room with one course to fill in to complete the next term's class schedule. When I got to the front of the line that course was all filled up with prior registrants (they probably weren't out as late the night before). But there was this course called Trade Unionism that was offered at the exact same times, so I quickly signed up for it so I could get out of that stifling room. My intent was to figure out later what I'd actually do for the final course I needed.

The problem was, I had to get the professor offering Trade Unionism to sign a drop form. I decided the easiest way to do this was to go to the first day's class and have him sign it there. So I got to the classroom in plenty of time to take a seat at the front, so I could intercept the professor on his way in and get off to my substitute class. Unfortunately, this rolly poly, bushy-haired professor in an old gray tweed jacket with a blue working man's shirt and a black tie (he fit precisely my stereotype of a labor racketeer) sauntered to the front of the room, sat down and, before I could get to him, started lecturing and gesturing wildly about strange ideas. Conflict at work is a natural thing; unions have a key role in a democratic society and perform important economic functions; management shapes the workplace and the climate of the labor-management relationship: Marx was only half right – conflicting interests were built into employment relationships, but would persist under all economic systems not just capitalism; government policy must mediate among these different workplace interests to produce an efficient economy and equitable, democratic society, and so on. What was this all about? Barbash was so intriguing and these ideas so challenged my thinking at the time, that I never left his class or the field, to which he introduced to me.

These were among the best of years for another reason. I met Kathy, where else for a couple of local Wisconsin kids, but in our local "teenage" bar (a bar that could sell beer but not liquor to 18–21 year olds). She grew up in the neighboring small town of Two Rivers and was pursuing her nursing degree in Milwaukee. We got married on a hot summer day in 1969 and began our mutual adventures with her supporting us as an intensive care nurse in a Madison hospital while I focused on graduate school.

THE INDUSTRIAL RELATIONS RESEARCH INSTITUTE (1969–1973)

Barbash and several other very good undergraduate teachers, Al Filley, Jim Stern, and Dick Miller, encouraged me to apply to the University of Wisconsin Industrial Relations Research Institute for graduate school. This was after I went through a couple of disillusioning interviews with potential employers, including one with General Electric. Somehow I couldn't see myself as the next Lemeul Boulware, that infamous Vice President of Labor Relations at GE in the 1950s who introduced "Boulewarism," the practice of presenting unions one first, firm, and final offer rather than negotiating in the more traditional back and forth fashion. I'm forever grateful (as, I'm sure, is GE). A funny coincidence: thirty years later I discovered the current head of labor relations at GE, Dennis Rocheleau, grew up in Two Rivers, essentially around the corner from Kathy's family. We both made the right choice and GE is much better off for our respective decisions!

Graduate school at the University of Wisconsin in 1969–1973 was as intense an intellectual and learning process as one could ever ask for. The campus was politically alive. In my first year of graduate school (and marriage), the National Guard was on campus three times, there were two student political strikes in protest of the Cambodian invasion and escalation of American bombing of North Vietnam, a teaching assistants' strike (we stayed out for about three weeks, settled for a little less than the university was offering prior to the strike but, of course, we won on principle!), and I lived through the uncertainty of drawing a marginal number in the initial selective service draft lottery. I remember taking a key masters' exam in a building where the ventilation system produced more tear gas residue than air conditioning. Kathy and I decided that, if our marriage survived all that in its first year, it would probably last forever. It has, and it will.

The IR field was poised for change and, as students at Wisconsin, we were determined to be the agents of the coming transformation. Industrial relations theory was like God – elusive, hard to know when you found it; received with skepticism and challenged by others, but something to be pursued nonetheless. The task was to search for a unifying theory of industrial relations – one that overcame what we saw as the limits of the prevailing paradigm developed by John Dunlop[1] and his colleagues Clark Kerr, Frederick Harbison and Charles Myers.[2] We admired these scholars for taking on the big task of trying to provide a more analytical model to guide research in our field and for taking a multidisciplinary approach to the task. But how could we accept their model as gospel in an era in which all authority was to be questioned and challenged?

This electric environment was matched by a remarkably talented group of fellow graduate students who went on to distinguished academic and professional careers around the globe. The group included, among others, Herbert Heneman III, Lee Dyer, Hoyt Wheeler, Stuart Schmidt, Myron Roomkin, Thomas Barocci, Thomas DeCotiis, Morley Gunderson, Roy Adams, Kenneth Mericle, Haruo Shimada, Eli Ramos, George Ogle and David Zimmerman. We were the beneficiaries of a demanding curriculum that challenged us to learn how to build and test theories and master the research methods and quantitative skills needed to advance the IR field. It instilled in us each a broad, multi-disciplinary perspective that I value and follow to this day.

When I started graduate school, I planned to major in collective bargaining, but after a year or so I quickly exhausted all available courses on this subject. Wise, but not so gentle, counsel from Dick Miller led me to extend my program to major in organizational behavior (OB). "You might want to give it a try so that you can publish in some place other than *Labor Law Journal* for the rest of your life" was the unsubtle way he put it. He urged me to take a course in organization theory being co-taught by Larry Cummings and George Huber. Because I doubted that this stuff offered anything of value, I spent most of the semester arguing with them about how issues like conflict, power, competing interests, decision making, and change were treated in the OB literature. Larry and George turned out to be great teachers, sparring partners, mentors, co-chairs of my dissertation committee, and friends. They not only put up with my skepticism they channeled it into an appreciation for behavioral science theories and methods and into a way of doing research that has stuck with me ever since. I continue to be a skeptical consumer of and part-time contributor to the organization theory literature (cf. Kochan & Rubinstein, 2000).

Wisconsin's tradition also instilled the basic normative foundations of our field and for my work. The "Wisconsin Idea" stressed that scholars have a responsibility to society – they should work to address problems with a public policy or societal perspective in mind, rather than take the goals of firms, or for that matter the goals of workers or their unions, as a normative frame of reference. This reflected the traditions that John R. Commons brought to the Wisconsin School of Industrial Relations in his pioneering historical, empirical and public policy work in the early years of the 20th century. The work he and his students carried out in those early years not only set the normative and analytical foundations for the IR field, but also laid the foundation for the labor and employment policies enacted in the 1930s as part of the New Deal.[3] Such was the legacy we inherited and were expected to uphold.

The biggest public policy problem facing the IR field when I was in graduate school was the emergence of collective bargaining in the public sector. Laws were being passed, unions were organizing, strikes and impasses were occurring that ranged from the comic (Chicago Social Workers trying to take on Mayor Daley's machine) to the tragic (the sanitation workers' strike that took Martin Luther King Jr. to Memphis on April 4, 1968). So public sector collective bargaining seemed a natural topic to take up as a student interested in collective bargaining.

The idea of studying public sector collective bargaining had added appeal. It offered the chance to mix theory and empirical research, and to apply a mix of behavioral and institutional methods. And the topic was largely uncharted. Whereas lots of descriptive and prescriptive work on the topic could be found, there was little theory or evidence to structure thinking about the problems facing public sector policy makers, unions, or employers. Even Don Schwab, our exacting teacher of research methods (and another sparring partner over various issues in the area of human resource management.), approved of my choice of topic. As only Don could put it: "You should stay focused on collective bargaining research. Anything you do will be better than what's out there now."

One burning question that seemed to beg for an answer was why bargaining in the public sector seemed to depart from the principles and norms that had built up over the years in the private sector. Was it that its participants were simply not yet experienced enough to conform to how bargaining worked in the private sector? Or was there something deeper about the institutional and political setting of the public sector that caused these differences? Specific questions abounded in the literature. Who is the employer in the public sector? Why do involved parties seem to make end runs around formal negotiators to elected representatives? Why do politics seem to intrude when things heat up and an impasse or strike is threatened? What could be done to improve the bargaining process?

I had actually gotten my feet wet on this topic in my first "real world" exposure to these questions. Perhaps I was still trying to figure out what had happened and why. As an undergraduate I did a semester's work-study stint in the City of Madison's Personnel Department. At the time, the firefighters were negotiating with the city. The big issue in negotiations was wage parity with the police. As in most cities in the country, there had been a tradition of parity and the city's chief negotiator, recruited from Chrysler to bring his private sector experience to bear on city bargaining, was determined to break parity in these negotiations. So he assigned me the task of doing some research on this topic and drafting a policy paper on this topic. I dutifully complied and wrote what I thought was the definitive report that would clearly show the logic of why police should be paid more than firefighters. My first lesson in real-world politics was about to unfold.

My report was to be presented to the city's Police and Fire Commission, a body not formally involved in the negotiations, but that had some ambiguous jurisdiction on this matter. Rather than present it, the city's negotiator "allowed" me to present the report and recommendation to the Commission at a breakfast meeting. The Chair of the Commission was a faculty member in the School for Workers at the University, and an advisor to many unions on job evaluation, safety, and wage setting. Needless to say, he didn't think much of my report, tore apart the recommendations with the gusto and the skill of an experienced advocate and analyst, and basically ate me for breakfast! So much for the role of research in negotiations, I thought. What I didn't realize until I wrote up this case as part of my Master's thesis was that this was all part and parcel of the politics of city government bargaining. The Commission favored parity, the chief negotiator did not, and this was the Commission's opportunity to try to demonstrate its displeasure with the city's position in negotiations. I had naively thought because they were part of management they should be on "our side."

In case you wonder what happened in those fateful negotiations – we ended up with a three-day firefighter strike over the parity issue. It was settled in the mayor's office in one of those classic face-saving compromises. The principle of parity was to be preserved but firefighters would be paid one cent per year less than police officers. As far as I know that differential remains to this day! So, who won and who lost in that strike? Clearly one penny a year per firefighter was not really worth putting the good citizens of the city through a three-day disruption in fire protection.

That process – how to explain the complicated mix of intraorganizational bargaining and conflict[4] and what several of us later termed multilateral bargaining, became the topic of my dissertation. The answer to the question of what is different about the public sector is that it inherently has multiple parties, and for this reason does not conform to traditional bilateral negotiations. The division of power within management is there for good political/democratic reasons. Our forefathers built the separation of powers into our governmental institutions. Moreover, elected and appointed officials care more about preserving their power and authority than about any presumed norms of "effective" negotiations in which each side has one spokesperson and internal conflicts are resolved either prior to negotiations or privately as the bargaining process unfolds. The theory of multilateral bargaining that I developed from my masters thesis case study, and then tested in a sample of 326 firefighter-city government negotiations, suggested that this was not just a temporary artifact of inexperience. It reflected the political dynamics and setting of public sector organizations and, therefore, was likely to endure. It has.

My dissertation allowed me to apply the mix of institutional, behavioral, and economic theories and methods that I believed were needed to modernize the study of collective bargaining. To my total surprise, this approach seemed to take. My dissertation was awarded the "best dissertation" prize of the American Psychological Association's Division of Industrial and Organizational Psychology. I didn't consider myself a psychologist, but was very happy to see that this type of work was of interest to and respected by I/O psychologists.

CORNELL (1973–1980)

My dissertation also served me well because it helped land a job at Cornell's New York State School of Industrial and Labor Relations (NYSSILR). To my mother's great relief, Kathy and I chose Cornell and Ithaca over the University of Chicago – she was afraid to have her youngest son, his wife, and Andy, her newest little grandson, in the big City of Chicago. She was relieved to learn that Ithaca was about the size of our hometown and far away from New York City!

Cornell and Ithaca served us well, both as a place to start a career and to expand our family. Before we left, we had adopted three more children, Sarah, Sam, and Jacob. But the initial reaction to my radical ideas for bringing quantitative research methods and behavioral science concepts to the study of collective bargaining didn't sit so well with some of the more senior members of the ILR Collective Bargaining Department. It seemed I was hired to fill the slot just vacated by a retiree – induced by that new ILR Dean, Robert McKersie, who was determined to change things. I'll never forget the memo this particular retiree sent me in response to my seemingly collegial act of asking for his comments on a paper. He wrote back that any paper that tried to use numbers to quantify how bargaining takes place will "clearly die the death it deserves." Real collective bargaining is more than numbers and by God real collective bargaining researchers should know better or learn quickly. I turned out to be a dismal learner – largely because of Bob McKersie's good advice: "Just treat him like your grandfather – listen respectfully, but don't necessarily take his advice. He can do no harm." All deans should be so wise and supportive of unsure assistant professors!

Bob McKersie was busy giving similar advice to other young faculty members at the time because he was leading the ILR School through a major generational transition as the School's founding fathers and mothers retired. He recruited a remarkable group of young scholars, including Lee Dyer, Tom Barocci, Tom DeCotiis, Sam Bacharach, Tove Hammer, Bob Stern, Bob Smith, Ron Ehrenberg, Bob Hutchins, Clete Daniels, Howard Aldrich, John Drotning, Jenny Farley, George Milkovich, Olivia Mitchell, and Roger Keeran. Together this group brought more mainstream social science and historical methods into the School's curriculum and research programs. The friendships we made with these folks, both through collaborative research with people like Lee Dyer and David Lipsky, and through the "family" gatherings we shared on holidays, have lasted to this day. The Dyer and Kochan families have kept up the tradition by celebrating Thanksgiving and other family milestones together ever since.

The Cornell years offered two other important opportunities that would shape much of my work and learning while in Ithaca. First, because New York State needed mediators and fact finders to help resolve the many local and state level bargaining cases that occurred each year, I got the opportunity to practice mediation and factfinding rather than just teach about such things. What an opportunity! Driving in the middle of the night or early morning on the winding deer-filled roads that connected Ithaca to the rest of New York State, often after a long and sometimes frustrating bargaining session, was only half the fun. The real fun, learning, and satisfaction came when the mediation bore fruit and produced that dynamic and creative flow from disagreement and impasse to settlement. I can safely say I never learned more in a shorter period of time than in the five or so years in which I had the opportunity to practice and learn mediation, factfinding, and arbitration.

The second opportunity was serendipitous. In 1974, one year after arriving at Cornell, the State amended its law governing collective bargaining for police and firefighters to provide for binding arbitration. The law was enacted as a three-year "experiment." At the end of three years, the legislature would once again decide if the controversial arbitration provision would be continued or abandoned and return to the prior situation of providing only mediation and factfinding followed, if necessary, by cities implementing whatever terms they favored. Again, what an opportunity! A natural field experiment was unfolding in front of us. After making a few inquiries with Robert Helsby and Harold Newman, the two top officials of New York's Public Employment Relations Board, the state agency in charge of resolving these disputes, it was clear they would welcome a "Cornell study" of the experiences under the law. They were quick to point out, however, that they had no funds to support such a study. That was okay with me because I had already heard of a division of the National Science Foundation (NSF) that was charged with funding well-designed public policy evaluation research. So I took a semester to write a NSF proposal and used the opportunity to propose a number of questions we might tackle as we carried out an evaluation of the policy issues at stake. The main question was whether or not we could put some deeper structure into understanding the labor mediation process. Most practitioners and some researchers considered mediation more a fine art than a science. I thought otherwise, in part, based on my own mediation experiences. If I could be successful as a mediator it couldn't be art! Luck maybe, art no.

This study was my first opportunity to mix public policy analysis of an important, and, as it turned out, highly visible and hotly contested political issue, with a systematic research analysis using a "quasi-experimental" (before-after with several comparison groups) design. It also was my first experience in building and supervising a team of very talented students (Moti Mironi, Jean Badenschneider, and Todd Jick) and faculty (Ronald Ehrenberg). The study consumed three years of my life, nearly cost me my marriage (Kathy still refers rather unkindly to "that red report" referring to the color of the cover), and reinforced the value of mixing policy and research analysis together. Everyone at home and work had to put up with the effects of the stress I felt over having to produce a report that would be used in the political debate over the future of the collective bargaining law whose extension the governor's office opposed, the police and fire unions favored, and to which the neutral state agency that administered the law had taken the risk of exposing its record and its future to this greenhorn assistant professor who spoke in regressions and other arcane terminology.

The project taught me a great deal about how to work with practitioners who have big stakes in the issues at hand and divergent and probably irreconcilable positions. In the end, I did recommend continuing the arbitration process, but making a whole host of changes in the way it was structured and how bargaining impasses would be handled. Each of the parties used our findings and recommendations to support its case, sometimes with logic that was diametrically contrary to the data. But they felt compelled to frame their arguments around the evidence provided by our study. In the end, the legislature and governor followed most of our recommendations and continued the arbitration provision. It remains on the books today. The project also produced two dissertations, multiple articles, and that "red report" ended up as a short book (Kochan, Mironi, Ehrenberg, Baderschneider & Jick, 1979). One of my fondest memories of this project is the many hours Moti Mironi and I spent debating the merits and limitations of arbitration. I started as a skeptic and he, given his lawyer's training, a proponent. By the end of the project we had reversed positions but were still in disagreement! Such is the intellectual and social process that builds strong, life-long bonds and friendships.

The culmination of my work at Cornell took the form of my first major book, *Collective Bargaining and Industrial Relations*. Technically, the first edition (published in 1980) was a textbook. It took my colleague Harry Katz, however, to actually turn it into a useful teaching text, nearly a decade later (Katz & Kochan, 1987, 1993, 1998). The real purpose of the book was to show how institutional, economic, and behavioral science concepts and methods could be combined to help bring a more analytical and systematic approach to the study of collective bargaining and industrial relations. Although poorly written and even more horribly edited, for its day, it did just what I was trying to do. It showed one could, in fact, mix these approaches creatively, use numbers sensibly, and advance our understanding of the IR field. Viewed with more than 20-years hindsight, this seems like no big deal. At the time, it was controversial and different and argued for how the field should bring the social sciences back into its research and teaching. The field has done so.

THE DEPARTMENT OF LABOR (1979–1980)

Sabbaticals are wonderful inventions. I recommend them to everyone. I had accumulated the right number of years (seven) to take a sabbatical from Cornell during the academic year 1979–80. What to do? We were happy at Cornell and in Ithaca. As mentioned earlier, three more adopted children were added to our family while we were there and Ithaca was a very supportive community for the diverse mix of nationalities and races now reflected in our family. So we had no expectation or burning desire to move on to another academic setting. But the lure of Washington was hovering around. After all, that's where real public policy is made, or so I naively thought.

It turned out that a number of faculty from industrial relations programs in different universities had been urging the Department of Labor to provide more research funding for IR research. We particularly wanted a program to support Ph.D. dissertations in our field, similar to the supportive program that had been in place for many years in the Employment and Training area. Because the industrial relations academic community had a friend and colleague in Ray Marshall serving as Secretary of Labor at the time, why not move on this idea now? And because I had all these wild and weird ideas on where research should go in our field, why not have me develop an agenda? So it was to be that the Kochans would take our sabbatical in Washington and I would be assigned to recommend to Secretary Marshall a program for research on industrial relations.

I was assigned to the Assistant Secretary for Policy Evaluation and Research for the one-year job. Peter Henle, the Deputy Assistant Secretary, was to be my boss. But Peter had enough of me after a month and decided to take a new early retirement package the government was offering. So, I was then on my own. But not really. Peter continued to offer wise informal counsel over the course of the year and has ever since. He and his wife, Theda, remain great friends of ours. Among other things, they introduced us to the quiet beauty of New Hampshire in the summer and we enjoy our visits to their summer home there each year.

So August 1, 1979 (yes, we moved to Washington in August) we packed the now four little kids in a Chevrolet Malibu station wagon that not only lacked air conditioning (who needed it in Ithaca?) but also, to our discovery, back-seat windows that Chevrolet's design geniuses decided really didn't need to open.

Our son, Sam, had more sense than his parents. The first Sunday after arriving, we again threw the kids in the car to go see the Washington sights. Waiting in a traffic jam to approach the Jefferson Memorial, 3-year old Sam had had enough of the heat. "I have a great idea," he proclaimed. "Let's go home to Ithaca and come back here at Christmas." Sam to this day has the most street-wise sense of the clan.

The year was a wonderful learning experience. It only took about two months to draft a report and research agenda. So, what was I to do for the other nine or so months? It turned out that Secretary Marshall was a kindred soul, an academic lonely for someone to talk to about ideas. And Ray loved (loves) to talk and tell stories. So I got to work on a wide range of special projects – I was sort of the Department's utility academic. I soon discovered it didn't matter if you had actually done research on a topic to be deemed an expert. I was the academic. If they needed a paper on a topic, whether it was what type of advanced notice for plant closing should the Secretary propose, or how to set up and keep together a tripartite steel industry labor-management group, or how to design an experiment to promote "voluntary compliance" with OSHA regulations and safety standards, or whatever, I could write a memo in a hurry (sometimes by 5 PM) that could be condensed down to the classic one page read for busy Assistant Secretaries, Cabinet members or even, heaven forbid, the President or his White House staff! So, as a free lancer moving without portfolio at an early career stage, I learned how Washington worked and how it didn't. Once again our practical son Sam described to a friend, on the way to pre-school in the back seat of our car, what his dad did for a living: "He goes to lunch." Apparently I had regaled the kids at the dinner table with tales of the interesting people I had been meeting in the heady DC environment.

The lasting effect that year was to give me a realistic picture of the Washington job scene for political appointees. It took the aura off the jobs that had lured me to Washington. I discovered that unless you had a very clear idea of what you wanted to accomplish and an environment that offered you a reasonable chance to get it done, the jobs are essentially reactive and firefighting activities on issues not of your own choosing and the agenda is largely out of your control. Moreover, you quickly become a captive of what 20-years later, another Secretary of Labor, Robert Reich, would describe as his feeling of being *Locked in the Cabinet*.[5] So, ever since that truly delightful and invigorating year, I have always been grateful that at the end of a day in Washington I can get back on a plane to go home to a job where I can speak my mind and control my agenda and still have a hand in policy debates and advice. Such are the beauties of life in the academy!

I learned another lesson from this experience, this time from grandfatherly advice Clark Kerr offered one day when he was kind enough to take time to meet with me to discuss the draft proposed research agenda I had prepared. He was in town because he was holding an arbitration hearing for a new contract covering the nation's postal workers. After discussing the report, he began to reflect on why the fields of labor economics and industrial relations had not developed more and deeper theory over the past twenty years, despite some promising beginnings in the work of John Dunlop and their collaborative work. His analysis (actually couched as advice to me) was to recognize that "you can't do it all." You can't produce new theoretical thinking if you are involved in solving the practical problems of the day as a policy maker or advisor in Washington (as so many in our field had done in the three decades after World War II). Policy or university administration and leadership require a different type of thinking – less open to deep study and critical reappraisal, more advocacy, more on-the-spot judgements, etc.

Small doses of public service of short duration can be helpful for applying and testing one's ideas on the run. Staying too long or spending too much time on such assignments may be invigorating and rewarding, but can dull the theoretical senses and writing style. Clark is absolutely right both about the value of short and time-limited exposure and the costs of long term capture. It's usually a one-way street.

MIT: THE 1980s

It turned out that we did not return to Cornell. Abe Siegel, then Associate Dean of the Sloan School at the Massachusetts Institute of Technology (MIT), suggested this was a good time for us to make a move. MIT was particularly attractive because it had a long and distinguished tradition in industrial relations and its Ph.D. program needed to be rebuilt, a task close to my heart.

Because Kathy and I couldn't answer our question of why not give Boston a try, we decided to accept Abe's offer.

Moving from Cornell to MIT and from the small quiet environs of Ithaca to the sprawling, confusing, and expensive Boston was a daunting and eye-opening experience. Navigating in Boston for an outsider is a learning experience of its own. They don't believe in street signs in Boston. I think the theory is that if you grew up here you know where you are and where you are going and, if you didn't, you don't belong here anyway! If Ithaca is great for its splendid central isolation, Boston is the opposite. Everybody seems to be just "passing through" or visiting one or another university at some point and would like to stop in. In fact, that's what makes Boston, Cambridge, and MIT so exciting and such an opportunity for continual intellectual challenge and learning. You are never alone, or at a loss for someone to talk to about your work. Moreover, the (often overrated) aura of the MIT and/or Harvard names makes one more visible and in demand for speaking and visiting requests than is probably warranted by the actual quality of one's work. As MIT President Chuck Vest once said to several of us, "I have a well worked out and proven formula, my wisdom goes up by geometric proportions the farther from Cambridge I travel." So one of the biggest challenges of being productive at MIT is managing one's time and avoiding getting one's ego caught up in the view that you know more than you actually do.

The move to MIT was also very good for our family. Ben, our fifth child, was born in Boston. Managing a household of five children and a husband who traveled a lot and worked long hours in the office and at home would try the patience of most mortals. I recognized from the first day I met her that my wife Kathy is no ordinary mortal. She not only held us all together as our four boys and daughter grew from infants through the tough adolescent years, along the way, she also managed to get her master's degree and become a Nurse Practitioner, thereby returning to the profession she had temporarily set aside when the children arrived.

Our personal and family choices put us in a rather unique, neither here nor there, sociological space. Both Kathy and I come from large families. Though we are close to our parents and siblings, none lives near to us and, therefore, our children didn't have the benefits of growing up in proximity to their grandparents and numerous cousins. So they and we missed that part of family life. At the same time, there were few others of our generation, and in our professional communities, who chose to have such a large family. To some our choice seemed quite unusual, if not odd. It didn't seem odd to us, however, especially that we have just sent Ben, our youngest child, off to college. Now sometimes we watch parents struggling with young children and wonder how we did it when we had, as we had at one point, four children under the age of eight. Selective recall is a good thing.

Arriving at MIT, in 1980, left me and my new colleagues feeling uneasy for another reason. Events in the IR field were becoming hard to predict and interpret. Industrial relations seemed to be changing in unpredictable and non-incremental ways. I remember the first sense I had of this. At Cornell I got to know the labor-relations executives and staff at Xerox Corporation because the company's main operations were located in Rochester, New York. They were frequent guest lecturers in my classes and I used Xerox practices to illustrate how bargaining works. So, after settling in at MIT, I visited Xerox headquarters in anticipation of starting a research project on some aspect of current industrial relations. To my surprise, it seemed like a different company. Instead of the steady as you go stable industrial-relations setting, management was talking about a new "quality of working life" experiment they had just negotiated into their collective bargaining agreement and the need to bring about bigger changes in their relationships to get manufacturing costs down, improve quality, and engage line management in the labor-relations process. I had seen and written about all of these developments separately in recent years but here it was, all in one package, from an organization I had least expected it from.

After reporting this back to my new MIT colleagues Bob McKersie (who had also moved from Cornell to MIT about the same time) and Harry Katz, we decided to each visit other firms to see what was going on. More shocks. Some firms were doing what Xerox was doing. But more were openly and (publicly rather than quietly and discreetly) proclaiming their "union-free environment" strategies. In the past, we could predict which company would behave this way by a simple metric – what percent of the workforce was unionized already. Those with high levels of unionization put a higher priority on working with unions and those with lower levels put top priority on remaining non-union (Kochan, 1980). But now all was out in the open. And, moreover, the strategies were out of control of industrial-relations professionals and being driven by human resource executives and line managers and chief executives. Something was afoot in our field that many of us had either missed or chosen to ignore. Our group was determined to change this state of affairs and to understand how and why our field of study and practice was changing and what the implications of these changes would be for theory, policy, and practice.

So began a decade long multi-faculty-multi student (and extremely challenging and engaging) research project on "Industrial Relations in Transition." We were blessed with outstanding colleagues including, Michael Piore, Henry Farber, Katherine Abraham, Tom Barocci, Phyllis Wallace, and Jim Driscoll, and, at later dates, Bob Thomas, Mary Rowe, Paul Osterman, Lisa Lynch,

Jim Rebitzer, and Maureen Scully. We were supported by a series of equally talented and dedicated graduate students such as Anil Verma, Janice Klein, Casey Ichniowski, Nancy Mower, Maryellen Kelley, Kirsten Wever, Joel Cutcher-Gershenfeld, John Chalykoff and Richard Locke, and one excellent post-doc, Peter Cappelli. Together we produced a considerable number of articles, edited volumes, specialized monographs, and one integrative book that challenged our field to change its prevailing paradigm to better understand the fundamental changes taking place. Indeed, that was the underlying argument in *The Transformation of American Industrial Relations* – that the field was undergoing fundamental changes that would in the end transform the post war or New Deal system in ways our incremental-cross sectional models wouldn't predict.

The book was well received. It won the Academy of Management's George R. Terry Best Book Award in 1988. But it also produced a storm of controversy, considerable interest, and debate among other scholars and practitioners, who divided into two camps – those of us arguing that the system of industrial relations as we knew it was undergoing a fundamental transformation and those who argued that we had overstated the case and that the current era was simply a short-term fluctuation that could be accommodated just fine by prevailing models. Our chief sparring partner on this was John Dunlop, the intellectual dean of our field for the past fifty years, author of the field's prevailing paradigm (Dunlop, 1958), and a former Secretary of Labor. This was to be the first chapter in an extended intellectual debate with a man whom I respect deeply and whom I now (but not then) consider a friend.

This project also taught me an important lesson, one that Harry Katz and Mike Piore in particular stressed. At the heart of any intellectually interesting question is some sharp debating point – there has to be someone or something that disagrees with your hypothesis, argument, or line of reasoning, and the consequences of that disagreement have to be clear and consequential. Otherwise, eventually the question of "so who cares" cannot be answered and the issue is likely to be forgotten, if not abandoned. The transformation argument met this test and sustained our group and, indeed, our field for more than a decade.

THE PETROCHEMICAL CONTRACTOR SAFETY STUDY

On October 23, 1989, a disastrous explosion at the Phillips Chemical plant in Pasadena, Texas, killed twenty-two workers, injured over two hundred others, and narrowly avoided sending toxic gas into the surrounding community. This accident triggered a debate over the role of contract workers because a contract crew, rather than a crew of regular employees, had been working on the tank that started the explosion and fire. The increased use of contract workers had been a major source of conflict in labor relations in the petrochemical industry for years. This incident brought the debate over whether contract workers (largely non-union) were not only taking away the jobs of regular employees (most of who were unionized), but also threatening the safety and welfare of those working in the industry and the communities in which petrochemical plants are located.

As a result of the pressure brought to bear on the Occupational Safety and Health Administration, Congress and the Secretary of Labor commissioned the John Gray Institute at Lamar University in Beaumont, Texas to conduct a study of the safety issues associated with the use of contract workers. Because years ago David Lipsky, Lee Dyer and I had done a small study of safety-and-health committees, the head of OSHA asked me to join an advisory committee he was creating to provide input to the study. I agreed, thinking I would go to one or two committee meetings, read drafts of a report, and offer whatever comments I might.

So began another intensive foray into the politics of labor policy, this time in the heart of political hardball country – the oil and chemical industry. After attending the first advisory group meeting and, unfortunately, offering a number of suggestions for how the study might be designed and conducted, John Wells, the project director, asked me to play a more active role and help with the actual research process. This changed my role and my relationship with the industry and labor representatives on the advisory committee. I was seen as a problem for the industry representatives, who really did not want this study conducted in the first place, and if it had to be conducted, certainly expected to control it's recommendations. At the advisory committee's second meeting, the informal leader of the industry representatives, a high-level Executive in one of the major oil companies, made what I thought was a rather weird comment. "You certainly write a lot don't you", he said. I mumbled something about that being part of my job. He went on to say, "I know, we had somebody read everything you've written, so we understand where you are coming from." The implication was not stated, but clear. The industry didn't particularly like my prior published writings and was putting me on notice to that effect.

That little exchange was a harbinger of what would become a hotly contested project. We conducted a survey of employers, contract firms, regular employees, and contract workers. Case studies were done to identify how different plants managed their contractors, and the relationships between safety practices and outcomes were analyzed. The results showed that, indeed, use of contractors had increased steadily over the past decade and their use was associated with higher accident rates, due primarily to the less experience, less training, and less supervision they received relative to regular plant employees. At the same time, a number of plants had developed very comprehensive safety management systems that were applied to selecting contractors and to supervising and training contract employees. These management systems, where implemented, sometimes against the advice of corporate lawyers who feared exposing the company to "co-management" liabilities, mitigated the negative effects of using contractors. Therefore, it was not the use of contractors per se that increased the risk of accidents, it was the failure by most companies and plants to adopt effective systems for managing across these workplace boundaries.

Not surprisingly, the first draft of our report produced sharp criticism from industry representatives. This was the only time in my experience where the same group not only disagreed with the substantive findings of work I was involved in, but went to great lengths to discredit the work and the research team, even to the point of investigating our backgrounds and putting pressure on OSHA to cancel the John Gray Institute research contract and getting members of Congress to challenge the legality of issuing the research grant to begin with. In the end, OSHA "received" our report and recommendations (Wells, Kochan & Smith, 1991), the head of OSHA, and his Deputy both left the agency. Although the industry never accepted our results, over the next several years most of the major petrochemical companies took steps to change their practices in ways consistent with our findings and recommendations. Such was the state of what we described as a failed industrial-relations system in this industry (Kochan, Wells & Smith, 1992). The unfortunate part of this story is that a decade later, OSHA, business, and labor are still debating who should be held responsible for the management of contract worker safety. The debate over co-management remains a piece of unfinished business, a point I will turn to at the end of this essay.

THE HUMAN RESOURCES NETWORK

In 1989 Ralph Gomory took over as President of the Alfred P. Sloan Foundation and announced at a MIT dinner talk his intention to create a series of industry centers at different universities focused on deepening our understanding of what was needed to restore their competitiveness. His concern was that too few contemporary academics had deep expertise in the technologies, institutions, and organizational practices that make specific industries productive and he wanted to change this. To his credit, he did. Today there are over a dozen such industry centers focusing on such sectors as apparel, autos, steel, financial services, telecommunications, semiconductors, computers, food, and construction.

Two years after launching this initiative, Hirsh Cohen, a Sloan Foundation Program Officer and assistant to Gomory, visited MIT and said they were hearing a set of common themes from these industry centers: Human resources matter a lot. Perhaps we should create a crosscutting network to study these issues in various industries. This was music to my ears. With the generous support of the Foundation we formed what has come to be called the HR Network. Our simple approach was to periodically bring together researchers studying innovations in work systems and human-resource practices to share ideas, methodological challenges and approaches, drafts of papers, and ideas for future work. Coordinating this network has been one of the more pleasant and easy things I've been involved in over the years.

Watching students from various centers come together and create their own networks that then sometimes produced joint projects has been especially exciting. This is the best part of this job – helping talented young people get involved in the IR field and go on to shape and lead it in new directions. Over the years our MIT group has been fortunate to attract an extremely talented set of Ph.D. students. Most have been very active in the HR Network. They are the nucleus of the next generation of scholars and leaders in our field. In addition to the 1980s contingent mentioned earlier, they include: John Paul MacDuffie, Gil Preuss, Christopher Erickson, Ann Frost, Marc Weinstein, Jody Hoffer Gittell, Saul Rubinstein, Rose Batt, Larry Hunter, Brenda Lautsch, Lucio Baccaro, Philip Hirschohn, Susan Eaton, Corinne Bendersky, Sean Safford, Isabel Fernandez, Forrest Briscoe, Matthew Bidwell and Natasha Iskander.

LIFE AS A TEAMSTER-NOMINATED BOARD MEMBER

One of the more bizarre learning experiences I've had was serving on the board of directors of two trucking firms (at different points in time). In the 1980s, the Teamsters Union negotiated a number of employee stock-ownership plans as quid pro quos for concessionary wage agreements with trucking firms that were struggling to survive in the post deregulation environment. As part of the package the Union demanded seats on the boards of these companies and recruited outside experts to take up these seats. I was asked to serve on two of these boards. The first experience was short-lived. Within a year of being appointed the company was merged with another trucking firm – an outcome necessary for the firm to avoid going bankrupt and to save most of it's employees' jobs.

The second experience was not much different in ultimate outcome, but considerably more memorable. At times it took on elements of a Charlie Chaplin tragic comedy. Picture the irony of representing a group of truckers on the board of a struggling company whose headquarters was in Beverly Hills! Once a month I dutifully flew across the country, first class of course, stayed overnight in the Beverly Hills Hilton, and listened to financial reports of a company slowly but steadily going downhill. I had a comrade-in-arms on the board. Wayne Horvitz, a former Director of the Federal Mediation and Conciliation Service, and a friend of long-standing, also represented the Teamsters. We were a caucus of two on a board with seven other West Coast owners, financiers, and other cronies of the CEO/part-owner of the company.

After about six months of falling revenues, the board decided it needed to look for someone to acquire the firm. Here is where the real battles began. The CEO simply wanted a deal that would get as much of his money out of the transaction as possible, regardless of the consequences for the company's employees or it's future. So, at one point, he reported that he had located a suitable purchaser for the company and outlined the general terms of the proposed deal. It took only a few questions from Wayne and me to sense that something did not sound right, at least for those of us who had the interests of the employees in mind. So we did some checking through our Teamster contacts about the reputation of this would-be buyer. It seemed that this potential buyer had purchased other trucking firms before and then simply stripped the assets and closed down the firms, thereby, throwing their employees out of work and confiscating a good part of their pensions.

We thought it better for the Teamsters to report their prior experience with this potential buyer directly to our board rather than have us deliver the message. It turned out the Teamsters were holding a meeting of their Executive Board in Palm Springs about the time of our next scheduled board meeting. So picture the following. Mario Puzo could not have written a better script. Wayne and I fly to the west coast and meet the CEO and several fellow board members at the Santa Monica airport. There we board a private jet to fly to Palm Springs. Upon arrival the Teamsters have cars waiting to take us to a hotel where we are to have a private meeting with Billy McCarthy, their ailing President, his General Counsel (a fellow Bostonian who set up the meeting on our behalf), and two vice presidents of the union who had experience with this prospective buyer.

We walked in and sat down in the large, but now empty conference room – except for a wheezing (from emphysema) hunched over President wearing dark glasses and his bodyguard and fellow officers. I couldn't help but think we were actually in Hollywood, not Palm Springs. For the next hour we listened to these Teamster representatives tell our fellow board members to beware – the company we were considering selling the firm to was essentially a bunch of crooks. It would not be in our interests, and certainly not in our employees' interests, to follow through. The message was delivered!

All along I just kept wondering if the wheezing Billy McCarthy was going to die before our meeting was over. He didn't. In fact he lived to be indicted for his own misdeeds! At the end of the meeting, we said thanks, returned to our waiting cars and waiting jet, and returned to Santa Monica to consider other options. A memorable, if not inspiring, experience in labor relations and corporate governance in the trucking industry. Eventually the company did get sold to a buyer, only a little more reputable than the one we avoided.

One other ironic experience involved the same mix of characters. We had to meet again with Billy McCarthy on another issue, a few months later. This time it was more convenient to meet him at a hotel in Washington, D.C. where the AFL-CIO convention was taking place. By coincidence, the day we agreed to meet was also the day that the famous Polish labor leader and president of Poland, Lech Walesa, was to address the convention. We agreed to meet McCarthy in his suite following Walesa's speech. As it turned out Walesa finished about the time we arrived. As we got off the elevator on the way to our meeting, Walesa walked by, smiled, and said hello. A few minutes later as I sat in McCarthy's suite listening to him raise the issue of the day, I had the distinct feeling that within ten minutes I had seen close up the best and the worst labor has to offer in the world! That image completely dominates any recollection of how we resolved the question we came to discuss.

Aside from these memories, I actually learned a lot about the pros and cons of serving on corporate boards, albeit these might not have been the most representative cases to support any generalizations. It is clear that having someone speaking for employee interests and human resource issues expands the agenda of typical board meetings and the factors considered in making strategic decisions. This can work to the mutual advantage of shareholders and the workforce, but only if decisions taken at this level are supported and reinforced throughout an organization. On its own, board representation can at best be a defensive strategy for protecting employee interests from harmful or just plain stupid decisions. But board representation is extremely valuable in supporting and sustaining strategies aimed at utilizing a workforce's knowledge and skills. The strategic challenge is that it takes power to get a seat on a board, but then it takes an integrative perspective and mode of interaction to be influential in board decisions and actions.

THE SATURN PROJECT

The insights gained from these board experiences were helpful in another project, namely the decade-long study that Saul Rubinstein and I carried out at the Saturn Corporation (Rubinstein & Kochan, 2001). Our group at MIT had worked closely with Don Ephlin from the United Auto Workers (UAW) and Al Warren at General Motors (GM) throughout the 1980s. Don and Al were the champions within their respective organizations for the ideas that led to Saturn's founding. From the beginning, Saturn was created to serve multiple purposes. It was designed to: (a) show that small cars could be built profitably in the U.S.; (b) preserve jobs for American workers and UAW members that otherwise had been moving to lower wage countries; and (c) serve as a learning laboratory for both GM and the UAW. Partnership principles were built into Saturn from the shop floor to the highest levels of management and between the company and its suppliers and retailers. As such, it became the most far reaching and the most controversial experiment in labor-management relations, co-management, and corporate governance carried out in America in the last twenty years.

Over time, as its initial champions retired, Saturn lost the support of top GM and UAW leaders, new product allocations were delayed, and its early promise and impressive marketplace success eroded as its original product aged. Whether it will rebound and use its partnership principles to good advantage in the future remains to be seen. Regardless of the ultimate fate of Saturn, I believe society would be better off if we had more organizational experiments like this to learn from and to foster a debate over how the corporation of the future can best meet its multiple responsibilities to shareholders and other stakeholders.

THE DUNLOP COMMISSION

By the 1990s, I thought the debate over how industrial relations had changed was over. No one seriously believed we would return to the stable days of collective bargaining and labor-management relations envisioned by the New Deal system and that dominated the period from the 1940s through the 1970s. The real debate was what changes in labor law and related policies, and what new strategies for the labor movement and for managers of industrial relations and human resources, were needed to adapt to a more competitive environment, changing technologies and workforce, and new concepts about how to gain competitive, strategic advantage from a firm's workforce. The election of Bill Clinton and a Democratic majority in Congress seemed to offer a ray of hope that we might finally get on with the task of reforming labor law – something that failed in 1975–1976 and again in 1979–1980, and then was abandoned as hopeless during the Reagan-Bush years.

I was not alone in hoping something could be done. I had been asked by the Clinton campaign and then by the transition team to write a memo on what should and could be done to reflect the candidate's, and now the new President's, opportunity to focus on these issues. I did so and stressed the obvious: The world has changed in fundamental ways and calls for equally fundamental changes in labor law and the role of government. But labor and business remained locked in an irresolvable impasse over labor law. Left to their own devices these two groups will not reach a compromise. But much of what the President wants to achieve at the micro level of the economy will be impossible without modernizing labor law and changing the country's labor-management climate. So the President should articulate a clear statement of the principles that will underlie a new labor policy suited to the times (I offered five points I thought should anchor a new policy) and then ask for labor and management to work with him and his administration to figure out how to achieve and implement these principles. But it would be fruitless to simply create a blue ribbon labor and management group to try to find a common solution on their own. There was no deal to be made and in fact, no one could identify the key players who could make such a deal on behalf of the diverse business and labor interests and workforce of the day.

Robert Reich, the newly announced Secretary of Labor, agreed with this point of view. The day after his confirmation we met and he indicated that he and the administration agreed with the ideas in the memo (others much more influential than me were giving him the same advice) and that they planned to set up a group to do this with a charter along the lines outlined in my memo. So I thought we might get somewhere.

Fast-forward three weeks. On a late Friday afternoon a call came to me at MIT from Robert Reich. After chatting for a couple minutes he reiterated that he was about to publicly announce formation of a commission to work on these issues, that he wanted me to be a member and, to my surprise and somewhat shock, that he planned to ask John Dunlop to chair it. My immediate reaction was that this would set us back into the old debate about whether anything was new or not and that this would not serve the country well. But this was not a call to ask what I thought, but to alert me that this was the way it was going to be.

So began The Commission on the Future of Worker-Management Relations, a.k.a. the Dunlop Commission. Now our differences were of more than simple academic interest and debate. Like it or not, we had to try to work together, along with a distinguished group of two other former Secretaries of Labor, a former Secretary of Commerce, two CEOs, a retired labor leader and several other academics. The first year involved the collective efforts of Commission members and most of the business and labor leaders and representatives of women's organizations that appeared before the Commission to convince the chairman that, in fact, the world had changed and new approaches to law and policy were needed. To John's eternal credit, he came around to share this view, slowly, incrementally, and only when it became clear to him that business and labor leaders saw themselves in a different world. So after a full year of regional and national hearings, and considerable and sometimes rather heated internal debate, we issued a "Fact Finding" report that outlined our analysis of the current state of affairs in the IR field. That report, I believe, provided a reasonably solid foundation for then going on to propose policy recommendations in what was to be the second report of the Commission.

My hope was we would recommend a complete overhaul and updating of labor and employment law. This would include stronger penalties against employers that violated or thwarted workers' rights to join a union, options for new forms of representation and participation suited to meet the diverse needs and preferences of the modern workforce, experimentation with alternative forms of dispute resolution, and flexibility for employers and unions in compliance with labor law and employment law to adapt workplace regulations to fit their varying needs (Kochan, 1998). These were controversial views, both within the Commission and with some traditionalists in the labor movement and the business community.

Alas, it was too late to get anything constructive done. In the mid-term elections of 1994, the Gingrich Republican Revolution took over majorities in both houses of Congress and the short window of opportunity for the Clinton Administration to do something constructive on labor policy had closed. In the end, the Commission issued a rather watered down report, still in John's mind one that might forge a compromise. In a word, our report fell on deaf ears. In fact, it was worse than that. My views became identified by some in the labor movement as favoring a change in the law that would bring back company dominated unions and further undermine independent unionism and collective bargaining. Whereas this was not what I was advocating, reputations have long tails in Washington and for years, even now, I still have to deal with this perception by some in the labor movement.

So ended our chance to change national policy. For the remaining six years of the Clinton Administration labor and employment policy fell off the radar screen and, like most other domestic policy issues, eventually took a back seat to the Clinton scandals. Vice President Gore then took the overly cautious road of avoiding these issues in his campaign for fear of alienating either labor or business by taking controversial positions. So the national impasse continues, and outdated labor and employment policies remain the law of the land.

MODERNIZING THE FEDERAL MEDIATION AND CONCILIATION SERVICE

One satisfying experience during the Clinton years bears mention. Clinton appointed my now good friend John Wells as Director of the Federal Mediation and Conciliation Service and we once again co-conspired on how to modernize that agency. I had worked with FMCS in various informal advisory roles over the years and knew the agency and many of its staff well. It needed a major transformation in outlook, role, and strategy or it would continue to decline as collective bargaining shrunk and the number of strikes it needed to resolve declined. To John's credit, he initiated a strategic review of the agency, brought in a large number of new mediators and national staff, and built strong relations with the key Congressional committees that oversaw the FMCS budget. He asked Joel Cutcher-Gershenfeld and me to design and conduct a first ever national customer (labor and management) survey of the agency and its activities (Cutcher-Gershenfeld, Kochan & Wells, 1999). Today FMCS is repositioned to support both labor and management parties using modern problem solving and partnership tools, new negotiations techniques for interest-based bargaining, and even an innovative virtual meeting tool that is well suited to support problem solving and negotiations among multiple parties scattered across multiple locations.

THE IIRA AND IRRA YEARS

Over the 1990s, I devoted a great deal of time to the two major professional associations in the IR field, the International Industrial Relations Association (IIRA) and the Industrial Relations Research Association (IRRA). The former is our worldwide association and the latter is its North American counterpart. I served as President of the IIRA from 1992–1995 and of the IRRA from 1999–2000. Both are among my most pleasurable and satisfying experiences to date.

Presiding over an international association of professionals in any field is a daunting task in cross cultural and global communications, learning and organizing. The IIRA holds a World Congress every three years. It was our task to organize this event in the U.S. in 1995. Because this would be the first World Congress to be held in the U.S., we wanted it to be a special event and one that made an intellectual mark on the IR field. To do so, we started nearly five years earlier to create several international research networks and urged these networks to mount studies of how different industrial-relations systems were adapting to the same pressures that were transforming the U.S. system. One network focused on the Organization for Economic Cooperation and Development (OECD) countries and another on the developing economies in Asia. Other groups came together around specific crosscutting issues such as the changing processes and institutions of dispute resolution or around specific industries such as banking, telecommunications, or autos. Each of these produced significant new research findings and built new professional alliances, and generated lively debates and discussions when the networks reported on their work at the World Congress.

Thanks to the remarkable organizing skills of Susan Cass, our Congress Coordinator, and the creative work of our newly hired administrative assistant, Karen Boyajian, the Congress exceeded all our expectations. Looking out at the 1,000 or so of the most accomplished and talented academics, government officials, and professionals in the IR field gathered at the opening ceremony, with my family members in the front row, was one of the most rewarding sights I could imagine. It takes enormous amounts of time and the commitment of a large number of people and organizations to make such an event successful and I'll be forever grateful to all who contributed. My deepest gratitude and admiration go to Susan and Karen. Their work on this and other projects have gained acclaim from our colleagues around the world as a showcase for the power of teamwork.

The IRRA was formed in 1947 in the wake of the wave of strikes that exploded in the U.S. after the war. It is a unique association in that it brings together academics across multiple disciplines who share an interest in working with professionals from business, labor, government, and the mediation-arbitration communities. Holding this coalition together and satisfying its members' varying interests for research and applications is a significant challenge, but one that brings out the best features of the IR field. I know of no other field where there is this type of close interaction of researchers with practitioners of such diverse interests!

The IRRA was facing a long period of decline in membership and in its sense of direction. It too needed to undergo a transformation by broadening the issues it addressed and by re-engaging scholars from the multiple disciplines that make up the IR field. So a number of us started a multi-year renewal effort that actually began when we celebrated the IRRA's 50th anniversary in 1997. One major initiative was to launch a new practitioner-oriented magazine, *Perspectives on Work*, devoted to engaging the membership in debates and dialogue on how we might work together in "shaping the workplace of the future." Once again Susan Cass, now fully recovered from the World Congress, took up the task of Managing Editor for *Perspectives* and led the design of what has been recognized as an innovative and useful publication – the one valued most by existing IRRA members and the one that helped us turn around the decline in membership.

In January, 2000, we organized the annual Industrial Relations Research Association (IRRA) meetings. I chose "Rebuilding the Social Contract at Work" as the theme for the meeting and the topic of my Presidential Address (Kochan, 2001). Regional meetings were held leading up to the national meeting to discuss local issues and specific topics such as work and family policies. We worked hard to broaden the membership base to bring new, younger scholars and practitioners into the organization. The participants in the different sessions were encouraged to look ahead at the challenges of the future. As a result, those who summarized the meeting for an issue of *Perspectives* expressed a sense of optimism that our profession has the ideas and research base needed to reverse the growing income gap between the rich and poor, resolve the impasse in national labor and employment policies, encourage and nurture the growth of new labor-market intermediaries and non-governmental organizations (NGOs) that are sprouting up around the world, and build "the next generation unions."

THE LABOR MARKET TASK FORCE PROJECT

My ideas on how to rebuild the social contract and update America's labor-market institutions are not mine alone. They reflect the shared ideas of the faculty and students in our group at MIT and the network of former students and colleagues we work with around the country. Our ideas are laid out in more detail in our recent book *Working in America: A Blueprint for the Labor Market* (Osterman, Kochan, Locke & Piore, 2001). The book is the culmination of a project led by Paul Osterman from our group. With support from the Ford and Rockefeller Foundations, we held a series of meetings and conferences over a four-year period with leading business, labor, government, and community leaders to explore what innovations in work were occurring on the front lines. Two hypotheses drove our effort. The first is the broad one already introduced: Work and the workforce have been changing faster than the institutions, policies and practices governing work and employment relations. The resulting gap is an important part of the explanation for growing disparities in income and the stresses and frustrations felt by many in the workforce and in our institutions, even during the prosperous 1990s. The second hypothesis driving this effort is that if solutions to this problem are to be found, they most likely already exist and are being developed in local innovations somewhere in the country. So we focused on identifying these islands of innovation and then asked what would be needed to bring them up to a national scale so that our overall society and economy might benefit. So, we now have produced our "blueprint" for the labor-market policies and institutions of the future. Whether anyone in a position of power is listening and willing to act on the blueprint remains to be seen.

DIVERSITY RESEARCH AND PRACTICE

Over the years I have gradually gotten drawn into research and practical efforts, at both MIT and in industry, to promote the effective management of diversity. I am not sure exactly how or why this happened. Perhaps it reflects my personal interests and the make-up of our family. Perhaps it is because I believe this is one of the biggest and most important management challenges and responsibilities of our time. At MIT, I've chaired the Sloan School's Diversity and Community Committee and now chair an MIT Committee on Campus Race Relations. My interest in doing something about this issue was stirred when I (and others) noticed that although the Sloan School had made significant progress in recruiting more women, minorities, and international students, it was doing little to help build the skills our students and faculty needed to work and learn effectively in a diverse environment. As a result, not surprisingly, conflicts, communications problems, and incidents of harassment were on the rise. A subgroup of our Diversity Committee, led by Maureen Scully and Mary Rowe, developed a set of intervention/training exercises to work on building these group-process skills. We drew on the analogy of being a bystander in a group or team setting where someone's words or actions were unconsciously hurtful to others. Our MIT-wide Committee is now taking a similar approach starting right at Freshman Orientation and working up through the tough problem of recruiting and then building a supportive environment for women and minority faculty. It is nice to see a university trying to practice what it preaches!

An industry group heard about our efforts and asked me to organize a team to study the "business case" for diversity in industry. So we now have a Diversity Research Network examining the management and organizational strategies and processes needed to translate workforce diversity into positive business and personal results. The key hypothesis driving the research, consistent with what we experienced at MIT, is that diversity per se will not automatically produce higher performance. In fact it might just as likely have a negative effect. To make diversity pay off for an organization and for the people involved requires management and organizational strategies that enhance communications, problem solving, constructive conflict, and conflict resolution. The task is to build skills in these organizational processes throughout a workforce. Working on these issues, both at MIT and through our research, brings together a professional interest with a set of values I feel strongly about. It is nice, indeed, when these two spheres of life come together.

REWARDS AND REINFORCEMENTS

Periodically, people are kind enough to take the time to exaggerate one's contributions with an award. Two that I've received are great sources of personal satisfaction because they reflect traditions I value deeply. One is a career achievement award received in 1996, from the Academy of Management's Personnel and Human Resources Division named in honor of Herbert Heneman Jr. Herb led the Industrial Relations Center at the University of Minnesota for many years and personified the image of scholar-activist-practitioner I most admire. Receiving an award in his name was very special.

Each year the Boston Labor Guild, a unique labor-management education and outreach program of the Catholic Archdiocese, gives an award to an academic or other neutral party for contributions to the labor-management community. Being given this award in 1998 was especially gratifying because the mission and work of the Labor Guild reflects the best of our Catholic social doctrines and traditions. My mother was especially pleased to get a picture of Kathy and me with Boston's Bernard Cardinal Law and the Labor Guild's Director, Father Ed Boyle!

LOOKING AHEAD: THE JOB UNFINISHED

This leads up to where things stand at the present moment. Some interesting work has been done, but the job far is from finished. And indeed, we cannot stand still and wait passively for the "blueprint" to be acted on by others. Nor can we be content that we have answered all the questions or identified policy and institutional changes that will work for workers or for all time into the future. We need to continue to broaden our view of the IR field – to take seriously the statement that industrial relations (or to use a more modern label, work and employment relations) encompasses the study and practice of all aspects of work and the institutions that support them. We need to again rethink our theories and methods, and reach out to draw in the best scholars from different disciplines who share an interest in these issues and build on some of the recent methodological and conceptual advances of systems modeling, network analysis, organizational economics, and so on. And we need to be open to ideas for new institutions and policy solutions that might look at first like they challenge or compete with current approaches. Out of these innovations, I believe, will come the intellectual foundations for updating our national policies and institutions, whenever the political conditions make it possible to do so.

Of all the open issues, the one I find most intriguing and promising, as an avenue for making progress is the contemporary challenge of integrating work and family life. This takes me back to my family farm analogy. There, work and family were one and the same. Today, we may be back to this same situation in a world where more members of households are participating in the paid labor force and technology allows the boundaries of work, home, and leisure time to be blurred, and the service-oriented economy demands 24 by 7 coverage.

So perhaps the next intellectual and public policy challenge is to figure out how to better integrate work and family life in ways that respond to both the needs of the workplace and the aspirations and expectations of workforce members, as well as to the needs of families and communities who share time and space with the world of work. My colleague Lotte Bailyn and I, at the urging and with the support of the Sloan Foundation, have combined efforts to create a Center for the Workplace and Working Families at MIT. Our goal is to encourage the various stakeholders who share interests and responsibilities for these issues to experiment with ways to better integrate work, family and community responsibilities. Stay tuned – this is a big part of the unfinished work.

A TENTATIVE LESSON

Writing this type of introspective essay offers a chance to reflect and draw some lessons from one's life experiences. One lesson strikes me as the thread linking the various projects described here. It is the value of what Hal Leavitt has labeled "hot groups."[6] These are intellectually alive groups that have come and gone in academic circles and together produced important innovations that no single member could have generated alone. Leavitt described two he had experienced in the 1950s and 1960s: (1) the Carnegie Mellon group of Herbert Simon, Richard Cyert, James March et al.; and (2) the MIT group led by Kurt Lewin and Douglas McGregor.

I think I've been privileged to be part of at least one such hot group – the extended network of faculty and students at the MIT Industrial Relations Section from the time of the Transformation project and book in the 1980s, through the HR Network's studies of workplace innovations or what some call "high performance work organizations," and most recently through the Labor Markets' Task Force Project. The leadership of Bob McKersie through most of these years has been nothing but inspiring. Working with highly talented students and colleagues who have very different and sometimes hotly contested views and ideas, but who share a common commitment to a larger cause, is the ultimate rewarding experience in academic life.

My hope is that we will continue in this tradition and build a new and expanded "hot group" that lights a fire not only under us, but among those researchers and professionals who share a concern for building a world of work that produces efficiency, equity, dignity, and wholesome families and communities.

Like the farmer whose cows are always waiting to be fed and milked, our work is not yet finished. It probably never will be. It, however, is too dynamic and important to leave lie fallow for too long. Although, like good field management, it is probably wise to give it a short rest from time to time to keep it fertile ground for new ideas and growth. On a personal level, that's one function of family, and of our family's quiet little retreat on New Hampshire's Pine River Pond. It's the best of both worlds – very much like Wisconsin, without the cows in waiting.

PUBLICATIONS

1971

City Employee Bargaining with a Divided Management. Madison: Industrial Relations Research Institute.
Interplant Transfer and Terminated Workers: A Comment. *Industrial and Labor Relations Review*, 24(3), 442–446.

1972

With Stuart M. Schmidt. The Concept of Conflict: Toward Conceptual Clarity. *Administrative Science Quarterly*, 17, 359–370.

1973

Correlates of Public Sector Bargaining Laws. *Industrial Relations, 12*, 322–337.
Resolving Management Conflict for Labor Negotiations. Chicago: International Personnel
   Management Association.

1974

Collective Bargaining and the Quality of Work: The View of Local Union Activists. With Lee Dyer
   & David Lipsky, *Annual Proceedings of the Industrial Relations Research Association*,
   150–162.
With Thomas A. DeCotiis. Professionalization and Unions in Law Enforcement. *National
   Symposium on Police and Labor Relations, International Association of Chiefs of Police*,
   41–50.
A Theory of Multilateral Bargaining in City Governments. *Industrial and Labor Relations Review,
   27*(4), 525–542.

1975

City Government Bargaining: A Path Analysis. *Industrial Relations, 14*(1), 90–101.
Determinants of Power of Boundary Units in an Inter-organizational Bargaining Relationship.
   Administrative Science Quarterly, 20, 434–452.
With Hoyt N. Whueler. Municipal Collective Bargaining: A Model and Analysis of Bargaining
   Outcomes. *Industrial and Labor Relations Review, 29*, 46–66.

1976

With Stuart M. Schmidt. An Application of a Political Economy Approach to Effectiveness:
   Employment Service-Employer Exchanges. *Administration and Society, 7*, 455–475.
With Lee Dyer. A Model of Organizational Change in the Context of Union-Management
   Relations. *Journal of Applied Behavioral Science, 12*, 58–78.
With L. L. Cummings & George P. Huber. Operationalizing the Concept of Goals and Goal
   Incompatibilities in Organizational Research. *Human Relations, 29*, 527–554.
Theory, Methodology and Policy Evaluation in Collective Bargaining Research. *Twenty-ninth
   Annual Proceedings of the Industrial Relations Research Association*, 238–248.

1977

With John Anderson. Collective Bargaining in the Public Service of Canada: An Evaluation of
   Some Policy Recommendations. *Relations Industrielles, 32*, 234–249.
With John Anderson. An Examination of the Dual Impasse Procedures in the Federal Public
   Service of Canada. *Industrial and Labor Relations Review, 3*, 228–301.
With Hoyt N. Wheeler. The Impact of Unionization of Public Sector Supervisors. *Monthly Labor
   Review, 100*, 44–48.
With Richard Block. An Interindustry Analysis of Bargaining Outcomes: Preliminary Evidence
   from 2-Digit Industries. *Quarterly Journal of Economics*, 431–452.

With Stuart Schmidt. Interorganizational Relations: Patterns and Motivations. *Administrative Science Quarterly, 22*, 220–234.
With Lee Dyer & David Lipsky. Union Attitudes Toward Management Cooperation. *Industrial Relations, 16*, 163–172.
With Lee Dyer & David Lipsky. *The Effectiveness of Union-Management Safety Committees,* W. E. Upjohn Institute for Employment Research.

1978

With Jean Baderschneider. Dependence on Impasse Procedures: Police and Firefighters in New York State. *Industrial and Labor Relations Review, 31*, 431–449.
The Politics of Interest Arbitration. *The Arbitration Journal, 33*, 5–9.
With Todd Jick. The Public Sector Mediation Process: A Theory and Empirical Examination. *Journal of Conflict Resolution, 22*, 209–240.
With Mordechai Mironi, Ronald G. Ehrenberg, Jean Baderschneider & Todd Jick. *Dispute Resolution Under Factfinding and Arbitration: An Empirical Analysis.* New York: American Arbitration Association.

1979

How American Workers View Trade Unions. *Monthly Labor Review, 102*, 23–33.
With Stuart M. Schmidt & Thomas A. DeCotiis. Superior-Subordinate Relations: Leadership and Headship. *Human Relations, 28*(3), 279–294.
The Dynamics of Dispute Resolution in the Public Sector. *Public Sector Bargaining.* Benjamin Aaron, Joseph Grodon & James Stern, (Eds), Bureau of National Affairs, Annual Research Volume of the Industrial Relations Research Association, 150–190.

1980

Industrial Relations Research: An Agenda for the 1980s. *Monthly Labor Review, 103*, 20–25.
Labor Management Relations Research: The Role of the Department of Labor. *Annual Proceedings of the Industrial Relations Research Association*, 8–15.
Collective Bargaining and Organizational Behavior Research. In: Barry Staw & L. L. Cummings (Eds), *Research in Organizational Behavior* (Vol. II, pp. 129–176). Greenwich: JAI Press.

1981

Empirical Research on Labor Law: Lessons from Dispute Resolution in the Public Sector. *Illinois Law Review, 1981*, 161–181.
With Jean Baderschneider. Estimating the Narcotic Effects: Choosing Techniques that Fit the Problem. *Industrial and Labor Relations Review, 35*, 28–38.
An American Perspective on the Integration of the Behavioral Sciences Into Industrial Relations. In: Andrew W. J. Thomson (Ed.), *Industrial Relations and the Behavioral Sciences in Britain.* London: Saxon House.
With David E. Helfman. The Effects of Collective Bargaining on Economic and Behavioral Job Outcomes. In: Ronald G. Enrenberg (Ed.), *Research in Labor Economics*, Vol. III. Greenwich: JAI Press.

Step by Step in the Middle East from the Perspective of the Labor Mediation Process. In: Jeffrey Z. Rubin (Ed.), *Dynamics of Third Party Intervention: Interdisciplinary Perspectives on International Conflict*. New York: Praeger.

1982

Review Symposium: Collective Bargaining and Industrial Relations (paper prepared in response to a symposium devoted to my collective bargaining book). *Industrial Relations, 21,* 115–122.

Edited with Daniel J. B. Mitchell & Lee Dyer. *Industrial Relations Research in the 1970s: Review and Appraisal*. Madison, WI: Industrial Relations Research Association.

With John Godard. Canadian Management Policies, Structures and Practices under Collective Bargaining. In: Morley Gunderson & John Anderson (Eds), *Union Management Relations in Canada*. Toronto: Addison Wesley.

Toward a Behavioral Model of Management Under Collective Bargaining. In: Gerald Bomers & Richard Peterson (Eds), *Conflict Management and Industrial Relations*. Boston: Kluwer.

1983

With Robert B. McKersie. Collective Bargaining: Pressures for Change. *Sloan Management Review, 24,* 59–65.

With Harry C. Katz. Collective Bargaining, Work Organization, Worker Participation: The Return to Plant Level Bargaining. *Labor Law Journal, 34,* 524–529.

With Harry Katz and Kenneth Gobeille. Industrial Relations Performance, Economic Performance and Quality of Working Life Efforts: An Inter-Plant Analysis. *Industrial and Labor Relations Review, 37,* 13–17.

Collective Bargaining and Income Policies in a Stagflation Economy. *Rapporteur's Report in Proceedings of the Sixth World Congress of the International Industrial Relations Association*. Kyoto, Japan.

With Anil Verma. Negotiations in Organizations: Blending Industrial Relations and Organizational Behavior Approaches. In: Max Bazerman & Roy Lewicki (Eds), *Negotiating in Organizations*. New York: Sage Publications.

Worker Participation and American Unions: A Case Study. In: Frances Bairstow (Ed.), *1983 McGill Industrial Relations Conference Proceedings*.

1984

With Robert B. McKersie & Peter Cappelli. Strategic Choice and Industrial Relations Theory and Practice. *Industrial Relations, 27,* 16–39.

With Michael Piore. Will the New Industrial Relations Last? Implications for the Labor Movement. *The Annals of the American Academy of Political and Social Science, 473,* 177–189.

With Peter Cappelli. The Transformation of the Industrial Relations and Personnel Function. In: Paul Osterman (Ed.), *Internal Labor Markets*. Cambridge, MA: The MIT Press.

Challenges and Choices for American Labor (Ed.). Cambridge, MA: The MIT Press.

With Harry P. Katz & Nancy Mower. *Worker Participation and American Unions: Threat or Opportunity?* Kalamazoo, MI: W.E. Upjohn Institute for Employment Research.

With Michael Piore. U.S. Industrial Relations in Transition. The Growth and Nature of the Non-union Sector Within a Firm, with Anil Verma; and Worker Participation and American Unions, with Harry Katz & Nancy Mower. All in: Kochan (Ed.), *Challenges and Choices Facing American Labor.* Cambridge: The MIT Press.

1985

Comment on What Do Unions Do? *Annual Proceedings of the Industrial Relations Research Association*, 365–368.

With Harry Katz & Mark Weber. Assessing the Effects of Industrial Relations and Quality of Working Life Efforts on Organizational Effectiveness. *Academy of Management Journal*, 28, 509–527.

With Thomas A. Barocci. *Human Resource Management and Industrial Relations: Text, Readings and Cases.* Boston: Little Brown.

1986

With Robert McKersie & John Chalykoff. Corporate Strategy, Workplace Innovation, and Union Members. *Industrial and Labor Relations Review, 39*, 487–501.

With Boaz Tamir. Collective Bargaining and New Technology. In: Greg Bamber & Russell Lansbury (Eds), *New Technology: Perspectives on Human Resources and Industrial Relations.* London: Allen and Unwin, 1989. Also in Proceedings of the Seventh World Congress of the International Industrial Relations Association, Hamburg, West Germany.

With Anil Verma. Macro Determinants of the Future of the Study of Negotiations in Organizations. In: Roy J. Lewicki, Blair H. Sheppard & Max H. Bazerman (Eds), *Research on Negotiations in Organizations (1, 1986b, pp. 287–310).* Greenwich: JAI Press.

1987

With Harry Katz & Jeffrey Keefe. Industrial Relations and Productivity in the U.S. Automobile Industry. *Brookings Papers on Economic Activity, 3*, 685–715.

Strategies for Sustaining Innovations in U.S. Industrial Relations. *Journal of State Government*, 60, 30–35.

Human Resource Management and Business Life Cycles: Some Preliminary Propositions. In: Archie Kleingartner & Carolyn S. Anderson (Eds), *Human Resource Management in High Technology Firms* (pp. 183–200). Lexington: Lexington Books.

Labor Arbitration and Collective Bargaining in the 1990s: An Economic Analysis. In: Walter J. Gershenfeld (Ed.), *Arbitration 1986: Current and Expanding Roles* (pp. 44–59). Washington, D.C.: Bureau of National Affairs.

With David Lewin, Peter Feuille & John Delaney. *Public Sector Labor Relations: Analysis and Readings.* Thomas Horton and Daughters Publishers, 1977. Second edition, 1981. Third edition published by Lexington Books, 1987.

With Harry C. Katz. *Collective Bargaining and Industrial Relations: From Theory to Policy and Practice.* Homewood: Irwin, 1980. Second edition, 1987.

1988

The Adaptability of the U.S. Industrial Relations System. *Science, 15*, 287–292.

With Paul Osterman & John Paul MacDuffie. Employment Security at DEC: Sustaining Values Amid Environmental Change. *Human Resource Management Journal.*

The Future of Worker Representation: An American Perspective. *Labour and Society, 13*, 184–201.

With John Paul MacDuffie. Human Resources, Technology, and Economic Performance: Evidence from the Automobile Industry. *Annual Proceedings of the Industrial Relations Research Association*, 159–171.

With Kirsten Wever. Industrial Relations Agenda for Change: The Case of the United States. *Labour, 2*(2), 21-56.

On the Human Side of Technology. *ICL Technical Journal*, 391-400.

Enhancing Industrial Relations Innovations in the United States. In: *New Departures in Industrial Relations* (pp. 5–10). National Planning Association.

Looking to the Year 2000: Challenges for Industrial Relations and Human Resource Management. In: K. Newton, T. Schweitzer & J. P. Voyer (Eds), *Perspective 2000, Proceedings of a Conference Sponsored by the Economic Council of Canada* (pp. 203-217).

With Joel Cutcher-Gershenfeld & Anil Verma. Recent Developments in U.S. Employee Involvement Activities: Erosion or Transformation? In: David Lipsky & Donna Sockell (Eds), *Advances in Industrial Relations*. Greenwich: JAI Press.

1989

With John Chalykoff. Computer-Aided Monitoring: Its Influence on Employee Job Satisfaction and Turnover. *Personnel Psychology, 42*, 807–34.

With Robert B. McKersie. Future Directions for American Labor and Human Resources Policy. *Relations Industrielles, 44*, 224–244.

1990

With Anil Verma. Comparison of Changes in U.S. and Canadian Industrial Relations. *Labor Law Journal.*

1991

With Kirsten Wever. American Unions and the Future of Worker Representation. In: George Strauss, Daniel Gallagher & Jack Fiorito (Eds), *The State of Unions*. Madison: Industrial Relations Research Association.

Employee Participation, Work Redesign and New Technology: Implications for Manufacturing and Engineering Practice. In: Gavriel Salvendy (Ed.), *Handbook of Industrial Engineering*. New York: John Wiley.

With Paul Osterman. Internal Labor Markets and Employment Security. In: Katherine Abraham & Robert McKersie (Eds), *New Developments in Labor Markets*. Cambridge: The MIT Press.

1992

With Robert McKersie. Human Resources, Organizational Governance, and Public Policy: Lessons from Experimentation in the 1980s. In: Kochan & Useem (Eds), *Transforming Organizations* (pp. 169–186). New York: Oxford University Press.

With Lee Dyer & Rosemary Batt. International Human Resource Studies: A Review and Critique. In: David Lewin et al., (Eds), *Research Frontiers in Industrial Relations and Human Resource Management*. Madison: Industrial Relations Research Association.

Edited with Michael Useem. *Transforming Organizations*. New York: Oxford University Press.

With Ben Whipple. Bringing Research to the Classroom: The MIT Auto Case. *MIT Management*, Winter, 27–33.

With John C. Wells & Michal Smith. The Consequences of a Failed IR System: Contract Workers in the Petrochemical Industry. *Sloan Management Review*, 79–89.

With James Rebitzer. The Management of Contract Workers and the Risks of Accidents: Evidence from the Petrochemical Industry. *Annual Proceedings of the Industrial Relations Research Association*, 325–331.

1993

Canadian Labor Policy and Research at a Crossroads. *Proceedings of the Canadian Industrial Relations Association.*

Crossroads in Employment Relations: Approaching a Mutual Gains Paradigm. *Looking Ahead*, February.

With Lee Dyer. Managing Transformational Change: The Role of Human Resource Management Professionals. *The International Journal of Human Resource Management*, 569–590.

Toward a Mutual Gains Paradigm for Labor-Management Relations. *Labor Law Journal*, 454–464.

Trade Unionism and Industrial Relations: Notes on Theory and Practice for the 1990s. *Annual Proceedings of the Industrial Relations Research Association*, 185–195.

Principles for a Post New Deal Employment Policy. In: Clark Kerr & Paul Staudohar (Eds), Labor Economics and Industrial Relations: Markets and Institutions, Cambridge: Harvard University Press.

With Saul Rubinstein & Michael Bennett. The Saturn Partnership: Reinventing the Local Union. In: Bruce Kaufman & Morris Kleiner (Eds), *Alternative Models for Employee Representation*. Madison: Industrial Relations Research Association.

Teaching and Building Middle Range Industrial Relations Theory. In: Roy Adams & Noah Meltz (Eds), *Industrial Relations Theory* (pp. 353–380). New Brunswick: Scarecrow Press.

1994

With Lee Dyer. HRM: An American View. In: John Storey (Ed.), *Human Resource Management* (pp. 332–351). London: Routledge.

Industrial Relations and Human Resource Management in Korea: Implications for Further Reforms. In: Y. H. Kim (Ed.), *Korea's Political Economy*. San Francisco: Westview Press.

With Paul Osterman. *The Mutual Gains Enterprise*. Boston: Harvard Business School Press.

With Michael Smith, John Wells & James Rebitzer. Human Resource Strategies and Contingent Workers: The Case of Safety and Health in the Petrochemical Industry. *Human Resource Management, 33*, 55–78.
Labor and Employment Policies for a Global Economy. *Industrial Law Journal*, South Africa, *15*, 689–707.
With Marc Weinstein. Recent Developments in U.S. Industrial Relations. *The British Journal of Industrial Relations, 32*, 483–504.
With Harry C. Katz & Robert B. McKersie. *The Transformation of American Industrial Relations.* New York: Basic Books, 1986. Second edition, 1994.

1995

With John Paul MacDuffie. Do U.S. Firms Invest Less in Human Resources?: Training in the World Auto Industry. *Industrial Relations, 34*, 147–168.
With Richard Locke & Michael Piore. Reconceptualizing Comparative Industrial Relations: Lessons from International Research. *International Labour Review, 134*(2), 139–161.
With Jody Hoffer Gittell & Brenda Lautsch. Total Quality Management and Human Resource Systems: An International Comparison. *The International Journal of Human Resource Management*, 201–222.
Using the Dunlop Report to Achieve Mutual Gains. *Industrial Relations, 34*, 350–366.
Edited with Richard Locke & Michael Piore. *Employment Relations in a Changing World Economy.* Cambridge: The MIT Press.
Edited with Anil Verma & Russell Lansbury. *Human Resource Management in Asian Economies.* London: Routledge.
With Marc Weinstein. The Limits of Diffusion: Recent Developments in Industrial Relations and Human Resource Practices. In: Richard Locke, Thomas Kochan & Michael Piore (Eds), *Employment Relations in a Changing World Economy.* Cambridge: The MIT Press.

1996

The American Corporation as an Employer: Past, Present, and Future. In: Carl Kaysen (Ed.), *The Corporation in Modern Society: A Second Look* (pp. 242–268). New York: Oxford University Press.
With Susan Eaton. A Grass-Roots Experiment to Resolve Workplace Problems. *Negotiation Journal, 12*(2), 175–179.
Launching a Renaissance in International Industrial Relations Research. *Relations Industrielles, 51*, 247–263.
With Susan Eaton. New Ideas on Resolving Workplace Disputes: Examples from the U.S. and Abroad. *Negotiation Journal, 12*(2), 113–117.
With Casey Ichniowski, David Levine, Craig Olson & George Strauss. What Works at Work: Overview and Assessment. *Industrial Relations, 35*, 299–333.

1997

With Russell D. Lansbury. Changing Employment Relations and Governance in the International Auto Industry. *The Journal of Management and Governance, 1*(1), 85–102.
Rebalancing the Role of Human Resources. *Human Resource Management Journal, 36*(1), 121–127.

With Russell D. Lansbury & John Paul MacDuffie. *After Lean Production: Evolving Employment Practices in the World Auto Industry*. Ithaca: Cornell University Press.

With Joel Cutcher-Gershenfeld. Dispute Resolution and Team-Based Work Systems. In: Sandra E. Gleason (Ed.), *Workplace Dispute Resolution – Directions for the 21st Century*. East Lansing, MI: Michigan State University Press.

1998

Human Capital and the American Corporation. *Perspectives on Work*, 2(1), 7–12.

Beyond Myopia: Human Resources and the Changing Social Contract. In: Ferris (Ed.), *Research in Personnel and Human Resources Management* (pp. 199–212). Greenwich: JAI Press.

Crossroads in Employment Relations: Approaching a Mutual Gains Paradigm. In: James A. Auerbach (Ed.), *Through a Glass Darkly: Building the New Workplace for the 21st Century*. Washington, D.C.: National Policy Association.

What Is Distinctive about Industrial Relations Research? In: Keith Whitfield & George Strauss (Eds), *Researching the World of Work: Strategies and Methods in Studying Industrial Relations* (pp. 31–45). Ithaca: Cornell University Press.

With Joel Cutcher-Gershenfeld & John Calhoun Wells. How Do Labor and Management View Collective Bargaining? *Monthly Labor Review*, 121(10), 23–31.

Labor Policy for the Twenty-First Century. *University of Pennsylvania Journal of Labor and Employment Law*, 1(1), 117–131.

1999

How to Update Employment and Labor Policies for the 21st Century. *Perspectives on Work*, 3(2), 12–17.

Reconstructing America's Social Contract in Employment: The Role of Policy, Institutions, and Practices. *Chicago-Kent Law Review*, 75(1), 137–152.

The Changing Nature of Work: Implications for Occupational Analysis. Committee on Techniques for the Enhancement of Human Performance: Occupational Analysis, Washington: National Academy Press.

With Deborah Ancona, Maureen Scully, John Van Maanen & D. Eleanor Westney. *Managing for the Future: Organizational Behavior and Processes*. Cincinnati: South-Western College Publishing, 1996. Second edition.

2000

With Harry C. Katz. *An Introduction to Collective Bargaining and Industrial Relations*. New York: McGraw Hill, 1992. Second Edition.

With Richard Chaykowski, Joel-Cutcher-Gershenfeld & Christina Sickles Merchant. *Facilitation Conflict Resolution in Union-Management Relations: A Guide for Neutrals*. Ithaca: Cornell/Perc Institute on Conflict Resolution.

Edited with Margaret M. Blair. *The New Relationship: Human Capital in the American Corporation*. Washington: Brookings Institution Press.

An Agenda for the President. *Challenge*, November/December, 5–14.

With Saul Rubinstein. Toward a Stakeholder Theory of the Firm: The Saturn Partnership. *Organization Science*, 11, 367–386. (Lead article).

With Brenda Lautsch & Corinne Bendersky. Massachusetts Commission Against Discrimination Alternative Dispute Resolution Program Evaluation. *Harvard Negotiations Law Review, 5,* 233–278.

On the Paradigm Guiding Industrial Relations Theory and Research. *Industrial and Labor Relations Review, 53,* 704–711.

Rebuilding the Social Contract at Work: A Call to Action. *Proceedings of the Industrial Relations Research Association 52nd Annual Meetings* (also reprinted in Perspectives on Work), 1–25.

2001

With Paul Osterman, Richard Locke and Michael Piore. *Working in America: Labor Market Institutions for the New Century.* Cambridge, MA: MIT Press, forthcoming, Fall, 2001.

With Saul R. Rubenstein. *Learning from Saturn: Possibilities for Corporate Governance and Employee Relations.* Ithaca, NY: Cornell University Press.

ACKNOWLEDGMENTS

I would like to thank Kathy Kochan, Richard Locke and Robert McKersie for their helpful suggestions on an earlier draft. For a remarkably parallel and extremely well told story of the sights, sounds, and work associated with growing up on a farm in a rural Midwestern community, I highly recommend, Howard Cohn, *The Last Farmer.* New York: Harper and Row, 1988. My son Andrew gave me this book for Christmas a number of years ago. I found myself reliving much of my youth in the pages of this vivid memoir.

REFERENCES

1. Dunlop, J. T. (1958). *Industrial Relations Systems.* New York: Holt.
2. Kerr, C., Dunlop, J. T., Harbison, F., & Myers, C. (1960). *Industrialism and Industrial Man.* Cambridge: Harvard University Press.
3. Kaufman, B. E. (1993). *The Origins and Evolution of the Field of Industrial Relations.* Ithaca, NY: Cornell ILR Press.
4. Walton, R. E., & McKersie, R. B. (1965). *A Behavioral Theory of Labor Negotiations.* New York: McGraw Hill. Reprinted in 1997 by Cornell University Press.
5. Reich, R. B. (1997). *Locked in the Cabinet.* New York: Alfred Knopf.
6. Leavitt, H. J. (1996). The old days, hot groups, and manager's lib. *Administrative Science Quarterly, 41,* 281–300.

FINDING MYSELF IN THE RIGHT PLACE AT THE RIGHT TIME, BUT NOT ALWAYS

Richard T. Mowday

One of the courses I have taught at the University of Oregon in recent years is a career planning course offered in cooperation with our campus Career Center titled Career Mentoring in Business. The purpose of the class is to help students plan for a career after graduation by gathering information on jobs or occupations they think might be attractive. We put students in touch with people working in these jobs and students conduct informational interviews. The questions students ask range all over the board but generally focus on what a specific job is really like and how one can best prepare to work in that area. The underlying message we try to convey to students is that careers need to be carefully researched and planned.

In the process of reflecting on my own career for purposes of writing this chapter, it was embarrassing to note how my own career had unfolded in ways that were neither planned nor intended. I found a huge disparity between the advice I had been giving students in the classroom and what I actually did when I was a student. Although I've never told my students about the hypocrisy of the career advice I've been giving them, perhaps I should as a cautionary tale ("be careful, or this could happen to you!)".

Although I've never considered myself a particularly lucky individual, the story of my academic career is repeatedly finding myself in the right place at the right time. I have had the extraordinary good fortune to find myself around talented people who were doing exciting work or who pointed me in the right

Management Laureates, Volume 6, pages 243–267.
Copyright © 2002 by Elsevier Science Ltd.
ISBN: 0-7623-0487-1

direction at critical junctures. I've also never considered myself a terribly talented or gifted individual. In fact, in addition to being a poster child for wayward careers, I may be proof positive that performance depends on both ability and motivation, and that deficits in the former can be compensated for by increases in the latter.

I must admit that the thought of writing an autobiographical account of my career is a bit intimidating. And if I paused for a moment to contemplate who might find my career interesting, I probably wouldn't bother. But having agreed to write the chapter, I feel compelled to give it my best shot. The usual approach to writing an autobiographical account of one's career is to take things in chronological order. Although I intend to honor this tradition by first saying a few words about my formative years, I'll depart from this format somewhat by discussing the three areas of research, service, and teaching. There is still a quasi-chronological order underlying these three areas because I've found that at different stages of my career I've sequentially focused my attention on different aspects of the professorial role. Although most professors are always simultaneously engaged in different activities reflecting research, teaching, and service, the relative emphasis given to each of these areas can and does shift over the course of a career.

Before telling my story, I should add a warning about what follows. What I have to say is based on what I remember, which may or may not be exactly what happened. I would not deliberately say something I know to be false, but time has a way of blurring memories. I have never been one to look backward in life. Rather than reflect on events that have taken place, I'm more inclined to move on to the next task. I've blamed my poor memory on this tendency, but it may be a convenient fiction.

FORMATIVE YEARS

I was born in 1947 in Oakland, California, the second of two sons of parents who never completed college, but who valued education nonetheless. The first fortuitous event of my life came in second grade when my family moved across the bay from Alameda to Palo Alto. My father had taken a job at Kodak in the Stanford industrial park and Palo Alto in the 1950s, not yet the frenetic Silicon Valley of today, was an idyllic place to grow up. As a child, I have fond memories of spending hours on end exploring my neighborhood and the foothills behind the Stanford campus with my buddies.

Growing up in the same community as Stanford University was both a blessing and a curse. The best part of having Stanford in my backyard was spending time on campus attending sports camps and sporting events. Sports was a preoccupation when I was growing up. As a schoolboy, I could attend all of Stanford's home football games except the "Big Game" with Cal for a dollar a season. We "junior rooters" were relegated to the worst section in Stanford stadium, but it took only a little initiative and even less imagination to sneak into the best seats in the house. On a really good day, we could talk our way into the press box. All the professional football teams who came to the Bay Area would stay at Rickey's Hyatt House just down the street from my home. Although the hotel discouraged it, I used to haunt the place as a youngster collecting autographs from some of the greatest football players of that era. Although I'm not sure anyone has been counting, I've probably been thrown out of Rickey's Hyatt House more times than anyone else on the face of the earth. Of course, I'd always find a way to sneak back in.

The downside of living next door to Stanford was that every time one of their professors itched, students in the Palo Alto school district scratched. We were the guinea pigs, or so it seemed, for every new standardized test and wacky educational idea to come down the pike. The wackiest of the ideas that I recall concerned how to teach math. Around junior high, someone decided it would be a good idea to teach math in base 7. I'm not absolutely certain that some Stanford professor was responsible for this, but I've blamed Stanford all these years nonetheless. A career in mathematics was probably only a remote possibility, but spending a year in the twilight zone of base 7 shut that door for good.

I was an indifferent student in high school. I found it fairly easy to get decent grades without studying too hard, so my attention turned to social activities and work. I took a night job delivering prescriptions for a pharmacy because I got to drive a cool Jeep and I thought that might impress the girls (this was neither the first nor last time that I was wrong about something). I had more fun in high school than any young man had a right to have. Perhaps for that reason, I remember less about those years than I should.

When it came time to graduate in 1965, I hadn't really given much thought to going to college. Even in those days, it was just expected that you would go to college but somehow planning for that eventuality never seemed to make it on to my radar screen. I didn't have the grades, test scores or initiative to get into a top school and as a result I headed off to San Jose State University. I imagine this was a great relief to my parents. After sending my older brother to Brown, financing an education at a state university must have seemed like a bargain. The other great relief, I'm sure, was getting me out of the house.

Although San Jose State didn't have the academic reputation of Stanford or Berkeley in the Bay Area (at football games Stanford students referred to San Jose as the place where the sewer met the bay), it did offer some remarkable academic opportunities. Many Ph.D students at Stanford and Berkeley were unwilling to leave the Bay Area after receiving their degree, even at the cost of working at an institution of perceived lower quality. Although most of the faculty members were first rate, a couple of them were truly strange. One instructor in the Management Department was a fervent believer in para-psychology. We spent more time during the introduction to management course talking about energy fields and an individual's aura, which he claimed to be able to see, than discussing Koontz and O'Donnell, the authors of the text in the course. He had a loyal following among a small group of students, although I must admit that I was unable to see his aura. Who knows how my career might have turned out if I had been able to see it.

Perhaps because I had so much fun in high school, by the time I enrolled in college I was ready to settle down. This was facilitated by the fact all my high school buddies headed up to Chico State, although for academic reasons they didn't stay there for long. Also, the fact that the government was drafting people to serve in the Vietnam war helped focus the attention of many students. For the first time, however, I found school interesting and my grades reflected it. I discovered I had a passion for a number of different areas, ranging from philosophy to Asian history to ceramics. Because I dabbled so widely across the different curricula, it took me more than the usual four years to graduate. I think I had qualified for minors in three or four areas as a consequence of my intellectual curiosity. But because I was practical (and, at the time, didn't know better), I majored in business or, more precisely, a field called Manpower Administration.

Actually, this was a fortuitous choice because it put me in touch with a young assistant professor named J. Malcom Walker. Mal was a doctoral student at Berkeley who was doing his dissertation research on academic governance. He hired me as a research assistant to comb through the archives of San Jose State. It was my first taste of research and even though I was untrained I found it quite interesting. Mal was the first person to encourage my interest in the study of organizations. I recall he gave me a copy of March and Simon's Organizations when I asked about good books to read in the area. I admired the precision and logic of their analysis and propositions.

But Mal's greatest influence over my career was the advice he provided me when it came time to graduate. One day he inquired about my plans after graduation and, not having any, I told him I'd probably get a job in business. His response, which I recall quite vividly, was to predict that my family would starve if they had to rely on my business skills for survival. Mal advised me to go to graduate school instead and told me about a new program that was starting up on the Irvine campus of the University of California. Mal was instrumental in introducing me to Lyman Porter who had recently moved to Irvine from Berkeley.

Actually, Irvine wasn't necessarily my first choice for graduate school. Perhaps seeking an adventure farther away from home, I applied to the New York State School of Labor and Industrial Relations at Cornell and was accepted. Because Cornell was a private school, it was quite a bit more expensive than what I would pay as an in-state student at Irvine (there was no tuition at the University of California in those days). I called Larry Williams at Cornell and told him I really wanted to come to Ithaca but would need financial aid to do so. Larry's response, as I recall, was that he also wanted me to come to Cornell, but not that badly. With that, I was off to Irvine.

STUDYING EMPLOYEE-ORGANIZATION LINKAGES

In 1970 I enrolled in the M.S. program at the Graduate School of Administration (now the Graduate School of Management) at Irvine and I definitely found myself in the right place at the right time. The program was several years old and I think there were almost as many faculty members as students. I recall that my master's class had about fourteen students, with only eight of us left after the first term. We actually had seminars with more faculty members than students. The faculty, with a few notable exceptions, was excellent. One instructor was so bad, though, that we students actually refused to attend class (in fairness to that instructor, he was asked to teach outside his area). Our protest resulted in a school-wide faculty, student, and staff retreat.

One of my first courses was a year long seminar on the study of organizations co-taught by Robert Dubin and Lyman Porter. Dubin led the first quarter and at his insistence we spent our time reading and discussing the classic books in management. Dubin wanted us to appreciate the fact that many of the theories and ideas that we were reading in the more current literature were not entirely new. It was an important lesson.

One of the nice things about being at a new, smaller school was that it gave students a great deal of independence and flexibility. Although there was an established curriculum, it wasn't very extensive. This meant that you spent a lot of time doing independent studies when you wanted to learn something about an area not covered in an existing class. Thinking back on it, I think this was excellent preparation for being an academic. I also remember students would sometimes organize classes to backfill around the curriculum. For example, when we decided we needed to learn more about research methodology than the standard course offered, the students organized an advanced seminar. We needed a faculty sponsor for the course, but asked him not to attend because we thought it might slow us up.

The best part about Irvine for me was a research project funded by the Office of Naval Research (ONR) that Porter and Dubin had underway. The project focused on organizational attachments, with Dubin studying his concept of central life interest and Porter working on organizational commitment. I think I was hired on as a research assistant in my second year and joined a team of very talented doctoral students, including Rick Steers, John VanMaanen, Bill Crampon, Gene Stone, and Joe Champoux. This was when I first began to learn the craft of research and it was a tremendously exciting environment. Moreover, the entire field of organizational behavior was exciting and intellectually stimulating in the early 1970s. There were many empirical questions that remained unanswered and intense debates raged about theories that had not yet grown stale. Expectancy theory had been around for a while but, had yet to be adequately tested. Fiedler's contingency theory of leadership was receiving considerable attention and some were critical of its empirical support, although not Fred. Hackman and Oldham's job design model had just appeared and many researchers rushed to test its predictions, including the ONR group at Irvine. Port was excellent in bringing in visiting faculty and speakers. I remember seminars with Larry Cummings, Ed Lawler, Vic Vroom, Fred Fiedler, John Campbell, and Marv Dunnette. Again, having little career direction, when I finished the M.S. program I stayed around to enter the doctoral program simply because I was having so much fun.

On the ONR project I worked most closely with Port. He had developed the Organizational Commitment Questionnaire (OCQ), which was used in a number of studies to examine the effects of commitment on performance, turnover, and absenteeism.

One of my very first published papers (Mowday, Porter & Dubin, 1974) was a study of the relationship of subunit employee commitment to the performance of bank branches. My early foray into publishing hardly gave me realistic expectations about the journal submission process. As I recall, we submitted the paper to *Organizational Behavior and Human Performance* and it was accepted with almost no revisions. I thought this profession was going to be a breeze. Again, it was not the first or last time I was wrong about something.

Although we went on to publish a number of papers on organizational commitment and other topics, perhaps the best known paper to emerge from this line of work was a validation of the OCQ that appeared after I graduated in the *Journal of Vocational Behavior* (Mowday, Steers & Porter, 1979). At one time, it was the most cited paper in the history of the journal. Steers and Porter allowed me to be the lead author on this paper, although at the time I didn't know why. Now I know. Hardly a week has gone by in all these years when someone seeking permission to use the instrument has contacted me. I think Steers and Porter, both far smarter than I am, saw this coming.

Although I've published a number of papers in a variety of areas, I think my favorite was a chapter I did with Steers that appeared in Cummings and Staw's series on *Research in Organizational Behavior* (Steers & Mowday, 1981). The first part of the paper was devoted to presenting a model of turnover in organizations. To me, it was pretty standard boxes and arrows type of work and one of my doctoral students, Tom Lee, subsequently tested the model in his dissertation (Lee & Mowday, 1987) But the second half of the chapter was, I think, quite innovative for the time. Although most previous research in the area of turnover tried to predict who would leave, we explored the consequences for individuals of the decision to stay or leave. This allowed us to apply a number of important theories from social psychology to understanding how individuals react both to their own decisions and to decisions made by others.

The work organizational commitment that Port had undertaken struck me at the time, as it still does (Mowday, 1999), as important. Commitment seemed to be a very useful explanatory construct with respect to predicting important behaviors. In addition, I believe organizations benefit from employee loyalty and the willingness to go the extra mile. Moreover, I also think employees find meaning in their careers and the ties that bind them to organizations. The accumulated work we did in the area of commitment, turnover, and absenteeism was summarized in a book titled *Employee-Organization Linkages* (Mowday, Porter & Steers, 1982).

Although most of my research during the time I was a graduate student was associated with the area of organizational commitment and employee turnover, I chose to do my dissertation on power and upward influence processes in organizations. My curiosity in this area was piqued by watching one of the deans of a small school at Irvine get his way on important decisions even though his school was far less powerful than the others on campus. Observing this individual made me realize that influence was not just a matter of how much power you possessed, but also of how effectively you used it. I did a small study of upward influence processes among school principals that led to two published papers (Mowday, 1978, 1979). Port chaired my dissertation and Henry Tosi, who was visiting Irvine for the year, was on my committee. Actually Henry was quite instrumental in my successful completion. Because my samples were small, I feared that Port would not accept my study results as valid evidence. Henry offered to "take care of Port" and apparently he did.

Although I've emphasized employee-organization linkages in discussing the Irvine years, there was another, more important, linkage that was established at that time. When I arrived on the Irvine campus, the GSA had what was euphemistically known as the "research collection." In actual fact, it was a puny library. I befriended a young woman, Mary Nelson, who worked in the research collection, perhaps in hopes of getting special library privileges. Over the next several years it became clear to me that it was privileges of another sort that I was really after and Mary and I were married after I completed my oral exams. Mary later went from working in the research collection to serving as an assistant to the Dean and my dissertation chair, Port. I feared this might hurt my chances for graduation. I knew Port thought it was time for me to leave because he told me so. I suspect he was a good deal less excited about the prospect of losing Mary, however. In 1975, Mary and I packed up our possessions and headed off to my first teaching job at the University of Nebraska, Lincoln.

SERVING THE PROFESSION

Lyman Porter was a marvelous mentor, as has been documented on a number of occasions (cf. Stephens & Sommer, 2001). One of the things Port taught me was that although research productivity and publications were the coin of the realm in academia, service on the campus in which one works and to the broader profession was also important. Port was a great role model. In addition to remaining highly productive as a researcher, he served as dean, was a member of numerous campus committees, and held several offices in professional associations.

I attended my first meeting of the Academy of Management meeting in 1974, Port's year as President. The meeting was held in Seattle and, as I recall, about 700 people attended. It was a wonderful experience. For the very first time, I felt a bond with a larger group of scholars who shared my interest in understanding behavior in organizations. When I wasn't interviewing for a job, I attended all the paper sessions and symposia I could cram into the day. It was a stimulating and exciting environment for a doctoral student. Although I was vaguely aware of a status hierarchy in the field, it was at this meeting that I learned my place in it. I attended Port's Presidential Reception, which in those days he had to pay for out of his own pocket. I was leaning against a column in Port's suite and Fred Fiedler (who I had once met when he gave a talk at Irvine) came up to introduce himself. Five minutes later, I had sidled around the column facing the other side of the room and up comes Fred. I guess I had made a huge impression on him the first time, because he introduced himself again! If I wanted to have greater stature in the organization, it appeared that I would have to work at it.

I first became active in service at the Academy by serving on the program committee for a meeting of the Western Academy of Management in 1978. Little did I know then what a slippery slope my service involvement in the Academy would become. I could provide details about the many ways in which I've found to get involved in the Academy, but I would run the risk of boring the reader. Suffice it to say that I found it difficult to say no when asked and my involvement in one area inevitably led to requests to be involved in other areas (no good deed goes unpunished). Instead, let me mention two roles that I played in the Academy that were especially important in my career and particularly rewarding.

I joined the editorial review board of the *Academy of Management Journal* (*AMJ*) as an assistant professor in 1980 when John Slocum was editor. Four years later, the newly appointed Editor, Janice Beyer, asked me to become the first consulting editor for the journal. I had become acquainted with Jan when, as officers of our respective Academy divisions, we worked together on organizing the doctoral consortium at the annual meeting jointly sponsored by the Organizational Behavior, Organizational and Management Theory, and Organizational Development divisions We worked well together and I jumped at the chance to work with Jan on the journal. She proved to be a wonderful colleague and mentor. Although I had always thought of myself as a good reviewer, it was Jan who really taught me the craft of reviewing. Jan was a tough task master, although no tougher on others than she was on herself. As consulting editor, I was reviewing over 100 papers a year. At the end of her term as editor, I believe Jan was instrumental in my appointment as editor to succeed her. Because I have already written about my term as editor of *AMJ* (Mowday, 1993, 1997b), there is little need to tell the story again here. But being editor was a tremendous personal learning experience because it exposed me to areas of the Academy that I would not otherwise have taken the time to read. I came away from the experience with much greater breadth, although some might say I was an inch deep and a mile wide.

The other memorable experience I have had in the Academy happened when I was elected as an officer. I had previously lost two elections to office in the Academy and I sometimes thought that losing was the best of all worlds. You got credit for being willing to serve but didn't actually have to do the work. My third election for office proved the charm, though. Serving as an officer in the Academy gives you a unique perspective on the organization and it puts you in contact with a large number of members who work quietly behind the scenes to make things happen. These are the people at the annual meeting who run placement, recruit exhibitors to the Academy, and make sure there is water and audio visual equipment in the meeting rooms. I was tremendously impressed then, as I continue to be today, that the Academy of Management accomplishes so much with literally hundreds of volunteers. In many ways, it is inspiring.

My year as President of the Academy was 1995–1996. There were several things I wanted to accomplish during my term. First, my time as a officer made me aware that although the Academy celebrates research at its meeting and in its journals, many Academy members come from teaching schools or are engaged in the application of management knowledge as consultants. The Academy served the needs of researchers quite well but did not honor or celebrate achievements in other areas. Following Boyer (1990), I made expanding our definition of scholarly contributions a major theme of my Presidential address (Mowday, 1997a). Not only did I want to recognize the importance of the different ways our members contributed to the profession, I also wanted to provide more services to those with interests in teaching and applying management knowledge. Although I can't claim credit for this, the growth of what are now called the Professional Development Workshops has created an annual meeting that is far more inclusive and does a far better job of meeting the needs of the Academy's diverse members.

A second area in which I had hoped to nudge the Academy was its relations with the external environment. It seemed to me that important changes were taking place in business education but that groups like the Academy of Management didn't have a seat at the table when these changes were discussed. Instead, the American Assembly of Collegiate Schools of Business (AACSB), which represented business school deans, was the dominant player in determining the new directions business schools might take. During my year as president, I reached out to the professional associations representing the other business disciplines, including accounting, finance, and marketing. I tried to organize a meeting of the presidents of the business faculty associations, although that effort proved unsuccessful. Such a meeting was subsequently held under the auspices of AACSB, though.

Finally, as president I was concerned that even if we were able to develop strong linkages with the other professional associations and/or AACSB, we wouldn't know what to do with them because the Academy had no strategy or clearly articulated goals. The Academy's Board of Governors had undertaken strategic planning efforts on several occasions over the years and we did so again during my term as president. Moreover, the strategic planning process was expanded beyond the board by including many Academy members in Vision Task Forces at the 1996 annual meeting in Cincinnati. Under the leadership of Michael Hitt, who followed me as president, a number of task forces were formed to translate the ideas emerging from the Vision Task Forces into ideas that could be implemented. Unfortunately, this effort seemed to lose steam and we never converged on a strategic plan that could guide the Academy in making future decisions. I was pleased to see, however, that under Andy Van de Ven's presidential leadership strategic planning once again became a priority within the Academy. More importantly, Andy was able to push this effort far more effectively than I did and an outstanding strategic planning document has emerged from the effort.

As the title of this chapter implies, although I've more often than not found myself in the right place at the right time, there have been occasions when the opposite was true. One of those occasions concerned service at the University of Oregon. I have always tried to play an active service role in the university, including serving on many committees, as Department Head on several occasions, and as Academic Direcor of our executive MBA program. The one time this inclination worked against me was when my college was looking for a new dean in the mid-1990s. As members of the search committee, we were told that there was a phase in the search process in which it is important to ask whether a candidate was good enough for the position. Once the process converges on a short-list of candidates, however, it is time to stop asking questions and time to sell, sell, and sell.

Our search process had converged on Tim McGuire, Deputy Dean at Carnegie Mellon's Graduate School of Industrial Administration. Trying to be a dutiful committee member and to convince him to take the job, I told Tim that I was committed to doing whatever it would take to make his deanship successful. I was totally unprepared for his response, which was to ask me to become associate dean. I had never wanted to become an associate dean, in large part because I thought it only made sense to do so if you aspired to become a dean. I had no such aspirations but Tim trapped me like a rat. I felt I had no alternative to accepting his offer and thus began a brief interlude in academic administration. Working with Tim was at first invigorating and exciting. He was a high energy, positive, and "ready-shoot-aim" type of leader.

Unfortunately, my time as associate dean overlapped with my term as president of the Academy. Trying to balance the responsibilities of these two demanding jobs simply got the better of me. I had an obligation to the Academy, but in working for an activist dean I had numerous other administrative responsibilities heaped on my plate while I continued to teach in the college's MBA core. I found myself dropping balls left and right. The final straw came after a four-day trip to New York to recruit MBA students. I had planned to take a dozen student group papers with me on the trip for grading because feedback was due on the Monday after my return. Unfortunately, for some reason the papers weren't available before my departure. I was supposed to return to Eugene on Sunday afternoon but my flight was delayed due to mechanical problems. I arrived home in the early evening, stopping first at the office to pick up the papers that needed to be graded that night. I hadn't seen my family in four days, I faced a long night of grading, and then I received a call from Tim McGuire. He didn't really need to talk with me but his wife, also an academic, wanted to talk about the importance of having a working paper series in the college, a topic so pressing that it couldn't wait until I got back in the office. After a tiring journey home, I found myself on a Sunday evening wanting to be with my family, needing to grade a stack of papers, but being forced to talk with the Dean's wife about an issue I didn't consider a high priority. That was the last straw and I wrote my letter of resignation the next morning. Although there were things I did as associate dean that were fun, there were many more that were not. Moreover, I'm not sure it was a job that I was particularly good at. Even so, my resignation may have been well timed. When Tim McGuire resigned quite suddenly some time later, a new associate dean who had been on the job all of about thirty minutes became interim dean.

Even though service to my college has not always been an entirely positive experience, my involvement in the Academy has been. In fact, every role that I have been asked to play in the Academy, both large and small, has been a rewarding experience because of the dedicated people I was able to meet and work with. Although it is still good advice for young assistant professors to pay the most attention to their research in the early years, I will never regret my involvement in the Academy early in my career. Not only did it change the trajectory of my career in positive ways, I was able to meet and work closely with many talented and dedicated people. Looking back, being recognized by my fellow Academy members with the Distinguished Career Service Contributions Award at the 2000 annual meeting was one of greatest honors of my career.

BECOMING A COLLEGE TEACHER

Because Irvine didn't have an undergraduate program in business, and university policy prevented graduate students from teaching fellow graduate students, I had never taught a class before arriving for my first faculty position at the University of Nebraska, Lincoln. I don't think my initial efforts at being an instructor were very good. In fact, years later when I was President of the Academy of Management making the rounds of the regional meetings, the person introducing me said "you probably won't remember, but I was a student in one of your very first classes at Nebraska." Taken somewhat by surprise, all I could think of to say in return was "God, I'm sorry."

When I joined the profession, teaching did not have the same degree of importance in judging faculty performance as it does today. This was again a case of being in the right place at the right time because as a brand new assistant professor I didn't have a clue about how to facilitate student learning. I think I showed up for my first one hour lecture to my undergraduate organizational behavior class with a nineteen-page outline. I managed to get through a page and a half of the outline before the hour ended. I made every rookie mistake in the book. I failed to think about my audience and presented the theory and research in the field of organizational behavior as I had learned it as a Ph.D student rather than how an undergraduate student might. I felt that my job as an instructor was to lecture for the full class period instead of breaking things up with discussions or case analyses. Finally, because I had only limited work experience I did not take as much time as I should to show the relevance of the concepts being presented to solving real managerial problems in organizations. Even though I wasn't a very good instructor early in my career, luckily my colleagues at Nebraska failed to notice or were too polite to say anything about it.

Although I've always worked hard at becoming a better classroom instructor, it was not until I moved to the University of Oregon and took my first sabbatical in 1983 that I gave serious thought to teaching effectiveness. I was promoted and tenured 1981 so some of the pressure to publish or perish was behind me. My first sabbatical was spent at The Amos Tuck School of Dartmouth College. Tuck was a school quite different than any I had experienced up until that time because it took good teaching very seriously. At Oregon in those days, a faculty badge of honor was to chase students away from your classes to decrease their size or to offer an elective so obscure that few students were interested, and some my colleagues were quite adept at it. At Tuck it was exactly the opposite. The "stars" on the faculty were Brian Quinn and John Hennessey because they could fill their MBA electives and still have long waiting lists of students trying to get in.

At Tuck I was very fortunate to be taken under John Hennessey's wing. He taught a very popular elective titled Dilemmas in Management using the case method, an approach with which I was not very familiar. John was kind enough to allow me to sit in his class. We frequently met before class and John would explain his teaching goals for the day and how he intended to achieve them. After class, we would debrief and John would explain the reason why he had done specific things during the class. I also visited Harvard and watched one of their outstanding instructors teach a course. This experience totally changed my approach to teaching, both in terms of my specific approach in the classroom and in the importance I attach to student learning. Moreover, I've found teaching far more rewarding as a result of my experience at Tuck.

There was one teaching tip that John Hennessey passed along that I have not followed, however. John taught a very large class (70 students) using the case method and in which students were required to provide a written analysis of a large number of cases. I recall asking John how he found the time to read and grade all those cases. John explained to me that he didn't. John would scan each written case analysis and assign a grade based on this ballpark assessment. Only if a student complained would he read the case word-for-word. Few ever complained. I don't think the students ever caught on to John's grading method, but I've never felt comfortable applying this technique in my own classes.

One of the greatest changes I've seen take place in academia concerning the role of professors is the increasing importance of teaching excellence today compared when I entered the field. Having two sons currently in college, one for which I'm paying out-of-state tuition, I'm not sure it is such a bad change. It is has dramatically raised the hurdle assistant professors must jump over to be tenured and promoted, however. In tenure decisions at Oregon our expectations for research have not diminished and, if anything, may have increased. But now you also have to be an excellent teacher. It is simply more difficult today than in the past. Again, I must have been in the right place at the right time because I'm not sure I would be promoted today based on my teaching effectiveness in the late 1970s and early 1980s.

CHANGES I HAVE OBSERVED ACROSS THE YEARS AND SOME I HAVEN'T

As I reflect back over my career, it's apparent that much has changed. For one thing, I've changed. For another thing, the field of organizational behavior has changed. Finally, business education as an area of professional education has changed and promises to continue to change. Although change seems to be a constant in life, there are also several things in my career that have remained remarkably stable.

Personal Changes

When I first entered the profession in 1975, I was an energetic young researcher who felt that my highest calling in life was conducting empirical research and publishing the results in academic journals. One reason was the reward system that existed at the time placed higher value on research than other things. The path to salvation and, not coincidentally, tenure lay through published research that made contributions to the existing knowledge base in the field. When I looked for research questions to investigate, I was more often guided by theoretical issues and holes in the empirical research literature that needed to be plugged than by problems faced by managers or ways to improve the practice of management. Practical considerations were never completely out of my mind, but testing and extending academic theory, refining methodologies, and extending research knowledge were the dominant influences on my research.

In retrospect, I wish I had been a bit better tuned into what was happening in organizations and the concerns of managers and employees. I think a better dialogue between the academic world and the world of practice would increase the vibrancy of the organizational behavior field. I once tried to arrange a sabbatical in industry because I thought I would learn a lot from working side-by-side with managers. I almost had a deal worked out, but it fell through at the last moment. I was never completely sure why this happened, but I think it boiled down to the fact that the company wasn't quite sure what to do with me. I like to believe that I could have added value to the company, although they may not have perceived the same value in having an academic in their midst as I did. I spent that sabbatical on another university campus and, although I spent my time productively, I'm not sure I learned as much as I would have from spending time in a very different environment. I think it is useful to get outside your comfort zone every once in a while. It is something we don't encourage enough. I've always admired my fellow doctoral student, John Van Maanen, for his approach to research that involves immersing himself in organizational contexts. I also admire Steve Kerr for his willingness to put the skills he honed as a faculty member and dean to the test in the business world as Vice President for Leadership Development at General Electric.

It concerns me more today than it did in the past that researchers more often write only for other researchers and less often take the time to translate their ideas into concepts managers can understand. We have several excellent outlets for such work, including the *Academy of Management Executive*. But it's unclear how many managers read *AME* or whether an article appearing in that journal (or others like it) carries the same weight on campus as one published in the *Academy of Management Journal* or the *Academy of Management Review*. I'm not arguing that theory and research are unimportant, only that the field of organizational behavior may benefit from a better two-way linkage between research and practice.

Another way in which I've changed over time is the dominant focus of my activities. The first third of my career to date (it's not quite over yet) was heavily invested in research and publications. The next third I invested more time and energy on service activities. In the final third, I think I'm devoting more of my time to teaching than to either research or service. Thus, my career might be characterized by a sequential attention to different facets of the professorial role. Although I've enjoyed each stage of my career and found the different activities in which I've engaged rewarding, I'm not sure this was the best way to do it. Instead, I might have been better served by a more balanced focus across the professorial roles over time. At a minimum, it has resulted in a "lumpier" publication record than might otherwise have been the case. Maybe I *am* the poster child for wayward careers (don't let this happen to you!). What is unclear at this point is where my attention will be directed in the next phase of my career. I'm engaged in several research and writing projects that I find exciting. Maybe I'm coming full circle (or, alternatively, regressing).

One thing that hasn't changed much over the course of my career has been the university where I work. My first teaching job was at Nebraska and I stayed there only two years. I didn't leave Nebraska because of dissatisfaction with the school. On the contrary, it was a great place to work with wonderful colleagues like Fred Luthans, Sang Lee, Art Kraft, and John Cullen. Instead of being pushed out of Nebraska, I was pulled out when Oregon had a faculty opening that would bring us back to the West Coast and closer to our families. I've been at Oregon ever since because Eugene is a nice community, I have had wonderful colleagues in my department (Warren Brown, Alan Meyer, Mike Russo, Peter Sherer, Rick Steers, Jim Terborg, Buddy Ungson, and Marc Weinstein), and my wife and family weren't willing to go anywhere else. However, I wonder sometimes if maybe I should have been more willing to move between universities. I certainly would have been better off financially. Also, the environment in which you work can be an important source of stimulation and changing your environment can have the benefit of putting you outside your comfort zone. Of course, sabbaticals do that to a certain extent but you don't make the same investment in a university where you are spending a sabbatical as in the school you work for.

Another thing that has remained remarkably stable over the years is my work habits. One down side of having Port as a role model was how hard he worked. Before I was married and my wife put her foot down, I was more often than not spending seven days in the office. She made me cut back to six. Even after being promoted to full professor, I still put in six days a week in the office, although my Saturdays have grown shorter over the years and I miss a few now and then. I remember telling Mary that one of the benefits of an academic career was that you had summers off. I've always worked in the office during the summer and Mary still asks: "which summer is it that you get off?"

Academic careers can be all consuming. Looking back, I'm not sure I've exhibited the healthiest work-family balance and I fear that has come at a cost to my family, including my sons Graham and Garrett. Although I have always tried to make sure that I didn't neglect my family, Mary bore the brunt of the responsibility in shepherding their homework while I was otherwise engaged in reviewing manuscripts, preparing for class, or traveling. Given how well my sons have turned out, perhaps that was for the better. I might have messed it up.

Changes in the Field of Organizational Behavior

I have also witnessed changes in the field of organizational behavior over the course of my career. As I've indicated, when I entered the field it was incredibly vibrant and exciting. There were intense theoretical debates and empirical questions that demanded to be answered. Clearly, within the Academy of Management the Organizational Behavior Division was the place to be. Although the OB Division remains the largest within the Academy, it is no longer clear to me it is where the action is. Instead, I think the more macro areas such as the Business Policy and Strategy Division have come center stage in terms of research interest and activity. Clearly, considerable research continues to be done in OB, but it seems less focused on new theories or ideas. As Dubin predicted, many of the "new concepts" are old ideas that have been repackaged. Just for fun one day in an OB doctoral seminar I was teaching, I put my belief to the test. I took a ten-year-old program from Academy of Management meeting and randomly selected a dozen or so titles of papers presented in the OB Division portion of the program. I did the same thing for the most recent meeting of the Academy of Management meeting. Randomly ordering the titles on a piece of paper, I asked the doctoral students to indicate at which meeting each paper had been presented. The fact that they couldn't distinguish research done ten years ago from research being done currently reinforced my belief that perhaps not much new was being done.

In suggesting that the field of OB has lost some of its vibrancy, I am too good a methodologist not to recognize that there may be an alternative explanation for the phenomenon I perceive. Maybe the field of OB is doing just fine but I've lost some of my interest and vibrancy. Although I cannot totally rule out that hypothesis, it still seems to me that the excitement I once witnessed in the field of OB has diminished. That may be the lament of each generation, however, as they prepare to pass the torch to the next.

Changes in Business Education

The final major change that I've seen during my career is in business education itself. There was a time when business education was not held in high regard on most campuses, and rightfully so. It was not very rigorous because it was neither guided by theory nor supported by empirical research. I think Warren Bennis' (1966, p. 182) historical description of business education sums up the status of the field rather nicely.

> In American universities – the less said about European universities, the better – business education, where it did exist, was disreputable, non- or antiscientific. It provided a haven for fools, adventureres, and the anemic heirs of industrialists who needed a college degree on the minimum of brains and the maximum of tuition, and it was taught as conventional wisdom cum moral uplift by successful, and hopefully, inspirational practitioners. Business education ranked in the academic hierarchy somewhere between football and a curiously indigenous American course known colloquially as home economics, a curriculum cocktail of cooking, etiquette, and good housekeeping.

As business education developed, the increasing emphasis on research, often published in top social science journals, has enhanced the stature of business schools on campus. At the same time, however, we may have moved farther away from the very phenomena we wish to understand (the practice of management).

In recent years, there has been a definite pendulum swing in the other direction. Business school deans place increasing emphasis on program rankings, relevance, and making strong connections with alumni and practicing managers. As higher education, at least at public schools, has become much more dependent on private giving there are strong pressures to please alumni, most of whom are less impressed by our research achievements than by other things. My own dean seems more excited when I, or one of my colleagues, is quoted in the popular press than when we publish in top journals. In fact, he is moving to add a new dimension to our performance evaluations reflecting visibility and interactions with practicing managers. Unquestionably, attention in the press is important to increasing the visibility of my school and, as I've argued above, I think we have much to learn from two-way interactions with managers. My concern is that we may be moving too far away from good scholarship in our quest for greater relevance.

One manifestation of the increasing emphasis placed on practice in business schools is the increasing role played by adjunct instructors who come not from academia but from business organizations. Part of the motivation of employing adjuncts is that they are much cheaper than tenure track faculty. Budgetary implications aside, I think there is also a belief among some that individuals who have extensive experience in business can do a more effective job training students than tenure track faculty. In fact, at my school we have a required course for seniors on leadership (which I introduced into the curriculum) that is moving in the direction of being only taught by adjuncts. Although the administration won't say so explicitly, the premise seems to be that only business practitioners have knowledge about leadership skills in organizations. Personally, I enjoy having adjunct instructors around because they bring a different perspective on issues. I believe it is wrong, however, to think that their perspective is the only one of value for students or that tenure track faculty members have little of value to contribute.

The increasing emphasis on practice runs the risk of losing sight of the value-added contribution that we bring to business education. Relevance and rigor are often discussed as if they are opposite ends of a continuum. Jim March wisely warned us, however, that there could be no relevance without rigor (Schmotter, 1995). I have come to appreciate the importance of relevance as my career has progressed. Perhaps not surprisingly, given my training as a researcher, I would hate for the quest for relevance to come at the expense of rigor and good scholarship. In the vast marketplace for ideas in business, the market segment representing relevance without rigor is already crowded. This observation can be verified by browsing the business trade-book section of any bookstore. We are better served by playing from our competitive advantage of pursuing relevant research questions with high levels of rigor.

SUMMING THINGS UP

In discussing these changes, the reader may have perceived a contradiction in my feelings. On the one hand, I argue for a greater concern for practical matters in the research that we do. On the other hand, I am concerned about the increasing emphasis placed on practice in business education. Perhaps this reveals an underlying ambivalence on my part, but I don't think so. What I think it reflects is a growing belief that greater balance is needed in all of our academic endeavors. Research that only informs, and is only informed by, other research distances us from the phenomena we wish to understand. In addition, instruction that is informed only by practice and that is not supported by a solid foundation of theory and research knowledge runs the risk of returning to the business schools of old.

CONCLUSION

That's my tale. It is hard for me to believe that I am closer to the end of my academic career than to the beginning. The journey has taken me along paths

I never could have anticipated, but I've never for a moment regretted the years I've spent as a professor. Even if I never intended to become one, it still feels like I'm in the right place at the right time, at least on most days.

PUBLICATIONS

1974

With L. W. Porter & R. Dubin. Unit performance, situational factors, and group attitudes in spatially separated work groups. *Organizational Behavior and Human Performance, 12,* 231–248.

With L. W. Porter, R. M. Steers & P. Boulian. Organizational commitment, job satisfaction, and turnover among psychiatric technicians. *Journal of Applied Psychology, 59,* 603–609.

1977

The need to train more sophisticated consumers of organizational behavior knowledge. *The Organizational Behavior Teaching Journal, 2,* 23–26.

With R. M. Steers. The motivational properties of tasks. *Academy of Management Review, 2,* 645–658.

With E. F. Stone & L. W. Porter. Higher-order need strengths as moderators of the job scope – job satisfaction relationship. *Journal of Applied Psychology, 62,* 466–471.

1978

The exercise of upward influence in organizations. *Administrative Science Quarterly, 23,* 137–156.

With L. W. Porter & E. F. Stone. Employee characteristics as predictors of turnover among female clerical employees in two organizations. *Journal of Vocational Behavior, 12,* 321–332.

1979

Equity theory predictions of behavior in organizations. In: R. M. Steers & L. W. Porter (Eds), *Motivation and Work Behavior* (2nd ed.). New York: McGraw Hill.

Leader characteristics, self-confidence, and methods of upward influence in organizational decision situations. *Academy of Management Journal, 22,* 709–725

With R. M. Steers. *Research in Organizations: Issues and Controversies.* Santa Monica: Goodyear Publishing.

With L. W. Porter & E. F. Stone. The interaction of personality and job scope in predicting turnover. *Journal of Vocational Behavior, 14,* 78–89.

With R. M. Steers & L. W. Porter. The measurement of organizational commitment. *Journal of Vocational Behavior, 15,* 224–247.

With C. Shreisheim, & R. Stogdill. Leader-group interactions. In: J. G. Hunt & L. L. Larson (Eds), *Crosscurrents in Leadership.* Carbondale: Southern Illinois University Press.

1981

Viewing turnover from the perspective of those who remain: The influence of attitudes on attributions of the causes of turnover. *Journal of Applied Psychology, 66,* 120–123.

With R. M. Steers. Employee turnover and post-decision accommodation processes. In: L. L. Cummings & B. M. Staw (Eds), *Research in Organizational Behavior* (Vol. 3). Greenwich: JAI Press.

With U. Sekaran. A cross-cultural analysis of the influence of individual and job characteristics on job involvement. *International Review of Applied Psychology, 66,* 51–64.

With D. G. Spencer. The influence of task and personality characteristics on employee turnover and absenteeism incidents. *Academy of Management Journal, 24,* 634–642.

1982

Expectancy theory approaches to faculty motivation. In: J. Bess (Ed.), *New Directions for Teaching and Learning: Motivating Professors to Teach* (No.10). San Francisco: Jossey-Bass.

With L. W. Porter & R. M. Steers. *Employee-Organization Linkages: The Psychology of Commitment, Absenteeism, and Turnover.* New York: Academic Press.

1983

Beliefs about the causes of behavior: The motivational implications of attribution processes. In: R. M. Steers & L. W. Porter (Eds), *Motivation and Work Behavior* (3rd ed.). New York: McGraw Hill.

Intrinsic job characteristics, extrinsic job characteristics, and work design. In: R. Harre & R. Lamb (Eds), *The Encyclopedic Dictionary of Psychology.* Oxford: Basal Blackwell.

With D. G. Spencer & R. M. Steers. An empirical test of the inclusion of job search linkages into Mobley's turnover decision process model. *Journal of Occupational Psychology, 56,* 137–144.

1984

Organizational strategies for adapting to high rates of employee turnover. *Human Resources Management, 23,* 365–380.

With C. S. Koberg & A. W. McArthur. The psychology of the withdrawal process: A cross-sectional validation test of Mobley's intermediate linkages model of turnover in two samples. *Academy of Management Journal, 27,* 79–94.

1985

With R. M. Steers & G. R. Ungson. *Managing Effective Organizations.* Boston: Kent Publishing.

1987

With T. W. Lee. Voluntarily leaving an organization: An empirical investigation of Steers and Mowday's model of turnover. *Academy of Management Journal, 30,* 721–743.

With R. M. Steers. Employee turnover from organizations. In: R. M. Steers, & L.W. Porter (Eds), *Motivation and Work Behavior* (4th ed.). New York: McGraw Hill.

1989

With J. G. Morita & T. W. Lee. Introducing survival analysis to organizational researchers: A selected application to turnover research. *Journal of Applied Psychology, 74,* 280–292.

1992

Out of the tangled thicket: Persistence in the face of failed conventional wisdom. In: P. Frost & R. Stablein (Eds), *Doing Exemplary Research.* Newbury Park: Sage Publications.

With T. W. Lee, S. J. Ashford & J. P. Walsh. Commitment propensity, organizational commitment, and voluntary turnover: A longitudinal study of organizational entry processes. *Journal of Management, 18,* 15–32.

1993

Reflections on editing *AMJ. Journal of Management Inquiry.*

With R. I. Sutton. Organizational behavior: Linking individuals and groups to organizational contexts. *Annual Review of Psychology, 44,* 195–229.

With J. G. Morita & T. W. Lee. The regression-analog to survival analysis: A selected application to turnover research. *Academy of Management Journal, 36,* 1430–1464.

1997

Reaffirming our scholarly values. *Academy of Management Review, 22,* 335–345. (a)

The quest for relevance. *Journal of Management Inquiry, 6,* 27–30. (b)

The journal editor as well-intentioned steward. *Academy of Management Journal, 40,* 1442–1449. (c)

Celebrating forty years of the Academy of Management Journal. *Academy of Management Journal,* 1400–1413. (d)

With S. Nam. Motivating more effective university teaching: The implications of expectancy theory. In: J. L. Bess (Ed.), *Teaching Well and Liking It: Motivating Faculty to Teach Effectively.* Baltimore: Johns Hopkins University Press.

1998

Dialogue: The Academy of Management has a useful role to play in shaping future business education. *Academy of Management Review, 23,* 12–13.

1999

Reflections on the study and relevence of organizational commitment. *Human Resource Management Review, 8,* 387–401.

In Press

With K. Colwell. Employee reactions to unfair outcomes in the workplace: The contributions of Adams' equity theory to understanding work motivation. In: G. Bigley, L. W. Porter & R. M. Steers (Eds). *Motivation and Work Behavior* (7th ed.). New York: McGraw Hill.

With J. P. Burton & J. E. Butler. Lions, tigers, and alley cats: HRM's role in Asian business development. *Human Resource Management Review.*

REFERENCES

Bennis, W. G. (1966). *Changing Organizations.* New York: McGraw Hill.

Boyer, E. L. (1990). *Scholarship Reconsidered.* Princeton: The Carnegie Foundation for the Advancement of Teaching.

Schmotter, J. W. (1995). An interview with Professor James G. March. *Selections.* McLean, VA: Graduate Management Admissions Council, *11*, Winter, 1–8.

Stephens, G. K., & Sommer, S. M. (2001). Lyman Porter: A celebration of excellence in mentoring. *Journal of Management Inquiry, 10*, 190–196.

Greg R. Oldham

STUMBLING INTO ORGANIZATIONAL BEHAVIOR

Greg R. Oldham

When I was growing up, I never wanted to be an academic. Perhaps I would become an engineer, or, if that didn't work out, maybe a social activist of some sort. But I had no interest in a profession that was in any way connected to the field of education. It seemed to me that the job of an academic was to stand up in front of a group of students and deliver lectures. That had absolutely no appeal to me – in fact, I could imagine few activities that were less attractive.

Since I now find myself writing an essay about my life and career as an academic, I guess it would be appropriate to say, "My plans changed." Why did they change? As I reflect, I believe I just stumbled around searching for something I could get excited about when I happened to bump into the field of Organizational Behavior in the late 1960s. After that initial contact, the people I met, and the contexts that surrounded me, influenced my decision to pursue a career as an academic and to focus my energies on the kind of research that I have been conducting for nearly thirty years. In the pages that follow, I discuss the journey I have taken, and highlight some of the major events and opportunities that shaped my career as a Professor of Organizational Behavior.

MY EARLY YEARS (1947–1965)

I was born in Inglewood, California, a city a few miles from Los Angeles. For the entire period of time I lived in Inglewood, my father was employed by Douglas Aircraft Company. I believe he was a foreman or a leadman on a production line. My mother was a homemaker and was responsible for caring

Management Laureates, Volume 6, pages 269–302.
Copyright © 2002 by Elsevier Science Ltd.
All rights of reproduction in any form reserved.
ISBN: 0-7623-0487-1

for me and my sister, who was about four-years older. When my mother needed support on the home front, she received it from my maternal grandparents, who were semi-retired and lived nearby.

My family was very close, and we were involved in many activities together. But I mostly remember the road trips – the countless hours my parents, sister, grandparents, and I spent touring the country by car. We started taking these trips when I was one (I understand I was a good traveler at that age), and we took one every summer until I turned 15. Our trips lasted between two and four weeks, and we went to every state, except North Dakota. I have never really understood why we missed that one; perhaps my parents felt that if you have seen one Dakota, you have seen them all. I do recall we had fun, playing games in the car, seeing the sites, and dining at "interesting" roadside diners and restaurants.

I attended public schools in Inglewood through the third grade. When I turned nine, we moved to La Mirada, a little town about 20 miles from Los Angeles. La Mirada wasn't (and isn't) much of a town, and there wasn't much to do there. But the houses and schools were fresh and new, there was little crime, and there was plenty of space for kids to run around. These were the sorts of things my parents valued at the time, and La Mirada provided all of them. In addition, about the time we moved, my father decided to take a job with a new company, Metro Steel. His job with Metro involved selling prefabricated buildings, and he was responsible for sales in the geographic area surrounding La Mirada.

My father had no experience as a salesman and knew absolutely nothing about prefabricated buildings, or the steel industry. However, he dedicated himself to learning the tasks and responsibilities associated with this new job, and after a period of adjustment, he became quite successful. My father's decision to accept this new job, and his subsequent success, had a big impact on me at the time. In fact, as I reflect, I think all of the events surrounding his new position had much to do with my developing an appreciation for the value of hard work, perseverance, and determination.

While I was growing up in La Mirada, my mother was most involved in the lives of my sister and me. My mother was a full-time homemaker, and after her marriage never took a job outside the home. She essentially dedicated herself to my sister and me, and regarded her "job" as creating a supportive and stimulating home environment in which my sister and I could reach our potential. There was never any doubt that our success and well-being were my mother's primary concerns, and she would always take it upon herself to address any obstacles that might interfere with our ability to achieve.

I spent twelve years in La Mirada. My elementary, junior high-school and high-school years were generally happy. I recall a few disappointments, mostly involving breakups with girlfriends. However, I can recall few incidents that I would characterize as traumatic. In general, I was a very good student, participated in a variety of sports, had a solid core group of friends, and was involved in a number of activities at school, ranging from theatre to editing the school yearbook. I cannot say that I was exceptionally competent at, or particularly passionate about, any one subject in school or any of my extracurricular activities. Rather, I had a wide range of interests and achieved some measure of success in most academic areas and in nearly all of my other activities.

As a result of these successes, adults started to develop high expectations of me – expectations that I could accomplish nearly anything I set my sights on, and that I would be successful no matter what the activity. This group included my teachers, extended family, neighbors and most important to me – my mother. She was subtle, but seldom missed the opportunity to articulate her expectations and to remind me that everyone in our family was counting on me to do well in pretty much everything I tried. On reflection, this was a lot of "stuff" for a kid to carry around. But at the time, I don't recall having any problems with the expectations. Most things came easily to me in those early years, and I felt the expectations were appropriate given some of the successes I had experienced. I now believe that I internalized many of these high expectations and standards, and that they had a substantial impact on the way I conducted myself throughout my career.

Although neither of my parents attended college, there was never any doubt that my sister and I would. My parents began emphasizing the importance of a college education from the time I was in the first grade. Their argument was fairly straightforward – a college education was necessary if you were to have a secure job, a successful career, and a fulfilling life. They never discussed specific colleges, academic programs, or the potential financial gains that might be associated with a college degree. Instead, they focused on the overall value of a college education for future well-being and indicated that my sister and I had little choice but to attend.

My sister was the first member of my family to go to college. She attended California State University-Fullerton, just a few miles from La Mirada. There, she majored in education and became an elementary school teacher. When it was my turn to consider colleges, I decided to apply to only one: the University of California. I didn't investigate other public or private universities in California, and never considered the possibility of attending an out-of-state college. In fact, I really didn't collect all that much information about the

University of California. All I knew was that many of my friends were applying to that University and that my academic record exceeded the standards for admission. In retrospect, I probably should have conducted a much more thorough analysis of possible colleges and universities. But at the time, I didn't consider choice of college to be a particularly important event, and felt I had all the information I needed to make an intelligent choice.

In those days, students applied to the University of California system, and did not designate in their application materials particular campuses within the system. Once admitted to the system, applicants were required to rank order the campuses of choice, and were admitted to those campuses on a first come, first served basis. I was admitted to the University, and decided to consider only those campuses that were relatively close to La Mirada. I wanted to remain close to my family, and three campuses would allow me to do that: UCLA, UC-Riverside, and a brand new campus, UC-Irvine. Irvine was the smallest, and I found it the most hospitable of the three. In addition, I thought attending a new campus might be a real adventure. But most significantly, most of my closest friends had decided to attend UCI, and attending would give me a chance to maintain those friendships, as well as remain close to my family. I never thought about the quality of the faculty, the breadth of programs, or the social opportunities at UCI. Irvine just "felt right," and I decided to go with my instincts and to become part of a "charter" class that would be the first to complete all four years at UCI.

MY COLLEGE YEARS (1965–1969)

It was an interesting time to be a student at UCI. I think there were only a thousand or so undergraduates, four or five buildings, and no traditions. Still, my friends and I thought we were in a special place that was destined to become a great university. And, from an academic perspective, UCI turned out to be a wonderful choice for me. UCI had been successful in attracting a number of outstanding faculty members who were among the best in their fields. Because there were few graduate students around during that time, these faculty taught nearly all of my classes. As a result, not only were many of the classes on the cutting edge of current research, but I also had the opportunity to establish relationships with several faculty members who later were to have a profound impact on my career.

When I arrived at UCI, I decided to major in engineering. Actually, at the time, I had no idea what it was that engineers did, or what types of classes they were required to complete. All I knew was that one of my hometown neighbors was an engineer, that he was smart, and that I liked him. That was all the information I needed. I was confident that I would be successful in this major because I had been told by so many people for so many years that I could achieve success in whatever field I chose.

Well, I was not successful. For the first two quarters at UCI, I did not do well academically. The combination of my skills, study habits, and the first year curriculum didn't match, and I nearly dropped out of UCI as a result. Those first two quarters at UCI were among the low points in my life – and the first time I had ever struggled academically.

Of course, it turned out that my academic difficulties during those first two quarters were a blessing in disguise. I attributed all of my academic problems to my college major, and felt that if I were to achieve success and remain at Irvine I had to change majors. Following pretty much the same "non-strategy" I used in selecting a college, I did not conduct a systematic search or an evaluation of possible majors. Instead, I made what I thought was an obvious choice. I had done well in one social science course I completed during the second quarter, found the content much more interesting than that of the other few classes I had taken, and simply decided to switch out of engineering and into the Social Sciences Department. I never thought about the implications of this switch, or seriously considered any other major. I just wanted to settle quickly on a major I felt comfortable with and move on with my life. Thoughts of jobs, careers, and opportunities would come later, after I had achieved some academic success.

The social science curriculum at UCI was interdisciplinary, and I was able to take courses ranging from "Social Psychology" to "Dream Therapy" to "Cross-cultural Sociology." Most important, the classes were small and I had individual contact with a number of excellent faculty members including, Jim March (who was Dean of Social Sciences at the time), Barbara Foley Meeker, and Duran Bell. After my setback during the first year, I dedicated myself to improving my academic standing, and did well in my final three years at UCI.

During my entire stay at UCI, I held summer jobs. The first summer I worked as a service station attendant; the remaining summers, I held a variety of jobs with Steelcase, the office furniture manufacturer. It was at Steelcase that my interests in work and organizations began to develop. My first job there involved dipping drawer parts (e.g. partitions) into a tank of gray paint, and then hanging the parts on an overhead conveyor line that lead to a dryer. I have a vivid recollection of every single aspect of that job, including the exact smell of the paint! I next moved to a job that required me to remove the dried painted parts from the conveyor line and stack them on pallets, in neat little piles. Fortunately, I didn't spend much time on either of these jobs, as I was promoted pretty quickly. However, I did learn some things about the mind-numbing qualities of repetitive, machine-paced work, and the methods employees use to exercise some control over line speed (i.e. I figured out how to sabotage the paint line). In my last several jobs at Steelcase, I was responsible for assembling different types of drawers and cabinets. Compared to my jobs on the paint line, this was enriched, meaningful work, and gave me a chance to appreciate the sense of accomplishment that was associated with building a product from beginning to end.

During the second quarter of my junior year at UCI, I started to think about possible topics for my required senior project. My work at Steelcase had peaked my interest in work and organizations, and I was looking for an opportunity to apply my social science background to topics that were related. But I didn't have any idea if this were possible, and if there was a field of study related to social sciences and organizations. I knew that the UCI Social Sciences Department offered no courses on such an applied topic. Then, while in the UCI library one day, I stumbled onto a textbook titled "industrial sociology." I skimmed a few chapters of this book, and it seemed to be just what I was looking for. So, I began searching for a faculty member in the social sciences who knew something about industrial sociology and who might be willing to sponsor my senior project.

One day I bumped into a friend of mine who had just come from a meeting with faculty member from UCI's Graduate School of Management. At the time, I didn't know that the Graduate School of Management existed – I believe it occupied the top floor of a small shopping center somewhere across campus. My friend indicated that this professor had applied interests in industrial sociology, held a joint appointment in the Social Sciences Department, and seemed open to talking with undergraduates. He urged me to make an appointment to see the faculty member, a fellow by the name of Lyman Porter. I made the appointment, not realizing at the time that my meeting with Porter would provide a direction for my professional life and career.

During our initial meeting, Lyman suggested a few books and articles for me to read over the summer of my junior year. After reading this material, it didn't take me long to realize that he wasn't a sociologist. Instead, I was reading books and articles in the areas of industrial and organizational psychology, and Organizational Behavior. This was my first contact with this material, and I found it extremely interesting and relevant, given my summer work experiences. Lyman agreed to sponsor my senior project, and I completed it on the topic of organizational commitment.

During my senior year, I was enthusiastic about the material I was covering in my classes, and in my senior project. I still had high expectations of myself, and by that time, I had developed some solid work habits and had begun taking my academic work pretty seriously. However, I was also anticipating graduation, which in those days meant being drafted into the Army and sent to Viet Nam.

I was interested in one last challenge, something I could feel passionate about, before being drafted. My classes had been going well for some time, and Lyman had been very supportive during the period I spent with him. I was starting to believe that attending graduate school was something I could get excited about, and that I might just have the potential to do well in it. So, at this time, I made the decision to pursue a master's degree. I recall that at the time I never gave any thought to pursuing a Ph.D. – that seemed far too distant a goal. And I didn't consider the implications of obtaining a master's degree for future employment – I thought I would probably be killed in Viet Nam, anyhow. All I knew was that I wanted to continue my education in some field that was related to the work I had been doing during my senior year.

When considering various graduate school programs, I decided to focus on those that were interdisciplinary and that had a real applied focus on organizations. I also wanted the program to be located somewhere other than southern California, the place I had lived my entire life. I guess my interest in the interdisciplinary part was based on my experiences in UCI's Social Science Department. But I can't exactly recall why I was so anxious to leave California. Perhaps it had to do with the friends I had at UCI. I wouldn't say that they were frivolous, but they certainly didn't take their academic work as seriously as I was taking mine at the time. I know that I felt I might find friends who were more like me outside of California.

I recall discussing my plans with Lyman. He suggested that programs in Industrial Relations might be appropriate given my interests and background. Industrial Relations programs were often interdisciplinary and offered courses that generally fit my interests. I remember taking Lyman's advice, going to the UCI library and paging through some graduate school catalogs describing programs in Industrial Relations. I was particularly attracted to the programs at Purdue and the University of Minnesota. I applied and was accepted by both, but for reasons that are a little unclear after all of these years, I was most attracted to the Purdue program. Perhaps it was because Purdue seemed a little more interested in me than Minnesota. Or maybe the Minnesota winters frightened me. Whatever the reasons, I recall discussing my preference with Lyman. He indicated that he thought I would do well in either program. That was all I needed to hear. I didn't talk with any other faculty member or collect any additional information. I was off to Purdue in the summer of 1969.

MY TIME IN WEST LAFAYETTE (1969–1970)

It turns out that I didn't have much more than a "cup of coffee" in West Lafayette – I lived there for a total of nine months. But those were important months in my professional development, and I now look back on those times with fond memories.

When I arrived at Purdue, I think the faculty and students thought I was somewhat peculiar. After all, what kind of person moved from southern California (i.e. Nirvana) to a small town in the middle of Indiana? When I told people that I was paying out-of-state tuition for the pleasure of living in these conditions that simply reinforced their view that I was crazy.

Perhaps my decision to move to West Lafayette was a little unusual, but the Purdue Industrial Relations program was a perfect fit for me at the time. My fellow students were much more focused on their academics than my friends at Irvine. That may have been a function of the fact that my Purdue colleagues were graduate students with clear interests, or, in contrast to my friends in California, they had a serious case of midwestern work ethic. Or maybe it was just because there wasn't much else to do in West Lafayette except work. Whatever the reason or reasons, the work habits of my friends and colleagues at Purdue were more like mine, and I felt very comfortable there.

Most of my classes were interesting and gave me a general idea of the range of possible topics in the field of Industrial Relations. I recall taking classes in Industrial Sociology, Industrial/Organizational Psychology, Collective Bargaining, Organizational Communication, and Organizational Behavior. I also recall the stimulating discussions we had in many of these classes and thinking that the material fit well with my interests. Further, I began to feel that Organizational Behavior was the most interesting and relevant of all the topics, and that it was something that I could get very excited about.

The best part of my experience at Purdue involved my interaction with the faculty connected to the Industrial Relations program and the Business School. These included, Paul Johnson, Bob Bain, and Howard Fromkin. Johnson was my advisor, and he was an extremely supportive and encouraging guy. He had high hopes for me, and let me know it. It wasn't long before he got me a job as his research assistant that paid for my tuition and gave me a chance to conduct some empirical work. I have always felt indebted to him. Fromkin was also incredibly supportive. At Paul Johnson's recommendation, I had stopped by Fromkin's office one day. He was generous with his time, and over a period of several months he gave me excellent advice about the field of Organizational Behavior, and my possible future in it.

I did very well in my classes at Purdue, and was particularly excited by the content of my Organizational Behavior and I/O Psychology courses. But the possibility of an all-expense paid vacation in Viet Nam still lingered. I had passed my physical exam for the service, and expected to be drafted at any time. Then, I believe toward the end of my first semester at Purdue, Richard Nixon initiated the draft lottery. I recall the evening that the lottery was conducted. My friends and I were huddled around a small radio waiting to hear the numbers that were connected to our birthdays. Small numbers were "bad," and I believe any number above 180 was considered "good." My number was *very* good (350), and after that evening, there was little chance that I would be drafted.

At that point, I decided to become a little more serious about my future plans. I knew that I could continue in the Industrial Relations master's program, get my degree and delay a decision by a year or so. But that seemed like a waste of my time. I already knew that I wanted to focus on the field of Organizational Behavior. And I wanted to be involved in something that would really stretch me academically and personally.

I had maintained my relationship with Lyman Porter, and I remember calling him one day and discussing my future. I recollect indicating that I wanted to move on to a Ph.D. program in some field related to Organizational Behavior. I don't think I really understood what would be involved after I received the Ph.D. (e.g. teaching, research, service, or anything like that), all I recall is that I wanted to learn more about Organizational Behavior and be a part of a program that would really challenge me.

Lyman had been a visiting professor at Yale a year or two before I met him, and he felt that Yale's Department of Administrative Sciences would be a perfect fit for me. I have never really understood why he thought that Yale was the place for me, but, in retrospect, he gave me terrific advice. Lyman told me that the Organizational Behavior faculty at Yale had a wide range of interests and was absolutely first-rate. And he was so confident that I would be admitted to the program and thrive there he indicated that I really needn't bother considering others. I don't remember collecting much information about the Yale program or the research of the Administrative Sciences faculty. I simply relied on Lyman's knowledge of the program and of the Organizational Behavior field and decided to apply to Yale.

I also recall that I was not at all convinced that I would be admitted to Yale – after all, it was an Ivy League university! So, after discussing my interests with Howard Fromkin, I decided to apply to the OB doctoral program at Purdue, as well. I was admitted to both programs, but was more attracted to Yale based on Lyman's recommendation, the thought of attending an Ivy

League university, and because I thought the program would be extremely difficult and challenging. Moreover, Yale offered a Fellowship (versus Purdue's assistantship), which meant that I would be paid ($140 a month, I believe) just for being a student. What a deal! I still remember the day Ed Lawler, who was on the Yale faculty at the time, called to let me know I had been admitted. I was so excited that I decided right then to accept the offer of admission. I returned to California for the summer (this time to work in a meat-packing plant). Then, I was off to Yale in August of 1970.

MY YEARS IN NEW HAVEN (1970–1973)

This was an exciting time in my life and the period when things started to fall into place in my career. I joined the OB doctoral program in the Administrative Sciences Department with seven other doctoral students: Jan Blom, Paul Boulian, Jim Carlisle, Stan Kaufman, Frank Satterthwaite, Lloyd Suttle, and Jerry Young. I believe all but Young and I took non-teaching jobs upon completing the program. Ph.D. students from earlier classes who were present at the time I arrived included Dave Brown, Bob Kaplan, and John Wanous.

Administrative Sciences was not a Business School; it included only two groups of faculty: Operations Research and Organizational Behavior. The OB faculty at the time was very young and included only one senior person – Chris Argyris. The other faculty were untenured associate and assistant professors: Clay Alderfer, Bliss Cartwright, Richard Hackman, Douglas "Tim" Hall, Ed Lawler, Roy Lewicki, Andrew Pettigrew (a Visitor), Ben Schneider, and Gerrit Wolf. I believe all of the junior faculty were in their late 20s, or possibly early 30s, when I arrived in 1970.

I had done very well at Purdue, but I recall being a little intimidated during the first few months at Yale. During an initial session for new Ph.D. students, Chris Argyris had made a few remarks suggesting that all of us were unlikely to make it through the program. That scared me, but more troublesome was the fact that many of my fellow doctoral students had received their undergraduate degrees from Ivy League universities like Princeton and Yale. I don't think I had ever met an Ivy League graduate before I arrived in New Haven, and I initially felt that they were my intellectual superiors. The bottom line was that I just wasn't confident that I could compete on an equal footing with graduates of Ivy League universities.

During my first year at Yale, I took micro-organizational behavior seminars from Alderfer, Hall, and Lawler, and a macro-organization theory course from Pettigrew. It didn't take me long to realize a couple of things. First, I could do as well in any of my classes as my fellow students, regardless of the origin of their undergraduate degrees. The education I received at UCI and Purdue was first rate and had prepared me well for Ph.D. level classes. Also, I learned that I was much more interested in subjects involving individuals and groups in organizations than I was in subjects involving organization structure and the organization's environment. They just seemed more relevant to me, based on my summer work experiences and the classes I had completed at Purdue.

The seminars at Yale included only a few students and were incredibly challenging and stimulating. I know that I learned as much from the in-class discussions with faculty and students as I did from the assigned readings. I think all the students were rewarded for developing new ideas and theoretical frameworks and figuring out innovative ways of testing them. I was doing very well in my classes and, at the same time, doing a lot of non-required reading outside class, trying to learn as much as possible about OB and about the research of the Yale faculty. I recall becoming completely absorbed in the subject during that first year and starting to develop a real passion for the field. I was also becoming intense and developing a strong determination to succeed in the program and to have a major impact on the field.

One of the major emphases in the Yale Ph.D. program involved establishing a relationship with one faculty member and working with him on individual projects, including the required pre-dissertation research project. I had heard from Howard Fromkin at Purdue that Richard Hackman was a very competent, young, and energetic guy whom I should consider as an advisor. I had already read some of Richard's published work, thought it was interesting, and decided to stop by his office one day. I recall that we hit it off, and that he seemed interested in working with me. Without talking with any other faculty member, I asked him to serve as my advisor on my pre-dissertation research project. He agreed, and I never seriously considered anyone else as an advisor after that.

Through my readings, I had become interested in research on leadership and goal setting and decided that I wanted to integrate the two areas and conduct a study on the effects of various leadership characteristics (e.g. legitimacy and trust) on individuals' acceptance of assigned performance goals. Richard helped me design a laboratory study to test my ideas. I conducted the study and obtained some interesting findings. I recall working hard on the write-up, feeling very good about it, and thinking that I had written a publishable piece of work. I submitted the write-up to Hackman expecting to be praised for my efforts. After telling me how much potential I had, he returned the manuscript to me with his comments. If I recall, all but one of my sentences had been crossed out and replaced with one of his! Looking back, this was a real learning experience, and I benefited greatly from it. At the time, however, I didn't react that way. I took the criticism personally, felt humiliated, and became defensive.

In fact, I was so disappointed in myself that I considered leaving the Ph.D. program. Richard noticed my reaction (it would have been hard not to), discussed his reasoning with me, and I soon agreed to stay on, to use his critique as constructive feedback and to push forward. This paper was eventually published in the *Academy of Management Journal*, largely due to the time and effort Hackman devoted to the piece.

I had been receiving positive feedback about my potential from Richard and other faculty, and by my second year, I had redefined success. I no longer considered it as simply doing well in the Ph.D. program. Now, I was determined to be the best graduate student in the program. I think the best way to characterize me at that time is "driven." The high standards that I had internalized as a kid growing up were still present, and I had found a subject area that I could feel passionate about. I was very intense and determined to make an impact.

After completing my pre-dissertation project, I began thinking about my dissertation. I was still interested in leadership and, in particular, attempting to identify some alternative ways that leaders might enhance the motivation and performance of employees. And I had become fiercely independent. I wanted to work with Hackman because I respected him and thought he was an excellent scholar. However, I wanted my independence and didn't want to conduct research that was in any way connected to his specialty. That wasn't a problem with the area of leadership – Richard wasn't interested in the topic, and didn't know all that much about the leadership literature. It was perfect situation! I continued to work with Richard on my dissertation, and he gave me the independence to think about leadership in different ways. Richard always emphasized that I should be trying to conduct research that would completely change the way people think about organizations – not research that simply extends what we know. He also suggested that the successful people in the field simplify concepts; they don't make them more complex. I tried to take this advice to heart in working on my dissertation, and in my subsequent research.

Most of our discussions about my dissertation took place, not in the office, but in Richard's fishing boat. Both of us enjoyed fishing, and we spent many hours on the water discussing my dissertation. I have great memories of those times, and Richard and I became really good friends during our fishing expeditions. We didn't catch many fish, and always seemed to have plenty of time to discuss my dissertation and research strategies in general. I certainly learned a great deal about research during those discussions. But I think I learned most about how to interact with doctoral students. Richard took me and my ideas seriously. He was able to establish high standards and expectations of me, but at the same time be encouraging. I have learned that it isn't all that easy to interact with doctoral students in this way, and he was a master at it.

Organizational Behavior faculty began steadily leaving Yale during my second and third years in the program. For a variety of reasons, Argyris, Cartwright, Hall, Lawler, and Schneider left. Vic Vroom and two visitors, Bob Sobel and Tom Taber, replaced them. Because of this turnover, I had a difficult time forming a dissertation committee. I finally convinced Alderfer and Wolf to join Hackman as committee members. None of them had a strong interest in leadership, the subject of my dissertation. But they were supportive and willing to let me take something of a risk with a dissertation topic, which is what I was looking for at the time. Alderfer and Hackman were especially helpful in helping me find a research site for the dissertation. They were working with a large retail firm at the time and persuaded the manager to allow me to collect my dissertation data in several of its stores.

I enjoyed working with Hackman on the dissertation and appreciated the independence and freedom he gave me. However, I wasn't satisfied with the fact that we had not really established a collaborative working relationship. We were not at the time working on a project as colleagues; rather, he was serving as an advisor for the research I was doing independently. I recall stopping by his office one day and sharing this frustration with him. He indicated that he was thinking about starting a new project in the area of job design, and would be meeting in a few days with two consultants (Bob Janson and Ken Purdy) from the Roy Walters Consulting firm, who were interested in collaborating with him on this project. He asked me to join the meeting to see if I had any interest in participating in the project. I had some interest in job design. I had read much of the work that had been published in the area, had given a lecture on that topic to a class that Wolf was teaching, and recalled the importance of the work itself when I was at Steelcase. So, I attended the meeting with Hackman, Janson and Purdy, and it eventually led to our early work on Job Characteristics Theory (JCT).

My participation in this project was just a great experience – probably the best academic experience I had in graduate school. And it was good for lots of reasons. First, Richard and I had a good personal relationship, and we worked very effectively together as colleagues. We continuously challenged one another, and I don't recall either of us becoming upset or defensive in the process. At the time, Richard was most interested in the job characteristics and measurement parts of the model we were developing, and I was more interested in individual differences (e.g. Growth Need Strength), and the implications of the model for organizational change. Thus, our interests tended to complement one another, without substantially overlapping. I recall many of our discussions involving the job characteristics that should be included in the model, how they should be defined, how they might affect different psychological states, and how individual differences might moderate many of these relations. I also recall that the discussions were terrific. Richard considered me a full partner in the work – he listened to my ideas, and took them seriously. The second major reason the project was an excellent experience was that it provided me with an opportunity to manage a large field research study. Janson and Purdy had consulting relationships with several organizations, and Hackman and I were given an opportunity to collect JCT data in those organizations in return for Janson and Purdy's involvement in the project. I traveled with Janson and Purdy to several of the organizations and was given full responsibility for data collection and for managing the projects on site. My experiences with data collection on this project, in addition to the data collection for my dissertation, had a substantial impact on the way I have conducted research during my entire career.

The work we completed on JCT has had a much bigger impact than I expected it would when we began working on it. I certainly thought the research was good and the topic timely, but I had no idea that it would be among the most frequently cited research ever published in the OB field. And I really didn't think it was nearly as creative or significant as my dissertation research. Now that, I thought at the time, was important work! Unfortunately, people in the field didn't exactly see it that way. Although the article based on my dissertation, "The Motivational Strategies used by Supervisors: Relationships to Effectiveness Indicators," was published in a top journal (*Organizational Behavior and Human Performance*) and was cited frequently immediately after publication, interest in it diminished quickly. I don't think it has been cited more than a handful of times in the past ten years.

After a little more than two years at Yale, I decided to go on the job market. Although I had submitted for publication the paper based on my pre-dissertation and one other paper, I had not published anything. My work on Job Characteristics Theory was still in the data analysis stage, and my dissertation data had just been collected. But I was anxious to go on the market, and Hackman and the other faculty thought I was ready and encouraged me to move forward.

Looking back, I'm not sure why I was in such a hurry to leave Yale. I was certainly happy with my work and the professional relationships I had established. Perhaps, I just wanted to demonstrate to myself, friends, and family that I could be among the youngest ever to receive a Ph.D. in Organizational Behavior at Yale. Maybe I was looking for a new challenge – I had taken all the OB classes at Yale that interested me. Maybe I was tired of being poor – I had been given an increase in my fellowship to about $180 a month, but still had a bit of a problem making ends meet. Or maybe I just thought that leaving was an easy way to get away from my girlfriend at the time. She was using the "M" word quite a lot, and I definitely wasn't ready for that. In any case, I wanted out.

I interviewed at many of the top business schools in the country, including the University of Chicago and Carnegie Mellon, and did not do well. Certainly, my difficulties in these interviews count among the major setbacks in my professional life, and I still have many of the bruises to prove it. I don't think I'll ever forget one senior member of the Chicago faculty standing up in the middle of my presentation and announcing to all that he had better things to do with his time than listen to me. He then left the room, crossing right in front of me! I had never experienced anything like that before, and I didn't have a strong desire to experience it again.

Looking back, I was ill prepared for my job interviews. I had not given a practice job talk at Yale or participated in mock interviews with Yale faculty. I simply presented my dissertation research and expected the offers to pour in. After all, I was a Yale Ph.D. student! The offers didn't come right away. My lack of preparation showed, as did my poor presentation skills. I had given a total of two lectures while I was in graduate school, because graduate students had fellowships and typically did not offer regular classes to Yale under-graduates. I was not at all polished or prepared for questions from the audience.

As with many of my early experiences, the fact that I did poorly during my initial interviews turned out to be a blessing. I was very status conscious when I was in graduate school, and I would have probably accepted an offer from one of those private business schools if I had received one. But looking back, there really wasn't much of a fit between the kind of research I was doing and the expectations of those programs. I seriously doubt that I would have been happy, productive or successful in any of those programs.

I received a call late in the recruiting period from Ken Rowland of the University of Illinois at Urbana-Champaign. Rowland indicated that an offer Illinois had made to a senior person had just been rejected, and that they were interested in interviewing me for a junior faculty position. I accepted the invitation to interview and came away from it with a very positive reaction. I thought my job talk went a bit better than my earlier presentations, but from what I was told after I accepted the job, it still didn't go all that well. The faculty at Illinois were not impressed with my leadership research, but thought the work I was doing with Hackman on JCT had some potential.

The Illinois faculty at the time was young and very talented. In addition to Rowland, they included, Bobby Calder, Dave Cherrington, Jeff Pfeffer, Jerry Salancik, and Barry Staw. Only Rowland had tenure; the others were assistant professors. In addition, there were outstanding faculty in other departments, including Jeanne Brett and Joe McGrath in Psychology, and George Graen and John Kimberly in Labor and Industrial Relations. After my interview, I recall feeling that the intellectual and research climates at Illinois were comparable to those at Yale. I thought I could be comfortable at Illinois, and that the colleagues would be supportive and stimulating.

I received an offer from Illinois and accepted it almost immediately. I think I might have had one or two other offers at the time, but I liked the colleagues, the climate and the opportunity at Illinois. I wasn't concerned with the size of community, the location, or the social/cultural opportunities – only with an opportunity to do my research in a supportive environment with bright, interesting colleagues.

I moved to Urbana-Champaign in August of 1973. I was 26 years old, single and still self-assured. Although my difficulties during the job interview process had certainly dented my self-confidence, I was able to deal with this by attributing most of my setbacks to a lack of preparation and experience, not to a lack of competence. And I was anxious to start my career so that I could demonstrate to the people in the programs that had rejected me, as well as to others in the field, that I could do high quality research and have a successful career.

MY LIFE IN URBANA-CHAMPAIGN (1973-PRESENT)

I could not have found a better place to start my career than the University of Illinois. When I arrived, I had extremely high personal standards for scholarship developed during my time in graduate school. I was not only determined to produce high-quality research, but to have a major impact on the field. I was intense and completely absorbed in, and passionate about, my research. Urbana-Champaign provided the ideal environment for me – there were few distractions in the community, and it was populated by other academics who were also passionate about their work. It was just a perfect fit! My work habits were reinforced by those of others in the OB program and elsewhere on campus.

My first year at Illinois was basically a post-doctoral experience. I learned how to teach, essentially by being thrown into the classroom for the first time in my life. I also learned that there were approaches to research other than those I had been taught at Yale. When I arrived, I believed the world revolved around

Yale and the research strategies followed by the faculty there. However, I soon realized that others had different perspectives on research that were just as legitimate as those at Yale. Perhaps the most important lesson I learned during that first year, though, was to take my work and myself less seriously. Actually, Barry Staw taught me this lesson in an indirect way. He indicated that he did research "just for the fun of it." When he initially mentioned this to me, I thought it a strange and inappropriate way to think about one's research program. At that point, I didn't do research for the fun of it – I did it to change the way that other academicians and the public in general thought about organizations. Over time, though, I began to accept Staw's perspective as a much healthier approach. So, I began taking on new research projects that seemed like they would be fun to pursue, hoping that other people in the field would find my work interesting and significant. This is still the approach I take in my research program.

I learned soon after accepting the position at Illinois that the Organizational Behavior program would have a new look upon my arrival. Calder, Cherrington and Pfeffer had resigned to take positions elsewhere. And Lou Pondy of Duke University had accepted an offer to become a full professor in the program. In retrospect, it was Pondy's decision to accept this position that really set things in motion for OB at Illinois. Pondy was extremely charismatic, and an intellectual force – one of the smartest people I had ever met. He was a program builder and saw his role as creating a strong intellectual climate within the OB program, and increasing the visibility of the program both nationally and locally. I always felt that Lou was less concerned with his own research agenda than he was in creating an interdisciplinary OB program with a strong focus on idea exchange. In that respect, then, he was an ideal person to lead a group of young assistant professors. Lou made contacts everywhere, and was constantly promoting me and my research, and that of my colleagues, to people inside and outside the university. Lou and I had nothing in common personally or professionally, but I could not have asked for a better senior colleague at that stage of my career.

So, my first year was a great experience. I had a group of bright, energetic colleagues and Lou Pondy creating a culture that knit us altogether. We felt we were on our way and that we might be able to create one of the best OB programs in the country. And we were able to attract some outstanding young faculty. In 1974, we hired Manny London, Keith Murnighan, and Dave Whetten. All remained at Illinois for many years and have gone on to have very successful careers.

Things really started to come together for me in 1974 and 1975. Hackman and I finished two of the papers based on the job design project I started in graduate school and submitted them for publication. The first paper focused on the development of the Job Diagnostic Survey (JDS), and we submitted it to the *Journal of Applied Psychology*. Richard was excited about publishing this piece because he thought the JDS might receive lots of attention in the field. Was he ever right on target! That paper was accepted and turned out to be one of the most frequently cited in all of Organizational Behavior. Simultaneously, we submitted a paper targeted to a practitioner audience to *California Management Review*. This paper described our approach to work redesign, and included a section on implementing changes in the design of work, which was the special interest of our coauthors, Janson and Purdy. Those papers were published in 1975 and, as a result, I started getting a lot of recognition almost immediately. Academics and practitioners started asking me to deliver lectures on job design and asking to be placed on my mailing list for reprints. I didn't have a reprint mailing list, and I was quite surprised that people were that interested in me and my work.

In 1975, Hackman and I finished our final paper based on the project with Janson and Purdy and submitted it to *Organizational Behavior and Human Performance*. This paper presented our statement of Job Characteristics Theory, and provided its first test. The paper was published in 1976 and seemed to capture a lot of attention from people in the field. I was soon overwhelmed by the response, in terms of both invitations for me to discuss the theory and the numbers of papers based on the theory that were submitted to journals that I was asked to review. It was pretty clear to me at this point that I was going to be recognized as an expert on the topic of job design, despite the fact that this was only a secondary interest in graduate school.

About this time, I was visiting an organization in Chicago, discussing with managers and employees the possibility of conducting a work redesign intervention. I recall that during some of my meetings, employees were telling me that they would be interested in having their jobs redesigned, but only after several problems with the work context were addressed (e.g. controlling supervisors and poor pay structures). I began thinking at that point that Job Characteristics Theory did not address the effects of the work and organizational context, and that several contextual elements should be integrated into the model if we were really to understand how people reacted to the nature of their jobs. I was able to test some of these ideas in this same organization by examining the extent to which people were satisfied with several elements of their context. The argument was that people would only respond positively to well-designed jobs when they were relatively satisfied with their context; otherwise, they would focus their attention on contextual elements themselves. The sample was small and the results were pretty weak, but they did suggest that satisfaction with the context influenced the way employees responded to their work. That paper was submitted to *Human Relations*, and eventually published in 1976.

I had mentioned to Hackman my idea about the relevance of organizational context to Job Characteristics Theory and my frustration with having only a small sample on which to test this idea. He indicated that he had a data set that would be appropriate to test the idea that employees must be satisfied with the surrounding organizational context if they were to respond well to enriched jobs. He invited me to return to Yale in the summer of 1975 to work on the data, along with one of his current students, Jone Pearce. I agreed to return, and Jone, Richard and I began discussing the role of the organizational context in JCT. During these discussions we concluded that, if people were to respond positively to well-designed jobs, they not only had to be satisfied with various elements of the organizational context, but also be desirous of growth satisfactions at work (i.e. have high Growth Need Strength). The Growth Need Strength argument was already part of JCT, and adding the organizational context piece seemed to strengthen and enrich the theory. We were able to test these ideas with Richard's data set and put together a paper demonstrating that individuals with high Growth Need Strength and high context satisfactions were most responsive to well-designed, enriched jobs. This paper was published in 1976 in the *Journal of Applied Psychology* and resulted in our modifying Job Characteristics Theory in later publications by incorporating satisfaction with the organizational context into the JCT model.

Most of the papers I have described were in press in 1975, along with the paper from my dissertation (*Organizational Behavior and Human Performance*) and a few others papers I had been developing. My research was going well, and I had also become reasonably effective in the classroom. I found teaching much more enjoyable than I expected I would when I was a kid growing up in California. In 1975, my department head, Ken Uhl, let me know that he wanted to put me up for promotion. This seemed early to me, and I initially told Uhl that I wasn't interested. I had been at Illinois for a little over two years, and I felt as though I had not yet lived up to my personal standards for scholarship.

Uhl told me, in essence, that my standards were too high, and he persuaded me to allow the process to move forward. The department and the College of Commerce and Business Administration approved my case. When it got to the University Promotions and Tenure Committee, however, I was rejected. This Committee confirmed what I believed all along – I was too young and not established enough to warrant promotion to a tenured position at Illinois. I was disappointed and somewhat shaken by the news. And Ken Uhl was not at all happy with the decision. He was a big supporter of mine, and a very persistent fellow. He fought the decision – the Vice-Chancellor eventually overturned it – and I became an associate professor with tenure in 1976. At the time, I was 29 years old, and feeling "overrewarded" given my professional accomplishments. I recall feeling a good deal of pressure to be more productive and do better research than before.

The years 1975 and 1976 brought additional changes. Barry Staw, probably my closest colleague at the time, decided to leave for another position. It was a difficult adjustment for me because Barry was a wonderful colleague with whom I could discuss my work and who would always have a different take on it. Also, during that period, I became interested in establishing a working relationship with a doctoral student similar to what I had had with Hackman. I missed that kind of interaction, and thought I had learned some things from Richard that I wanted to apply to my own work with doctoral students.

There were no students in the Ph.D. program at Illinois who had any interest in me or my work – most of the current students wanted to work with either Pondy or Rowland. However, I was able to identify someone I thought might be appropriate when I was teaching a combined undergraduate/graduate course in Organizational Behavior. There was a Labor and Industrial Relations master's student who was head and shoulders more competent than anyone else in the course. His name was Dan Brass, and I somehow persuaded him to join the OB Ph.D. program the following year and to work closely with me.

Dan's decision to join the program was significant, not only because he had the potential (now realized) to be an excellent scholar, but also because one of the projects on which he and I would eventually collaborate would set in motion an entirely new research stream for me. I recall that Dan stopped by my office one day and told me that the newspaper organization where his wife, Karen, was managing editor had decided to change physical spaces – they would be moving from a traditional office layout to something called an "open plan" office. I had never heard of that type of office, and I knew nothing about the office design literature or the related literature in environmental psychology and architecture. I was intrigued and thought this might present an opportunity for me to stretch my research interests and to conduct an experimental or quasi-experimental study on the effects of this new physical space on employee reactions. Dan discussed the possibility with his wife, and she arranged for us to have access to what would become my first quasi-experiment.

The results of the study were interesting and demonstrated that the open office had a generally negative effect on responses, which were due to changes in the way people responded to their jobs and social opportunities. The paper was published in *Administrative Science Quarterly* in 1979. And I continued to publish articles on that topic through 1998, involving several of my graduate students (e.g. Anne Cummings, Yitzhak Fried, Doug May, Lee Stepina and Jing Zhou) in that program of research. Research on the physical environment was just plain fun, and it allowed me to really extend myself – to learn an entirely new literature and a new way to conduct research. Moreover, I think my research in that area underscored the fact that I had become interested in many of elements of the organizational context, not just the work itself.

Also in 1977, I married a woman I had been dating for about a year, and my first son, Kyle, was born about eighteen months later, in 1979. Although I expected my son's arrival to have something of an adverse effect on my research productivity, there didn't seem to be much of an impact. In fact, even though I was spending a considerable amount of time with him, I think the quality of my work actually improved. I guess I had not accounted for the possibility that his arrival would have such a positive impact on my positive mood states and that my improved mood would more than counteract the effects of the time away from the office! I recall that the years after Kyle's birth were among the happiest of my life. I just loved being a father, and felt that I now had two real passions in my life – my work and my son. Who could ask for more than that?

In 1979, Hackman and I were wrapping up our book, *Work Redesign*. We had been working on this piece fairly steadily since 1977 and hoped that it would have an impact on both academic and practitioner audiences. Our effort was to summarize what we knew about the design of work, how it fit into an organizational context, and about strategies for actually changing the structure of jobs. The publication of this book in 1980 seemed to start a new flurry of job design research. I think the attraction to this area was multi-faceted. Academics could identify with the importance of the work itself, because most were absorbed in their own jobs. Moreover, we provided a clear and testable theoretical framework for the effects of work on people, and we offered a set of instruments that would allow for the test of this framework.

It is no secret that Hackman and I received a good deal of criticism about the Job Characteristics Theory and about the instrument designed to test it (i.e. the JDS). Some people in the field have suggested to me that because many of the theory's major propositions were not confirmed, that I should feel guilty about spending so much of my time on JCT research. Nothing could be further from the truth. I think Hackman and I posed some interesting, timely questions that captured the attention of many people, and that resulted in numerous research studies. I think the field is better as a result, regardless of whether the original model we posited was valid and the instruments we developed were perfect.

In the late 1970s, I offered seminars on the design of work, and had the opportunity to interact with many doctoral students from the OB program, Department of Psychology, and the Institute of Labor and Industrial Relations. I found that I really enjoyed the intellectual stimulation associated with working with Ph.D. students. One student from the Department of Psychology, Howard Miller, asked if I would offer an advanced independent study on the topic of job design. I agreed, and our discussions ultimately turned to an analysis of the effects of the social context on employees' responses to their jobs. In discussing these issues, we finally moved to an examination of how the jobs held by coworkers might affect individuals' reactions to their own jobs and how social comparison models might help us to explain these possible effects. I had data that would allow us to explore these issues, and we were able to demonstrate that individuals' responses to their own jobs were more positive when they were comparable in complexity to those of their colleagues. Our results were not strong, but intriguing, and we published them in *Human Relations* in 1979.

Shortly after the publication of this work, I was recommended for promotion to full professor. Although when I arrived at Illinois I was interested in being on a fast track to promotion, I felt this promotion, like the first one, was premature. I had only been at Illinois for six years, and I just didn't think that I had accomplished enough or had had enough impact on the field to warrant a full professorship. I had accomplished some things, but had not met my own personal standards for scholarship.

Once again, my department head disagreed, and persuaded me to allow the promotion process to move forward. Unlike my first promotion, this one went smoothly, and I became a full professor in 1980. Looking back, I believe I was promoted based on the impact of my work in the area of job design and on the potential significance of my work on the physical environment. I had only published one paper on that latter topic (with Brass, in *Administrative Science Quarterly*), but it had received positive reviews and a pretty good "buzz" among my colleagues in the field.

The research with Howard Miller started me thinking about the integration of research in the areas of job design and social comparison. Specifically, I was interested in the possibility that individuals' responses to their jobs may not simply be a function of the jobs of their colleagues at work, but also of other potential comparative referents (e.g. their past jobs, future jobs). Along with a team of graduate students who had taken a course with me (Gail Nottenburg, Marcia Kassner, Gerald Ferris, Don Fedor, and Marrick Masters), we tested these ideas in a local organization. We found that employees there compared their work to that of several other referents. Moreover, when their jobs were comparable in complexity to those of their referents, they had the highest levels of motivation. These findings were consistent with what might be predicted by social comparison theories, and we published the paper based on this study in *Organizational Behavior and Human Performance* in 1982.

I began to receive a good deal of attention for this paper, especially from social psychologists interested in social comparison and equity theories. At about the same time, one of my former students, Lee Stepina of Florida State University, indicated that he would like to collaborate on a related project and that he had located an organization that he thought would be interested in participating in the research. At that time, I was working closely with Carol Kulik, who had joined the OB Ph.D. program. Carol had been an undergraduate in our Psychology Department, and I had recruited her to the OB program. She, along with Julie Brand from the OB program and Maureen Ambrose of the Psychology Department, agreed to become involved in this project. We designed a study that was basically an extension of my earlier work, except that we developed a systematic framework of the types of referents individuals might use, including the nature of the referent and a time dimension (e.g. coworkers I had in a previous job, the job I hope to have in the future). We also extended our analysis to job facets other than the work itself, such as supervisory behavior and pay. Again, we obtained interesting results that were consistent with social comparison theory predictions – employees exhibited the most negative responses when they felt disadvantaged on each job facet relative to their comparative referents. We published two papers from these data in 1986, one in *Organizational Behavior and Human Decision Processes* and the other in the *Academy of Management Journal*.

During this period (1984), my second son Todd was born. I was very involved with his care, and spent a substantial amount of time at home and away from my work. This was all worthwhile, and I enjoyed observing his development so much that I actually considered returning to graduate school part time to get a second Ph.D. in developmental psychology. I was very much involved in being a father and couldn't imagine anything more worthwhile than to understand child development better. However, when I then thought about the amount of time that the pursuit of this degree would require and the implications for the time I spent with my children and the research I still enjoyed in OB, I quickly put thoughts of a second Ph.D. on the back burner. It is still there.

Among the worst events for me during the 1980s was the death of Lou Pondy. He was only 49 years old when he passed away in 1987. Lou had been the glue of the OB group, and its emotional leader since I arrived in 1973. His loss was devastating to the spirit of the OB program, and for some time we were without a real direction. Many members of the group stepped up and took on elements of Lou's role, but things were never the same. Despite the fact that we continued to hire outstanding faculty (including, Joe Broschak, Lorna Doucet, Matt Kraatz, Carol Kulik, Huseyin Leblebici, Mike Moch, Greg Northcraft, Mike Pratt, and Mary Waller), the spirit was never quite the same. Illinois still provided a stimulating intellectual climate, but the energy and excitement have never been at the same levels as when Pondy was alive.

In the 1980s through the early 1990s, I was quite involved in consulting. My primary area was the design of work, although I did complete a few projects involving an organization's physical space. I was working with some of the largest organizations in the country, and things were going extremely well. I was fortunate to be able to consult in a way that few academics ever have an opportunity. Namely, I was directly involved with employees and managers and actually responsible for designing jobs for individuals and groups within work units. That is, I was not only involved in teaching work design concepts, but I was actually restructuring jobs in organizations. The experience was exhilarating – to be able to actually put into place many of the ideas about which I had written was terrific, and to observe the positive reactions when the changes had intended effects was even better. Also, I soon learned that the experience made me much more credible when I spoke about job design issues to students and managers in the classroom. I was no longer simply a theorist and a researcher. I had become something of a practitioner who could discuss practical problems and pitfalls associated with jobs and organizational change.

There were some costs, however. I was spending much of my time on airplanes and away from my children. I was finding that increasingly difficult. I wanted to enjoy them during the short time they would be with me. Also, these activities had an adverse impact on my research. I found it very difficult to wear two hats simultaneously – that of a researcher and of a consultant. So, I started cutting back on the consulting and spending more time in Champaign dealing with my research, writing and children.

But conducting research and engaging in my normal activities became much more difficult in 1990, when my wife and I divorced. I had experienced few problems or setbacks since I had moved to Illinois, but I counted this as a major failure on my part. I was simply not able to hold together my marriage and my family unit. I was extremely upset, and felt that I no longer had the support system I felt I needed to be happy and productive. Moreover, I thought I would lose contact with my children, who were the most important people in my life. I was in a great deal of pain for a year or two after the divorce, and my research program really suffered.

As it turns out, the divorce had very positive long-term effects. I was happier divorced than I was married. And I think I grew as a person. I learned to take my work and myself less seriously, and to relax some of the standards and expectations I had for graduate students and myself. Moreover, I was able to maintain contact with my children and to develop a strong bond with them. My research program began to perk up again in 1993, and I was again focused on my work, excited by ideas, and interested in working with Ph.D. students.

One of my doctoral students, Christina Shalley, had completed her dissertation in 1989 on the topic of goal setting and creativity, and I began to find work in the general area of creativity to be very interesting. I was particularly interested in integrating my interest in the organizational context with the creativity of individual employees. It seemed to me that we knew little about the effects of the organizational context on creativity, and if there were individual differences in the way contextual characteristics affected the creative accomplishments of individuals.

Christina graduated and accepted a position at the University of Arizona, and I was interested in attracting another student to work with me on research involving creativity. By this time, I knew that I found research projects most personally rewarding when I was able to work with a doctoral student in a collaborative fashion in much the way that I had worked with Hackman when we were developing JCT. I enjoyed that type of faculty-student interaction, and most of my earlier students seemed to respond well to it, as evidenced by the fact that most have gone on to have very successful professional careers.

The first student I was able to persuade to work with me on the topic of creativity was Anne Cummings. After she was admitted to the OB doctoral program, we initiated a study that examined how two elements of the organizational context (i.e. the nature of the work and supervision) had effects on individuals' creative responses at work, and how these effects differed according to an employee's personality. We were able to demonstrate that individuals exhibited the highest creativity when they had creative personal-ities, worked on complex jobs, and were supervised in a supportive, non-controlling fashion. This paper was published in *Academy of Management Journal* in 1996, and it seemed to attract quite a bit of interest from other academic researchers. Another one of my students during that period, Jing Zhou, also became interested in creativity and wrote her dissertation on the effects of feedback type and style on creativity. Cummings's dissertation focused on creativity as a function of a person's position in a social network. Nora Madjar, one of my current students, is interested in the effects of support and information from a variety of groups on individuals' creativity at work.

She, one of my colleagues, Mike Pratt, and I have published one paper in the *Academy of Management Journal* on this topic that demonstrated that support and encouragement from family and friends influenced individuals' creativity at work. Nora's dissertation is designed to extend this work.

I continue with work in this area today, and I am still intrigued by the possibility that it might be possible to set up contextual conditions to prompt creative idea generation as well as the expression of these ideas. In particular, I am working on understanding contexts that prompt both the generation of new, creative ideas at work and individuals' willingness to share those ideas with others. I am optimistic about this work and hope that it draws some attention and stimulates additional research activity.

I should say a few words about my participation in the leadership of the Academy of Management. I was asked to run for Chair of the OB Division in the mid-1980s and was fortunate enough to be elected. I enjoyed the position, but certainly wasn't looking for other opportunities to participate as an officer in the Academy – I was too busy playing with my kids and doing my own research. I recall that around 1990, a member of the Academy's Board of Governors, Art Bedeian, called and asked if I would consider running for President of the Academy. Frankly, I was surprised that anyone would be interested in me running for that office. I pretty much did my own thing in the OB division, and didn't know much about the other divisions in the Academy. I thought long and hard about running, and eventually agreed because I thought it was an honor to be asked and because I thought it would stretch me a bit as an academic. Again, I was fortunate enough to win the election and spent the early 1990s as a member of the Academy's Board, and in 1993 as its President.

Although serving the Academy did take me away from my research program, I enjoyed the entire experience and wouldn't change a thing about my decision. I was able to meet some great people in the field and to gain a better appreciation for the kind of work that people do outside OB.

It was shortly after my term ended as President of the Academy that my Dean, Howard Thomas, decided to award me the C. Clinton Spivey Distinguished Professorship in Business Administration. Like my promotions to associate and full professor, I wasn't comfortable accepting this professorship because I wasn't confident that my contributions to the field warranted it. But I was happy that Howard and others felt differently, and I agreed to accept the position. I still feel grateful to Howard and to the University of Illinois for the tremendous amount of support they have provided me over my entire career.

CONCLUSIONS

Putting together this account of the people and contexts that influenced my decision to become an academic and that shaped my work and research interests has proved very enlightening. If someone had simply looked at my vita or a schematic representation of my career, they might have gotten the idea that it had been both easy and all the result of a carefully calculated career strategy. But I hope that my essay has put to rest both of these possible impressions. First, it definitely has not been easy. I have had many setbacks and difficulties during my career as an academic, and dealing with them has often been a struggle. I don't believe that I have ever questioned my skills or abilities as a result of these setbacks, but instead have tried to use them as opportunities to reflect on how I might improve my work and myself. As to the second point, I have never followed a particular strategy that I thought would result in a successful career. Most of my career choices were the result of just stumbling around and making decisions based on my instincts at the time, rather than following a deliberate and well-crafted master plan.

Would I choose this career and profession if I had it to do over? Obviously, that is a complicated question. Certainly, I've had great fun, and my life has been immeasurably enriched by the experiences I've had in the OB field and by the people I've have had an opportunity to meet. But I honestly believe much of what I wrote in this essay – that I simply stumbled into this profession and that my decision to become an OB professor was largely a function of the people and experiences I had early in my life. If I had not met Lyman Porter in 1968, I'm quite sure I would be doing something else today. Would I have been as happy or as successful? Hard to say, but I know I would have had fun trying.

PUBLICATIONS

1974

With J. R. Hackman. The Job Diagnostic Survey: An instrument for the diagnosis of jobs and the evaluation of job redesign projects. *Psychological Documents*, 4, 148, Ms. No. 810.
With E. E. Lawler & D. T. Hall. Organizational climate: Relationship to organizational structure, process and performance. *Organizational Behavior and Human Performance*, *11*, 139–155.

1975

With J. R. Hackman. Development of the Job Diagnostic Survey. *Journal of Applied Psychology*, *60*, 159–170.

The impact of supervisory characteristics on goal acceptance. *Academy of Management Journal*, *18*, 461–475.

With J. R. Hackman, R. Janson & K. Purdy. A new strategy for job enrichment. *California Management Review*, *17*, 57–71.

1976

Organizational choice and some correlates of individuals' expectancies. *Decision Sciences*, *7*, 873–884.

The motivational strategies used by supervisors: Relationships to effectiveness indicators. *Organizational Behavior and Human Performance*, *15*, 66–86.

Job characteristics and internal motivation: The moderating effects of interpersonal and individual variables. *Human Relations*, *29*, 559–569.

With J. R. Hackman. Motivation through the design of work: Test of a theory. *Organizational Behavior and Human Performance*, *16*, 250–279.

With J. R. Hackman & J. L. Pearce. Conditions under which employees respond positively to enriched work. *Journal of Applied Psychology*, *61*, 395–403.

With M. London. Effects of varying goal types and incentive systems on performance and satisfaction. *Academy of Management Journal*, *19*, 537–546.

With D. J. Brass. Validating an in-basket test using an alternative set of leadership scoring dimensions. *Journal of Applied Psychology*, *61*, 652–657.

1977

With M. London. A comparison of group and individual incentive plans. *Academy of Management Journal*, *20*, 34–41.

The design of work. In: B. Wolman (Ed.), *International Encyclopedia of Neurology, Psychiatry, Psychoanalysis, and Psychology* (Vol. 11, pp. 443–446). New York: Van Nostrand-Reinhold.

1978

With B. M. Staw. Reconsidering our dependent variables: A critique and empirical study. *Academy of Management Journal*, *21*, 439–449.

1979

With H. E. Miller. The effect of significant other's job complexity on employees reactions to work. *Human Relations*, *32*, 247–260.

With J. R. Hackman & L. P. Stepina. Norms for the Job Diagnostic Survey. *Psychological Documents*, 9, 14, Ms. No. 1819.

With D. J. Brass. Employee reactions to an open-plan office: A naturally occurring quasi-experiment. *Administrative Science Quarterly*, *24*, 267–284.

1980

With J. R. Hackman. Work design in the organizational context. In: B. Staw & L. Cummings (Eds), *Research in Organizational Behavior* (Vol. 2, pp. 247–278). Greenwich, CT: JAI Press.
With J. R. Hackman. *Work redesign*. Reading, MA: Addison-Wesley.

1981

With J. R. Hackman. Relationships between organizational structure and employee reactions: Comparing alternative frameworks. *Administrative Science Quarterly, 26*, 66–83.

1982

Work redesign: Enhancing productivity and the quality of working life. *National Forum, 62*, 8–10.
With G. Nottenburg, M. K. Kassner, G. Ferris, D. Fedor & M. Masters. The selection and consequences of job comparisons. *Organizational Behavior and Human Performance, 29*, 84–111.

1983

With C. T. Kulik. Motivation enhancement through work redesign. *Review of Higher Education, 6*, 323–342.
With N. L. Rotchford. Relationships between office characteristics and employee reactions: A study of the physical environment. *Administrative Science Quarterly, 28*, 542–556.

1985

With C. E. Shalley. Effects of goal difficulty and expected external evaluation on intrinsic motivation: A laboratory study. *Academy of Management Journal, 28*, 628–640.

1986

With C. T. Kulik, M. L. Ambrose, L. P. Stepina & J. F. Brand. Relations between job facet comparisons and employee reactions. *Organizational Behavior and Human Decision Processes, 38*, 28–47.
With C. T. Kulik, L. P. Stepina & M. L. Ambrose. Relations between situational factors and the comparative referents used by employees. *Academy of Management Journal, 29*, 599–608.

1987

With C. E. Shalley & J. F. Porac. Effects of goal difficulty, goal-setting method, and expected external evaluation on intrinsic motivation. *Academy of Management Journal, 30*, 553–563.

With Y. Fried. Employee reactions to workspace characteristics. *Journal of Applied Psychology,* *72,* 75–80.

With C. T. Kulik & J. R. Hackman. Work design as an approach to person-environment fit. *Journal of Vocational Behavior, 31,* 278–296.

1988

With C. T. Kulik & P. H. Langner. Measurement of job characteristics: Comparison of the original and the revised Job Diagnostic Survey. *Journal of Applied Psychology, 73,* 462–466.

Effects of changes in workspace partitions and spatial density on employee reactions: A quasi-experiment. *Journal of Applied Psychology, 73,* 253–258.

With C. T. Kulik. The Job Diagnostic Survey. In: S. Gael (Ed.), *Job Analysis Handbook for Business, Industry, and Government* (Vol. 2, pp. 936–959). New York: Wiley.

1991

With C. T. Kulik & L. P. Stepina. Physical environments and employee reactions: Effects of stimulus-screening skills and job complexity. *Academy of Management Journal, 34,* 929–938.

1992

With C. T. Kulik. Work design. In: E. Gaugler & W. Weber (Eds), *Handbook of personnel* (2nd ed., pp. 363–374). Stuttgart: Poeschel Verlag.

1995

Job characteristics. In: N. Nicholson (Ed.), *The Blackwell Encyclopedic Dictionary of Organizational Behavior* (pp. 263–264). Oxford: Blackwell.

Job enrichment. In: N. Nicholson (Ed.), *The Blackwell Encyclopedic Dictionary of Organizational Behavior* (pp. 270–271). Oxford: Blackwell.

Job rotation. In: N. Nicholson (Ed.), *The Blackwell Encyclopedic Dictionary of Organizational Behavior* (p. 272). Oxford: Blackwell.

Growth need strength. In: N. Nicholson (Ed.), *The Blackwell Encyclopedic Dictionary of Organizational Behavior* (pp. 208–209). Oxford: Blackwell.

With A. Cummings, L. J. Mischel, J. M. Schmidtke, & J. Zhou. Listen while you work? Quasi-experimental relations between personal-stereo headset use and employee work responses. *Journal of Applied Psychology, 80,* 547–564.

With A. Cummings & J. Zhou. The spatial configuration of organizations. In: G. Ferris (Ed.), *Research in Personnel and Human Resources Management* (Vol. 13, pp. 1–37). Greenwich, CT: JAI Press.

1996

With A. Cummings. Employee creativity: Personal and contextual factors at work. *Academy of Management Journal, 39,* 607–634.

With A. Cummings, L. J. Mischel, J. M. Schmidtke, & J. Zhou. Can personal stereos improve productivity? *HRMagazine, 41*(4), 95–99.
Job design. In: C. Cooper & I. Robertson (Eds), *International Review of Industrial and Organizational Psychology* (Vol. 11, pp. 33–60). New York: Wiley.
With Y. Fried & A. Cummings. Job design. In: M. Warner (Ed.), *The International Encyclopedia of Business and Management* (Vol. 3, pp. 2419–2429). London: Thomson Business Press.

1997

With A. Cummings. Enhancing creativity: Managing work contexts for the high potential employee. *California Management Review, 40*, 22–38.
With C. E. Shalley. Competition and creative performance: Effects of competitor presence and visibility. *Creativity Research Journal, 10*, 337–345.

1998

With A. Cummings. Creativity in the organizational context. *Productivity, 39*, 187–194.
With Y. Fried & A. Cummings. Job design. In: M Poole & M. Warner (Eds), *The IEBM Handbook of Human Resource Management* (pp. 532–543). London: Thomson Publishing Co.
With J. Zhou & A. Cummings. Employee reactions to the physical work environment: The role of childhood residential attributes. *Journal of Applied Social Psychology, 28*, 2213–2238.

1999

With B. I. Gordon. Job complexity and employee substance use: The moderating effects of cognitive ability. *Journal of Health and Social Behavior, 40*, 290–306.
With J. Zhou. Expected evaluation and creative performance: Effects of evaluation approach, type, and individuals' creative personality characteristics. *Best Paper Proceedings of the Academy of Management National Meeting.*
With B. I. Gordon. Employee job complexity and substance use. *Best Paper Proceedings of the Academy of Management National Meeting.*

2001

With J. Zhou. Enhancing creative performance: Effects of expected developmental assessment strategies and creative personality. *Journal of Creative Behavior, 35*, 151–167.

In Press

With N. Madjar & M. G. Pratt. There's no place like home?: The contributions of work and non-work sources of creativity support to employees' creative performance. *Academy of Management Journal.*
With N. Madjar. Preliminary tasks and creative performance on a subsequent task: Effects of time on preliminary tasks and amount of information about the subsequent task. *Creativity Research Journal.*

Stimulating and supporting creativity in organizations. In: S. Jackson, M. Hitt, & A. DeNisi (Eds), *Managing Knowledge for Sustained Competitive Advantage*. San Francisco: Jossey-Bass.

With Y. Fried & A. Cummings. Job design. In: M. Warner (Ed.), *The International Encyclopedia of Business and Management* (2nd ed.). London: International Thomson Business Press.

With C. T. Kulik. Work design. In: E. Gaugler, W. A. Oechsler, & W. Weber (Eds), *Handbook of Human Resource Management* (3rd ed.). Stuttgart: Poeschel Verlag.

MANAGEMENT LAUREATES:
A COLLECTION OF
AUTOBIOGRAPHICAL ESSAYS

Edited by Arthur G. Bedeian

VOLUME 1: 1992
H. Igor Ansoff
Chris Argyris
Bernard M. Bass
Robert R. Blake
Elwood S. Buffa
Alfred D. Chandler, Jr.
Larry L. Cummings
Keith Davis
Fred E. Fiedler
Jay W. Forrester
Robert T. Golembiewski

VOLUME II: 1993
Frederick I. Herzberg
Robert J. House
Edward E. Lawler, III
Paul R. Lawrence
Edmund Philip Learned
Harry Levinson
Edwin A. Locke
Dalton E. McFarland
John B. Miner
Henry Mintzberg
William H. Newman
Charles Perrow

VOLUME III: 1993
Lyman W. Porter
Edward H. Schein
William H. Starbuck
George A. Steiner
George Strauss
Eric L. Trist
Stanley C. Vance
Victor H. Vroom
Karl E. Weick
William Foote Whyte
James C. Worthy

VOLUME IV: 1996
Kathryn M. Bartol
Janice M. Beyer
Geert Hofstede
John M. Ivancevich
Fred Luthans
Jeffrey Pfeffer
Derek S. Pugh
John W. Slocum, Jr.

VOLUME V: 1998
Arthur G. Bedeian
C. West Churchman
David J. Hickson
Thomas A. Mahoney
Andrew M. Pettigrew
Karlene H. Roberts
Wickham Skinner

VOLUME VI: 2002
John Child
George B. Graen
Donald C. Hambrick
Michael A. Hitt
James G. Hunt
Thomas A. Kochan
Richard T. Mowday
Greg R. Oldham

NAME INDEX